History
of
Ancient Greece

History
OF
Ancient Greece

Edited by
W. and R. Chambers

Athens ‡ Manchester

History of Ancient Greece

Old Book Publishing Ltd

Book Cover Design: Old Book Publishing Ltd

Copyright © 2011 Old Book Publishing Ltd
All rights reserved.

Title of original: History of Ancient Greece
Originally published in 1855

ISBN–10: 1-78107-075-X
ISBN–13: 978-1-78107-075-8

EDITOR'S NOTE

Old Book Publishing Ltd takes care in preserving the wording and images of the original books. For this reason we have invested in technology that enables us to enhance the quality of such reproduction. This investment helps overcome problems encountered when reproducing old books, such as stains, coloured paper, discolouration of ink, yellowed pages, see-through and onion skin type paper.

This reproduction book, produced from digital images of the original, may contain occasional defects such as missing pages or blemishes due to the original source content or were introduced by the scanning process.

These are scanned pages and the quality of print represents accurately the print quality of the original book, though we may have been able to enhance it.

As this book has been scanned and/or reformatted from the original we cannot guarantee that it is error-free or contains the full content of the original.

However, we believe that this work is culturally important, and despite its imperfections, have elected to bring it back into print as part of our commitment to the preservation of printed works.

Old Book Publishing

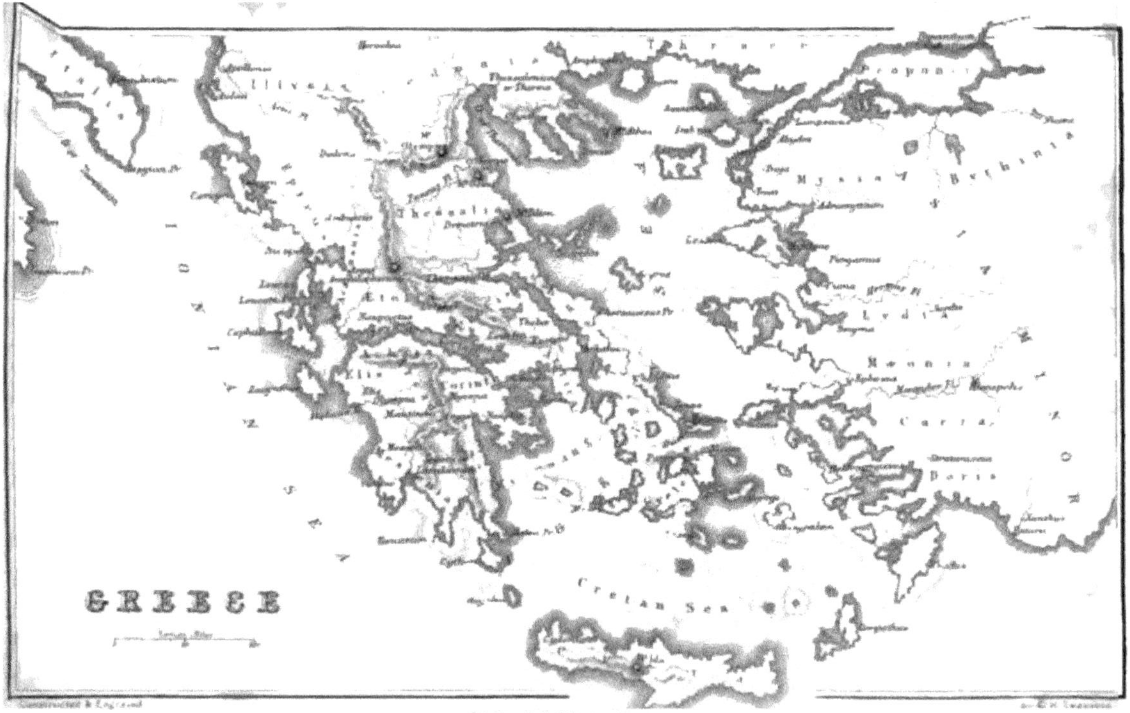

Edinburgh W & R Chambers

*CHAMBERS'S EDUCATIONAL COURSE.—EDITED BY
W. AND R. CHAMBERS.*

HISTORY

OF

ANCIENT GREECE

LONDON
W. AND R. CHAMBERS 47 PATERNOSTER ROW
AND HIGH STREET EDINBURGH
1855

Edinburgh:
Printed by W. and R. Chambers.

PREFACE.

THE elucidation of the History of Greece, as is well known, has made greater progress during the last few years, than at any other period since the revival of learning. While the Germans have composed numberless treatises and dissertations on almost every matter connected with Greek antiquity, it has been the honour of England to produce two great works, in which the materials thus collected by many labourers are combined and arranged into continuous narratives. We allude, of course, to the Histories of Ancient Greece by Bishop Thirlwall and Mr Grote, which, it has been justly remarked, are calculated to throw into the shade all previous attempts of a similar nature. It has been felt that even our school histories require to be rewritten, so that the rising generation may not have, like their fathers, to unlearn in maturer years what they were carefully taught in their youth.

In compiling the present volume on this interesting subject, we have chiefly taken Grote as our guide; and this because his work seemed more full and satisfactory than that of Thirlwall as to the delineation of facts and characters; the work of Thirlwall appearing, in comparison, more a dissertation on the history, than the history itself. Of course, we could not go the whole way with Mr Grote in that strong political bias which has caused his work to be characterised as 'an able and partial pleading, not only for democracy, but also for ochlocracy, as much as if he had been hired by the Athenian Demos to panegyrise their excellences, and veil their crimes.' It has been our aim merely to collect the facts, representing them as impartially as possible, and leaving them to make their own impression.

Not, however, all the facts. The space proposed did not admit of doing justice to every character, or relating every event; and as every one has felt that a skeleton history, briefly enumerating many occurrences, engages no interest, and leaves no impression, we have rather studied to bring out the leading features of the history in a mode to command the interest of the youthful reader, hoping that at a future time he will make a further acquaintance with it through works on a larger scale.

November 5, 1855.

CONTENTS.

	PAGE
GEOGRAPHY OF ANCIENT GREECE,	1
THE HELLENES, OR PEOPLE OF ANCIENT GREECE,	4
THE GODS OF GREECE,	7
LEGENDS OF APOLLO,	16
MYSTERIES,	19
ORACLES,	22
THE OLYMPIC AND OTHER GAMES,	22
THE AMPHICTYONIC COUNCIL,	24
HEROIC LEGENDS,	25
THE ARGONAUTIC EXPEDITION,	31
WAR OF THE SEVEN AGAINST THEBES,	31
THE SIEGE OF TROY,	33
ANCIENT EPIC POETRY OF GREECE,	35
THE GREEK CLANS, OR GENTILE CLASSIFICATION,	38
EARLY MIGRATIONS,	39

HISTORIC AGES.

INTRODUCTION,	43

FIRST PERIOD.

776—500 B.C.

GENERAL VIEW OF THE GREEK STATES,	44
EARLY GOVERNMENTS,	47
EARLY GREEK COLONIES IN ASIA AND THE ISLANDS,	49

CONTENTS.

	PAGE
SICILIAN COLONIES,	53
ITALIAN COLONIES,	58
GROWTH OF THE GRECIAN STATES,	62
ARGOS,	62
SPARTA,	63
MESSENIAN AND OTHER WARS OF SPARTA,	68
ATHENS,	77
LITERARY RETROSPECT,	102

SECOND PERIOD.
500—478 B.C.

THE IONIC REVOLT,	104
WAR BETWEEN PERSIA AND GREECE,	112
MILTIADES, THEMISTOCLES, AND ARISTIDES,	116
BATTLE OF MARATHON,	118
END OF MILTIADES,	121
AFFAIRS OF GREECE AFTER THE BATTLE OF MARATHON,	123
PREPARATIONS FOR A RENEWAL OF THE WAR,	125
PREPARATIONS FOR DEFENCE,	129
THERMOPYLÆ AND ARTEMISIUM,	132
SALAMIS,	139
PLATÆA AND MYCALE,	148
HERODOTUS,	162

THIRD PERIOD.
478—404 B.C.

FOUNDATION OF MARITIME POWER AT ATHENS,	164
FALL OF PAUSANIAS,	167
ADVENTURES OF THEMISTOCLES,	169
ATHENS THE LEADING STATE OF MARITIME GREECE,	171
PERICLES AND CIMON,	173

	PAGE
DIFFERENCES BETWEEN ATHENS AND SPARTA—PROGRESS OF ATHENIAN POWER,	176
THE THIRTY YEARS' TRUCE—SPLENDOUR OF ATHENS,	180
OPENING OF THE PELOPONNESIAN WAR,	183
A NEW CALAMITY—THE PESTILENCE,	187
PROGRESS OF THE PELOPONNESIAN WAR,	190
SURRENDER OF PLATÆA,	194
SPHACTERIA,	196
FROM THE EIGHTH TILL THE ELEVENTH YEAR OF THE WAR—THE HELOTS—BRASIDAS—DELIUM—AMPHIPOLIS—PEACE OF NICIAS,	200
ELEVENTH AND FOLLOWING YEARS OF THE WAR—ALCIBIADES,	206
THE SYRACUSAN EXPEDITION,	211
CONSEQUENCES OF THE DEFEAT AT SYRACUSE—THE FOUR HUNDRED,	225
THE WAR ON THE ASIATIC COAST,	229
LYSANDER AND CYRUS THE YOUNGER—BATTLE OF ÆGOSPOTAMOS—THE DECARCHIES—HUMILIATION OF ATHENS,	230
THE THIRTY TYRANTS—RESTORATION OF THE DEMOCRACY—DEATH OF ALCIBIADES,	236
HUMILIATION OF THE ELEANS AND MESSENIANS,	240
LITERARY RETROSPECT,	240
SOCRATES,	241

FOURTH PERIOD.

404—371 B.C.

THE TEN THOUSAND GREEKS,	242
LYSANDER AND AGESILAUS,	250
AGESILAUS IN ASIA,	252
COMBINATION AGAINST SPARTA—BŒOTIAN WAR,	255
CORINTHIAN WAR—CORONEA,	257
DESTRUCTION OF THE MARITIME EMPIRE OF SPARTA,	259
REBUILDING OF THE ATHENIAN WALLS BY CONON,	260
CAMPAIGNS OF AGESILAUS IN THE CORINTHIAN TERRITORY,	261

CONTENTS.

	PAGE
PEACE OF ANTALCIDAS,	262
OLYNTHIAN WAR,	264
PELOPIDAS THE THEBAN,	266
THEBAN WAR—EPAMINONDAS,	269
BATTLE OF LEUCTRA,	271

FIFTH PERIOD.

371—338 B.C.

PROGRESS OF THEBES—JASON OF PHERÆ,	275
DECLINE OF SPARTAN POWER IN PELOPONNESUS—ARCADIAN FEDERATION,	276
INDEPENDENCE OF MESSENIA,	277
ASCENDANCY OF THEBES—ITS WARS IN THESSALY AND PELOPONNESUS,	279
DEATH OF PELOPIDAS,	281
BATTLE OF MANTINEA,	282
LAST DAYS OF AGESILAUS,	284
PHILIP OF MACEDON,	285
SACRED WAR,	289
PHILIP AND THE OLYNTHIANS,	294
SACRED WAR RESUMED,	296

SIXTH PERIOD.

338—300 B.C.

ARREST OF PHILIP'S PROGRESS,	307
ALEXANDER THE GREAT,	310
SUCCESSORS OF ALEXANDER,	334
THE ROMANS IN GREECE,	340
INDEX,	343
SYNCHRONISTIC TABLE,	351

HISTORY OF GREECE.

GEOGRAPHY OF ANCIENT GREECE.

1. THE mountain-chain called Olympus and the Cambunians, which commences near the Ægæan Sea, or the Gulf of Therma, about the 40th degree of north latitude, is prolonged to the west, under the name of Mount Lingon, till it reaches the Adriatic. The countries south of this chain comprehend that known to ancient history as Greece or Hellas. The only break in this natural rampart was the celebrated Vale of Tempe, through which the river Peneius finds its way into the sea, a little to the south of Olympus. At a point about midway between the Ægæan and Ionian Seas, this mountain-range is intersected by the still greater chain called Pindus, which strikes off nearly southward, and forms the western boundary of Thessaly; and, at about the 39th degree, Pindus sends forth the lateral chain of Othrys, which supplies the southern boundary. To the west of Pindus is the mountainous country of Epeirus, through which the Achelous, the largest river of Greece, flows towards the Gulf of Corinth. Such was northern Hellas.

2. The Gulf of Ambracia on the west, and that of Malia on the east, contract the country into a comparatively narrow space, south of which lies the peninsula of Central Greece. Its northern barrier is formed by another lateral branch from Pindus, called Œta, the only entrance

being the narrow opening celebrated as the Pass of
Thermopylæ, between the termination of Œta and the sea.
In Central Greece, and at the point of junction with Œta,
the chain of Pindus divides into two great branches:
one strikes to the south-east, under the names of Parnassus, Helicon, Cithæron, and Hymettus, reaching the
sea at Sunium; the other diverges to the south-west, under
the names of Corax and the Ozòlian mountains. The
eastern branch formed the following districts:—

3. *Doris*, a narrow plain between Œta and Parnassus;
Phocis, occupied chiefly by the heights of Parnassus, and
containing the famous oracle of Apollo at Delphi; the
small district of *Locris*, containing the Pass of Thermopylæ; *Bœotia*, a large hollow basin enclosed by mountains,
and containing many independent cities celebrated in
history, as Thebes, Platæa, Tanagra, Thespiæ, Coronea,
and Leuctra; *Attica*, a foreland stretching into the sea
to the south-east, and shut off on the land-side by the
mountains of Cithæron and Parnes, which divide it from
Bœotia; *Megaris*, a small mountainous territory formed
by a prolongation of Cithæron, skirting the shores of the
Corinthian Gulf.

4. The western ramifications of Pindus formed the
district of the *Ozolian Locris*, a wild mountainous country,
so called to distinguish it from the eastern district of the
same name; *Ætolia* and *Acarnania*, separated by the
river Achelous, are also mountainous, and, like Locris, were
long the haunts of rude and predatory tribes.

5. Southern Greece consists of the peninsula called
Peloponnesus, or 'island of Pelops,' the connecting Isthmus
of Corinth being so narrow that this tract was regarded as
an island. Its form was anciently compared to the leaf
of the plane-tree or of the vine; and the modern name,
Morea, is derived from its resemblance to a mulberry leaf.

6. The mountains of Peloponnesus diverge in all directions from the centre to the sea. The middle region,
called Arcadia, is surrounded by a ring of mountains,
broken only on the western side, where the river Alpheius
finds a passage towards the Ionian Sea. Achaia was a
narrow tract lying between the Gulf of Corinth and

GEOGRAPHY OF ANCIENT GREECE. 3

the lofty range which forms the northern barrier of Arcadia. It was intersected by offsets from the Arcadian mountains, with fertile valleys between. Argolis, to the east of Arcadia, included the territories of several independent states, chiefly those of Corinth and Sicyon. South of Arcadia were Laconia and Messenia, separated from each other by the lofty mountains of Taÿgetus, running from north to south, and terminating in Cape Tænarum (now Matapan). Elis was the tract between the Ionian Sea and the western mountains of Arcadia, whose offshoots covered much of its surface. The river Alpheius flows through its principal valley, celebrated as the Plain of Olympia, in which stood the city of Pisa.

7. The numerous islands studding the shores of Greece appear as outlying peaks of the various mountain-chains already mentioned. The long, lofty, and naked backbone of Euboea, opposite the coasts of Boeotia and Attica, appears as a prolongation of the Ossa and Othrys mountains. Further south is the group which was called the Cyclades, and to the east of these the Sporades, near the coast of Asia. To the south of these groups lie two large islands—Crete and Rhodes; and off the southern coast of Laconia, the island of Cythera. Between Attica and Argolis was the Saronic Gulf, containing the celebrated island of Salamis, which was reckoned part of Attica; here, too, was Ægina, its hated rival. In the Ionian Sea were—Corcyra, opposite Epeirus; Ithaca and Cephallenia, opposite Acarnania; and Zacynthus, near the coast of Elis.

8. From this brief sketch, it might be judged that the people whose history we are to trace, inhabited one of the most mountainous territories in Europe; but besides the chains we have mentioned, there were innumerable minor ramifications and scattered peaks; few extensive plains, and even few continuous valleys; while irregular mountains, alternating with numerous but isolated vales and land-locked basins, formed the leading features of the country.

9. Greece was but scantily supplied with water, the winter-rains soon running in torrents off the limestone

hills, and leaving behind either dry ravines or insignificant streams. The climate varied in different localities; but was probably more healthful, on the whole, than it is at present, owing to the more general cultivation of the soil. The principal vegetable productions were wheat, barley, and flax, with the vine and the olive. The limestone mountains supplied excellent materials for military structures; and the rich veins of marble with which they abounded, were singularly favourable to the labours of the architect and the sculptor. Silver was found at Laurium, in Attica; but otherwise Greece was not rich in the precious metals. Iron was found in Laconia, and both copper and iron in the island of Euboea.

THE HELLENES, OR PEOPLE OF ANCIENT GREECE.

10. The configuration of Hellas, as described in the preceding pages, was peculiarly calculated to foster a large number of independent communities, separated from each other by mountain-chains, but open to foreign intercourse by the sea, which, in consequence of its numerous indentations, was accessible to almost every state of Greece. Accordingly, we find that each of the principal cities was founded in one of the small plains or valleys we have described, and grew up in solitary independence of all the world besides. The Greek owned no authority beyond his own city walls, and enjoyed no privileges beyond its territorial jurisdiction. A few miles from this loved spot, he found himself a stranger and an alien, where he could acquire no landed property—could contract no marriage— could claim no protection against wrong, nor sue for redress in case of injury; but here, in his native city, he found all that he deemed essential to a dignified existence; and the denizen of Athens, Corinth, or Thebes, looked with scorn upon such people as the Epeirots, the Ozolian Locrians, the Ætolians, and the Acarnanians, who long maintained their separate village residence, instead of amalgamating into cities, and preserved with it their primitive rudeness and disorderly pugnacity. Such had no consecrated acropolis or agora, no ornamented temples and porticos,

no theatre for music and recitation, no gymnasia for athletic exercises, no fixed arrangements for transacting business with regularity and decorum ; and without these, there was nothing to satisfy in the Greek mind the exigencies of social order, security, and dignity.

11. To a modern reader, accustomed to large political aggregations, it requires a certain mental effort to suppose a time when even the smallest town clung so tenaciously to its right of self-legislation : nevertheless, this multiplicity of self-governing cities was a phenomenon common to ancient Europe, and placed it in singular contrast with the extensive monarchies of Asia ; but it appears more marked among the Greeks than anywhere else ; and doubtless they owed it to the multitude of insulating boundaries which the configuration of their country presented.

12. Though politically disunited, the inhabitants of Greece had some intimate bonds of union. They were, according to their own belief, all of one blood, boasting their descent from one common ancestor, HELLEN, after whom they called themselves Hellenes, while they stigmatised every other people as barbarians. They all spoke the same language, though broken into numerous dialects ; so that, except in rare cases, every Greek understood every other Greek ; and whatever might be the diversity of their manners or character, there were some important points in which they resembled each other, while they differed from the most celebrated of the surrounding nations. Polygamy, the selling of children into slavery, the deliberate mutilation of the person, and the immolation of human victims to the gods, generally prevailed among the contemporaneous Egyptians, Carthaginians, Persians, and Thracians ; but such practices were utterly abhorrent to the Hellenic mind. On the other hand, the cultivation of gymnastic exercises by public contests was common to all the Hellenes, but unknown, so far as appears, to any of their neighbours.

13. This people were united, likewise, by a community of religion and literature. They worshipped the same gods, and held sacred the same localities. They had a

common stock of legends, maxims, and metaphors embodied in the works of Homer and other early poets, which were familiar to all, and acknowledged by all as the standards of literary language. So also the councils called Amphictyonies, and the games known to us as the Olympic, the Pythian, the Nemean, and the Isthmian, which are understood to have arisen out of religious fraternisation, presented opportunities of mutual intercourse to brethren habitually isolated from each other. Thus each petty community, nestling apart amidst its own rocks, was sufficiently isolated from the rest to possess an individual life and attributes of its own, yet not so far as to exclude it from the sympathies of the remainder; so that an intelligent Greek, maintaining at least occasional intercourse with numerous communities of half-countrymen whose language he understood, and whose idiosyncrasies he could appreciate, had access to a larger mass of social and political experience than any other man could obtain at that early age of the world. Perhaps it is thus that we are partly to explain that knowledge of human nature, that power of touching the sympathies common to all ages and nations, which pleases us so much in the old epic authors of this people.

14. There is some difficulty in explaining how the Hellenic people became known to the Romans, and through them to modern Europe, only by the name of Græci or Graii; but it is a common occurrence, even in our own day, that a people receive among foreigners a name quite different from their domestic one. The term *barbarian*, which, we have said, they applied to all other nations, seems at first to have merely expressed one not of Hellenic blood, conveying doubtless a feeling of antipathy, as well as a note of distinction; but after the Greeks or Hellenes became a more refined people than any of their neighbours, a barbarian easily came to signify an individual belonging to an uncivilised tribe or people.

15. By what circumstances, or out of what elements, this Hellenic family was formed, we know not. The legends, indeed, mention such people as the Pelasgi, the Leleges, the Curetes, and others, as previous inhabitants,

of Greece, and historians have endeavoured to compile from their conflicting statements a supposed narrative of the past; but there exists no evidence to explain how the Hellenes acquired those great national characteristics, of which we find them possessed from the earliest period known to us.

16. As little do we know of the foreign influences which were brought to bear on them. The legends tell of a colony led from Egypt into Attica by Cecrops, to whom is ascribed the foundation of Athens, and the introduction there of the arts of civilised life. Argos is said to have been founded in like manner by Danaus, an Egyptian, taking refuge in Greece, with his fifty daughters, from the persecution of their suitors. Another colony is said to have been led from Asia by Pelops, after whom the southern peninsula was called Peloponnesus. And yet another is said to have been founded at Thebes, in Bœotia, by Cadmus, a Phœnician, from whom the Greeks learned the art of writing. Doubtless, the use of letters was derived from the Phœnicians; but with this exception, there is little trace of the impress of any of these nations in the earliest Greeks—rather an obvious and fundamental contrast of character.

17. The religious and historic legends to which we have referred as the common property of all the Hellenes, and the festivals which drew so many of them together at certain seasons, exercised so great an influence on the character and history of this remarkable people, that they demand more special notice.

THE GODS OF GREECE.

18. The legendary history of Greece begins with a history of the gods, whom it represents as both pre-existent and superior to men; and it gradually descends first to heroes, then to the ordinary race of human beings.

19. The numerous gods of ancient Greece were conceived after the model of human nature, but not on the same scale. They had the same appetites, passions, and affections that disturb the soul of man; but were at the

same time invested with immensely greater powers, and gifted with immortality. Beings thus imagined, were, of course, peculiarly suitable subjects for adventure and narrative; and the inventive fancy of the Greeks had full play in the fabrication of legends illustrative of their respective characters and attributes.

20. The earliest mythical events are the proceedings of certain gigantic agents—the collision of certain terrific forces, which were ultimately reduced under the more orderly government of Zeus or Jupiter, with whom begins a new dynasty, and a different order of beings.

21. Zeus divided the sovereignty of the universe with his two brothers—Poseidon (Neptune) and Hades (Pluto).

Pluto and Proserpina.

He retained for himself the æther and the atmosphere, together with the general presiding function; Poseidon obtaining the sea, and administering subterranean forces generally; while Hades ruled the world of shades. These deities, with their sisters and divine progeny, comprehended the gods worshipped by the early Greeks. Twelve were especially called the great Olympic gods, being supposed to dwell on the heights of Mount Olympus, and to form the divine agora, or council of the gods, which was held there. We must briefly introduce these twelve to the reader, with their leading characteristics; and in doing so, we shall give those Latin synonyms for their names, which, as they are the most familiar, will hereafter be used.

22. (1.) Zeus or Jupiter, the chief of the gods, is said to have been the son of Saturn, one of the Titans, who sprang from Uranus and Ge. Saturn, foreboding destruction to himself from his own children, swallowed them as soon as they were born. However, his wife Rhea contrived to conceal the birth of Jupiter, who thus escaped, and grew to manhood, when he by stratagem induced his father to disgorge the five previous children— Vesta, Ceres, Juno, Neptune, and Pluto. Jupiter now determined to wrest the power from Saturn and his brothers, the Titans; and a long and desperate struggle took place, in which all the gods and goddesses took part, and universal nature was convulsed. The thunderbolts of Jupiter at length prevailed; and Saturn, with the other Titans, were irrevocably imprisoned in Tartarus. Saturn was afterwards known under the name of Chronos, as the god of Time, and was represented under the figure of an old man, holding a scythe in one hand, and a serpent, with its tail in its mouth, in the other. Jupiter is always represented as seated on a throne, with thunderbolts in his right hand, and an eagle by his side.

Saturn.

Jupiter.

23. (2.) Poseidon or Neptune, the Earth-shaker and Ruler of the Sea, was second only to Jupiter in power. The island of Calaurea was his favourite residence. He was also the patron god of the Isthmus of Corinth, and

10 HISTORY OF GREECE.

some other places. He is represented as a half-nude man, drawn in a chariot over the sea by water-horses,

Neptune.

and having a crown on his head, and a trident, or three-pronged sceptre, in his hand.

24. (3.) Apollo, son of Jupiter, the god of Prophecy, Music, and Song, is represented as a handsome young man, with a lyre and a bow.

Apollo.   Vulcan.

25. (4.) Hephæstus or Vulcan, the god of Fire, and a great artificer in metals. Having been born weak and

THE GODS OF GREECE. 11

deformed, he was thrown down from Olympus, and alighted on the island of Lemnos, where he was kindly received, and which continued his most favoured abode, though other volcanic islands—as Lipara, Hiera, Imbros, and Sicily—were reckoned also his workshops. During the best period of Grecian art, he was represented as a vigorous man, with a beard; and characterised by his hammer, or some other tool, his oval cap, and a dress which leaves the right arm and shoulder uncovered.

26. (5.) Ares or Mars, the god of War, delighting in the

Mars.

din of battle, the slaughter of men, and the destruction of towns. He was hated by the other gods; and his worship in Greece was not very general. He is often represented as an armed man in a chariot, with an inferior goddess named Bellona at his side.

Mercury presenting a Soul to Pluto.

27. (6.) Hermes or Mercury, the god of Eloquence, the messenger of the gods, the inventor of the lyre, which he transferred to Apollo, and the patron of knavery. He is characterised by sandals with wings, which carried him

rapidly over sea and land; a wand called caduceus, which he bore as herald; and a travelling-cap, which in later times was furnished with two wings.

28. (7.) Hera or Juno, the wife of Jupiter, a beautiful

Juno.

but unamiable goddess. She quarrelled much with her husband, and persecuted his children. She was worshipped in many parts of Greece, but particularly in Argos, where she had a splendid temple, as well as in Samos. She is usually represented as a majestic female of mature age, with a beautiful forehead, and large eyes widely open. Her characteristics are a diadem, veil, sceptre, and peacock.

Minerva.

29. (8.) Athena, Pallas, or Minerva, the goddess of Wisdom and War, is the type of composed, majestic, and unrelenting force. She is said to have issued in full armour from the head of Jupiter, and to have been inaccessible to feminine sympathies. She is characterised by the formidable ægis and crushing spear; and in the centre of her breastplate or shield, appears the head of Medusa the Gorgon. She was worshipped in all parts of Greece, but was especially the tutelar divinity of the city of Athens and the soil of Attica. The story ran that Neptune

contended with her for this honour, and that the gods determined to give possession to whichever of the two should confer the most useful gift on mankind: whereupon Neptune struck his trident on the ground, and the horse appeared; Minerva planted an olive-tree, and was declared the victor. The city was named after her, and the magnificent festival of Panathenæa was celebrated there in her honour. The owl, the serpent, the cock, and the olive-tree were sacred to her.

Diana.

30. (9.) Artemis, or Diana, the twin-sister of Apollo, and goddess of Hunting, is, like him, armed with a bow and arrows. Unlike him, she was ever unmoved by love. As Apollo had charge of the sun, so had Diana of the moon. As a huntress, she is represented with her limbs bare and her breast covered; her accessories being either the bow, quiver, and arrows, or a spear, stags, and dogs; but as goddess of the Moon, she wears a long robe and a veil, with a crescent rising above her forehead. The Ephesian Diana was an Asiatic divinity, quite distinct from the Greek one.

31. (10.) Aphrodite or Venus, the goddess of Love and Beauty, is generally represented with her son Eros or Cupid. The principal seats of her worship were the islands of Cyprus and Cythera. The myrtle, the rose,

Venus.

the apple, and the poppy were sacred to her; likewise
the sparrow, the dove, the swan, the swallow, and the iynx.

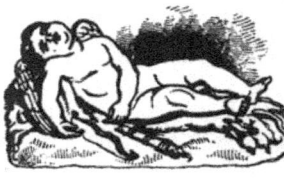
Cupid.

32. (11.) Hestia or Vesta, the goddess of the Hearth, or rather of the fire burning there, was a chaste and home-keeping maiden divinity, believed to dwell in the inner part of every house. The first part of every sacrifice was presented to her, as goddess of the sacred fire on the altar, and solemn oaths were sworn by her. It was on the hearth that refugees, entering a house, implored protection of the inhabitants; and every town had a sacred hearth, where the goddess had her especial sanctuary, and where she protected suppliants. When a colony was sent out, the emigrants took fire from their native town, to kindle that on the hearth of their new home.

33. (12.) Demeter or Ceres, the goddess of Agriculture, acquired much importance in Greece, and was worshipped with great splendour by the Athenians, who pretended that agriculture had been practised first in their country, and under the immediate tuition of this goddess.

Ceres.

Works of art represent her fully attired, wearing a garland of corn-ears, or a simple ribbon, and holding a sceptre, corn-ears, or poppy; sometimes also a torch, and the mystic basket.

34. Besides these, called the twelve great gods of Olympus, there was an indefinite number of others, some of whom were little inferior in power and dignity. Such

were Helios or Sol, Bacchus, the Muses, the Nereides, the Nymphs, &c. There were also monsters, the progeny

Bacchus.

of the gods—as the Harpies, the Gorgons, Cerberus, the Centaurs, the Dragon of the Hesperides, Xanthos and Balios, the immortal horses, &c.

Centaur.   Hebe.

35. Some deities performed special services for the greater gods—as Iris, a messenger of the gods; Hebe, who waited upon them, and filled their cups with nectar; the Horæ, who guarded the doors of Olympus, &c.

36. It was thus that all nature was imagined to be moving and working through a number of personal agents;

all things in earth and heaven, as well as the earth itself and the solid heaven, were considered as endowed with appetite, feeling, sex, and other attributes of humanity. In the view of a Greek, the description of the sun, as given by a modern astronomer, would have appeared repulsive and impious; for the sun in his eyes was the god Helios, whom he saw mounting his chariot every morning in the east, riding on triumphantly to the height of the heaven, reaching it at mid-day, and arriving in the evening in the western horizon with horses fatigued and needing repose. In the course of his journey, Helios delighted to gaze on certain favourite spots where his cattle were pastured; he also had sons and daughters upon earth; his all-seeing eye could penetrate everywhere; but often he turned away to avoid contemplating scenes offensive in their nature. And so of the rest. To us these now appear but pleasing fancies, but to the Greeks they were venerated realities.

37. The gods were propitiated by animal sacrifices, of which the bones only and the fat were presented to them; likewise by offerings of fruits, oils, and fragrant odours; and by the dedication of lands and treasures to their service. Every king was the priest of his subjects, and every father sacrificed for his family.

LEGENDS OF APOLLO.

38. To give some idea of the legends attached to these divinities, it may suffice to mention the principal ones belonging to Apollo, whose worship was widely diffused in every branch of the Hellenic race, and forms one of the most ancient and strongly marked features of its history.

39. The narrow, rocky, uninviting island of Delos was the accredited birthplace of Apollo. Here his mother, Latona, persecuted by Juno, found shelter to give birth to the infant. Hardly had he tasted the nectar and ambrosia which formed the immortal food of the gods, when he burst his swaddling-bands, displayed his divine strength, claimed his bow and harp, with his special function of announcing to men beforehand the designs of Jupiter.

According to a promise made by Latona to the islanders, Delos was ever after preferred by Apollo as his residence; and there the Ionians, with their families, congregated periodically from their respective cities to do him honour. The countless ships, and wealth, and elegance, of these multitudes had the air of an assembly of gods. Dance and song, and athletic contests, graced the solemnities; the Delian maidens sang hymns in praise of the god, as well as of Latona his mother and Diana his sister, intermingling these with adventures of foregone men and women, to the delight of the listening throng. So runs the strain of the blind bard of Chios, who himself had found favour at this festival.

40. But Delos was not an oracular spot; and Apollo descended from Olympus to choose one where he might manifest himself as the revealer of futurity. Many different places did he inspect; and at length would have fixed on the fine plain and frequented fountain of Delphusa or Tilphusa; but Delphusa, proud of the beauty of her own site, would not have her glory eclipsed by that of the god; and she persuaded him that the chariots which contended in the plain, and the cattle which watered at the fountain, would disturb the solemnity of his proceedings. He was thus induced to proceed to the southern side of Parnassus, where he chose a site overhanging the harbour of Crissa. It was near a fountain, guarded by a terrific serpent, which Apollo slew with an arrow, and allowed the carcass to rot in the sun. Hence the place was called Pytho, and the god as here worshipped, Python or the Pythian Apollo.

41. After his temple had been built, he discovered with indignation that Tilphusa had cheated him, and he went back to resent the fraud. This he did by throwing into her fountain a great crag, which obstructed the limpid current; he also established an altar for himself in a neighbouring grove, where men worshipped him as Apollo Tilphusios, because of his revenge upon the once beautiful Tilphusa.

42. Apollo now required special ministers to take care of his temple and sacrifice, and to pronounce his responses

at Pytho. Descrying a ship containing 'many and good men,' bound on traffic from Crete to Peloponnesus, he determined to secure them for this service. Therefore, assuming the form of a dolphin, he splashed about and tossed the vessel so as to alarm the mariners, while he also blew a strong wind, which drove it into the Corinthian Gulf, and finally ran it aground in the harbour of Crissa. The terrified crew did not dare to land; but Apollo, standing on the shore in the form of a vigorous youth, revealed himself as the author of their compulsory voyage, and announced the honourable functions to which he intended to promote them. They followed him, accordingly, to the rocky Pytho on Parnassus, chanting the solemn Io-Pæan, as it was sung in Crete, while Apollo marched with lofty step in front, playing on the harp. He led them to the temple and site of the oracle, directing them to worship him as Apollo Delphinius, because he had first appeared to them as a dolphin. They asked how they were to live in a place destitute of corn, and wine, and pasture; to which he replied, that their lot should neither be toil on the one hand, nor privation on the other; that they should live by the offerings which crowds of pious visitors would bring to the temple, needing only the knife to be ever ready for sacrifice. He then appointed them guardians of his temple, and ministers of his feasts, warning them, that if they should ever be guilty of insolence or wrong, they should be subject to slavery, and that for ever.

43. These two legends of Delos and Delphi form but a very insignificant fraction of the stories that were once current respecting the great and venerated Apollo. They are specimens, and very ancient specimens, to convey what these divine myths were, and what was the peculiar character of Greek faith and fancy. The oft-recurring festivals of the gods occasioned a constant demand for new stories respecting them, or at least for new forms and varieties of the old ones. Each deity had many surnames, temples, groves, and solemnities; and to each of these was attached more or less of mythical narrative, which the poets found as a popular belief, and embodied,

adorned, and diffused in their songs. These myths harmonised with each other in their general types only, but differed irreconcilably in details. Provided the poet maintained the general keeping, taking care that his story corresponded to the characteristic notions which his hearers had of the god, he might indulge his fancy without restraint in the particular incidents.

44. Nor was it only the general types and attributes of the gods that stimulated the propensity of this people to frame mythical stories. The details of every temple and its locality, with the peculiar rites and ceremonies belonging to it, were connected with traditional narratives, which lent a certain dignity even to the minutiæ of divine service. These were preserved and recounted to the curious stranger by the local guides and guardians of the holy places, and afforded inexhaustible materials for poetry.

MYSTERIES.

45. About the sixth century before the Christian era, various religious novelties were introduced into Greece from Egypt, Asia Minor, and Thrace, attaching themselves chiefly to the worship of Bacchus and Ceres, who were easily identified with deities of similar attributes worshipped in those countries. Such were the special mysteries, schemes for religious purification, and orgies in honour of some particular god, distinct both from the public and the family solemnities of primitive Greece, celebrated apart from the citizens generally, and approachable only through a certain course of initiation. They were generally under the superintendence of hereditary families of priests, who imparted the rites to voluntary disciples. Occasionally, the disciples of such mysteries united in permanent brotherhoods, bound by ascetic vows and periodical solemnities. These special religious services, superinduced as they were upon the old public sacrifices of the chief on behalf of the people, and of the father on his family hearth, were especially in requisition during times of public calamity, when the gods were supposed to be displeased, and the ordinary routine of worship and

sacrifice appeared insufficient to appease them. And as great exactitude was held to be necessary in the performance of these peculiar services, the class of priests, or Hierophants, who alone were familiar with the ritual, acquired a highly influential position.

46. These rites, especially those in honour of Bacchus, were in many cases furious and ecstatic, especially among the women, who had everywhere occasional meetings of their own, apart from the men. At a stated time every three years, crowds of females, dressed in fawn-skins, and bearing the consecrated thyrsus, flocked to the solitudes of Parnassus, Cithæron, or Taÿgetus, and passed the night in dancing by torch-light, clamorously invoking the god, and abandoning themselves to the most frantic excitement; while the men celebrated noisy revels in the streets, playing the cymbals and tambourine, and carrying the image of the god in procession. It was understood that those who surrendered themselves to these ecstasies in the prescribed manner, procured immunity from such frenzies for the future; while those who resisted the inspiration became obnoxious to the displeasure of the god. It is to be remarked, that the Athenian women never perpetrated these wild extravagances, though they had some exclusively female congregations, and mournful solemnities accompanied with fasting. The legends upon which all these practices were founded were sacred stories, which were known only to the initiated, and which it was sacrilege to repeat in public.

47. The legend connected with the Eleusian mysteries was in substance the following :—Proserpine, the daughter of Ceres, had been seized by Pluto while she was gathering flowers in a meadow, and was carried off to become his wife in the world of shades. The disconsolate mother wandered for nine days and nights by torch-light in search of the maiden; and at length Helios (Sol), the 'spy of gods and men,' revealed the truth to her, and, moreover, that Jove had permitted the abduction. Ceres, in anger and despair, renounced the society of Olympus, abstained from nectar and ambrosia, and wandered fasting upon earth. Thus she came to Eleusis, where she was found

by the daughters of the prince sitting in the form of an old woman by a well. She said she wanted employment as a nurse, and the damsels effectually used their good offices to have her intrusted with the care of their only brother, a new-born infant. Here she refused to taste wine, begging for a peculiar mixture of barley-meal and mint-water. She gave the child no food, but anointed him with ambrosia, and he grew like a god; every night she plunged him in the fire, and took him out unhurt. She would have rendered him immortal, but for the interference of the mother, who one night witnessed the process. The goddess now revealed herself, assumed her own divine form, and directed that a temple and altar should be erected to her on the neighbouring hill, where she was to be served with orgies of her own prescribing. Her injunctions were obeyed, and she took up her abode in the temple, still pining with grief. She withheld from mortals her beneficent aid; the barley which was sown that year never sprung up, and the human race was in danger of starvation. Jupiter sent various deputations of goddesses to implore her to relent; but she would be satisfied with nothing except the restoration of her daughter, which Jupiter was obliged at length to effect. Ceres was now reconciled both to the gods and to men; the buried seed came up in abundance, and she returned to Olympus. She was obliged, however, to allow Proserpine to spend three months of every year with Pluto, departing always at seed-time; the reason being, that she had not remained utterly fasting in the lower world, but had eaten a pomegranate seed.

48. The small town of Eleusis derived great importance from the solemnities connected with this myth, consisting of processional marches, and other observances suggested by the legend. Besides, the Athenians declared that the arts of agriculture had been first taught by Ceres to a man of Eleusis, and that themselves had been the medium of communicating its blessings to all the rest of mankind.

ORACLES.

49. A distinguishing characteristic which continually meets us in the history of the Greeks, is their anxiety to penetrate the future, and their unwillingness to commence any enterprise without ascertaining that the gods were propitious to it. The divine will was supposed to be announced by visions, dreams, and various omens—as thunder, lightning, eclipses, the flight or the notes of birds, the entrails of sacrificial victims, but especially by oracles. The most ancient of these oracles was that of Dodona, in Epeirus, where Jupiter announced his will by the whistling of the wind through lofty trees. In order to render the sounds more intelligible, vessels of brass were suspended on the branches, to be driven against each other by the wind; and the sounds thus procured were interpreted by the aged women who had the charge. This oracle was afterwards superseded to a great extent by the one at Delphi, which was built round one of the openings of a deep cavern in the side of Mount Parnassus. An intoxicating vapour arose from this chasm, over which the priestess called Pythia sat on a tripod when the oracle was consulted. The words she uttered, after inhaling the vapour, were believed to be the revelations of Apollo, and were communicated in hexameter verse by the attending priests to the inquirers. This oracle in time proved a powerful engine of political influence, and its wealth became immense, from the numerous and costly offerings of its votaries.

THE OLYMPIC AND OTHER GAMES.

50. The celebrated games called the Olympic, the Pythian, the Nemean, and the Isthmian, are understood to have been great religious festivals; the gods gave their sanction to recreation, and there was the closest connection between common worship and common amusement. It is impossible to trace the origin of these solemnities, which was anterior to all history. It would seem that the habit

of neighbouring tribes or villages joining in sacrifice at each other's festivals, was one of the earliest usages of Greece ; and to partake of the recreations which followed the religious observances, was a matter of course. As Greece emerged from the turbulence of the heroic age, the village festivals became city festivals, and thus the once humble gatherings at Elis and Delphi swelled into the pomp and confluence of the Olympic and Pythian games.

51. The most ancient as well as famous of these festivals, was that celebrated in the plain of Olympia, in the territory of Elis, and near an ancient temple of the Olympian Jove. It was celebrated every four years, which interval was called an Olympiad ; and the first register of a victor's name, which occurs in 776 B.C., supplies the earliest historic record of Greece—that from which the dates of later historians were calculated. At first, the amusements lasted but a single day, and consisted only of foot-races in the stadium ; but various trials of strength and skill—as wrestling, boxing, throwing, and chariot-racing—were afterwards introduced, and the time was prolonged. The management of the whole festival was in the hands of the Eleans, and their territory was considered sacred during its continuance, so that to invade it would have been a sacrilegious act. The number of spectators was immense, and included deputies from the different states, vying with each other in the number of their offerings and the splendour of their retinue, to support the honour of their respective cities. The only prize given to the victor was a garland of wild olive ; but it was reward enough that his name was proclaimed before assembled Hellas ; that his statue was erected in the sacred grove of Jupiter at Olympia. He returned to his home in triumphal procession, and was rewarded by his fellow-citizens always with distinguished honours—sometimes with substantial benefits.

52. The Pythian games, second only to the Olympic, were celebrated in the third year of each Olympiad, on the plain of Cirrha, and under the protection of the Amphictyons. The Nemean were held every two years, in honour

of the Nemean Jove, and in the valley of the same
name between Phlius and Cleonæ ; the Isthmian, by the
Corinthians, on their own isthmus, in honour of Neptune.
In the Pythian, Nemean, and Isthmian games, contests
in music and poetry were added to gymnastics and races.
The concourse which these festivals collected, afforded
the poet, the philosopher, the historian, and the artist,
the best means for making their works known, while to
the merchant it opened a scene of busy traffic.

THE AMPHICTYONIC COUNCIL.

53. Sometimes the tendency of the Greeks to religious
fraternisation took a form called Amphictyony. A certain
number of cities entered into partnership for the celebration
of periodical sacrifices to the deity of a particular temple,
which was supposed to belong to them all, and to be under
common protection. Probably there were unions of this
kind that never acquired a place in history; and among
those that did, one which embraced twelve tribes or sub-
races gained pre-eminence, and came to be distinguished as
the Amphictyonic Council. Its meetings were held every
spring at Delphi, and every autumn at Thermopylæ.
They were attended by sacred deputies, including a chief
and certain subordinates from each Amphictyonic town,
accompanied, as it seems, by numerous volunteers, for purposes of religion, enjoyment, or commerce. The original
and most important function of this body was to watch
over the wealthy temple at Delphi, in which all had an
interest, as may be gathered from the Amphictyonic oath :
' We will not destroy any Amphictyonic town, or cut off
from it running-water in time of peace ; and if any one
shall do so, we will march against that city and destroy it.
If any one shall plunder the treasures of the god, or shall
be privy to its being done, or shall take treacherous counsel
against the things in his temple at Delphi, we will punish
him with foot, and hand, and voice, and by every means in
our power.' In process of time, the Amphictyons took a
larger view of their own functions, and from being first
a purely religious convocation, their council became both

religious and political, and finally more political than religious. But it seems to be a mistake to view it as a national congress charged with defending the common interests of Greece, or entitled to command universal obedience. Its first establishment must have been long before the date of any historic records, for it included races scarcely heard of afterwards, as the Dolopes and Malians, on a footing of perfect equality with the Dorians and Ionians.

54. The Pythian festival, in its first humble form of a competition among bards to sing a hymn in praise of Apollo, was doubtless of immemorial antiquity; but the first multiplication of the subjects of competition, and the first introduction of a continuous record of the conquerors, dates from the time when it came under the presidency of the Amphictyons; after which, the games became crowded and celebrated.

HEROIC LEGENDS.

55. Having briefly noticed the principal gods of Greece, and some of the usages connected with their worship, we come to the genealogies which connect them with historical men.

56. In the retrospective faith of a Greek, the idea of worship was closely connected with that of ancestry; every association of men traced its union to some common progenitor, and that progenitor was either the god they worshipped in common, or some semi-divine being closely allied to him. Every Greek loved to look back to his gods through an unbroken line of ancestry, and to boast a genealogy filled not only with the names, but the splendid adventures of those who were little removed from the divine. These genealogies constitute the supposed primitive history of Hellas, but it is impossible to distinguish the historical truth they may contain from the fictitious creations which embellish them. Their number exceeds all computation, but we shall glance at some of those most intimately connected with the succeeding history.

57. The wickedness of the earth, says one of these

legends, provoked Jupiter to send an unremitting and terrible rain, which laid the whole of Greece under water, except the highest mountain-tops, on which a few stragglers found refuge. Deucalion, the son of Prometheus, who was a son of the Titan god Iapetus, was saved, with his wife Pyrrha, in a chest or ark which his father had forewarned him to construct; and after floating on the water for nine days, he settled on the summit of Mount Parnassus. He now prayed that companions might be sent to them; and, accordingly, Jupiter directed them to throw stones over their heads, which, when they had done, those cast by Pyrrha became women, and those by Deucalion men, over whom he reigned as king in Thessaly. One of the sons of this pair was Hellen, the great progenitor of the people previously called Greeks, but henceforth Hellenes. It was, however, maintained by many that Hellen was the son of Jupiter, and not of Deucalion. Hellen had three sons by a nymph—Dorus, Xuthus, and Æolus. Æolus inherited the dominion in Thessaly, but his descendants occupied a great part of Central Greece, and became widely diffused, especially on the coasts. Dorus and his descendants occupied the country on the northern side of the Corinthian Gulf. Xuthus received Peloponnesus, and had two sons, Achæus and Ion, the progenitors of the Achæans and Ionians. Thus the four great branches of the Hellenic race became masters of Greece, the previous Pelasgic inhabitants either disappearing before them, or being incorporated with them. The Dorians and Ionians became, in historical times, the two leading races, represented by the Spartans and Athenians respectively; but in the heroic ages described in the ancient legends, the Achæans were the most distinguished, as being the most warlike of the races.

58. The first few generations of the family thus established in Greece are called the Heroic race, and the period in which they lived, the Heroic age—a time when, as posterity believed, feats of superhuman strength were achieved by mortals, and divine interference in human affairs was frequent and familiar. Two of the heroes, Hercules and Theseus, we must notice, on account of their connection with subsequent history.

59. Hercules, the greatest of all the Grecian heroes, was the son of Jupiter by Alcmene, the wife of Amphitryon, king of Thebes, in Bœotia, who adopted him as his own son. By a stratagem of Juno, Hercules was deprived of the empire which Jove had designed for him as the descendant of Perseus, and it became the inheritance of Eurystheus, another grandson of Perseus. She likewise sent two serpents to destroy him in his cradle, but the infant hero strangled them with his hands. As he grew up, he was sent to tend Amphitryon's cattle; a huge lion made great havoc among them, and Hercules, slaying him, wore the skin ever afterwards as his ordinary garment, and the mouth and head as his helmet. The gods made him presents of arms, and he usually carried an immense club, which he had cut for himself in the neighbourhood of Nemea. After various adventures, he consulted the oracle of Delphi as to where he should settle, and was instructed to live at Tiryns, and serve Eurystheus for twelve years, after which he should become immortal. Hence the twelve labours, performed at the bidding of Eurystheus.

60. In these are realised the great objects of all ancient heroism—the destruction of monstrous evils, and the acquisition of wealth and power. Such, on a magnificent scale, was the overthrow of the Nemean lion and the Lernean hydra; the seizure of the girdle of Mars from Hippolyte, queen of the Amazons; the fetching of the golden apples of the Hesperides, guarded by a hundred-headed dragon. But in the case of Hercules, as in others, we perceive human faults which demanded expiation. Having, in a fit of passion, slain his friend Iphitus, he was smitten with sickness, from which he obtained deliverance only on condition of another servitude; on which he became the slave of Omphale, queen of Lydia, and spun wool with a distaff. The time of this servitude having expired, he undertook various warlike adventures, and married a lady called Deianira, whose jealousy became the cause of his death. Fearing that she might be superseded in his affection by Iole, a maiden whom he had captured, Deianira steeped a tunic in a liquid which she had been led to believe would secure his regards to herself. This was, however, a deadly

poison; and no sooner had the hero put it on, than he was seized with excruciating pains. In vain he strove to wrench it off; it stuck to his flesh, which tore away with it. Willing to hasten his end, Hercules, after desiring his son Hyllus to marry Iole, ascended Mount Œta, raised a pile of wood, placed himself on it, and directed it to be set on fire. While it was burning, a cloud came from heaven, and carried him, amid peals of thunder, to Olympus, where he was made immortal, was reconciled to Juno, and received her daughter Hebe in marriage. He was consequently worshipped throughout Greece both as a god and a hero, the sacrifices offered to him consisting chiefly of bulls, boars, rams, and lambs.

61. After the death and apotheosis of Hercules, his children were persecuted by Eurystheus; the Athenians offered them shelter, and Eurystheus invaded Attica, but perished in the enterprise. His sons fell with him, so that the Heracleids were now the only representatives of Perseus. They made an effort to recover their rightful possessions, but were met at the isthmus by the combined forces of the Ionians, Achæans, and Arcadians, then inhabiting Peloponnesus. Hyllus, the eldest of the sons of Hercules, proposed to determine the contest by single combat, the condition being, that if he were victorious, the Heracleids should be restored; but if vanquished, they should forego their claim for a hundred years. Echemus, the hero of Tegea, accepted the challenge, and Hyllus was slain, in consequence of which the Heracleids retired, and resided with the Dorians, under the protection of Ægimius, the son of Dorus, till the stipulated period of time had expired.

62. The most ancient name in Attic archæology is that of Erechtheus, said to have been born of the Earth, but adopted by Minerva, and reared by her in her temple at Athens, where annual sacrifices continued to be offered to him. But the great Attic hero was Theseus, a contemporary and relative of Hercules, whose exploits he imitated.

63. We shall advert to two specimens of his prowess. The Amazons—a race of female warriors, who continually appear in the old legends, and were universally believed in as having once existed—had scarce recovered from

the aggressions of Hercules, when Theseus attacked and defeated them, carrying off their queen, Antiope, which injury they avenged by invading Attica. They crossed the Cimmerian Bosporus on the winter-ice, and penetrated even into Athens, where, after a desperate and long doubtful struggle, they were finally overcome by Theseus. No legendary story appears to have worked more deeply into the national mind of Greece, than that of this hard-fought battle in the heart of Athens. The Attic antiquaries of succeeding ages pointed out the exact position of the two contending forces; while the sepulchral edifice called the Amazonian, the tomb or pillar of Antiope, near the western gate of the city, and the sacrifices which were offered to the Amazons at the periodical festival of the Thesia, were all so many religious mementos of the victory.

64. Another famous adventure of Theseus was connected with the Minotaur. Minos, the ruler of Cnossus, in Crete, and his brother Rhadamanthus, were sons of Jupiter by Europa, daughter of the Phœnix. Androgeos, the son of Minos, having vanquished all competitors at an Athenian festival, was induced to contend with the bull of Marathon, and perished. Minos made war upon Athens, to avenge his death, aided by his father Jupiter, who sent pestilence and famine into the city. The Athenians were at length obliged to accept peace on any terms; and Minos required that seven youths and seven maidens should be sent to Crete every ninth year, to be devoured by a monster, half-bull, half-man, in a labyrinth, out of which no one could find a passage. The third period for despatching victims had arrived, and Theseus, craving the aid of Neptune, and receiving assurance that Venus would extricate him, offered himself as one of the fourteen. On his arrival at Cnossus, he at once captivated the affections of Ariadne, the daughter of Minos, who furnished him with a sword, with which he killed the Minotaur, and a clue of thread, by which he retraced his way out of the labyrinth. This done, he set sail from Crete with his companions, carrying off Ariadne also. On his way home, he stopped at Delos, to offer a grateful sacrifice to Apollo

for his escape ; and danced, with the young men and maidens he had rescued, a dance in imitation of the convolutions of the labyrinth. It had been agreed between him and his father, that if he returned in safety, he should hoist white sails, instead of the black ones usually carried on this mournful embassy ; but Theseus forgot to make the change ; and his father watching the returning ship, and concluding that his son had perished, threw himself into the sea. The ship was carefully preserved by the Athenians, being constantly repaired with new timbers down to the time of Phalereus Demetrius ; and every year she was sent to Delos with special envoys and a solemn sacrifice. During her absence, the city was held to abstain from all acts of public impurity, so that no one might be put to death even under judicial sentence till its return.

65. The historians of later ages attributed to Theseus the qualities of a far-sighted politician, as they have given to Minos the character of a great maritime conqueror, a stern lawgiver, and the originator of the Syssitia, or public meals afterwards introduced at Sparta. But it is difficult to shew any grounds for such statements, except the reverence with which the memory of Theseus was regarded, and the repulsive feelings which attached to Minos.

66. We now pass from the legends of individual heroism to some of the great collective expeditions of those days.

THE ARGONAUTIC EXPEDITION.

67. During the age of Hercules, Jason, a prince of Thessaly, undertook an enterprise, afterwards celebrated as the Argonautic Expedition. Æson, his uncle, had usurped his throne, and consented to restore it only on condition that Jason should bring from Æa (Colchis), a region on the east of the Black Sea, a golden fleece, which was there hanging on a tree in the grove of Mars, guarded by a sleepless dragon. The most renowned heroes of the time, including Hercules and Theseus, united with Jason in the enterprise; and the adventurers were called Argonauts, after the vessel which was built for it. When they arrived, the king, Æetes, promised to give Jason the fleece if he would yoke two fire-breathing oxen, with brazen feet, plough with them a piece of land, sow in the furrows the teeth of the dragon slain by Cadmus, and vanquish the warriors that would spring from this seed. Medea, the daughter of Æetes, who was skilled in magical arts, furnished Jason with the means of accomplishing all; and when her father still delayed to surrender the fleece, she put the dragon to sleep, seized the treasure, and set sail with the adventurers. Æetes pursued them in vain; and after much circuitous voyaging, they safely reached their home.

WAR OF THE SEVEN AGAINST THEBES.

68. Another celebrated expedition of the heroic age was the 'War of the Seven against Thebes.' Laius, forewarned that any son whom he might beget would kill him, caused Œdipus to be exposed on Mount Cithæron as soon as he was born. Here the herdsmen of Polybus, king of Corinth, chanced to find the infant, and took him to their master, who reared him as his own. When Œdipus grew to man's estate, he became uneasy about his parentage, and went to Delphi to consult the oracle. Here he

was warned not to return to his country, else he would slay his father and marry his mother. Deeming no other city but Corinth to be his birthplace, he avoided it, and quitted Delphi by the road leading to Bœotia and Phocis. By the way, he met Laius in a chariot; the insolence of one of the attendants brought on an angry quarrel, and Œdipus killed his unknown parent. Proceeding to Thebes, he found it vexed by a terrible monster called the Sphinx, whose ravages were to cease only when a riddle which she propounded to the Thebans was solved. Œdipus was happy enough to discover the answer, and obtained the promised reward, which was no less than the throne and the hand of the widowed queen, Jocaste, whom he married, all unknowing that she was his mother. The gods afterwards revealed the dreadful facts to mankind, and Jocaste hanged herself in an agony of sorrow. The mind of Œdipus became alienated; and again and again he cursed his sons, Eteocles and Polynices, praying the gods that they might fall by each other's hands. After his death, these sons quarrelled about the succession; and Polynices being driven from Thebes, found shelter with Adrastus, king of Argos, who gave him his daughter in marriage, and undertook to restore him to his rights. He is said to have engaged five chiefs in the enterprise, making seven with Polynices and himself—that is, one to assault each of the seven gates of Thebes. The two brothers proposed to decide the matter by single combat, and both fell; so that the issue was still undetermined. A desperate conflict ensued, in which the assailants were slain, and Adrastus alone survived out of the seven. Their defeat was avenged after some years by their sons, whose expedition is called that of the Epigoni. They succeeded in establishing the son of Polynices on the throne; but Adrastus lost his son in the conflict, and sorrow cut short his own life. He was worshipped as a hero at Argos and Sicyon. These sieges of Thebes are, in traditionary celebrity, second only to that of Troy, which occurred soon after.

THE SIEGE OF TROY.

1. Rhoeteum; 2. Canteum; 3. Tumul. Ajacis; 4. Tumulus Achillis; 5. Tumulus Patrocli; 6. Sigeum; 7. Templ. Apollinis; 8. Iliumnovum; 9. Tumulus Antilochi; 10. Tumulus Aesyetis; 11. Troja sive Ilium; 12. Pergamum; 13. Thymbra.

69. The sacred city of Ilium, or Troy, was built on a plain in Asia Minor, near the shores of the Hellespont. On one occasion, as Paris, the son of Priam the king, was tending the sheep on Mount Ida, the three goddesses, Juno, Minerva, and Venus, were brought thither, that he might decide a dispute that had occurred as to which was the most beautiful. He awarded the palm to Venus, who thereupon promised him the possession of Helen, wife of the Spartan Menelaus, the fairest of living women. At her instance, ships were built for his voyage, and he was hospitably received and entertained at Sparta. During a temporary absence of Menelaus in Crete, Venus brought about an intrigue between Helen and the guest, and they eloped, taking with them a large sum of money belonging

to Menelaus. The king, hearing of this perfidious abuse of his hospitality, hastened home ; and after consultation with his brother, Agamemnon, king of Mycenæ, and the venerable Nestor, king of Pylos, the outrage was made known throughout Greece, and its princes were solicited to aid in avenging it. Ten years were spent in preparing an expedition, and ten more in besieging Troy. The goddesses Juno and Minerva took an active part on the side of the Greeks. Among their heroes were the distinguished warriors Ajax and Diomedes, and the sagacious Nestor ; while Agamemnon, the commander-in-chief, scarcely inferior to them in prowess, had also a high reputation for prudence in council. But the most conspicuous of all were Achilles and Ulysses (Odysseus). Achilles was a beautiful youth, born of a goddess, swift of foot, fierce in temper, and irresistible in strength ; Ulysses, no less efficient from his wisdom and eloquence in counsel, and the combination of daring courage with deep scheming. Among the Trojans, the most striking hero was Hector, a son of Priam, forming a well-marked contrast with his effeminate brother Paris.

70. Troy was to remain invincible so long as a certain statue of Minerva, called Palladium, the gift of Jupiter himself, remained in the citadel. The daring Ulysses, disguising himself, found means to enter the city, and steal this away. Another stratagem secured the victory. The Greeks, by his direction, constructed a great hollow wooden horse, in which they placed a hundred of their best warriors, the rest sailing away, under pretence of abandoning the siege. The Trojans, coming out of their city to see what their enemies had left, were sorely puzzled with the great horse, which they brought into the city, making a breach in the walls to admit it. During a night of riotous festivity, when all were off their guard, the signal was given for the return of the Greeks by one whom they had left for that purpose ; the warriors rushing out of the horse, were joined by the rest, and the city was overpowered. Troy was utterly destroyed, and Helen resumed her union with Menelaus.

71. The return of the Grecian chiefs from Troy,

furnished poetical materials hardly less copious than the siege itself. Many suffered shipwreck in attempting to reach their homes; and those who succeeded, found their places occupied by usurpers, their lands overrun by enemies, or wasted by neglect, their families ruined by jealousy and discord, and their cities distracted by faction and sedition.

72. Thus, between the war and its consequences, the divine race of heroes was exhausted, and none other such arose to supply their place.

73. To analyse such fables as these, and to elicit from them any particular facts, seems fruitless, in the absence of all other data but what the legends supply. The religious memories, therefore, the poetic inventions, and the items of fact, if such there be, must for ever remain inseparable, as they were originally blended by the poet for the amusement or edification of his auditors.

74. The general public of every part of Greece were perfectly familiar with the legends of their own locality; the numerous festivals, processions, and other public rites, as well as the oracles and prophecies which circulated in every city, tended to keep them alive in every memory. Abundant relics also preserved in the cities and temples, served as mementos and attestations of the legendary events; such was the sceptre of Pelops and Agamemnon, the work of Vulcan, which was still to be seen at Chæronea, in Bœotia, in the days of Pausanias; such also were the tombs of the heroes, and 160 A.D. numerous chapels and sanctuaries, said to have owed their existence to mythical personages.

ANCIENT EPIC POETRY OF GREECE.

75. Long before the period of literature, properly so called, the praises of the gods, and the exploits of heroes, were embodied in verse, and sung from generation to generation. The myths to which we have referred passed into the verses of the poets, where they were multiplied and transformed in various ways; and in process of time numbers of these, at first short and unconnected lays, were

combined and arranged so as to form continuous narrative or epic poems. There was a large number of such poems extant in ancient Greece, but they are all lost except the *Iliad* and *Odyssey*, ascribed to Homer, celebrating the siege of Troy, and the subsequent adventures of Ulysses. The controversies of the learned concerning the person and the works of Homer are endless. At least seven cities of Asiatic Greece laid claim to his birth, and most of them had legends of his romantic parentage, his blindness, his poverty, and the life he led as an itinerant bard. On the other hand, the poetical *gens* called Homerids, who lived in historical times in the island of Chios, regarded him not as a mere man, but as a divine or semi-divine progenitor and *eponymus*—that is, a name-giving ancestor or chief—whom they worshipped in common, and in whom the individuality of every member of the gens was merged. The compositions of each Homerid were called the works of Homer, the names of the various individual bards perishing, while that of the common gentile father increased in renown through the genius of his self-renewing sons. Such manufacture of fictitious personality was a familiar and habitual process in the Greek mind. No less disputed is the date to be assigned to these celebrated poems : about the middle of the ninth century before the Christian era, is probably near the mark ; it could not be much later; and if earlier, it increases the wonder, already great enough, that these works should have come down from so remote a period.

76. The legends thus embodied in song, were not read by individuals apart, but recited either in short fragments before private companies, or as continuous narratives at public festivals, and they constituted the whole intellectual stock of the people for several ages.

77. Besides the poetic charm attaching to these works, they are interesting to us, as revealing the state of society among the Greeks at that early age ; for as antiquarian research was then unknown, Homer's pictures of life and manners must have been those of his own day.

78. The *Iliad* and *Odyssey* represent a state of society in which there is no such thing as law. The king or

chief defends and governs his people according to immemorial usage; and is responsible to none but Jove for the exercise of his authority. Yet is he not such an august tyrant as the monarchs of the East. Ulysses builds his own bed-chamber, constructs his own raft, and boasts of being an excellent ploughman. The wife and daughters of a prince not only spin, weave, and embroider, but fetch water from the well, and assist to wash garments in the river. The nobles or chiefs are distinguished by their warlike prowess, and numerous slaves. War is the grand profession, commerce is little cultivated, and the mechanical arts are known but to a few. Simplicity of feeling, reverence for age, and delicacy towards the female sex, appear in these warriors combined with considerable elevation of sentiment, derived from the belief that the gods take a deep interest in all their proceedings. Their virtues and their defects are those of a people above the savage state, but possessing only the rudiments of the high civilisation afterwards attained. On the whole, the condition and character of the heroic Greeks bear no inconsiderable resemblance to those of chivalrous Europe in the middle ages, or even the clans of the Scottish Highlands a century ago; making allowance for differences resulting from climate and religion. There is the same reliance on the higher qualities of the aristocratic few, rewarded by protection to the many; the same force of family relations, hospitality to the stranger, and protection to the suppliant—forming the brighter features of the picture; the same lawlessness in peace, ferocity in war, and despondency in misfortune—combining to form the darker side.

79. Hesiod, supposed to have flourished a considerable time after Homer, probably about 700 B.C., is the great authority as to the genealogy and history of the gods. Homer, in common probably with other epic poets of his day, supplies only some isolated narratives, besides passing allusions to the well-known legends. But the work of Hesiod is an ancient and genuine attempt to furnish a consecutive history of the divine foretime, and therefore the narratives in his theogony obtained an extensive

circulation among the Hellenes, and such a firm hold on the national faith, as could not be easily shaken by the philosophy of later times.

THE GREEK CLANS, OR GENTILE CLASSIFICATION.

80. In order to convey an idea of what is called the gentile classification of the ancient Greeks, we shall give a brief account of the Ionic section, as that best known to us, including as it does the population of Attica, Eubœa, the Cyclades, and a portion of the Asiatic coast.

81. The Ionians were distributed in four phylæ, or tribes, called Geleontes, Hopletes, Ægikoreis, and Argadeis ; but neither the primitive import of these names, nor the date of their introduction, is now ascertainable. Each tribe comprised three *phratræ*, and each phratrē thirty *genē*, or gentes. A *genos*, or gens, was a kind of clan, bearing a patronymic name, and including a number of families bound together by common religious rites, and enjoying the exclusive privilege of priesthood to a god or demigod supposed to be their ancestor. They had also a burial-place in common, and certain reciprocal rights and obligations in reference to the succession of property and other matters. The phratrē bond was less intimate ; but still it included some mutual duties and common privileges, besides a certain periodical attendance on religious ceremonies, under the presidency of a Phylo-Basileus, or tribe-king. Lastly, all the tribes were united in the common worship of Apollo Patrons, their tutelar god and father Ion having been the son of Apollo.

82. Such was the primitive religious and social distribution of the inhabitants of Attica, as distinguished from the various political classifications to which they were afterwards subjected. It was founded on those principles and tendencies of the Greek mind which have been already noticed, which led them always to combine the idea of ancestry with that of worship, and a communion of blood with a communion of special religious ceremonies. Each family had its own commemorative rites in honour of the manes of its ancestors, celebrated by the master of the house, and

witnessed only by the members of the family; and the larger unions called gentes, phratries, tribes, were formed by an extension of the same principle. To what extent each gens was at first based on actual relationship, we know not; but in historical times, gentilism was extended by artificial analogy, so as to embrace strangers in blood. The Highland clans of Scotland, and the Irish septs, are similar examples of enlarged and factitious family unions.

EARLY MIGRATIONS.

83. The localisation of the various sections of the Greeks at the earliest period of authentic history, by no means corresponds with that described in the Homeric poems. To account for this, we are told that, sixty years after the destruction of Troy, the Thessalians, who originally dwelt in Epeirus, migrated into the region now called Thessaly, expelling or subjugating the previous inhabitants. A still more important movement was that which settled the Dorians in Peloponnesus. The general facts are undoubted; but the details are purely traditional.

84. When the time came, says the tradition, for the Heraclid family to claim their heritage in Peloponnesus, they were represented by Temenus, Cresphontes, and Aristodemus, sons of Hyllus. Under their leadership, the Dorians, a northerly section of Greeks hitherto little known, invaded the peninsula. At the bidding of an oracle, they resolved to proceed by sea, and thus avoid marching by the Isthmus of Corinth, where Hyllus had been slain. The Ozolian Locrians gave them a port, afterwards called Naupactus, for building their vessels. Here Aristodemus was struck with lightning, and died; but his brothers prosecuted the enterprise with unabated vigour. Oxylus, an Ætolian, served them as a guide, and they landed on the coast of Achaia. According to the legends, a decisive victory over Tisamenus, the great potentate of Peloponnesus, made them masters of the whole peninsula; but this is probably a grouping of many successive events into one, for poetical effect. It is believed that the conquest was the work of several years.

85. At the division of the territory, Oxylus received the fertile land of Elis, as the recompense of his services; and on appeal to the lot, Argos fell to Temenus, Messenia to Cresphontes, and Sparta to the infant sons of Aristodemus.

86. The settlement of Oxylus and his Ætolians in Elis included, as a concomitant of supremacy, the administration of the temple at Olympia; and in consideration of this sacred function, which afterwards ripened into the presidency of the great Olympic games, their territory was solemnly pronounced inviolable. The Epeans, who previously inhabited the country, were either expelled or merged in the new-comers, henceforth called Eleans. From Argos, the children of Temenus proceeded to occupy Trœzen, Epidaurus, Ægina, Sicyon, and Phlius; while Sparta long continued to be governed by two joint kings, descended respectively from the two sons of Aristodemus.

87. Corinth is said not to have been connected with the triple partition above mentioned, but to have been Dorised somewhat later, under another leader. Hippotes, a descendant of Hercules, but not through Hyllus, had been provoked to slay Carnus, a prophet who appeared at the camp of Naupactus, endeavouring to discourage the adventurers. For this crime, Hippotes had been sent into exile; but his son, Aletes, returned at the head of a Dorian force, and overpowered Corinth.

88. The Arcadians, in the centre of Peloponnesus, resisted all attempts at invasion, and retained possession of their territory.

89. Of the Achæans dispossessed by the Dorian invasion, some remained in the condition of serfs; another portion took possession of the region now called Achaia, driving out the Ionians, who then sought refuge in Attica; while others joined in what is called the Æolic emigration, to be mentioned presently. The name Achæans, before so prominent, and sometimes used by Homer as a synonym for Greeks, is in future confined to the inhabitants of Achaia, and those of Achaia Phthiotis, north of Mount Œta.

90. The dispossessed Ionians were reserved for a brighter destiny. When Melanthus and the Nelid family

were compelled to abandon their kingdom of Pylos, they retired to Athens, where a fortunate adventure raised Melanthus to the throne. During his reign, and that of his son Codrus, large bodies of fugitives, escaping from the recent invaders throughout Greece, were harboured in Attica, and the Dorians became alarmed at this concentration of their enemies. A powerful force was accordingly mustered to invade the Athenian territory. The Delphic oracle promised them victory only provided they did not injure Codrus. Strict orders were issued accordingly ; but the oracle having become known at Athens, the generous king resolved to sacrifice himself for his country. Disguising himself as a peasant, he sought the Dorian camp ; provoked a quarrel, and was killed. No sooner was the event understood, than the invaders, despairing of success, abandoned their enterprise. In their retreat, however, they took possession of Megara, which now became a Dorian state. The Athenians declared that no one after Codrus was worthy to bear the name of king ; and his descendants were styled *archons*, holding the dignity for life. Such is the story that continued for centuries to warm the patriotism of the Athenians.

91. One of the sons of Codrus, displeased at missing the dignity of archon, resolved on seeking a new home. There was at this period an overflowing population accumulated in Attica, consisting chiefly of dispossessed Greeks of various sections. Various expeditions set forth to cross the Ægæan, chiefly under members of the Codrid family, whence the movement was called the Ionic migration, though it would seem the Ionians formed but an inconsiderable part in it. During their passage across the Ægæan, they formed settlements in the Cyclades and other islands ; and on their arrival in Asia, founded on or near the coast twelve independent cities—Miletus, Ephesus, Samos, Chios, Myus, Priene, Colophon, Lebedus, Teos, Erythrae, Clazomenae, Phocæa, and gave the name of Ionia to that portion of country which they thus occupied.

92. The movement called the Æolian or Bœotian migration, was somewhat earlier. Some of the dispossessed Achæans are believed to have been joined in Bœotia by a

number of its ancient inhabitants, and also by some of its Æolian conquerors, who led them to new homes in the east. The result was seven Æolian cities on the Asiatic coast, of which Cyme was the chief.

93. Some of the Dorian conquerors themselves were drawn into the current of emigration, and led bands of their own countrymen, and of the conquered Achæans, to settle in the south-western corner of Asia Minor and the neighbouring islands.

94. Though the history of these migrations is only traditional, yet it is in the main substantiated by subsequent facts; and it forms a necessary introduction to that part of Grecian history which rests on more reliable evidence. It accounts for the distribution of the Hellenes, as they are found at the dawn of authentic history : Peloponnesus divided unequally between Dorians, Arcadians, Ætolo-Eleans, and Achæans; while the islands of the Ægæan and the western coast of Asia Minor are peopled with Æolians, Ionians, and Dorians — the Æolians occupying the northern portion of this coast, with the islands of Lesbos and Tenedos; the Doric, the southern part, with the islands of Rhodes and Cos; while the Ionic held a position between them.

95. According to the received chronology, these events are succeeded by a period of nearly three centuries, concerning which we have little or no information, before we reach the earliest authentic chronology in the first recorded Olympiad, corresponding to the year 776 B.C.

HISTORIC AGES.

INTRODUCTION.

96. There can be no trustworthy materials for history except records made in writing at or near the time of the events related. It was not till the epoch known by the name of the First Olympiad, corresponding to the year 776 B.C., that the Greeks began to employ writing as a means of perpetuating the memory of historical facts; and, consequently, everything before that period is only traditionary narrative, which may contain a germ of historical truth, but in which it is impossible to distinguish between facts and their poetical embellishments. Having given the reader some idea of these legends, we now enter upon what is properly matter of history in regard to Greece.

97. Grecian history falls naturally into six periods:

I. From 776 to 500 B.C., or the period during which the various states and colonies of Greece pursued their separate career, without either alliance or collision with each other.

II. From 500 to 478 B.C., or the period of the struggles with Persia.

III. From 478 to 404 B.C., or the period of the Peloponnesian wars, in which the peninsular states were struggling against the supremacy of Athens.

IV. From 404 to 371 B.C., when the battle of Leuctra crowned the efforts of Thebes to attain to the headship of Greece.

V. From 371 to 338 B.C., when the battle of Chæronea rendered Philip the Macedonian master of Greece.

VI. From 338 to 300 B.C., or the period of the Macedonian supremacy.

98. Of these, the first may be viewed as a preparation for the other five, which present the acts of a historical drama connected by a sensible thread of unity. We shall adopt them as our order of distribution, interweaving in their proper places the important but outlying adventures of the Sicilian and Italian Greeks; introducing, likewise, such explanations concerning political organisation, philosophy, poetry, and literature, as are requisite to exhibit the multifarious activity of this people during their short but brilliant career.

99. 'After the generation of Alexander,' says Mr Grote, ' the political action of Greece becomes cramped and degraded, no longer interesting to the reader or operative on the destinies of the future world. The dignity and value of the Greeks from that time forward belong to them only as individual philosophers, preceptors, astronomers, and mathematicians, literary men and critics, medical practitioners,' &c. In all these respective capacities, especially in the great schools of philosophic speculation, they still constituted the great light of the Roman world; though, as communities, they had lost their own orbits, and had become satellites of more powerful neighbours.

FIRST PERIOD.

776—500 B.C.

GENERAL VIEW OF THE GREEK STATES.

100. As this is the period of detached histories, it is proper to present the reader with a general view of the various states bearing the Hellenic name, before relating the few events that are known to have occurred.

101. North of the Pass of Thermopylæ—between it and the mouth of the river Peneius, lived five tribes of Hellenes —the Magnetes, Perrhæbians, Achæans, Malians, and

Dolopes, together with certain Epeirotic and Macedonian tribes—all in a state of irregular dependence upon the Thessalians, a proud and disorderly noblesse, whose manners bore much resemblance to those of the heroic age. Here the finest horses in Greece were bred, and the Thessalian cavalry were justly celebrated, but the people make little figure in Grecian history.

102. In middle Greece, the Ozolian Locrians, the Ætolians, and the Acarnanians, lived chiefly in scattered villages, and unquestionably constituted the most backward of all the Hellenes; the people being always armed, ready for plunder, and often making aggressions on their neighbours, whose vengeance they escaped by flying to the inaccessible heights of their own territories.

103. To the east of them, the Locrians, Phocians, and Dorians, occupying the hilly country between Thessaly and Bœotia, were orderly town communities—small and poor indeed, but as well administered as the average of Grecian townships in early times.

104. In Bœotia, we find ten considerable cities, forming a sort of confederacy under the presidency of Thebes; but even of this important territory we know very little for above two centuries after the commencement of the historic era.

105. The condition of Attica, and the progress of the Athenian state, presenting as it does many interesting features, will demand a separate chapter.

106. Of the various races which occupied Peloponnesus, the Arcadians, Cynurians, and Achæans, are understood to have been aboriginal; the last having migrated from the southern to the northern part of it, while the other two had never changed their locality. The dominant race in the peninsula, the Dorians, were understood to be immigrants; so were the Ætolians of Elis, and some others of less note. The legendary account already given of their settlement, corresponds well with the condition in which we find them in historical times.

107. The dynasty of Aletes, in Corinth (see page 40), is said to have included twelve successive kings, of whom the fifth, called Bacchis, was so celebrated, that his

successors were named after him Bacchids, instead of Aletiads or Heraclids. In the reign of Antomenes, who was one of them, the Bacchiad family, numbering 200 individuals, resolved on the abolition of royalty, and constituted themselves a standing oligarchy. This occurred, however, before the time when our historical knowledge of the city begins. The Bacchids continued to form the governing caste, intermarrying usually among themselves, and annually choosing a president from their own number for the administration of affairs. Under them, we find Corinth in the position of a powerful maritime and commercial city. The foundation of such colonies as Corcyra and Syracuse in the eighth century B.C., evinces an appreciation of its maritime position; and we are told, that to the Corinthians is to be ascribed the first great improvement in ship-building—the construction of the trireme, or war-vessel, with a full deck and triple benches for the rowers. Four of these ships were made at Corinth for the Samians in 703.

108. As early as the fourteenth Olympiad, we find Megara an independent city of no mean consideration, and the mother of early and distant colonies. 720 B.C.

109. The rise and progress of Argos and Sparta will, like that of Athens, demand separate narration. These states make the earliest figure in the history of Greece Proper, while the colonies even claim a prior place, as their commercial, political, and intellectual development was earlier than that of any of the parent states.

110. We are here to remark, in reference to the social condition of the people, that, as a general rule, the cultivation of the soil by serfs in the country for the benefit of the citizens, prevailed throughout Greece; only in Laconia and Thessaly the thing was more marked, probably from the serfs being more numerous and high-spirited than elsewhere, and galled by the feeling of being fellow-Greeks with their masters; whereas elsewhere a large proportion of this class were purchased foreigners.

EARLY GOVERNMENTS.

111. Sparta was the only state which retained a kingly government during the brilliant period of Grecian history. It so happened that, for five centuries, neither of the two co-ordinate lines of Spartan kings was ever without some male representatives, so that the primitive notion of a divine right received no serious check, and never wholly expired in the tenacious mind of Sparta. The peculiar prerogatives which were spared to them, were in perfect harmony with this feeling. Their lineage was considered as connecting the whole state with a divine paternity; and as the chiefs of the Heraclids, they were the special donors of the soil of Sparta from the gods, the Dorian conquest having been sanctified and blessed by Jove only for the purpose of establishing the seed of Hercules in the valley of the Eurotas; they were by right priests of Jove, and offered the monthly sacrifices to secure his protection to the people; and whenever victims were offered to the gods, the skins and other portions were their perquisites. Nor is it to be omitted, in enumerating the privileges of a Spartan king, that he, assisted by two officers nominated by himself, and called *Pythii*, conducted all state communications with the temple of Delphi, and had the general custody of oracles and prophecies. In most of the Grecian states, such inspired deliverances were treasured up, and consulted in cases of emergency; but Sparta enjoyed frequent and intimate intercourse with the Delphic oracle; and as its responses were there attended to with more than usual reverence, the functions of the king were so much the more important as the medium of this intercourse.

112. It was far otherwise throughout the other cities of Greece Proper, as well as those of the colonies. Before the era of authentic history, the primitive kingships of the heroic ages had been abolished, and the government vested in some kind of oligarchy—a council deliberating collectively, deciding by the majority of votes, and electing some individuals of their own body as a temporary and accountable

executive. This government of the Few was the first form of republicanism in Greece. The age of democracy, or the government of the Many, was still distant, and the condition of the general mass of freemen appears to have been little affected by the change. The first check which the oligarchies received, and by which many of them were overturned, arose from usurpers called tyrants, or rather, despots, who availed themselves of prevailing discontents to compass the ends of their own ambition. Sometimes it was a magistrate, appointed to sway the executive for a time, who, at the expiration of his term of office, found himself able to retain it in spite of the electors. More frequently, it was a demagogue, who stood forward as the champion of the many in their grievances, acquired their confidence, and engaged their strength to put down the few, and exalt him in their stead. Sometimes a presumptuous rich man, without even the pretence of popularity, hired a body of retainers to seize the Acropolis, and place the government in his hands. It did also happen in several of the Greek states, that a citizen was formally invested with supreme and irresponsible power for a time, in order to meet some pressing emergency. Such an officer was called by the Greeks *Aesymnete*, and by the Romans, *Dictator*. As he was generally a man of ability, and always largely enjoyed the public confidence, he was sometimes so successful that his office was prolonged for life by those who originally appointed him; or otherwise he found himself strong enough to retain it, even in opposition to their wishes. The period between 650 and 500 B.C. witnessed the rise and fall of many such despots and despotic dynasties, of which the most celebrated were those of Corinth, Sicyon, and Megara. But there was in the Greek mind a deeply rooted antipathy, not only to usurped authority, but to anything like permanent or hereditary power vested in an individual; and though he was not always, in the proper sense, a tyrant, yet he generally incurred the hatred of his fellow-citizens sooner or later, and was obliged to surround himself with mercenary troops, and to use violence in order to put down disaffection. Even those who exercised a sovereignty with moderation, could never retain their popularity; for a position which dispensed with the restraints and obligations involved in citizenship, was understood to forfeit all title to the common sympathy and protection. The man who assassinated a despot, was considered worthy of public honour and reward; and a virtuous Greek would seldom have scrupled to carry his sword concealed in myrtle branches for the execution of the deed. Hence few of the despots lived to old age; still fewer transmitted their power to their sons; and very rarely did the dynasty reach to the third generation.

113. The Spartans were always ready to lend their powerful assistance towards the overthrow of these usurpers, but they seldom succeeded in restoring the oligarchy. The sway of the despot had done much to lessen the distance between the Few and the Many; for even the worst of them were more formidable to the rich than to the poor; and when they were removed, it was found impossible in most cases to reinstate the nobles in their ancient privileges. Hence arose a new struggle: the democracy demanded to be something.

114. The history of Athens will afford the most striking illustration of these successive revolutions.

EARLY GREEK COLONIES IN ASIA AND THE ISLANDS.

115. In a former chapter, it was mentioned that there were many separate and successive settlements founded by Greeks of different sections on the coasts of Asia Minor and the islands of the Ægæan before the earliest authentic chronology, and that a considerable number of Greek cities thus arose in these regions. For it is to be remarked that, unlike the procedure of our modern colonisation, the first thing a set of Greek emigrants did was to build a city with temples, gymnasia, and other structures necessary for the maintenance of religion, government, and social order, as they had seen them at home. As regards the relation of such a colony to its parent city, however,

there appears to have been no feeling of dependence on the one side, or claim of authority on the other. The connection was simply one of filial affection and religious veneration. The tutelary deities of the parent city were invited to preside over the newly conquered territory; temples were erected for them in the new acropolis as nearly as possible like those at home; their images were made after the old models; and the sacred fire, which was kept constantly burning on the public hearth, was taken from the altar of Vesta, in the senate-house of the mother city. The founder of a colony, called its œcist, was considered as the representative of the parent state, and as such was worshipped as a hero after his death; and when the colony became a parent in its turn, the new offshoot generally sought an œcist from the original mother-country. The same reverential feeling manifested itself in the religious embassies and offerings which a colony generally sent to honour the festivals of its parent city; but though the natural result of all this was a disposition on each side to afford help to the other in seasons of distress, yet obligation there was none, nor political tie of any kind. No more did the various colonies called the Ionic, the Æolic, and the Doric, form anything like confederations among themselves. Like their parent cities, each city was independent of all other; there was no provision for common defence against foreign enemies; no common tribunal, magistrate, or law, for the maintenance of internal tranquillity.

116. These colonists, in some cases, extirpated the previous inhabitants; in others, accepted them as fellow-residents; so that the Greek cities thus established, contracted a considerable admixture of Asiatic feelings and customs. They likewise acquired much greater activity and enterprise than the Greeks at home, and made rapid advances in wealth and power; while their brethren in Hellas Proper remained, for the most part, poor and proud, despising the arts of wealth, and prizing only those of war. We shall, therefore, glance at these colonies before tracing the progress of the mother-country.

117. The Ionian cities took the lead; and among them

Miletus was the most powerful at the earliest period of our knowledge; its celebrity being derived not merely from its own wealth and population, but from the great number of its colonies, established chiefly on the Propontis and Euxine, and said to have amounted to seventy or eighty. Ephesus acquired a large extent of territory, at the expense of the neighbouring Lydians; but it does not appear to have been very enterprising at sea, and it boasted few maritime colonies.

118. The large island of Eubœa formed the respective territories of six or seven cities, of which Chalcis and Eretria were the chief. Our earliest historical intimations represent these as the most wealthy and powerful of the Ionian cities in Europe, surpassing Athens, and rivalling Miletus. Then there were the Cyclades, of whose early wealth and importance some idea may be formed from the Homeric hymn to Apollo, in which the island of Delos is celebrated as the centre of a great periodical festival held by all the cities of the Ionic name, whether insular or continental, and frequented by the twelve Ionic cities of Asia Minor as well as by Athens and Chalcis in Europe. The description of the gathering is splendid and imposing—the number of the ships, the display of luxury in dress and equipments, the beauty of the women, the athletic games, and the competitions in song and dance, making an impression never to be forgotten. Another evidence of the importance of these insular cities, is found in the fact, that a scale of weight and money, derived through commerce with Asia, was naturalised among the Ionian cities under the name of the Euboic scale, because Chalcis and Eretria were the most actively commercial cities in the Ægæan; just as the commerce of Ægina among the Dorian states had given the name of Æginetan to the scale introduced by Phidon of Argos.

119. Between the years 700 and 530 B.C., the maritime activity of the colonial Greeks made immense progress; and the ships of Miletus, Phocæa, and Samos gradually spread over all those waters of the Levant that had once been exclusively occupied by the Phœnicians.

120. The progress of commerce and maritime discovery

among the Ionians, was coupled with the cultivation of the higher arts, and with the opening of new fields of intellectual culture. They early began to vie with each other in the splendour of their sacred edifices, and the works of art that adorned them. The temple of Juno at Samos, celebrated by the Father of Greek history as the largest he had ever seen, seems to have been commenced in the eighth century B.C.; and the art of casting metal statues is ascribed to a native of that place.

121. About the year 650 B.C., a band of Ionians and Carians having landed fortuitously on the coast of Egypt, were taken into the service of Psammitichus, and materially aided him in obtaining the throne. The consequence was that Egypt, which till then had been closed against all foreign settlers, was thrown open to the Greeks for permanent and friendly intercourse. The warriors to whom Psammitichus had been indebted, received grants of land on the Nile; and a number of Egyptian boys were committed to their care, that they might acquire the Greek language, and form a permanent class of interpreters between the two nations. The successors of Psammitichus pursued a similar policy; and the effect was that the Greek mind became enlarged by the wide field of observation thus presented; papyrus, the only writing-material then known, came into general use, to aid the progress of literature; and the fine arts made immense progress, probably from the Greeks obtaining from their new friends the knowledge of various technical processes, for want of which their genius had been cramped.

122. At the time when the Ionic colonies first went forth, the native populations of Asia Minor consisted of numerous inconsiderable tribes, presenting no formidable resistance to the successive bodies of Greek emigrants that settled on their shores. The Lydian monarchy, whose capital was Sardis, and whose territories bordered closely on those of the Ionic Greeks, began to display considerable strength about the year 700 B.C.; but still it appears to have been far from impeding their development. The Lydians were an industrious and wealthy people, and the Greeks derived from them not only a superior knowledge

of weaving, dyeing, and working in metals, but some commercial advantages, which became the principal source of their wealth; for the Lydians having no sea-board, carried on their trade to the Mediterranean through the Hellenic cities, as Miletus and Phocæa, which furnished the transport vessels. But Crœsus, the last king of Lydia, celebrated for his extensive dominions and countless treasures, was not satisfied to view the   560–546 B.C. independence of these flourishing cities ; and beginning with Ephesus, he subdued all of them under his own power. His rule, however, was mild and generous : he was satisfied with receiving a moderate tribute, and permitted them still to regulate their own affairs as heretofore. Moreover, he shewed much partiality for this intelligent people, as appears in his acquiring their language, consulting their oracles, enriching their temples, and conversing with their sages. We pursue their history no further here, because it will be convenient to take it up again as the connecting-link between the first and second periods of Grecian history.

SICILIAN COLONIES.

123. A long interval seems to have elapsed after the colonisation of the Asiatic coast and the Ægæan islands, before the state of Greece gave occasion to new migrations ; for it was not till about the eleventh Olympiad, that the stream of colonisation began to flow west-   735 B.C. ward. Cumæ, indeed, whose walls, during two centuries prior to 500 B.C., enclosed a large and prosperous population, with a surrounding territory both extensive and fertile, is supposed to have been founded in the eleventh or even twelfth century before the Christian era ; but with this exception, the earliest was Naxos, in Sicily, founded about 735 B.C., from which date these settlements multiplied rapidly. The hill which the colonists first occupied—an eminence of Taurus overhanging the sea—was marked by an altar of Apollo Archegetes, which continued to be a sanctuary common to all the Sicilian Greeks, and the shrine where sacrifice was always offered by the sacred envoys before

their departure for the Olympic and other festivals in the mother-country.

124. The Phœnicians had previously occupied various Sicilian promontories or islets for purposes of trade, but had sought no permanent establishment or territorial acquisition. They now abandoned these outlying factories, and concentrated their strength in three considerable seaport towns nearest Carthage; so that the east and south of Sicily, at least, were left open to the Greeks, with no other opponents than the native Sicels and Sicans, who were gradually driven from the coasts. In the year after Naxos was colonised from Chalcis, Corinth laid the foundation of the mighty Syracuse; and one colony rapidly followed another for five years, after which there seem to have been few arrivals for a long time. The little Sicel villages became gradually semihellenised and merged into subjects of Grecian towns. On the other hand, that the tastes and habits of the Sicels passed largely into the character of the Greeks located among them, appears in their literature, Sicily having been the birthplace of that coarse, rustic mirth which merged into comedy at Athens.

125. The history of the Hellenic cities of Sicily before the year 490, is very imperfectly known. During this obscure period—supposed to be about 570 B.C.—Phalaris made himself despot of Agrigentum. It is said that, under pretence of building a great temple to Jupiter Polieus on the citadel rock, he assembled and armed a number of workmen, whom he employed to overpower the constituted authorities; that he afterwards disarmed the citizens by stratagem, and committed unheard of cruelties far beyond the ordinary licence of Grecian despots. The story of a hollow bull of brass, in which he shut up and burned his victims, is more worthy of credit than it would be thought at first sight, being substantiated by subsequent historical facts. The tyrant at length became so intolerable, that the people suddenly rose against him. He was overthrown and slain, and a severe revenge was taken on the partisans of his tyranny.

126. About the year 509 B.C., the Spartan prince

SICILIAN COLONIES. 55

Dorieus led a body of emigrants to a territory in the north-west corner of Sicily, whence he hoped to expel the non-hellenic inhabitants, and form a settlement. But the Carthaginians, whose possessions were close adjoining, assisted in defeating this effort, in which the leader, with many of his followers, was slain. This was the first, so far as we know, of that series of contests between the Carthaginians and Greeks, which long held it undetermined whether the island should be part of Europe or of Africa.

127. Not long after the death of Dorieus, Gela began to attain a certain ascendancy over the other Sicilian Greeks under the despot Cleander; about 505 B.C. and after his death, his brother and successor, Hippocrates, extended his dominion over half the island. At the death of Hippocrates, the people revolted, refusing to acknowledge his sons; but Gelon, the commander of the cavalry, espoused the cause of the sons, and put down the people, after which he threw off the mask, and seized the sceptre for himself. A few years afterwards, the oligarchical order at Syracuse were dispossessed by their serf-cultivators, and the smaller 485 B.C. freemen called Demos; they invoked the aid of Gelon, who undertook to restore them, and to whom the insurgents surrendered without striking a blow. But instead of reinstating the oligarchs, he appropriated Syracuse to himself, and thither transferred the seat of his power. He greatly enlarged the city, strengthened its fortifications, transferred to it the whole population of Camarina, with more than half that of Gela, and rendered it the first city in Sicily. His own dominion was at the same time the greatest in the Hellenic world, embracing as it did not only Syracuse, but a considerable portion of the island, both Greek and Sicilian.

128. These circumstances partly explain how it happened that the Greeks at Corinth confederated to resist Xerxes, sent to solicit aid from Syracuse in 481 B.C. He was then imperial leader of Sicily, and could offer an immense force, besides furnishing provisions for the whole army of the Greeks. He refused, however; but whether

because he required to be recognised as generalissimo of the whole force, which was indignantly repudiated, or simply because he had full employment in defending himself at home, cannot easily be ascertained.

129. Certain it is that the same spring which brought Xerxes into Greece, witnessed a Carthaginian invasion of Sicily, probably according to a plan concerted with the Carthaginians by the Phœnicians on behalf of Persia. Hamilcar landed at Panormus in 480 with an immense force, described as including Phœnicians, Libyans, Iberians, Sigyes, Helisyki, Sardinians, and Corsicans—the first recorded example of those numerous mercenary armies which Carthage used to compose of various nations and languages as a security against mutiny. Hamilcar besieged Himera, to aid which Gelon sent an immense army, and completely defeated the Carthaginians, the general himself being slain. The numbers which have been handed down (about 150,000) as having fallen on the side of the invaders, are probably exaggerated; but doubtless the battle was hotly disputed, the victory complete, and the slain numerous, as well as the prisoners, who were divided as slaves among the cities in proportion to the troops furnished by each. Of course, the largest share fell to Syracuse and Agrigentum, where great numbers were employed on public works of defence, or ornament, or religious worship.

130. Most, if not all, of the Greek cities of Sicily now solicited the privilege of being enrolled as the dependent allies of Gelon. Even the Carthaginians sued for peace, which was granted on condition of their paying a large sum as the costs of the war, and erecting two temples, in which a permanent record of the treaty was to be made.

131. The conduct of Gelon, both at Syracuse and towards the dependent cities, appears to have been mild and conciliating. But he died not much more than a year after the battle of Himera, while its triumphs were fresh in every one's recollection. He left a son in tender years; and by his own direction, his authority 478 B.C. passed to two of his brothers. The real power, however, became vested in one of them, Hieron, a man of great energy,

SICILIAN COLONIES. 57

and munificent as a patron of the poets of his day, but jealous in his temper, cruel and rapacious in his government, and an enemy to freedom of speech among his subjects. His power seems to have been noway inferior to that of Gelon; indeed greater; for being provoked by Thrasydæus, tyrant of Himera and Agrigentum, he sent a force which completely defeated him; after which, the citizens sued for peace from the conqueror, and obtained it, doubtless on the condition of numbering themselves among his subject cities.

132. On the death of Hieron, the succession was disputed between his brother Thrasybulus, and his nephew, the son of Gelon. The Syracusans invoked the aid of the other cities of Sicily against Thrasybulus, proclaiming the dynasty of Gelon as the foe of freedom, and proposing universal independence as the reward of victory. The call was responded to with alacrity; a large force, both naval and military, came to succour the Syracusans; Thrasybulus was defeated, and obliged to retire to Locri, where he lived and died a private citizen.

133. Thus ended the powerful dynasty of Gelon at Syracuse, and its fall was the signal for an extensive revolution throughout the island. The despots 465 B.C. were all expelled, and governments more or less democratical were established in all the cities. The free governments, however, were at first exposed to much difficulty, from the collision of the returning exiles with the new citizens and mercenaries who had been domiciliated by the tyrants. These conflicts became so serious, that a general congress of the various cities was summoned to adjust matters. It was then determined that the exiles should be restored, and the Gelonian settlers expelled, a home being provided for them in the territory of Messene. Such was the reactionary movement in Sicily against the high-handed violence of the despots. The period of fifty years which followed was the most prosperous part of Sicilian history.

ITALIAN COLONIES.

134. Greek colonisation in Italy began nearly at the same time as in Sicily, and was marked by similar circumstances. The colonists were likewise of various origin— Æolian, Achæan, Dorian, Ionian, who planted themselves in positions of singular promise to the industrious cultivator, and founded the cities of Tarentum, Sybaris, Croton, Locri, and Rhegium.

135. The earliest as well as the most prosperous of these cities were Sybaris and Croton, both Achæan settlements, and situated on the Gulf of 720 & 710 B.C. Tarentum. The walls of Sybaris were fifty stadia, or nearly six miles in circumference; those of Croton were little less than twelve; and both enjoyed an extensive dominion from sea to sea across the peninsula, dividing between them the whole length of the Tarentine coast. The native tribes, which seem to have been petty rude communities, more pastoral than agricultural, became partially Hellenised; some of them dwelt in the Grecian towns, as domestic slaves; but most of them remained in the country region as serfs, intermingled with Greek settlers.

136. It was during the sixth century B.C. that these cities reached the maximum of their power, and were reckoned among the most flourishing communities of the Hellenic name. They even surpassed the prosperous cities of Sicily; while their luxury, organisation, industry, and political power, formed a striking contrast with Hellas Proper, which had poverty for a foster-sister. Five thousand richly caparisoned horse, we are told, formed the processional march in certain Sybaritic festivals; while the cavalry of Athens, even in her best days, did not number above 1200. The garments of these citizens were manufactured of the finest wool from Miletus, in Ionia. Next to the great abundance of home produce in corn, wine, oil, flax, cattle, fish, timber, the most important fact recorded is the great traffic with Miletus and other cities of Ionia.

137. Croton was particularly distinguished for the superior bodily habit of its citizens, attested by the number of

victors which it furnished to the Olympic games. It was, besides, famous for the skill of its surgeons and physicians.

138. We know little of the political organisation of these states. The supreme authority at Croton was vested in a council of 1000 persons, the heirs or representatives of the first settlers; but we are not told how the executive offices were filled.

139. The most remarkable circumstances deserving of notice in connection with this and the neighbouring cities, are connected with the sojourning of Pythagoras in Croton about 540–530 B.C. He was a native of Samos, and a man who professed to be inspired of the gods to reveal a new mode of life, and to insure the Divine favour to a select few, as the recompense of that strict ritual observance, austere self-control, and laborious training, both of body and mind, which he inculcated. His arrival at Croton, his preaching, and his conduct, produced an almost electric effect on the minds of the people, with a great moral reform, both public and private. Political discontent gave way to more serious anxieties; incontinence disappeared; luxury was discarded; and the women hastened to exchange their glittering ornaments for the plainest attire. No less than 2000 persons were converted at his first preaching; the supreme council of 1000 invited him into their assembly, and offered to constitute him their Prytanis or president; while his wife and daughter were accorded the leading places at all the religious processions. But it does not seem that Pythagoras accepted any official position, or exercised personally any political power. We have no satisfactory account of the nature or details either of his doctrines or his discipline; for neither he nor any of his immediate disciples left anything in writing. But it seems that a select body, about 300 in number, bound themselves by a sort of vow to him and to each other, and adopted a peculiar diet, ritual, and observances, as a token of brotherhood—though without any community of goods. Not least, there was an attachment of feeling among themselves, and a haughty exclusiveness towards all besides, such as no other fraternity could parallel. Such a band of men, standing high in wealth and station, came almost

unconsciously to mingle political ambition with religious and scientific pursuits, and gradually obtained great ascendancy over the government at Croton. Moreover, the influence spread to other towns, as Sybaris, Metapontium, Rhegium, Catana, Himera, where similar brotherhoods were formed: the Pythagorean order spread its net, and dictated the course of affairs throughout a large portion of Magna Græcia. It by no means follows that Pythagoras intended this. His scheme appears to have gone no further than the organisation of a private, select order of brethren, embracing his religious fancies, ethical doctrines, and germs of scientific thought; and this private society became politically powerful, because it attracted disciples from the wealthy and influential classes, and their individual influence became immensely strengthened by this union. But by and by it appeared that science, philosophy, and religion were kept for the private intercourse of the disciples, and nothing was seen and felt by those without but the political predominance of an ambitious fraternity. They now became as odious as they had once been popular; and their enemies were emboldened to employ extreme force against them. The Pythagoreans were attacked when assembled in their place of meeting, which was set on fire; many of the members perished; among whom, some say, was Pythagoras himself. A like violent suppression of the order took place in the other cities where it had obtained a footing; and we are told that these cities continued in a state of violent commotion, which was appeased only by the friendly exertions of mediators from the parent country.

140. Sybaris appears to have been a still more flourishing city than Croton. There had been a revolution here, in which Telys, a popular leader, had expelled the oligarchical government, banishing 500 of the leading rich men, and confiscating their property. He had then become despot of Sybaris, and the exiles threw themselves on the sympathy of the Crotons—a sympathy which they probably found the more readily, being one with them in the Pythagorean brotherhood. The despot demanded that they should be surrendered to him, which the Crotons refusing, he marched

against them at the head of a force reckoned at 300,000 ; and this in defiance of the strongest religious warnings, all the sacrifices having been unpropitious to the undertaking. A bloody battle was fought, in which the Sybarites were totally defeated ; and the very site of their city was rendered untenable by the conquerors, who, with this view, turned the course of the river Crathis so as to submerge it.

510 B.C.

141. The conquest and destruction of this, perhaps the greatest of all Hellenic cities, excited the deepest sympathy throughout the Hellenic world. From this time forward, the cities of Magna Græcia, like those of Ionia, declined in importance ; and their hitherto lofty relations with the rest of Italy underwent a change. The Lucanians and Bruttians spread southward, took possession of the inland territory, hitherto Greek, and left only the coasts to the Hellenes.

142. The Hellenic world presented a very different aspect in the fifth century B. C. from what it did in the sixth. In the sixth, the Greeks of Ionia, Italy, and Sicily were the great ornaments of the Hellenic name, carrying on more commerce with each other than either of them did with the mother-country, and boasting a much more advanced state of literature and art than Hellas Proper, as well as superior political influence. The military power of Sparta was indeed considerable at this time, but confined to Peloponnesus, as she had no navy to extend it. After the lapse of a century, the face of things was altered. The independence of the Asiatic Greeks was gone ; the power of the Italian broken ; while Sparta and Athens became the leading cities, and centres of action for the lesser states of Hellas.

143. These have been noted as some of the earliest and most important of the early colonies of Greece, but it is to be added, that similar establishments studded all the shores of the Mediterranean, which thus became a kind of Grecian lake ; and that Trapezus, on the furthest shores of the Black Sea, Cyrene, in Africa, and Massilia (now Marseille), in Gaul, were as essentially Greek states as Sparta or Athens ; having just the same bonds of union

with the cities of Greece Proper, that these had with each other. All had a communion of blood, religion, language, and literature; all appeared statedly, by their deputies, at the great national festivals; but all were politically independent of each other.

GROWTH OF THE GRECIAN STATES.

ARGOS.

144. At the earliest times of which there are authentic records—that is, as we have said, about seven centuries and a half before the Christian era—the states of Peloponnesus, held under the sway of the victorious Dorians, seem to have made the most important figure in the annals of Greece proper. Scanty as their annals are, they are less obscure and more interesting than those of the more northern states of Hellas. And among the Peloponnesians, Argos appears as the first power, being the head of a powerful confederacy of cities colonised from herself, and united in the common worship of Apollo Pythius, who had a temple in each of the cities, while his great cathedral, if we may so call it, was at Argos. Phidon, king of this state, who is reckoned to have lived about 747 B.C., and is represented as a descendant of Temenus the Heraclid, is one of the first really historical personages in Grecian history. It is said that he aimed at universal sovereignty in Peloponnesus; that he claimed the right of presiding at the Olympic games in virtue of his descent from Hercules; that he succeeded in expelling the Eleans; and that he celebrated one of these games (the eighth Olympiad) himself, in conjunction with the citizens of Pisa, who had been deprived of this privilege by the Eleans. But the Spartans interfered, defeated him, and destroyed his power; after which, we hear no more of him or the pre-eminence of Argos. But he left behind one striking and permanent trace of his influence, in the introduction of a copper and silver coinage, and a scale of weights and measures probably derived from Phœnicia, through the Asiatic Dorians. These were speedily adopted

SPARTA.

145. After the fall of Phidon, Sparta rose to the position of first among the Peloponnesian powers. Her ascendancy was mainly owing to her peculiar institutions, especially the rigorous military training and discipline of her citizens, unanimously ascribed by the ancients to the genius of the great Lycurgus. The date to be assigned to this distinguished man is disputed, but about the year 820 B.C. seems likely to be near the truth. There are various ways of telling the story of his life and labours, but the most probable is the following :—

146. Lycurgus belonged to the royal family of Sparta, being the younger brother of Polydectes, one of the joint kings. On the death of Polydectes, he might have succeeded as presumptive heir, and was encouraged to do so by his brother's widow, who proposed to marry him ; but Lycurgus with indignation rejected the offer, knowing that she was likely to become a mother ; and he consented to hold the reins of government only provisionally till the birth of the child, whom he presented to the people as the lawful heir and future ruler, giving him the name of Charilaus, 'the people's joy.' The vengeful widow now endeavoured to cast upon him the imputation of having designs against the life of the youthful king, whereupon Lycurgus deemed it prudent to withdraw for a time from his native country. It is said that he made the tour of Crete, Ionia, Egypt, Libya, Iberia, and even India, studying the polity of these countries, and conversing with their sages, with the view of improving the condition of his own city. Traditionary story also tells that he brought from Ionia a copy of Homer's poems, hitherto unknown in Peloponnesus.

147. During his absence, the young king grew up, and assumed the sceptre ; but the disorders of the state continually increased, and ere the return of Lycurgus, all parties were weary of the condition of things, and willing to submit to any change that promised peace and good order. With the view of applying a corrective, Lycurgus consulted the Delphic oracle, from which he received satisfactory assurances of divine support, together with some special injunctions which he was to take to Sparta. Thus prepared, he suddenly presented himself in the agora, surrounded by thirty distinguished citizens, whom he had gained to his projects, and who now appeared in arms for his defence. The king, though at first terrified, was no sooner made aware of his mission, than he stood forward to second it. There was for a time some opposition among the people, yet the bulk of them respectfully submitted to him, as a venerable descendant of Hercules, and, moreover, a missionary from Delphi.

148. The first proceeding of Lycurgus was to establish the Spartan senate, consisting of twenty-eight old men, with the two kings who sat and voted like the rest, making thirty members in all. The most important function of this council was that of a court of criminal justice, before which every cause was brought that involved the life of a citizen. To this was added a periodical assembly of the people in the open air, to hear the result of what had been concocted in the senate, and to accept or reject the measures proposed to them, without, however, any liberty of discussing them. It would seem that, a century afterwards, there was introduced a new executive directory of five men, called *ephors*, chosen from among the citizens, and that these greatly curtailed, and, indeed, almost wholly annihilated the political power of the kings, leaving, however, their religious prerogatives in full vigour. It is probable that the institution of the senate and the people's assembly did not originate with Lycurgus; that he only modified the details, and established on a firmer basis institutions previously existing in some shape or other.

149. The best critics are now of opinion that the great work of Lycurgus was the system of individual and personal discipline which he introduced, rather than any important political innovations. They reject the oft-told story of his having made a new division of all the landed property, as improbable, and supported on no sufficient

evidence; as also that of his having forbidden the use of gold and silver money, which, it is now believed, was unknown in Greece till introduced by Phidon, king of Argos, in the following century. There is no reason to suppose that Lycurgus attempted to make the poor rich, or the rich poor; but that he imposed upon both alike his system of subjugating discipline—the same fare and clothing; the same labours and privations; the same punishments and subordination; we may add, the same gentlemanly idleness—the object being to form a set of hardy, warlike, obedient, and self-sacrificing citizens, to whom the state was everything, and private interests and feelings nothing. The fundamental principle of the system was, that the Spartan should have no private interests whatever, but live only for the general good. Some of the details were such as these :—

150. A certain number of joint tables were appointed; every citizen was required to belong to some one of them, and no new member was admitted without the concurrence of the previous occupants. Each contributed from his own land a certain quantity of barley-meal, cheese, figs, wine, with a small sum of money for accessories; game was added by the labours of the chase; and whoever sacrificed a victim to the gods, sent part of it to the mess-table. These public messes were connected with the military distribution of the citizens, and a system of constant gymnastic exercise, with a rigorous discipline prescribed in detail. Every Spartan was obliged to commence this way of life in his seventh year, and he was not released from it till his sixtieth. During all this time, he spent his days in public exercises and meals, his nights in the barrack to which he belonged, an utter stranger to the independence of a separate home. Besides being trained to complicated movements in the military drill, he was subjected to other kinds of severe bodily discipline. He was inured to hunger and thirst, to the extremes of heat and cold; was obliged to tread every kind of ground barefooted, and to wear the same garment summer and winter. Nor this alone: the virtues of an accomplished Spartan included likewise the exhibition of a silent and motionless

deportment in public when action was not called for; the suppression at all times of external manifestations of feeling, and even the power of enduring bodily torture without complaint. To cultivate a daring and pugnacious spirit, two squadrons were often matched against each other—to fight, without arms indeed, but in right earnest, and with the fury of foes, under the eye of authority. To habituate them to endure suffering, they were at certain seasons scourged at the altar of Diana, and sometimes expired under the suffering without having betrayed it by word or gesture. To teach them strategy and secrecy, there were licensed expeditions for thieving, and severe punishment for those who allowed themselves to be detected in it. Every school-boy has heard of the Spartan youth who hid the stolen fox under his coat, and allowed it to tear out his bowels rather than expose it to view.

151. The literary education of these youths was but scanty; but they were taught to play on the lyre, and to sing martial songs or hymns to the gods.

152. The Spartan females were, at least in their youth, placed under a scarcely less hardy system of discipline. Lycurgus deemed that female slaves were good enough to sit at home spinning and weaving; but that women brought up in such occupations were not likely to fulfil what he considered their appropriate mission—that of giving birth to a splendid offspring. The Spartan damsels were taught to contend with each other in running, wrestling, and boxing, agreeably to the forms of the Grecian agones, while the presence of the citizens as spectators added animation to the scene. In like manner, the young women marched in the religious processions, sung and danced at particular festivals, and witnessed the gymnastic exercises of the youths; so that the sexes were constantly associated in public after a fashion repugnant to the feelings and usages of other Hellenic states.

153. It would seem that, in maturer years, especially after the lapse of some time from the first institution of these customs, the married women emancipated themselves from these obligations; accumulated property to a great extent; and maintained an ample and luxurious

establishment at home, while their husbands still went through the hard detail of their austere life. The beauty and vigour of the Spartan women were famous throughout all Greece, and the influence of their patriotism in sustaining that of the men is matter of historic celebrity. 'Return either with your shield or on it!' was the exhortation of a mother to her son on his departure for the field of battle.

154. Lycurgus was not, in the proper sense, a legislator. He positively interdicted the framing of written laws—that is, of formal and premeditated enactments on any particular subject. The wisdom and equity of the magistrate, unfettered by any code, were to decide in every case according to the recognised principles of the community.

155. This great man certainly realised his project of forming, in the eight or nine thousand citizens of Sparta, such habits of obedience, hardihood, and military aptitude, as are unparalleled in the history of nations; all with the most devoted attachment to the system he promulgated, and the most perfect submission of each individual to the public opinion; every one burning with emulation to distinguish himself within his prescribed sphere, and having little ambition for anything else. How a community was ever brought to submit to so rigorous a system of individual training, we are not permitted to discover. Doubtless, the influence of Lycurgus's own earnestness and energy was much; his acknowledged descent from Hercules, and his admitted authority from the Delphian god, were much; but these seem insufficient to explain the phenomenon, unless we suppose them aided by co-operating circumstances which history has not transmitted.

156. Respecting the condition of Sparta previous to the time of Lycurgus, we have no positive information whatever; but there is reason to believe that her territories were very limited—probably not extending beyond the lands immediately around the city. The subsequent records, scanty as they are, enable us to make out a progressive increase of power and dominion—such an increase as might naturally be expected from the military ardour and love of war which the institutions of Lycurgus were

calculated to inspire. The Spartans were now a body of professional and thoroughly disciplined soldiers, at a time when military discipline was little known in the other states of Greece. Their career of conquest went on— with some interruption, indeed—for nearly three centuries, till they were acknowledged masters of two-fifths of Peloponnesus.

157. The subjugation of Laconia Proper is very imperfectly narrated. Little is known of its pre-existing occupants, whom historians call Achæans; nor can we trace any difference between them and their Dorian invaders in respect of language or civilisation. But thus much is certain, that these people were gradually reduced to a state of feudal subjection under the name of Periœci, as we shall presently explain. We are also particularly told of the conquest of Helos, one of the maritime towns, and that, on account of the more than ordinary provocation which its inhabitants gave in the war, they were reduced to a state of absolute slavery; whence, according to various authors, the appellation of Helots came to be applied to all the persons held as slaves throughout Laconia.

158. The successful interference of Sparta with the usurpations of Phidon of Argos, appears as another manifestation of the progress of Spartan power; and this leads us to speak of the time when they undertook to subjugate their brethren, the Dorians of Messenia.

MESSENIAN AND OTHER WARS OF SPARTA.

159. From the earliest times of their establishment in Peloponnesus, the Dorians of Laconia and those of Messenia had a joint temple, and performed sacrifice in common to the goddess Diana, on the heights of Mount Taÿgetus. Here, on the occasion of one of these sacrifices, Teleclus, king of Sparta, was slain, and the quarrel was begun which issued in the struggles called the Messenian Wars. The Spartans asserted that Teleclus was murdered by the Messenians, as he was attempting to defend from the insults of the Messenian youth some Spartan damsels who were assisting at the sacrifice. The story of the Messenians

was, that Teleclus had laid a snare for them, by dressing some Spartan youths as females, and supplying them with daggers; and that Teleclus lost his life in the affray which ensued upon the discovery. The war, however, did not break out till some time after, when a new grievance arose.

160. A distinguished Messenian had been grossly injured by a Spartan, and was denied redress, whereupon he took his own revenge by aggressions on other Lacedæmonians. The Messenians, in their turn, refused to surrender him to Spartan vengeance, and the Spartans determined upon war. They made their preparations in silence, and without any formal declaration of hostilities, crossed the frontier, surprised the border town of Amphea, and put its defenders to the sword. The Messenians summoned their forces, and carried on the war with vigour. For the first four years, the Lacedæmonians made little progress, but in the fifth a great battle was fought, which, though indecisive, so weakened the Messenians, that they were obliged to shelter themselves on the fortified mountain of Ithome, and abandon the rest of the country. In this distressing situation, they sent to consult the Delphic oracle, and received the answer, that a virgin of the royal race of Æpytus must be sacrificed to the infernal gods for their deliverance. In a tragic scene which ensued, Aristodemus put his own daughter to death, and that rather by murder than sacrifice, so that the requirement of the oracle was not fulfilled. In the thirteenth year of the war, another hard-fought battle took place. The result was again indecisive, but the Messenian king was slain, and Aristodemus elected in his stead. In the fifth year of his reign, a third great battle was fought, when the Corinthians took part with the Spartans, and the Arcadians and Sicyonians assisted the Messenians. Now Aristodemus obtained a decisive victory, and the Spartans were driven back into their own territory.

161. It was now the turn of the Spartans to apply to the Delphic oracle; and the remaining events of the war, as related by the historians, exhibit a series of stratagems to fulfil the injunctions of the priestess, with prodigies in

which the divine displeasure appears against the Messenians. Aristodemus, agonised at the thought of having slain his daughter without saving his country, put an end to his own life. In the twentieth year of the war, the Messenians abandoned Ithome, and the Lacedæmonians razed its fortifications to the ground. The rest of the country was speedily conquered, and such of the inhabitants as did not withdraw to Arcadia or elsewhere were reduced to complete subjection. 'Like asses worn down by heavy burdens,' says the Spartan poet Tyrtæus, 'they were compelled to make over to their masters an entire half of the produce of their fields, and to come in the garb of wo to Sparta, themselves and their wives as mourners at the decease of a king or other important personage.'

162. The Messenians endured this degrading yoke for thirty-nine years, and their revolt against it at the end of that time goes by the name of the Second Messenian War.

163. Most of the Peloponnesian states took part in this struggle: the Corinthians on the side of Sparta; the inhabitants of Argos, Arcadia, Sicyon, and Pisa, on the part of Messenia. The first battle, which was fought before the arrival of the allies, proved indecisive, but the valour of Aristomenes, the Messenian leader, struck terror into the Spartans, and drove them again to the Delphic oracle. The god directed them—so the tradition goes—to apply to Athens for a leader; and the Athenians, with the view of nominally obeying the oracle, and yet rendering no real assistance, despatched Tyrtæus, who was a lame man, a schoolmaster, and withal a minstrel and poet. The Spartans received him with due honour; and when, by his martial songs, the fainting courage of the warriors was revived, and the discontents of the mutinous soothed, the credit of the oracle was fully established. So efficacious were his efforts, that to them mainly is ascribed the final success of the Spartans; and they testified their gratitude by making him a citizen of their state. His strains long maintained undiminished popularity among them, and he was looked upon as the great hero on the Spartan side in this struggle, as Aristomenes was the champion of the

Messenians. Victory, however, did not at first declare for the Spartans. In the second battle, they were defeated with great loss, through the treachery of an ally; but in the third, which was also the third year of the war, the Messenians suffered a signal defeat, and no longer ventured to meet the Spartans in the open field. After the example of the former war, they concentrated their whole force in the mountain-fortress Ira, where they maintained their position for eleven years. The Spartans encamped at the foot of the mountain, but Aristomenes made frequent sallies from the fortress, ravaging the lands of Laconia with fire and sword, and performing prodigies of valour in his various incursions. Thrice did he offer to Jupiter Ithometas the sacrifice called hecatomphonia, the exclusive privilege of the warrior who had slain a hundred enemies with his own hand. Thrice was he taken prisoner, but on two occasions marvellously escaped before he could be conveyed to Sparta. The third time, however, he was taken thither, and condemned by the citizens to be thrown, with fifty of his companions, into the deep rocky cavity of Keadas, in Mount Taÿgetus, which was a usual punishment for their criminals. His comrades were all killed by the fall, but Aristomenes reached the bottom unhurt. Seeing no means of escape, he was abandoning hope, and had wrapped himself up in his cloak to die, when he perceived a fox prowling about among the dead bodies of his companions. When the animal approached him, he grasped its tail, and following as it struggled to escape, he discovered the aperture by which it had entered, succeeded in crawling out himself, and to the surprise both of friends and foes, appeared again alive and vigorous at Ira. But again was he treacherously betrayed; and finding it impossible to maintain his position, he collected the bravest of his followers, forced his way through the assailants, quitted the country, and spent the remainder of his days at Rhodes.

164. Thus ended the second Messenian war. Its result was the total subjugation of the country. Some of the inhabitants, it is said, found sympathy among the Arcadians, who afforded them a new home, and gave them their

daughters in marriage ; but such as remained were reduced to a servitude probably not less galling than that which Tyrtæus describes them as having endured between the first war and the second. The Messenians now for a time disappear from the page of history ; and their territory henceforth appears as Western Laconia—a valuable acquisition to the conquerors, on account of the singular fertility of its valleys and plains.

165. We have yet to sketch the progress of Spartan conquest in the direction of Arcadia and Argolis, so as to conduct her to the maximum of her territorial possessions, and place her before the reader as the commanding state in Hellas.

166. The central region of Peloponnesus, called Arcadia, had not been subject to those immigrations which had given new masters to the surrounding states. Its population was a strong and hardy race of mountaineers, the most numerous Hellenic tribe in the peninsula, and withal among the rudest and poorest. They long retained their original mode of life in petty hill-villages, each independent of the other ; and though they had some religious festivals in common, yet the union of all who bore the Arcadian name was more loose and ineffective than that of the Hellenes generally. They had, however, some considerable towns, aggregations of villages ; and among the most important of these were Tegea and Mantinea, bordering on Laconia and Argolis. Both of these held several of the smaller Arcadian townships near them in a sort of dependence, and were anxious to extend this empire over others ; but Sparta had a strong interest in checking all schemes for the formation of local confederacies. She stood forward as the protectress of these smaller Arcadians, and kept the Mantineans within their own limits. It is impossible to say at what precise time it happened, that several of those which lay about the northern boundary of the Spartan territory were successively conquered and incorporated with it ; but it seems that the entire northern frontier of Sparta, still occupied by Arcadian inhabitants, had been brought into this position before the year 600 B.C. And now the victorious people contemplated nothing less

than to conquer the whole of Arcadia. Being encouraged, as they thought, by the Delphic oracle, to try their fortune against Tegea, they were defeated with great loss, and were compelled to labour as slaves in the very chains which they had brought to bind their expected prisoners. For one whole generation, we are told, their arms continued unsuccessful in this direction ; but at length the tide of victory turned, and thus it is said it occurred. The Spartans inquired at the Delphic oracle which of the gods they ought to propitiate, in order to secure success, and they were enjoined, in reply, to find and remove to Sparta the bones of Orestes, son of Agamemnon. But they knew not where the body of Orestes was deposited, and applied to the oracle for more specific directions. They were informed that he was buried at Tegea, in a place 'where two blasts were blowing under powerful constraint—where there was stroke and counter-stroke, and destruction upon destruction.' These mysterious words were by and by elucidated. During a truce with Tegea, Lichas, a Spartan, visited the place, and happened to enter the forge of a blacksmith, who casually mentioned to him, that while lately sinking a well in his outer court, he had come upon a coffin containing a body seven cubits long, and that in his terror he had left it undisturbed. It struck Lichas that this gigantic relic could be no other than the corpse of Orestes, especially as the situation exactly corresponded with the indications of the oracle ; for here were the 'two blasts blowing by constraint' in the two bellows of the blacksmith ; the hammer and anvil supplied 'the stroke and counter-stroke ;' and 'the destruction upon destruction' was found in the murderous weapons which were there forged. Lichas kept his secret till he could communicate it to the Spartan authorities, who then made a feint of banishing him under a criminal accusation. In the guise of an exile, therefore, he returned to Tegea ; prevailed upon the blacksmith to admit him to the premises ; and there exhumed and carried home the bones of the hero. After this fortunate acquisition, the Spartans were constantly victorious, and the Tegeans were at length obliged to acknowledge their supremacy, at least by becoming

about 560 B.C.

their subordinate confederates. They were not reduced to subjection, like the Messenians, but continued masters of their own city and territory, only upholding Sparta as the presiding power in Peloponnesus, and submitting to her orders in the disposal of their military forces.

167. It is uncertain at what time the Lacedæmonians became masters of the eastern coast of Laconia, and also of the district of Cynuria, all of which had belonged to the Argive confederacy; but the attempt of the Argives to recover it led to a combat memorable in the annals of Grecian heroism. It was agreed about 547 B.C. between the two powers that the possession of Thyrea, which was the place immediately in dispute, should be determined by a combat of 300 selected champions on each side, the armies of both retiring in order to leave the field clear. So equal was the fight, that only one Spartan and two Argives survived; and the latter, believing that all their opponents had been slain, hastened home to report their victory. But Othryades, the Spartan champion, remained on the field; despoiled of their arms the dead bodies of the enemy; and maintained his position till next morning, when both sides claimed the victory, and the dispute after all was decided by a general battle. The Spartans were victorious; and the brave Othryades, ashamed to return home as the sole survivor of the 300, fell upon his own sword in the battle-field. The possession of Thyrea was thus decided in favour of Sparta. This was her last territorial acquisitions. She was now possessed of a continuous dominion, comprising the whole southern portion of Peloponnesus, from the south bank of the river Neda on the western coast, to the northern boundary of Thyreatis on the eastern coast. Within this wide area, there was not one community pretending to independence; all were governed from this single city, and for the exclusive benefit of the citizens of Sparta.

168. The population of this extensive territory consisted of three classes—Spartans, Pericœci, and Helots. The first were the fully-qualified citizens, who resided in Sparta itself, fulfilled all the requirements of the Lycurgian code of discipline, and paid their quota to the *syssitia*, or public

mess. These alone were eligible to honours and public offices. They prosecuted no husbandry, trade, or handicraft; such occupations were incompatible with their prescribed mode of life, besides being positively interdicted. They were supported, therefore, from the produce of the lands round the city, which were cultivated by Helots, who retained a certain proportion for themselves, as the recompense of their labour. In case of any man ceasing to submit to the discipline, or becoming too poor to contribute his quota to the mess, he lost his franchise, and was numbered with the class called the *Inferiors*, in contradistinction to the *equals* or *peers*.

169. The Periœci were freemen and citizens, not of Sparta, but of some one of the townships of the conquered territories which have been described. These communities had no political power, but received their orders from Sparta. The term Periœci, which means 'dwellers round about,' was commonly used in Greece to denote native inhabitants, inferior in a political point of view to the fully-privileged burghers of a city, and did not mark any precise or uniform degree of inferiority; but in special reference to Sparta, it means native freemen and proprietors, grouped in subordinate communities, with more or less power of local management, but embodied in the Lacedæmonian aggregate, which was governed by the kings, senate, and citizens of Sparta. They carried on whatever home or foreign trade, or metallurgic enterprise, was found in the country, and in war they fought in the Spartan ranks as heavy-armed soldiers.

170. The Helots included the domestic slaves of the Spartans and Periœci, and also the rustic population of the country dwelling in small villages or detached farms, both in the district immediately around Sparta and also round the towns of the Periœci. They were serfs bound to the soil, which they tilled for the benefit of their masters; and their condition appears to have been somewhat similar to the villenage of the middle ages in Europe. They enjoyed their homes, wives, and families out of sight of their masters, and were never sold out of the country, probably never sold at all. Doubtless, this

class of men was found by the Doric conquest in the condition of villagers and detached rustics; but whether they were then in the servile condition to which the Spartans compelled them, and so much the subjects of scorn as they were pleased to render them, does not appear. In battle, they attended the Spartans and Periœci as light-armed infantry; and in case of distinguished bravery, the state sometimes presented them with their freedom. Such manumitted Helots, however, did not pass into the class of Periœci, but constituted a separate order, afterwards known as Neodamodes—a term signifying 'recently set free.' Whatever truth there may be in some of the tales related of the wanton and impolitic oppression of this class, it is certain that the treatment they received produced a deep-seated and inveterate detestation of their masters, and, as it has been expressed, 'they would gladly have eaten the flesh of the Spartans raw.' On the other hand, the Spartans lived under continual dread of Helotic revolt, and not without reason. A system of police or espionage called *crypteia*, seems to have been maintained over both the Periœcian townships and the Helotic villages, by the authorised employment of a number of active young Spartans, who went stealthily among them, and, it is said, quietly assassinated such as were considered formidable. The unpleasant position of these classes was aggravated by the fact, that these Helots were not like the slaves of other states—imported barbarians from different countries—but were genuine Hellenes, as much entitled as their oppressors to the protection of the Hellenic Jove, and personally differing from them only in the perfect training which was the Spartan prerogative.

171. The discontents of these subordinate classes were the great source of Spartan weakness. Her strength was derived, as we have seen, from the perfect discipline of her citizens at a time when military training was little practised in the rest of Greece. To this we must add the unparalleled steadiness of her government, which was maintained without revolution, and even without palpable alteration, for four or five successive centuries, in the midst of governments all of which were subject to more

or less fluctuation. It was the only government in Greece which could trace an unbroken and peaceable descent from a high antiquity, and from its reputed founder; and this was one of the main causes of that astonishing ascendancy which the Spartans acquired over the Hellenic mind, and which they appear not to have deserved through any superior ability in management of political affairs.

172. We have spoken of Sparta as a city, but it ought to be observed, that even in the days of its greatest power, it was not such in external appearance, but merely an agglutination of five adjacent villages. The unassailable character of its frontier, and the prowess of its inhabitants, supplied the place of walls, which, it is said, were strictly forbidden by Lycurgus. A striking contrast was thus presented between its humble appearance and the mighty reality of its inflexible government within, and its powerful influence without.

173. By the time to which we have now brought the history of Sparta, a kind of acquiescence in her superiority had become the habit of the Grecian 550 B.C. mind; and in this sentiment we recognise the first approach to anything like an aggregation among the various states of Greece.

ATHENS.

174. In the history of Argos and Sparta we have marked the progress of the principal Doric Greeks prior to 547 B.C. We now turn to the Ionic portion of Hellas during the same period.

175. The Ionic Hellenes comprehended the inhabitants of Athens, Eubœa, the Cyclades, many cities on the coast of Asia Minor, besides numerous colonies.

176. In compliment to the heroism of Codrus, who sacrificed his life for his country, it is said that the Athenians resolved no one after him should ever bear the title of king; and so that of *archon* (ruler) was conferred on his son, and afterwards enjoyed for life by eleven more members of the family in succession. In the year 752 B.C., this dignity was restricted to a duration of ten years; and

in 714 the office was thrown open to all the *Eupatrides* or order of nobility. Another more important change not only restricted the office to one year, but divided it between nine persons, each of whom bore the title, though one was called the archon *par eminence*. All this is but a traditionary, and, of course, unauthenticated account of the gradual change from monarchy to oligarchy in the government of Athens; the real history of Athens commences only with the institution of annual archons in the year 683 B.C. The duties of the executive were shared in the following manner : the first called *the archon*, and sometimes the *archon Eponymus*, because the year was distinguished by his name, was president of the body and the representative of the dignity of the state; while in his judicial functions he was the protector of widows and orphans, and the judge of all matters relating to the family. The second archon was called Basileus, because he exercised the 'kingly' prerogative of acting as high-priest of the people. To him were submitted all matters of religion and cases of homicide. The third archon was called Polemarch, or ' commander-in-chief,' as he was the head of the military force. The remaining six enjoyed the common title Thesmothetæ, or legislators ; not because they made the laws, but because their duties were chiefly judicial, and their decisions had the force of laws in the absence of a written code.

177. The senate or council—the only other political power at this early age—was the same that was afterwards called, by way of distinction, the Court of Areopagus, from its place of meeting, which was a rocky eminence called Mars Hill, opposite the Acropolis. It was, of course, formed of Eupatrides exclusively; and every archon became a member of it when his year of office expired.

178. As there were no written laws, the archons possessed an arbitrary power, which it appears they used chiefly for the benefit of their own order, and especially of their private friends, to the perversion of justice and the injury of the general body of free citizens ; and hence arose great discontent. The disorder at length 624 B.C. became so serious that Dracon, one of the archons, was

appointed to compile a code of laws for the guidance of the executive. The characteristic which has given celebrity to this code was its extreme severity, so that it was said to have been written not with ink, but blood. Light offences and grave ones were made equally punishable by death; and it is reported as the lawgiver's own justification, that he thought the smallest offence deserved the forfeiture of life, and he knew of no severer punishment for the greater. It would seem, however, that there has been some exaggeration as to this harshness; and that in the case of accidental or justifiable homicide, he actually softened the rigour of the existing usages.

179. The people of Athens were miserable enough under this severe legislation and aristocratic executive; and the dissatisfaction was favourable to revolutionary projects; yet the existing government received its first shock not from the oppressed many, but from a nobleman who aspired to despotism. This was Cylon, a patrician, who to his high family position added the personal distinction of having been a victor at Olympia, as a runner in the double stadium. He now conceived the project of seizing the Acropolis, and making himself master of the city. But before making so hazardous an attempt, he consulted the Delphic oracle, and was advised in reply to avail himself of the greatest festival of Jove for accomplishing his purpose. Concluding this to mean the Olympic games, Cylon, at the next recurrence of the festival, put himself at the head of a force partly furnished by his father-in-law, who was despot of Megara, and with this desperate band took sudden possession of the sacred rock of Athens. But the attempt excited general indignation, and the people hastened to assist the authorities in frustrating it; Cylon and his supporters were blockaded in the Acropolis, and reduced to the last extremity for want of provisions. The adventurer himself escaped by stealth; several of his companions died of hunger; and the rest, abandoning the defence, sat down as suppliants before the altar of Minerva. Here they were found by Megacles the archon, who, fearing that their death would pollute the sanctuary, promised to spare their lives on condition of their quitting

the spot; but as soon as they trod on profane ground, the promise was violated, and they were put to death. Some even, who contrived to throw themselves upon the altar of the Fates, near the Areopagus, received their death-blows on the sacred spot.

180. Though the conspiracy was thus put down, its suppression drew after it a long train of calamities. There was a large body of the people who believed that a dreadful act of sacrilege had been committed, such as must bring down divine vengeance, and who therefore clamoured for judgment against the perpetrators of the deed. A public trial was long evaded, but at length submitted to, not, however, till several of the guilty were dead. The accused pleaded that the goddess herself had withdrawn her protecting hand from the followers of Cylon, and abandoned them to their fate; for, said they, when the wretches were persuaded to quit the holy ground, they tied a cord round the statue of the goddess, and held by it for protection as they departed. But as they approached the altar of the Fates, the cord broke—the goddess thus refused to save them. The excuse was not accepted; the surviving perpetrators of the deed were banished from Athens, and the bones of those who were dead were cast forth beyond the border. Nor only so: the whole of the powerful family of the Alcmæonidæ, to which Megacles belonged, with their descendants for several generations, were regarded as a race tainted with the sin of sacrilege; and, in cases of public calamity, were liable to be singled out as those whose impiety had provoked the vengeance of the gods.

181. Meanwhile, the present punishment of the actual perpetrators did not suffice to quiet the religious susceptibilities and apprehensions of the community. They sank into grief and despondency; were continually seeing phantoms and hearing menacing voices; and were persuaded that the curse of the gods rested upon them as a people without abatement. The sacrifices offered at Athens availed not, nor could its prophets discover what else must be done to propitiate offended deity; but the Delphic oracle being applied to, directed them to invite a higher spiritual influence from abroad.

182. Under these circumstances, the Athenians invited to their city the venerable prophet and sage Epimenides, of Crete. It is at this time—that is, in the sixth century before Christ—that we have the first authentic record of religious fraternities by whom mystic rites and expiatory sacrifices were supposed to be performed with more than common effect. Epimenides was a celebrated member of such an order, and stood especially high in the favour of the Cretan Jove. He was thought to be supplied by the nymphs with constant food, as he was never seen to eat; and some reported that he had passed fifty-seven years in a miraculous trance, during which he had been favoured with divine revelations; though others asserted that that space of time had been spent in wandering among the mountains, studying the medicinal virtues of herbs. However this may be, it was now his task to restore mental tranquillity, and to banish from the city a pestilential disease under which the people laboured. In both he was completely successful. We know little with certainty of the details of his proceedings, but he is said to have turned out some sheep on Mars Hill, and directed certain persons to watch their movements, and mark the spots where they lay down, as Heaven-appointed sites for new altars. He established various lustral ceremonies, and issued new precepts for the regulation of worship. Doubtless some of the processes he enjoined had a direct influence in removing the epidemic, as well as an indirect power through the well-attested fact, that the people were assured and comforted. It is to be noted, too, that this sage associated himself with Solon, and was probably aided by his advice, while he no doubt contributed to raise the reputation by which this great man was able soon after to effect a revolution in the government.

183. Epimenides at length departed from Athens carrying with him the universal gratitude and admiration of the people, but refusing all other reward, except a branch from the sacred olive-tree in the Acropolis. According to a statement which was current in the days of one of his younger contemporaries, his life

596 B.C.

is said to have extended to 154 years, while the Cretans affirmed that he lived to 300.

184. We are now brought to a new era in Grecian history, furnishing the earliest known example of a genuine and disinterested constitutional reform. It is found in the establishment of that form of government at Athens which afterwards became the type of democracy throughout Greece.

185. It is likewise on the occasion of Solon's legislation which we are now to notice, that we obtain the first glimpse of the previous state of Attica—a sad and repulsive picture, indeed, replete with private suffering, as well as political discord.

186. The inhabitants were divided into three political parties, violently opposed to each other—the *Pedicis*, or noble and wealthy inhabitants of the plains; the *Diacrii*, or poor mountaineers of the north and east; and the *Parali*, or mercantile inhabitants of the southern coast, whose social position was intermediate between the other two. We have no particular account of the causes of discord between these parties. They had doubtless existed for some time; but now an aggravation of them arose in the shape of a general mutiny of the poorer against the richer, the consequence of a system of oppression which must be explained.

187. According to the law which once obtained here, as throughout a large portion of the world besides, every insolvent debtor was liable to be adjudged the slave of his creditor until he could find some means of satisfying his claim; and not only himself, but his youthful sons, his unmarried daughters, and his sisters, if under his protection —all of whom the law empowered him to sell. The poorer inhabitants of Attica had thus been driven into slavery in large numbers. Those who tilled the land, as dependent tenants or small proprietors, had incurred the misfortune by falling into arrears with reference to the stipulated proportion which they ought to have paid to the proprietor; or they had borrowed money from the more wealthy classes for the supply of their necessities, on the security of their own bodies and that of the persons of their families.

Upon some, too, this deplorable lot had fallen through the adjudication of unprincipled judges. Moreover, a great number of the smaller properties were under mortgage ; of which the token was a stone pillar erected on the land, and inscribed with the name of the lender and the amount of the loan. The proprietors of these lands had the prospect continually before them, that in case of any unfavourable turn of affairs, they and their families must be consigned to irremediable slavery. Thus had many been reduced to bondage in Attica ; others had been sold for exportation ; some had preserved their own freedom only by sacrificing that of their children ; while others had escaped it by quitting the country, to earn a miserable subsistence by degrading occupations in other lands. These evils had now attained such a point, that the mass of sufferers determined to extort some mode of relief. We are not informed as to the particular incident or incidents which immediately stimulated the outbreak ; doubtless there were such, as sparks that ignite a train which has long been prepared. However it was, such was the condition of affairs in 594 B.C., that the governing oligarchy were unable any longer either to enforce the laws against debtors, or to maintain their political power ; the people had become totally unmanageable, and those whose business it was to govern them, were fain to have recourse to the wisdom of Solon, and invest him with unlimited powers as dictator.

188. It is to be regretted that so little is known of the early life of this great man ; only we are told that he was a person of medium fortune, but of the purest heroic blood, tracing his origin to Neptune ; that his father had wasted his means by prodigality, which had compelled Solon, in his early years, to support himself by trade, and this had led him into many parts of Greece and Asia. Moreover, that he early displayed a talent for poetry—that is, for embodying in easy metre those sentiments which would now be expressed in prose ; for the age of prose-writing had not then arrived, and all authorship was in verse. He had gained considerable popularity by effusions which denounced the iniquity of

the existing system; and also, on one or two occasions, had distinguished himself in public affairs by deeds as well as words.

189. As all Grecian governments had hitherto been either oligarchical or despotic, we are not surprised to find that the friends of Solon urged him to multiply partisans, and to seize the supreme power. But his reply was, 'that despotism might be a fine country, but there was no way out of it;' and dismissing all views of personal aggrandisement, he applied himself faithfully to the task before him.

190. His first measure was one which completely relieved the poorer class of debtors. It cancelled at once all those contracts in which the debtor had borrowed on the security of either his person or his land; it swept all the mortgage-pillars from the landed properties, and left them free from past claims; it liberated those debtors who had been reduced to slavery by legal adjudication; it even provided the means of redeeming and bringing home many insolvents who had been sold abroad; and it provided that, for the future, the creditor might obtain judgment against the property of the debtor, but not in anywise against his person, to imprison, or enslave, or extort work from him. It further forbade every Athenian to sell or pledge any of the members of his family. This measure, called the 'shaking off of burdens,' though interfering with constituted rights, became, after a short interval, eminently acceptable, and all ranks concurred in a common sacrifice of thanksgiving. Further, as the creditors of these exonerated individuals might themselves be debtors to others, though their persons were in no danger, Solon resorted to the additional expedient of lowering the money-standard above 25 per cent., by which change the more substantial debtors acquired an exemption to the extent of about 27 per cent.

191. Lastly, Solon decreed the restoration of all citizens who had been condemned by the archons to civil disfranchisement, excepting only those who, after trial in the Prytaneum, had been condemned on the score of murder or treason—an amnesty implying the harshness with

which the archons had been wont to dispense this punishment.

192. The measure of Solon settled for ever the question to which it referred, and never again do we hear of the law of debtor and creditor disturbing Athenian tranquillity. The feeling which grew up under this monetary law, was one of high respect for the sanctity of contracts. Though all the existing mortgages had been rescinded by Solon, and the standard of money depreciated, as extreme measures to meet the present emergency, yet money was again freely lent upon similar security, mortgage-pillars were raised again, and remained undisturbed ; nor did there ever arise another demand for lowering the money-standard.

193. So great was the confidence which Solon had inspired, that he was now called upon to reorganise the political constitution for the better working of the government ; and this he did by introducing some radical changes. Setting aside the previous divisions of the people according to their *gentes* (see page 38), he distributed all freemen into four classes, according to the amount of their property. The first class comprised those whose annual income was equivalent to at least 500 medimni of corn ; the second, those who had at least 300 ; the third, those who had at least 200 ; while the fourth and most numerous class, included all those whose income fell below the value of 200 medimni. Those of the first class alone were eligible to the archonship and other high offices ; the second were regarded as the knights or horsemen of the state, as their property enabled them to keep a horse for this service. The third class formed the heavy-armed infantry, and were bound to provide themselves with full panoply as such. Besides these military services, each of these three classes was subject to taxation in the manner of a graduated income-tax—the highest class paying a larger percentage on their property than the second ; and the second than the third. The fourth class was exempt from all direct taxation, and their military service was only that of light-armed infantry, or heavy-armed in panoply provided by the state. They were likewise disqualified, as individuals, from holding

any public office, but in their collective capacity they were of much importance, as the election of the archons was vested in the popular assembly called Heliæa; and to this body, henceforth, all magistrates were made formally accountable for their conduct in office, and not, as heretofore, to the court of Areopagus. In order to guide this assembly in its proceedings, Solon created a preconsidering senate, of 400 members, whose business it was to prepare matters for discussion in the people's assembly, to convoke its meetings, and secure the execution of its decrees. This senate was chosen by the people from the three higher classes of the community. At the same time, the functions of the court of Areopagus were enlarged, and it was authorised not only to watch over the execution of the laws in general, but to observe the private morals of the citizens, and to punish the idle and dissolute.

194. Thus did Solon lay the foundation of democracy at Athens, by classifying the citizens according to their property instead of their lineage, and by familiarising even the poorest with the idea of protecting themselves by the peaceful exercise of a constitutional franchise. It was, however, only the foundation. The democracy, as a consummated system, such as it appeared in the time of Demosthenes and Æschines, was achieved by gradual steps, which will hereafter be traced.

195. The laws of Solon were written in the manner called *boustrophēdon*,* on wooden cylinders and triangular tablets, which were preserved, first in the Areopagus, and afterwards in the Prytaneum. Those laws which related to sacred matters were chiefly on the tablets; while those respecting secular concerns, or, as they were called, things profane, were on the rollers. It is difficult to form any correct judgment of this legislative code as a whole, because many subsequent additions were by the popular orators falsely ascribed to the wisdom of Solon. As far as we can judge, however, there appears to have been little attempt at systematic order or classification; and historians have generally been content with noting some

* That is, the lines reading, first, from left to right, then from right to left, like the course of the ox in ploughing.

of the most remarkable of the particular laws. Solon appears to have left unchanged the Draconian statutes on the subject of homicide, bound up as they were with the religious feelings of the people ; but he abrogated most of the rest, and substituted—in addition to the laws of debtor and creditor already described—certain provisions for the punishment of crimes ; detailed regulations about marriages and funerals; with others relating to the joint use of springs and wells, and for securing the respective interests of conterminous farmers ; and so on. Some of these are vague and general enough ; others, extremely minute.

196. Solon permitted the exportation of no agricultural produce, except olive oil, while he gave encouragement to the export of artisan labour ; his object probably being to promote manufacturing industry, rather than the culture of a soil naturally poor. He likewise suffered no immigrant to be received into citizenship unless he had irrevocably quitted his former abode, and had come to settle in Athens for the prosecution of some industrial calling ; in which case he received every encouragement, though placed in reference to political rights only among the fourth class of citizens, whatever his grade of fortune. Solon likewise directed the court of Areopagus to punish every citizen found living without any regular vocation ; and he exonerated a son from supporting his father in his old age, if that father had not taught him any art or profession in his youth.

197. These are matters especially deserving of notice, as manifesting a feeling favourable to sedentary industry, which, in most other parts of Greece, perhaps in all except Corinth, was looked upon as degrading. The general tone of opinion throughout the country recognised no occupations as perfectly respectable for a free citizen except arms, husbandry, athletic exercises, and music ; while the Spartans disdained even the prosecution of agriculture, and were admired for it throughout the Hellenic world, though they could not easily be imitated. The encouragement given at Athens to traders and artisans, multiplying as it did the number of town residents, was probably a

decided departure from the primitive temper of Atticism, which tended both to cantonal residence and rural occupation; but it led to the extension of her foreign commerce, and the improvement of her naval force, while, as a further consequence, it lent extraordinary vigour to her democratic government.

198. To Solon is also attributed the first enactments that empowered a man to bequeath his property as he pleased, in case of his having no direct heirs; while he laid down distinct laws for the division of property among the children when there were any, and among the more distant relatives, in case there should be neither children nor yet a will.

199. Another law which deserves particular notice, was that which pronounced any man dishonoured and disfranchised, if, in a time of sedition, he stood aloof and took no part with either side. It is obvious that in case of sedition or insurrection, the constituted authorities, having no standing military force at command, would probably be insufficient to restore peace, and, therefore, the sooner every citizen declared himself, the sooner the suspense would be over; while, on the other hand, nothing was likely to be more mischievous than the masses looking on till the struggle was past, and then submitting to the victor. But what is considered remarkable, is that the virtuous citizen is not by this law required to come forward in support of the government, but to come forward at all events either for or against—decisive and immediate action being the only thing insisted on. It appears as though there was as yet no positive standard round which the citizens could be pledged to rally under every possible circumstance.

200. Solon is said to have characterised his own laws as being not the best that he could have framed, but the best that the people could have been induced to receive; and it seems that they were proclaimed, inscribed, and accepted without demur. But it was not found easy for the people at once to understand and obey what they had so cheerfully consented to submit to; and the lawgiver was daily importuned with criticisms, suggestions, and

demands for explanation, which he feared might compel him to make alterations and unsettle his work. He therefore obtained leave of absence for ten years, and induced the senate and archons to take a solemn oath, that they would maintain his laws inviolate for that space of time. On departing from Athens, he visited Egypt and Cyprus.

201. During the absence of Solon, the old feuds between the Plains, the Coast, and the Mountain population had broken out afresh, and were at their height when the lawgiver returned : the first, headed by one Lycurgus ; the second, by Megacles, grandson to him who had suppressed Cylon's conspiracy ; and the third under Pisistratus, the cousin of Solon. Of these leaders, Pisistratus was the most able and dangerous ; and Solon, penetrating his ulterior design of making himself despot of Athens, did his best to restrain both him and the people in their perilous career. But neither Pisistratus nor his followers regarded his warnings ; and when matters came to a crisis, he proceeded thus :

202. Appearing one day in the agora of Athens in a chariot drawn by mules, both himself and the animals bleeding from wounds inflicted with his own hands, he threw himself on the sympathies of the people, assuring them that he had been nearly murdered for his zeal in defending their rights. The popular indignation was aroused ; an Heliæa was forthwith convoked, and it was proposed and determined, despite the remonstrances of Solon, that fifty club-men should be assigned a body-guard for his future security. This number was gradually increased, and Pisistratus soon found himself in a condition to throw off the mask, and seize the Acropolis. Megacles and the Alcmæonidæ, who were his principal opponents, immediately withdrew from the city, and Solon was left almost alone in a vain attempt to resist the usurpation. When remonstrance failed, the venerable sage, as a last appeal, put on his armour, and placed himself in military posture before the door of his house : no one dared to join him, and he renounced all further hope of successful opposition. His friends implored him to flee, and asked him

on what he relied for protection. He said, on his old age; and it is gratifying to learn, that his confidence was not misplaced. He remained unmolested by the despotism of Pisistratus, and died, as it is 560 B.C. thought, during the following year, at the venerable age of eighty.

203. The history of the next fifty years can be but imperfectly related, as few facts have been preserved. The power which Pisistratus had obtained by stratagem, and maintained by force, he exercised with moderation, not disturbing existing forms further than was necessary to insure to himself the control of the administration. Nevertheless, the general feeling was by no means favourable to his usurpation; and the terror and aversion it had excited presently appeared in the armed coalition of Megacles and Lycurgus, with their followers, for his overthrow. Pisistratus was in no condition to withstand this united force, and he was forced to leave the country. But the time came—we are not told how soon—when Megacles and Lycurgus quarrelled between themselves, and the former made overtures to Pisistratus. He undertook to aid him in recovering the sovereignty, stipulating for a prospective interest in it for his posterity, by the marriage of his daughter with the despot. The conditions were accepted; and a new stratagem was devised for obtaining possession of the citadel. A majestic-looking woman, six feet high, was arrayed in the costume and panoply of Minerva, the tutelar deity of Athens; she was surrounded with the processional accompaniments proper to this goddess, and placed in a chariot with Pisistratus at her side. Thus the exiled despot and his adherents drove up to the Acropolis, preceded by heralds, who cried aloud: 'Athenians! receive ye cordially Pisistratus, whom Minerva has honoured above all other men, and is now bringing back into her own Acropolis.' The citizens believed, worshipped, and obeyed; and the news spread among the country cantons, that Minerva had appeared in person to restore Pisistratus, who thus, without even the show of resistance, found himself in possession of the citadel and the government. His marriage with the daughter of Megacles was

celebrated according to the agreement; but he treated his bride with utter neglect, desiring that his heirs should be the sons of his former marriage, and that his race should not become one with that of the anathematised Alcmæonidæ. Megacles was so incensed at his conduct, that he undeceived the Athenians about the appearance of Minerva, and divulged the mode in which it had been got up. He also made peace with the third party, the adherents of Lycurgus, and assumed so threatening an attitude, that the despot again retired. This time he spent ten years in the island of Eubœa, where he made himself useful in political matters, especially to Lygdamis, whom he assisted to constitute himself despot of Naxos. He was rewarded with a body of auxiliary troops, and large sums of money, with which he hired mercenaries from Argos; and thus prepared, he returned to the conquest of his native city. He landed at Marathon, where he remained undisturbed, collecting his partisans both in town and country; and not till he marched with these towards the city, was any attempt made to frustrate his design. He now easily routed the force sent to oppose him, a third time found himself sole ruler of Athens, and took vigorous measures for rendering his authority permanent. He provided himself with a powerful body of Thracian mercenaries, whom he paid by taxes levied on the people. The Alcmæonidæ and their partisans having fled on his approach, he seized their children as hostages for their pacific behaviour, and placed them in the island of Naxos, under the care of Lygdamis. Nor did he neglect to propitiate the favour of the gods. With this view, he purified the isle of Delos, exhuming the dead bodies, and removing them out of sight of the temple of Apollo; and perhaps as a religious rather than a vengeful procedure, he razed to the ground the dwellings of the Alcmæonidæ; and disinterring the bones of the deceased members of that family, cast them out of the country.

204. This third and last despotism of Pisistratus was prolonged till his death, and transmitted to his heirs. It was not only exceedingly mild, but distinguished by the prosecution of several great public works, undertaken

perhaps both with the view of employing and of impoverishing the citizens. The temple of the Olympian Jove was begun on a prodigious scale, but left unfinished. Moreover, Pisistratus introduced what was called the greater Panathenaic festival, solemnised every fourth year. He bestowed great care in procuring full and correct copies of the Homeric poems, and improving the recitation of them at the Panathenæa—a proceeding for which posterity is deeply indebted to him. He also collected the works of other poets, and formed a library, which was thrown open to the public—a service doubtless of the highest value at a time when opportunities of reading and writing were so limited.

205. Pisistratus died in 527 B.C., at an advanced age, and in the thirty-third year from the time of his first usurpation. He left three sons—Hippias, Hipparchus, and Thessalus; the two former of whom succeeded him in the government. They are said to have maintained it with great mildness, interfering little with existing forms of law and justice, only taking care to keep themselves and their partisans in all the principal public offices. They adorned the city with many new structures; were punctual in the fulfilment of all religious obligations; and erected, in various parts of Attica, statues to Apollo, inscribed with short moral sentences, for the edification of the people. Hipparchus, in particular, inherited his father's literary tastes; cultivated the society of the most eminent poets of the day—it is to be remembered that all authors then were poets; and proved his zeal for genuine literature by banishing the mystic poet, Onomacritus, for interpolating the prophecies of Musæus. This state of things, however, was destined to undergo a change, arising from circumstances apparently trivial.

206. Harmodius and Aristogiton, two Athenian citizens, were attached to each other in the bonds of close mutual friendship. The former, having given offence to Hippias, was punished, not directly, but through an insult offered to his sister. She was summoned on one occasion to take her place in a religious procession as one of the basket-carriers, according to the usual customs. But

when she arrived at the place where the other maidens were assembled, she was dismissed with contempt, as one unworthy of the function, and the summons she had received was disavowed. Harmodius was exasperated; his friend Aristogiton espoused his quarrel, and they concerted a plan of vengeance with a few select associates. It was determined to avail themselves of the festival of the great Panathenæa, the only occasion on which an armed body could appear without exciting suspicion. It was usual in this festival for the citizens to form an armed procession, and the conspirators were to appear just like the rest, only carrying concealed daggers. The two leaders undertook to assassinate the two Pisistratidæ, while the rest of the conspirators defended them against the mercenary guards; and they reckoned on the spontaneous sympathy of the citizens, as soon as the first blow for liberty should be struck. The festive-day having arrived, Hippias was marshalling the citizens for the procession in the Ceramicus outside the gates, when Harmodius and Aristogiton approached to execute their purpose, and were astonished to observe one of their own accomplices in familiar conversation with Hippias. They concluded that they were betrayed, and hurried from the spot to secure at least the death of Hipparchus. Entering the city, they found him within the gates, and immediately slew him. The attendant guards killed Harmodius on the spot, but Aristogiton was for the moment rescued by the people. Tidings of these events were communicated to Hippias before they became known to the armed citizens whom he was preparing for the procession; and with singular presence of mind, he commanded them to drop their arms for a short time, and repair to another ground. They obeyed without suspicion, and he immediately directed his guards to take possession of the weapons thus abandoned. All the citizens whom he distrusted, especially those found with daggers, were seized; Aristogiton was put to the torture to discover his accomplices, and died under the suffering. Hippias remained undisputed master. This conspiracy occurred in 514 B.C., during the thirteenth year of the reign of Hippias, which continued four years longer; though some of the poets and even historians make no account of these years, and represent Harmodius and Aristogiton as having put down the Pisistratidæ, and restored freedom to Athens. They were afterwards commemorated both as the authors and protomartyrs of Athenian liberty; statues were erected to their memory, and their descendants were exempted from all taxes and public burdens.

207. Vengeance for the past, and fear for the future, now induced Hippias to lay aside the moderation with which the Pisistratid administration had hitherto been distinguished. He ruled with a rod of iron, and put many of the citizens wantonly to death. Still feeling insecure, and apprehending that he might need the shelter of an exile, he became anxious to secure the alliance of Darius, king of Persia, and with this view gavé his daughter in marriage to Æantides, the despot of Lampsacus, who stood high in the favour of the Persian monarch.

208. The same circumstances that rendered Hippias at once odious and apprehensive, tended of course to raise the hopes of his enemies, of whom the chief were the powerful Alcmæonidæ. Believing that the auspicious hour was come, they ventured on an invasion of Attica, but were defeated and repulsed by Hippias. His dominion now appeared secure. The Lacedæmonians were his intimate friends; Amyntas, king of Macedon, as well as the Thessalians, were his allies. But the exiles who had been beaten in the field proved more successful in operations of manœuvre.

209. The Delphian temple had been destroyed by an accidental fire in the year 548 B.C.; and after enormous exertions, the large sum (probably about L.115,000) necessary for its re-erection had been raised. 'The Alcmæonidæ, exiled from Athens, became the contractors for the work, and not only performed it in the most creditable manner, but displayed a generosity beyond their agreement, using Parian marble for the front, whereas the specified material was only coarse stone. The completion of the work is to be dated probably about a year or two after the death of Hipparchus—that is, more than thirty years after the conflagration. This liberal 512 B.C.

performance of so important an undertaking, procured signal reputation for the Alcmæonidæ throughout the whole Hellenic world; while the Delphians, to whom it was the most essential of all services, were unbounded in their gratitude. Clisthenes, the son of Megacles, and now the head of the family, availed himself of this feeling—backed, perhaps, by pecuniary presents—to work the oracle for political purposes, and call out the Spartans against his enemy Hippias. Whenever any Spartan presented himself to consult the oracle, either on public or private business, the answer of the priestess was, 'Athens must be set free;' and the constant reiteration of the mandate at length extorted a compliance, however reluctant. Reverence for the god proved stronger than friendship for the Pisistratidæ, and a force was sent by sea to expel the despot. He was, however, well prepared to receive it, having been reinforced by 1000 horse from Thessaly: the Spartans were driven back to their ships with great loss, and their commander slain. But this repulse only provoked them to fit out a larger armament, which marched into Attica by land, under the personal command of Cleomenes, the Spartan king. On reaching the plain of Athens, they were met by the Thessalian horse, which they repelled in so gallant a style, that they rode off at once, and returned to their own country. The Spartans then marched to Athens, and soon found themselves with the Alcmæonidæ, and other malcontents, in possession of the town. Hippias retired to the Acropolis with his mercenaries, and those of the citizens who sided with him, having provisioned it well beforehand. Yet, not altogether confiding in his position, he endeavoured to send his children away by stealth. They were taken prisoners, and to procure their liberation, Hippias consented to all that was demanded of him, and accordingly withdrew from Attica within five days. His expulsion was hailed with 510 B.C. joy by the vast majority of the Athenians. His principal partisans as well as his family accompanied him into exile, probably as a matter of course, without any formal sentence of condemnation; and an altar was erected in the

Acropolis, with a column commemorating the iniquity of the dethroned dynasty, and the names of all its members.

210. The mercenary troops with which the Pisistratidæ had surrounded themselves, disappeared with Hippias; Cleomenes also retired with his Lacedæmonians, leaving the Athenians free to settle their affairs without foreign interference.

211. It has been mentioned that the Pisistratidæ had generally respected the forms of the Solonian constitution. The nine archons, the senate of 400, the senate of Areopagus, and the occasional assemblies of the people, still continued, as well as the Timocratic classification or quadruple scale of income, with the corresponding scale of political franchise; but all subservient to the purposes of the reigning family. The pressure being now removed, these institutions were endued with reality and freedom; and there appeared again declared political parties, opposed to each other, under their respective leaders. On one side was Isagoras, the leader of the nobles; on the other, Clisthenes the Alcmæonid, with his singular claims on the gratitude of his countrymen. In what manner their opposition was carried on, does not appear; but we are told that Clisthenes being worsted, took the people into partnership, and thus brought about the Athenian democracy.

212. The political franchise or citizenship of Athens had hitherto been confined to the four primitive Ionic tribes, each composed of so many quasi-families—the *gentes* and the *phratries*. None of the residents in Attica, therefore, had any part in the political franchise, unless he belonged to some gens or phratry. But such non-privileged residents had now become extremely numerous, especially in Athens and Piræus, where it was most natural for immigrants to establish themselves; and the despotism had done at least this good, that by nullifying the powers of all alike, it had confounded the privileged and the non-privileged classes. The distinction could not now, perhaps, have been easily revived; the division into four Ionic tribes had become quite incommensurate with the condition of the population, and its revival for political purposes would probably have appeared an odious novelty, to which the

ATHENS. 97

excluded classes would not have submitted. However this may be, Clisthenes broke down the existing wall of privilege, and extended the political franchise to the hitherto excluded mass—that is, he disconnected the franchise altogether from the gentes and phratries, and redistributed the population into ten new tribes, which were purely local. Each tribe consisted of the enrolled proprietors and residents of a certain number of cantons or townships called *demēs*, with their legitimate sons on attaining the age of eighteen, and their adopted sons, whenever presented and sworn to by the adopting citizen. The Clisthenian constitution thus admitted to the political franchise not only all free native Athenians, but a large number of *metics* (immigrant tradesmen), and even some of the better classes of the slaves. It was a scheme approaching to universal suffrage, both judicial and political, the general slave population only being excluded.

213. It is important, however, to remark, that the demes which Clisthenes assigned to each tribe were in no case all adjacent to one another, and therefore a tribe did not correspond with any continuous portion of territory; consequently, could not have any peculiar local interests. The object, doubtless, was to avoid such local feuds as those of the preceding century, between the Plain, the Highlands, and the Coast. The city of Athens itself did not constitute either one deme or one tribe, but was distributed. Each tribe was a mere aggregation of demes for political purposes, without any interests peculiar to itself. It was named after some hero famous in ancient legend; it had a chapel, with sacred rites and festivals in honour of him; and the statues of all the ten eponymous heroes were placed in the agora of Athens, as fraternal patrons of the democracy. Each deme had its own demarch, its register of members, its collective or joint property, its public meetings and religious ceremonies, and its self-imposed taxes.

214. Clisthenes preserved, but with some modification, the main features of the Solonian constitution: there was still to be the public assembly or ecclesia; but it was to acquire new strength, and almost a new character, from the great accession of new members: there was to be the

preconsidering senate; but now enlarged to 500, taken equally from each of the ten new tribes : and there was to be, besides, the annual election of magistrates, and their annual responsibility to the ecclesia, the novelty of these high offices being thrown open to all classes. To render the ecclesia efficient, it was necessary that its meetings should be both frequent and free. The year was distributed afresh for all legal purposes into ten parts, bearing the name of *prytanies*, each marked by a solemn and freespoken ecclesia, convoked and presided over by senators called prytanes.

215. The judicial as well as the political powers of the people were extended; all public crimes were to be tried by the whole body of citizens above thirty years of age, in an assembly called Heliæa, convoked and sworn for this special purpose. It afterwards became necessary to divide the Heliæa into local courts ; and through time, the presidency of these became almost the only important function of the archons.

216. The new organisation of the tribes almost necessarily led to new military arrangements. The citizens were now marshalled according to their tribes, and ten strategi, or military generals, were appointed, one for each tribe, with two hipparchs for the supreme command of the horse; the third archon, or polemarch, still retaining in some sort his position—a joint command in the field, and an equal vote in the council of war—with these new functionaries.

217. Another remarkable institution of Clisthenes was *ostracism* (an arbitrary voting), by which a citizen might be banished for ten years, without either special accusation, trial, or defence. Before such a vote could be taken, it was necessary to debate and determine, in the senate and in the ecclesia, that the state of the republic was such as to warrant such a measure—that is, that it was in danger from the designs of some one or more individuals. This being decided, a day was appointed, the agora was railed round, with ten entrances left, one for the citizens of each tribe, and ten vessels for depositing the suffrages. Each citizen wrote upon a shell the name of the person whom he thought it desirable to banish, and placed it in the vessel.

At the close of the day, these votes were counted, and if 6000 were found to have been given against any one person, he was said to be ostracised. Ten days were allowed him to prepare for his departure, and no loss of property or other infliction was involved.

218. Such were the leading features of the first Athenian democracy—a novelty in many respects, appealing to a new set of feelings, and presenting a new set of duties in the daily life of every citizen. Perhaps the most unheard-of novelty, was the authentic recognition of a sovereign demos or people, with free speech and equal law; retaining no distinction of rank except the four classes of the Solonian property schedule. To many, this novelty was rendered precious by the fact, that it had raised them from the low position hitherto allotted to metics and slaves; while to all it furnished a splendid political idea, calculated to awaken the most ardent attachment, as well as a sense of responsibility and obligation to obedience.

219. It was received with the utmost cordiality, so that Isagoras, and the few advocates of the old regime who rallied round him, had no hope of successful opposition but by enlisting the powerful aid of Cleomenes and his Lacedæmonians. This Cleomenes readily promised, and sent a herald to Athens requiring the citizens to expel 'the accursed'—for so the Alcmæonid family were still called by their enemies. Clisthenes did not venture to resist the mandate, but voluntarily retired, so that Cleomenes, though arriving with but a scanty force, encountered little opposition, and found himself master of the city in conjunction with Isagoras and his partisans. He immediately expelled 700 families selected by Isagoras, as chief adherents of Clisthenes, and then proceeded to dissolve the new senate of 500. But this body refused to submit to dissolution; and the citizens beginning to manifest spirit and determination, Cleomenes and Isagoras were obliged to retire into the Acropolis. Here they were besieged by the citizens, and forced to surrender in two days for want of provisions. Isagoras, as well as Cleomenes and his troops, were permitted to depart unmolested; but the Athenian partisans, in this attempt to overthrow the new

constitution, were taken, condemned, and executed by the people.

220. Clisthenes was immediately recalled, with the 700 exiled families; but the fear of a new attack from Sparta induced him to send an embassy to Artaphernes, the Persian satrap at Sardis, to seek the alliance of Persia. The reply was, that the Athenians might be admitted to its alliance, if they chose 'to send earth and water to the Persian monarch.' The envoys promised this token of submission; but on their reporting the matter at home, the Athenians repudiated it with indignation.

221. It was at this time that the little Bœotian town of Platæa, being discontented with its treatment as a federative city of Thebes, seceded, and placed itself under Athenian protection. The Corinthians, as mediators in the quarrel, decided that it had a right to act so if it chose; and the Thebans, while submitting to the decision, retained a sullen enmity to Athens.

222. Meanwhile, Cleomenes had returned to Sparta, vowing vengeance against Attica, and determined to place Isagoras as despot over it. He summoned allies from the various states of Peloponnesus, but without explaining the object of the expedition to be taken; and at the same time concerted with the Bœotians and the Chalcidians of Eubœa, that they should simultaneously invade Attica on their side. But when the allied forces arrived at Eleusis, they learned the object that was in view, and expressed their entire disapprobation of it. Corinth especially was rather favourably inclined towards Athens; and even Demaratus, the joint king with Cleomenes, united in the general dissatisfaction. The whole army, therefore, broke up, and returned home without striking a blow; so that the Athenians had now only to combat their enemies on the north-eastern frontier. Here they gained a complete victory over the Bœotians; then crossed over into Eubœa, and obtained another so decisive as to terminate hostilities from this quarter. The Athenians now planted 4000 of their citizens as a kind of military colony upon the fertile lands of the Chalcidians —a policy which they afterwards pursued extensively, as

it both provided for their poorer citizens, whose estates had been diminished by the multiplication of their families, and also secured their domination in the conquered country. Such settlers were called *cleruchs*—that is, 'lot-holders,' and nearly corresponded with the military colonies of Rome in after-times.

223. The war between Athens and Thebes, however, still continued, to the great and repeated disadvantage of the latter; but the details which have reached us are scanty.

224. Meanwhile, Cleomenes and the Spartans were incensed at the late inglorious break-up at Eleusis, and still more so at the discovery they had recently made, that the injunctions so often repeated to them by the Delphian priestess for the expulsion of Hippias, had been elicited by fraud. They now sent for him, and summoned deputies from their allies to meet him at Sparta, and consult what might be done against Athens—not again risking the adventure of engaging their confederates without securing their concurrence in the object. This convocation of various states for the purpose of having a common object submitted to their consideration, is regarded as an important event in the political history of Greece—a new step towards a systematic conjunction of its many independent units. The allies having been assembled, and Hippias introduced, the Spartans expressed their sorrow for having dethroned him, their resentment and alarm at the insolence of the new-born democracy, and their desire to restore him, both as a reparation for past wrong, and as a means of keeping Athens in her proper place. But the proposition was met with a universal feeling of repugnance. The allies had no sympathy with Hippias, and no fear of Athens, but a profound detestation of the character of a despot. The Corinthian deputy was the principal speaker, adjuring the Lacedæmonians by the common gods of Hellas, not to plant despots in her cities, at least to try it for themselves at Sparta first, which they had never done. In vain Hippias replied by warning the Corinthians, that the time would come when they above all others would wish the Pisistratidæ back in Athens again.

No one believed him, and he was obliged to return to Sigeum.

225. Meanwhile, the energy of Athens developed astonishingly as the fruit of the fresh-planted democracy. So remarks Herodotus, after narrating their victories over the Bœotians and Chalcidians. 'Thus,' says he, 'did the Athenians grow in strength; and we may find proof not merely in this instance, but everywhere else, how valuable a thing freedom is, since even the Athenians, while under a despot, were not superior in war to any of their surrounding neighbours, but so soon as they got rid of their despots, became by far the first of all. These things shew, that while kept down by one man, they were slack and timid, like men working for a master; but when they were liberated, every man became eager in exertions for his own benefit.'

LITERARY RETROSPECT.

226. The distinguishing feature of the age which we have now reviewed, is the cultivation of lyric poetry, which began upon the coast of Asia and the neighbouring islands in the seventh century before the Christian era. Epic poetry, which had satisfied the desire for the marvellous in the infantile period of Grecian history, was on the decline, and an advancing civilisation and enlarged experience supplied new subjects for the Muse. The poetic art, hitherto occupied with action only, came to be employed on feelings and sentiments. And now no important event, either in the public or private life of a Greek, could dispense with the song: it was equally needed to solemnise the worship of the gods, to enliven the festive board, and to cheer the march to battle.

227. The enthusiasm excited by this new species of poetry, and the extent of its influence upon the people, appear from the esteem in which the lyric poets were held by their contemporaries; from the anxiety with which nations and individuals alike solicited their praise; and from the attention which even the legislatures bestowed on their works. Honour and wealth were lavished on

these poets; the citizens adopted them as guests; and the laws determined the musical modes they were to use in public.

228. The oldest of the lyric poets was Archilochus, the Parian, celebrated chiefly for his terrible satires, composed in iambic verse—the fruit, it is said, of a disappointment in love.

229. Many of the most renowned lyric poets flourished at Lesbos, which became a garden and a sanctuary of poetry. Here flourished Orpheus, whose head is said to have floated down the Hebrus with his lyre, and to have landed, still singing, on the coast of the island. Here, too, flourished Arion, famous for his dithyrambics; Alcæus, who, in manly strains, chastised the tyrants of his country; and here flourished Sappho, the tenth Muse, and the greatest of all the Greek poetesses.

230. Tyrtæus, an Athenian, whose warlike songs had so important an influence in the Messenian war, and Alcman, were the two great lyric poets of Sparta. In the later part of the lyric period, flourished Anacreon, who sang of love and wine; Simonides, who devoted his poetry chiefly to public life, to the celebration of noble deeds, and to the praise of the gods; and Pindar, the pride of Thebes, who dedicated his songs to the service of the Pythian Apollo.

231. At the commencement of the sixth century before Christ, there sprang up in different parts of Greece a number of men who obtained the appellation of the Seven Sages, on account of their practical sagacity. Their names are differently given; but those most generally admitted are Solon, Thales, Pittacus, Periander, Cleobulus, Chilon, and Bias. Most of them were actively engaged in the affairs of public life, and many of their wise sayings or maxims have been transmitted to posterity.

232. Out of the wisdom of the Seven Sages, as from a germ, sprang the philosophy for which Greece was afterwards so celebrated. The first beginnings of geometry and astronomy have been traced to Thales, the founder of the school called the Ionic.

SECOND PERIOD.

500—478 B.C.

THE IONIC REVOLT.

233. THE four sovereignties of Babylonia, with its wonderful city—Egypt, with its powerful king Amasis—Lydia, under Crœsus—and Media, under Astyages—were contemporaneously in a high state of prosperity, and more or less allied to each other, till from the mountainous region of Persia, which lies to the south of Media, issued a band of hardy warlike adventurers, hitherto living as agricultural or nomadic tribes, dressed in skins, and ignorant of the most common luxuries of life; but now, under the leadership of Cyrus, aspiring to conquest and dominion. The Median Astyages, whom some historians represent as the grandfather of Cyrus, was defeated and dethroned; in consequence of which, 559 B.C. the sovereignty of Upper Asia passed into the hands of Cyrus, who, with his warlike followers, went on thence from conquest to conquest. The stories that are told concerning the youth and early career of Cyrus, rest on but uncertain foundations, and are, besides, not necessary to our present purpose: that he was the first Persian conqueror, and that he overran a space including no fewer than 50 degrees of longitude, from the coast of Asia Minor to the Oxus and the Indus, are facts indisputable; but of the steps by which this was achieved, very little is known with certainty. Ecbatana, hitherto the chief city of Media, continued to be one of the capitals of this extensive empire, and the usual summer residence of the Persian monarchs; while Susa was the other, and their winter abode.

234. The war between Cyrus and Crœsus probably broke out shortly after the capture of Astyages, which

Crœsus, being his brother-in-law, desired to avenge. The first campaign proved indecisive. Before the second, Crœsus had engaged the Greeks to assist him; and the Lacedæmonians at least, had their ships ready and their troops embarking, when they heard that Crœsus was already ruined. Cyrus had pushed on to Sardis, and compelled him to fight before he could receive the expected reinforcements; he had been defeated, himself taken prisoner, and the Lydian monarchy destroyed. This event, so serious in its consequences to Hellas generally, took place in 546 B.C.

235. The Ionic Greeks of Asia whom Cyrus had invited, before the war, to revolt from Lydia, now implored that they might be tributaries to him on the same footing that they had enjoyed under Crœsus; but the conqueror angrily refused this to all except the city of Miletus; and they began to put themselves in a condition of defence. Besides strengthening their own cities, they sent a joint embassy to Sparta, imploring its succour. Though the request was refused, a Spartan commission was sent to Phocæa, to examine the state of affairs; and thence an envoy was despatched to Cyrus, to warn him that the Lacedæmonians would not suffer him to lay hands on any city of Hellas. The conqueror was provoked rather than intimidated by this message, which was the only show of assistance the Asiatic Greeks received from the mother-country.

236. Cyrus, presently quitting Sardis to prosecute his conquests eastward, took Crœsus along with him, and left his lieutenants to complete the subjugation of Asia Minor. One of these revolted, and the Greeks took his part; another was sent to reduce him, and after accomplishing this object, turned his sword against the Greeks themselves. The various Greek cities on the coast made a gallant but ineffectual resistance; where they could not be carried by storm, they were reduced by blockade, and thus one after the other compelled to acknowledge the sovereignty of Persia. Even the inhabitants of Lesbos and Chios, who were comparatively safe, as the Persians had no fleet to invade their islands, deemed it prudent to enrol themselves

subjects of the empire : Samos alone maintained its independence, and under the despotism of Polycrates, held its head higher than ever.

237. Harpagus, the general who had, on the behalf of Cyrus, subdued the Ionic and Æolic Greeks, now employed them as auxiliaries, and proceeded to the conquest of the south-western inhabitants of Asia Minor. The Doric Greeks in this direction offered but feeble resistance ; the Lycians only, in their chief town Xanthus, made a desperate defence. Having been worsted in the field, and blockaded in the city, they set fire to their dwellings with their own hands, leaving their women, children, and servants to be consumed in the flames, while the armed citizens marched out, and perished to a man in conflict with the enemy.

238. While Harpagus was thus employed, Cyrus had been extending his conquests toward the east. He took the city of Babylon, and incorporated its dominions with his own ; but in the following year, 538 B.C. while fighting against the Massagetæ, a nomade people beyond the Araxes, he was slain, and his empire devolved on his son Cambyses.

239. The stimulus which had been given to the pride and ambition of the Persians continued unabated, and Cambyses led them with success to the conquest of Egypt. In this enterprise, indeed, all the forces of the empire were engaged, including the Asiatic Greeks, both insular and continental, who, with the Phœnicians, supplied the maritime force.

240. It was the principal object of Darius, the successor of Cambyses, after suppressing some revolts, to organise this great empire. He divided it into twenty satrapies or departments, imposing upon each a certain annual tax, while the internal government was left pretty much in the hands of the former rulers. Yet did he not altogether forego the aggressive policy of his predecessors. He completed the conquest of the Ionic Greeks, by subjugating the important island of Samos ; but this not being a sufficient extension of the limits of his empire, he proceeded to the conquest of Scythia, his naval force consisting this time

entirely of his Greek subjects. To them was committed the task of throwing a bridge of boats across the Ister (Danube), and watching it until his return. It is reported, that intending to return home in another direction, he at first desired them to break it down, and follow him in his land-march, but afterwards consented, as a precaution against contingencies, to leave the Ionians in charge of it for sixty days; after which, they were to return home, concluding that he was not to be expected that way. They had remained at their post beyond the sixty days, when a body of Scythians appeared, urging them to break the bridge and retire, for Darius was in full retreat, and in great distress; his only hope was in the preservation of the bridge, and if it were destroyed, his fate would be inevitable, and their freedom secured. But the commanders of these Ionians were, for the most part, despots of their respective cities; and listening to the suggestion, that they would be unable to maintain their sovereignty without the Persian king, they preserved the bridge. Darius reached and crossed it; the Persian army was saved, and the Ionian Greeks lost the opportunity of throwing off the yoke. Histiæus of Miletus, who had chiefly swayed the determination of the Greeks on this occasion, received as his reward the town of Myrcinus, near the Strymon.

241. Darius, on his return to Persia, nominated his brother Artaphernes satrap of Sardis, and Otanes, instead of Megabazus, general of the forces on the coast. Having had reason to fear that Histiæus was collecting a power which might prove formidable to his own, he professed to need him as a friend and counsellor, and took him with him to Susa, allowing him to appoint Aristagoras in his place, as despot of Miletus.   512 B.C.

242. About six years afterwards, Hippias, the exiled despot of Athens, pressed his cause on the notice of Artaphernes, promising, that if restored to his sovereignty, he would hold it as subject to Persia. So favourably were his proposals received, that when the Athenians sent envoys to expostulate, and set forth the case that they had against Hippias, the reply of Artaphernes was, that they must receive back the despot, or prepare to meet the consequences.

Doubtless nothing less than an invasion of Attica was contemplated by the satrap, but other projects diverted him for a time.

243. The wealthy and populous island of Naxos was, like the rest of the Cyclades, as yet independent of Persia. When, however, the oligarchical rulers were expelled by a rising of the people, they repaired to Miletus, and implored the aid of Aristagoras to regain their power. The latter, not having sufficient force himself for an enterprise against the Cyclades, applied, through Artaphernes, to the Persian monarch, and was furnished with a large armament, composed both of Persians and the tributaries about the coast. It was alleged that this expedition was bound for the Hellespont; and its real design not being suspected at Naxos, no preparation was made for its repulse; till a dispute arising between Aristagoras and the Persian commander about precedence, the latter secretly apprised the islanders of their danger. The consequence was, that the most vigorous measures were taken for the defence; and after an unavailing siege of four months, the armament was brought back to the coast of Ionia.

244. Aristagoras now saw no way of discharging the obligation he had incurred with respect to indemnifying the Persian power for the cost of the fleet. He was seriously meditating a revolt, as the only alternative, when he received a message. Histiæus sent him a message urging him to rebel; for in case of a rising among the Ionians, Histiæus calculated that he would be sent to repress it, and would thus regain his freedom. The faltering resolution of Aristagoras was thus determined, and he convened his principal friends at Miletus, to concert the plan of revolt. It was forthwith resolved, as the first step, to enlist popular favour among the Asiatic Greeks by putting down all the despots, these being the chief instruments of Persian ascendancy. There was now a most favourable opportunity of doing a great part of this work by a single stroke, as the fleet was still on the coast, with many of the despots in command of their respective ships. These were seized at once, and delivered into the hands of their former subjects, who, for the most

part, dismissed them peremptorily, though without violence. Aristagoras himself laid down his authority at Miletus, and placed it ostensibly in the hands of the people. Throughout most of the other cities, a similar revolution was brought about; the despots were expelled, and the people became zealous for the revolt, as a strike for a double freedom. Being in possession of the fleet, they doubtless calculated on remaining masters of the sea; but the Persians procured a naval force from Phœnicia—a proceeding probably both new and unlooked for. Aristagoras now resorted to Sparta as the leading power in Hellas; but the Lacedæmonians were in no hostile relations with Persia, and did not choose to provoke a new enemy by meddling in the Asiatic war. The Athenians, who had already received tokens of hostility from Sardis, were more easily persuaded, and sent twenty ships across the Ægæan. Aristagoras, on his return, found the Persians besieging Miletus; but instead of combating them there, he ordered his forces at once to Sardis, where they easily possessed themselves of the town, Artaphernes having only troops enough to keep the citadel. But recalling his force from Miletus, and summoning help from all the neighbouring districts, the satrap soon found himself more than a match for the Ionians. Moreover, an accidental fire breaking out in the town, spread rapidly among the reed-built houses and thatched roofs. The people, thus driven from their dwellings, congregated in the market-place, and as reinforcements were daily crowding in, the position of the invaders became precarious. They made the best of their way back to the coast; and the Athenians betook themselves to their vessels, sailed home, and took no further part in the struggle. The burning of a place so important as Sardis, at once incensed the Persians and encouraged the revolters; the Greek cities near the Hellespont and the Propontis, as well as those of Cyprus, joined them, and the rebellion assumed a formidable character.

245. After a year spent in collecting forces, the Persians sent an army into Cyprus, by means of the Phœnician fleet. Shortly after the landing of the troops, the Ionian

fleet arrived, gave battle to the Phœnician, and obtained a brilliant victory. But the conflict on land went against the Cyprians, who were completely defeated, and the Ionian ships returned home. Meanwhile, an overpowering force had been brought to bear on the cities of the Asiatic coast; and the insurgents, though remaining masters of the sea, were everywhere worsted on land. Aristagoras, now despairing of success, took the resolution of retiring into Thrace, with all who chose to bear him company. But, soon after landing, he perished with most of his companions in besieging one of the towns.

246. Meanwhile, Darius had been enraged at the attack and burning of Sardis, which he understood had been carried into effect by the co-operation of the Athenians. It is said that he exclaimed: 'The Athenians! who are they?' and on receiving the answer, he asked for his bow, and shot an arrow as high as he could towards heaven, saying: 'Grant me, Jove, to avenge myself on the Athenians!' He had no doubt of the Ionians being speedily quelled, but he desired an attendant to say to him thrice every day at dinner: 'Master, remember the Athenians!'

247. It was now the time for Histiæus to offer his services, engaging not merely to quell the Ionian revolt, but also to add the great island of Sardinia to the empire; 'and this,' said he, 'I will do, before I take this tunic off my body.' Receiving a commission, accordingly, he hastened to Sardis, where he found the satrap Artaphernes better acquainted with his machinations than the great king at Susa had been. 'I will tell you, Histiæus,' said he, 'how the facts stand: it is you that have stitched this shoe, and Aristagoras has put it on.' The traitor, finding himself thus suspected, fled to the coast the same night, and thence passed over to Chios. Here he was apprehended on the opposite count, as being the confidant of Darius; but he was released on proclaiming himself to be not merely a fugitive from Persian custody, but also the first mover of the revolt. The Chians carried him back to Miletus, where he found the citizens altogether averse to the return of their former despot. Being repulsed in his efforts to enter the town, he returned to Chios, and thence to Lesbos,

where he obtained a few vessels, which he employed in piracies upon the Ionian merchant-ships as they passed in and out of the Euxine.

248. Meanwhile, Artaphernes was concentrating an immense force around Miletus, against which he was determined to employ all his energy. Not only the whole Persian army of Asia Minor, but the Cilician and Egyptian troops, fresh from the conquest of Cyprus, and even the conquered Cyprians themselves, were employed as auxiliaries; while the Phœnician fleet co-operated on the coast. The Ionians, knowing that it was impossible to meet such an array in the field, resolved that the Milesians should be left to defend their own walls, and that the whole force of the confederates should muster at Lade, an island close to Miletus, and remain on board the ships, which as yet had suffered no defeat. But there seemed to be no one commander to whom they were willing implicitly to submit, and in obedience to whom they would endure the steady toil and discipline necessary to prepare for the conflict. They began to resume their tents on shore; their camp became a scene of disunion and mistrust; the Samians even negotiated with the enemy, and engaged to desert on the day of battle. The bravery of the Chians proved no adequate counterbalance to the treachery and cowardice of the rest; and the defeat of the Ionic confederates was complete and irrecoverable.

249. The Persians were now in a position to attack Miletus by sea as well as by land; the siege was prosecuted with the utmost vigour, and the city soon taken by storm. Most of the men were put to the sword; those that were spared, were sent with the women and children to Darius, who assigned them a new residence. The treasures found in the temple at Branchidæ, which was pillaged and burned, went far towards defraying the expense of the expedition.

250. The conquest of Miletus, which occurred in the sixth year from the commencement of the revolt, was rapidly followed by the submission of the neighbouring towns of Caria; and ere the close of the following summer, the Persians had reconquered all the Greeks of Asia,

insular as well as continental. Those on the coast were treated with peculiar severity. The most beautiful of their sons and daughters were selected, and distributed among the lords of Persia, as captives; the cities, with their sacred edifices, as well as their humble homes, were delivered to the flames; and islands were swept as with the besom of destruction. Samos was made an exception, being spared as a reward for its desertion at the battle of Lade, and its despot was restored. Other despots also were reinstated; and the population was greatly changed, in consequence of new inhabitants being admitted to supply the loss sustained. Nevertheless, it cannot be credited that the Hellenic race was extirpated from the soil.

251. Amidst the sufferings of so many innocent persons, the fate of Histiæus awakens little compassion. During the break-up of the Asiatic Greeks, there were many who, not choosing to return home to an enslaved city, and having no settled plan for a new abode, put themselves under the temporary command of Histiæus, who led them to the plunder of Thasos. He was diverted from this, however, by the danger which threatened Lesbos from the Phœnician fleet. Repairing thither, he found such dearth of provisions, that he was obliged to cross over to the continent, to reap the standing corn on the fertile plains of Mysia. Here he was surprised by a Persian force, overpowered, taken prisoner, and carried to Sardis, where Artaphernes caused him to be summarily put to death by crucifixion, not waiting for the sentence of Darius, who, he feared, might even now spare the wretch's life out of gratitude for the preservation of the bridge over the Danube. The monarch did, indeed, disapprove of the precipitate execution, and he buried with honour the head which was embalmed and sent to him.

WAR BETWEEN PERSIA AND GREECE.

252. The intention of Darius to conquer Hellas was now no longer concealed; and Mardonius, at the head of a considerable force, was despatched in the ensuing spring for that purpose. Having marched as far as Cilicia, he

sent his army across Asia Minor to the Hellespont, while he himself proceeded by sea to Ionia. Here he dethroned the despots throughout the various cities of the Greeks, leaving the people to govern themselves, subject only to the Persian dominion and tribute. He then joined his troops at the Hellespont, crossed over into Europe, and began his march through the region of Thrace. All this territory had been reduced by Megabazus, without having afterwards joined in the Ionic revolt. Hence marching into Macedonia, the Persian army reduced a considerable portion of its inhabitants; while the fleet proceeded to double the promontory of Mount Athos, with the view of joining the land-force again at Therma. The sea around Athos was then, as it is known to be still, perilous to navigation; and one of the hurricanes to which it is liable overtook the fleet, destroyed 300 ships, and occasioned the loss of at least 20,000 men, who were either drowned or cast on shore to die of cold or be devoured by wild beasts. This disaster effectually checked the progress of Mardonius, who, besides, had sustained considerable loss with his army, and had been himself wounded in a conflict with some of the Thracians; so that he returned with shame into Asia.

253. Darius, though so much dissatisfied with Mardonius that he would not employ him again, was not at all less eagerly bent on the subjugation of Greece; nor was Hippias, who was still at his side, likely to allow his wrath against the Athenians to slumber. Orders were issued to the maritime cities to equip both horse-transports and ships of war for a new expedition; and heralds were sent to most of the cities, to require the usual tokens of submission—earth and water—by way of ascertaining the extent of the resistance to be anticipated. Most of the cities sent in their submission—among them Thebes and Ægina—prompted perhaps as much by their hatred to Athens as their fear of Persia; for it is to be remarked, that the hostilities which had grown out of the connection between Athens and Platæa, fourteen years before, had never terminated in anything like a peace, and hence, it was understood, arose the disposition of these cities to submit to the heralds of Darius. Very different was the reception of the royal

H

message at Athens and Sparta. The Athenians threw the herald into the *Barathrum*—a pit into which public criminals were sometimes precipitated; the Spartans tossed their visitor into a well, bidding him take thence earth and water for his master; nor can such conduct be accounted for—as the inviolability of heralds was an ancient and undisputed sentiment in Greece—unless we suppose that the message was considered so gross an insult, as to exonerate those who received it from observing the etiquette of ordinary hostilities.

254. The bonds were thus at once drawn closer between the Lacedæmonians and Athenians; and the latter now appealed to Sparta respecting the conduct of the Æginetans in giving earth and water to Darius, which, they said, was 'treason to Hellas,' and committed from a feeling of spite against Athens. A proceeding this, to be remarked as manifesting a recognised union between the states of Greece, with Sparta at its head. We formerly noticed the growing tendency of the Greeks to acknowledge the pre-eminence of this power; and afterwards we saw her summoning and leading a group of Peloponnesian allies; but now she appears as protector-general of something like a political aggregation, and the avenger of a panhellenic wrong. Argos had been the only state that refused to acknowledge this superiority, but it was now in no condition to dispute it. About three or four years before this time, a war had broken out between the two rivals—we are not told on what grounds—in which Sparta had completely worsted Argos, and prostrated its strength.

255. The interference which the Athenians sought, and which Cleomenes was disposed to exercise, in the case of the Æginetans was delayed for a short time, by the machinations of Demaratus, the collegiate king; but Cleomenes having succeeded in getting him dethroned, on account of illegitimate birth, and having obtained a colleague in his stead, the two kings went over to Ægina, and selected ten citizens of eminent wealth, station, and influence, to be placed in the hands of the Athenians as hostages for the good behaviour of the rest.

256. Meanwhile, an immense Persian force under Datis

and Artaphernes—this last being son of the satrap of Sardis, so named—had assembled on the plains of Cilicia, and thence embarked for Samos, the Ionic and Æolic Greeks forming an important part of the armament, and Hippias the exile despot accompanying it as a guide. The instructions given to the commanders were generally —to reduce to tribute all such Greeks as had not already given earth and water, but most particularly, to conquer Athens and Eretria, and bring their inhabitants as slaves into the king's presence.

257. Warned by the fate of Mardonius's expedition, they resolved not to proceed by Thrace and the Hellespont, but to steer right across the Ægæan from Samos to Eubœa, taking the intermediate islands on their way. Among these islands was Naxos, which had formerly stood siege so gallantly; but now struck with terror, its citizens offered no resistance whatever; they fled with their families to the tops of their mountains, while the Persians burned the town, capturing as slaves the few lingering inhabitants that fell in their way. Thus did the victorious Persians with all the islands of the Cyclades, except Delos, sacred to Apollo, which was spared, probably in deference to the religious feelings of the numerous Asiatic Greeks who formed part of the force. Reaching Eubœa at length, they took Carystus with little difficulty, and proceeded to Eretria. Here the inhabitants resolved on a defence, and sent to Athens for help, which was readily afforded. After a short resistance, Eretria surrendered, or rather was betrayed by some of its own people; the cleruchs fled to Athens in terror, the place was burnt, and the inhabitants taken captive.

258. Now one of the express objects of the expedition was achieved, and the Persian generals had little doubt of speedily accomplishing the other. After depositing the Eretrian and other captives on the neighbouring islet of Ægilia, the army re-embarked for Attica, and landed in the memorable bay of Marathon, on the eastern coast, according to the advice of Hippias, who again set foot on Attic ground, twenty years after his expulsion from the government.

MILTIADES, THEMISTOCLES, AND ARISTIDES.

259. At this period of Athenian history, the characters of the soldier, the magistrate, and the orator were intimately blended in every citizen who stood forward for eminence; the ten generals already referred to exercising for the most part considerable influence, both judicial and political. Certain it is that such a combination was found in the three men—Miltiades, Themistocles, and Aristides—who appear at this time as the leaders of the Athenian democracy, and who, there is reason to believe, held commissions as generals of their respective tribes.

260. Miltiades had been despot of the Thracian Chersonesus, whither he had been sent by Hippias. In this capacity, and as one of the dependents about 517 B.C. of Persia, he had been among the Ionians who accompanied Darius in his Scythian expedition; and it was he who had advised the destruction of the bridge which Histiæus and the other despots believed it their interest to preserve. What part he took in the Ionic revolt, we do not know, but that, while the Persian satraps were employed in suppressing it, he took the opportunity of expelling both the Persian garrison and the barbarous Pelasgi from the islands of Lemnos and Imbros. The extinction of the revolt portended no good to him, and, therefore, when Mardonius made his appearance in the Hellespont, Miltiades made his escape with all haste to Athens. On his arrival there, he was brought to trial for the despotism exercised in the Chersonesus, but honourably acquitted; and now he was chosen one of the ten annual generals of the republic, in the prospect of the Persian invasion. His character was one of great decision and bravery; yet a character formed in the school of the Pisistratidæ rather than in that of the democracy. It was otherwise with Themistocles and Aristides, who were men of middling station and circumstances, and not boasting a lineage of gods and heroes.

261. Themistocles is described to us as a man of immense *natural* talent—especially in this, that he perceived the

complications of a present embarrassment, and calculated the chances of a mysterious future with equal quickness and sagacity ; the right expedient seemed always to flash upon his mind, even in the most perplexing contingencies, without the least premeditation. He had had no advantages either of political education or experience, yet no business, however new, ever took him by surprise, or seemed to come amiss to him. At the same time, he had an unbounded passion, not only for glory, but for display of every kind ; nor was he at all scrupulous about the means, his morality being, on the whole, as reckless as his intelligence was eminent.

262. Aristides was inferior to Themistocles in resource, quickness, versatility, and power of coping with difficulties, but incomparably superior to him, and to his contemporaries generally, in integrity, public as well as private. He earned for himself the surname of 'the Just,' not only by his judicial decisions in the capacity of archon, but by his equity in private arbitration, and even his candour in political controversy ; displaying throughout a long public life, which was replete with tempting opportunities, an uprightness without flaw and beyond all suspicion. Such were the leading men at Athens at the time when the cleruchs from Eubœa brought home the tidings of the impending danger.

263. Doubtless the alarm was great ; a courier was sent to Sparta to solicit assistance, and performed the journey of 150 miles, on foot, in forty-eight hours. He reported that Eretria was already enslaved, and that their assistance was greatly wanted to avert the same fate from Athens. The Spartan authorities at once promised their aid, and engaged to march immediately after the full-moon ; but ancient law and custom forbade them to take a step during the quarter immediately before it, at least in this particular month ; and it was now unfortunately the ninth day.

BATTLE OF MARATHON.

264. The momentous question now to be settled at Athens was, whether to delay an engagement, waiting for Spartan help, to remain behind the walls for the defence of the city and the sacred rock, or whether to go out at once and meet the enemy in the field. The opinion of Miltiades, which influenced the casting vote of the assembly, was : 'that nothing could save the city from the influence of timidity and traitorous intrigue, but a bold, decisive, and immediate attack ; the success of which he was prepared to guarantee.' He was seconded by Aristides and Themistocles, while all the other generals agreed in surrendering to him the supreme command, instead of each taking his turn to exercise it for a day, according to the common practice of the democracy.

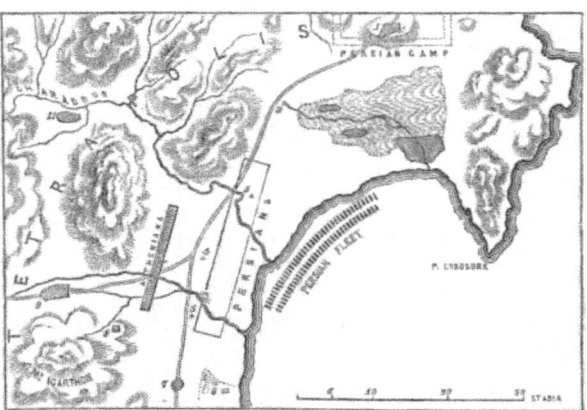

1. Tricorythus; 2. Macaria fons; 3. Tropæum; 4. Monumentum Miltiadis; 5. Tumulus Atheniensis; 6. Tpl. Minervæ; 7. Probalinthus; 8. Heracleum; 9. Marathon; 10. Oenœ.

265. The Athenian army, consisting entirely of heavily armed infantry, to the number of about 10,000, mustered on the rising-ground sacred to Hercules, near Marathon,

with the Persians occupying the plain below. As they reached this spot, they were joined by the whole force of the little town of Platæa, including about 1000 soldiers —a spontaneous effort of gratitude, which is considered one of the most affecting incidents in Grecian history. Of the numbers of the Persians, nothing is known, except that they were greatly superior to the Greeks. The aggregate number on board their ships must have been above 150,000 ; but what proportion of them were fighting-men, or how many actually did fight, we have no means of determining.

266. The plain of Marathon, situated near a bay on the eastern coast of Attica, is separated by the high ridge of Mount Pentelicus from Athens, with which it communicated by a road on the northern side, twenty-two miles long, and one on the southern, twenty-six miles. An amphitheatre of rugged heights separates it from the rest of Attica, with some steep and difficult paths over the lower ridges. The position of Miltiades was on some portion of the high ground, while the Persians occupied the plain, having their fleet ranged along the beach.

267. It was necessary for Miltiades to present a front as nearly equal as possible to that of the Persian host, for fear of being taken in flank, and with this view he made the central files but shallow, to occupy a large breadth of ground ; but the wings were made strong, that the attack might be effective on both sides.

268. As soon as the sacrifices in the Grecian camp exhibited favourable tokens, Miltiades, who had everything to gain by coming at once to close quarters, ordered his army to run over the mile which separated them from the enemy. This rapid advance, accompanied by the war-cry, or pæan, which always animated the charge of the Greek soldier, astonished the Persian army, and doubtless rendered their cavalry and archers comparatively harmless. The native Persians and Sacæ, which were the best troops in the army, were placed in their centre, which, therefore, pressed hard on the weak centre of the Greeks ; but the Hellenic wings routed the enemies opposite to them, and then staying the pursuit, relieved the centre, and put all

the Persian host to flight together. They hastened back to their ships, and, despite the efforts of the Athenians, secured a safe re-embarkation, leaving few if any prisoners, but a rich spoil of tents and equipments. Immediately afterwards, the Persian vessels were observed to take the direction of Cape Sunium; and at the same time a polished shield, discernible from afar by its brilliant surface, was seen glistening on one of the heights of Attica. There were, indeed, traitors within the country, partisans of Hippias, who had concerted to rise at Athens, and make this signal as soon as they were ready, that part of the Persian force might come round to co-operate with them. The intention was, that this diversion should have taken place while the main force of the Athenians was waiting at Marathon for the conflict. But the rapidity of Miltiades had so precipitated the battle, that it was over before the signal was made; and now, discerning the plot, he marched back his army with a celerity that dismayed the traitors; and the Persian generals, perceiving no movement on shore to encourage them, sailed away to the Cyclades. Thence they crossed the Ægæan into Asia, carrying with them the prisoners of war, whom they presented at the court of Persia, to await the pleasure of the Great King. When Darius saw them in his power, his wrath so far abated that, without personal injury, he settled them in a spot about twenty miles from Susa, where Herodotus conversed in Greek with their descendants many years afterwards.

269. To return to Greece. Immediately after the full-moon, 2000 Spartans set out from their own city, and, after a rapid march, reached the frontier in time to learn that all was over. They proceeded, however, to Marathon, to survey the battle-field, and returned home full of the praises of the victors.

270. The battle of Marathon, one of the greatest in ancient times, is considered to be without parallel, even in Grecian history. For it is to be remembered, that as yet the Greeks had not learned to despise the prowess of Persia in the field; on the contrary, the tide of Persian success had never yet been interrupted, and the

high-handed suppression of the Ionic revolt had spread terror and consternation among all the people of Hellas. The Athenians fought, therefore, not in the confidence of victory, but with the courage of desperation. The combat was, indeed, not a decisive one ; but it effected the first defeat that the Persians had ever sustained from the Greeks in the field. It was the exploit of Athens alone ; and as such, became the boast of poets and orators, repeated till it almost degenerated into commonplace ; yet the people themselves appeared never to weary of hearing it alluded to.

271. The unknown traitors who raised the bright signal-shield, took care not to betray themselves by any want of sympathy with the general triumph. Who they were, was never ascertained ; probably, in the exultation of success, no investigation was made ; so that the victory cost not a drop of intestine blood-shedding. When the Persian armament finally retired, the Athenians revisited the battle-field, to discharge the last duties to the dead. They had lost 192 warriors, to whose memory a tumulus was erected ; their names were inscribed on ten pillars on the spot, and the inhabitants of Marathon worshipped them along with their own heroes and with Hercules.

END OF MILTIADES.

272. The sequel of the history of Miltiades forms a melancholy contrast with his Marathonian heroism. It would seem as though, intoxicated with the admiration his conduct had excited, he lost his patriotism and his prudence together. He actually proposed to his fellow-citizens to equip seventy ships, with an armed force in proportion, to be placed at his discretion, declining to say what was its object ; but that he would enrich those who followed him. Such was the implicit confidence reposed at once in his judgment and his integrity, that the request was granted, and he sailed immediately for the island of Paros. Here he demanded of the inhabitants 100 talents, on pain of utter destruction. Whatever the pretence for this proceeding, the real motive is understood to have been,

that he had a private quarrel to avenge with one of the citizens. The Parians amused him with evasions till their defences were completed, when they set him at defiance; and he found himself unable to make any impression on the town, though he ravaged the open country. Next, he tampered—so we are told—with a woman, who induced him to visit by night a temple to which females alone were admitted, promising to reveal to him a secret which would put the town in his power. In pursuance of this adventure, Miltiades cleared the outer fence, and approached the sanctuary; but ere he reached it, he was seized with some sudden terror, ran away, and in leaping the same fence on his return, hurt his thigh severely, and became utterly disabled. In this state, he was placed on board ship; the siege was raised, and the armament returned to Athens.

273. The indignation of the citizens was extreme; and Xanthippus, father of the afterwards renowned Pericles, impeached Miltiades before the popular judicature as worthy of death, for deceiving the people and endangering his countrymen. The delinquent himself was unable to stand, or to say one word in his own defence, on account of the injured thigh, which was beginning even to shew symptoms of mortification. He lay on his couch before the assembled judges, while his friends made out the best case they could for him. It was impossible to defend, or even to palliate his recent conduct; but they appealed to his previous services; and the jurors were moved to commute the punishment to a fine of fifty talents. This, however, he did not live to pay; for the injured limb mortifying, he died within a short time, probably a very few days, and it was paid by his son Cimon.

274. Some historians have expressed great indignation at what they call the fickleness and ingratitude of the Athenian people in their treatment of the hero of Marathon; but there seems no just ground for such an aspersion. The crime of Miltiades is not disputed by any; and it would be unreasonable that a man who had rendered great services to the public, should receive as his reward a licence to betray his trust with impunity for the

future. Moreover, it seems natural that the unbounded confidence they had reposed in such a man, should only be the cause of a greater revulsion of feeling when they found that confidence abused. It could scarcely be expected, and ought not to have been presumed, that the recollection of his past services should do more than mitigate the deserved punishment. There seems to be no ground for the allegation, that Miltiades was imprisoned in default of payment.

AFFAIRS OF GREECE AFTER THE BATTLE OF MARATHON.

275. We are but scantily informed of the internal affairs of Greece after the repulsion of the Persians from Marathon. In the project of Cleomenes to dethrone his colleague Demaratus, he had tampered with the Delphian priestess; and this afterwards transpiring, awakened such displeasure in his subjects, that, fearing the consequences, he retired into Arcadia, and used his influence to induce its people to arm against Lacedæmon. The Spartans, alarmed in their turn, invited him back, with a promise of amnesty. But the habitual violence of his temper, aggravated, as it was said, by intemperate habits, merged into insanity; and notwithstanding the personal restraints laid upon him, he managed one day to get possession of a sword, with which he cut and mangled himself to death. So shocking an end was considered among the Greeks as a divine judgment for his misdeeds : they were not agreed as to which it might be of the many he had committed; but most of them pointed to the sin of corrupting the Pythian priestess as that which had brought down this special vengeance.

276. The fall of Cleomenes under these circumstances, emboldened the Æginetans to make a complaint at Sparta concerning the ten hostages which had been deposited at Athens by the joint kings. Leotychides, the surviving colleague, was accordingly brought to trial, and condemned to be delivered as a prisoner to the complainants, who

were, however, content with obliging him to accompany them to Athens, and to demand the hostages back. The Athenians refused, and the Æginetans took measures of retaliation, by capturing some sacred envoys of the Athenians as they were proceeding to a religious festival at Sunium. The consequence was an active war between Athens and Ægina. It began about the year 488 B.C., and was carried on chiefly in the form of frequent incursions and privateering expeditions, with various success, till the year 481 B.C.

277. During this war, an Æginetan citizen in exile devised a scheme, in concert with the Athenians, for effecting a democratic revolution at Ægina; but the movement failed through the delay which the Athenians suffered by having to borrow ships from Corinth. A large number of its partisans fell into the hands of the government: one of them, when led out to execution, broke from his bonds, and fleeing to the sanctuary of Ceres, just seized hold of the handle of the door when he was overtaken. His pursuers, finding it impossible to undo the grasp of their prisoner, severed his hands from his body, and then dragged him to execution. The guilt of this impiety was never cancelled, as we shall see, even by half a century of continued expiatory sacrifices.

278. It seems to have been the war with Ægina that first suggested to the Athenians the necessity of enlarging their naval force, and decided them to cultivate that character of maritime activity which afterwards proved so valuable.

279. After the removal of Miltiades in the manner before described, Aristides and Themistocles became the leading men at Athens. The former being chosen archon, exhibited such exemplary uprightness in his magisterial functions as to secure him the highest esteem from the general public. He was not without enemies, however—some of them sufferers by his justice, others simply jealous that he should be so constantly spoken of as the just man of Attica, as though all others were knaves. Such individuals naturally became partisans of Themistocles; and the political rivalry between the two became so bitter and so

perilous to the peace of the country, that, after three or four years, they themselves appealed to the people, and Aristides was banished by a vote of ostracism. We are not informed what were the particular points upon which they differed; but probably one of them was the development of the new and stirring element of naval power which was a favourite project with Themistocles, but which seems not to have accorded with the narrower and more stereotyped views of Aristides.

280. Besides the building of 200 ships, another most important naval undertaking was executed under the auspices of Themistocles. This was the forming and fortifying of a new harbour at Piræus, which possessed three separate natural ports, incomparably superior to the open bay of Phalerum, which had hitherto been the principal harbour.

281. It was fortunate that, at a time when money was so much needed, the public exchequer happened to be overflowing, as the result of some new enterprises at the silver-mines of Laurium. It is not known when the Athenians first began to work these mines, which were situated near the promontory of Sunium; but this is the first notice we have of their yielding a highly profitable result to the public exchequer. The sum now available was such, that a handsome dividend was about to be given to each citizen; but Themistocles persuaded the people to forego the promised distribution, and appropriate the money to the equipment of an efficient navy.

PREPARATIONS FOR A RENEWAL OF THE WAR.

282. The wrath of Darius against Athens was still unassuaged, and he made vigorous preparations for a renewed attack, directing the various satraps and sub-governors throughout Asia to provide the necessary troops, horses, and vessels. The empire was agitated for three years with this levy of forces, which the king resolved to lead personally against Greece. A revolt of the Egyptians only determined him to make one business of two

enterprises; but death interfered between him and them both. According to his nomination, his younger son Xerxes succeeded to the throne without opposition, and found everything ready for war, except his own inclination; for though a man of fine stature and soldier-like appearance, he inherited neither the courageous temperament of his father, nor his fierce animosity against the Hellenes. There was, meanwhile, a prior and pressing necessity for reconquering Egypt, which he did with the troops now at his disposal, and reduced its inhabitants to a state of more abject dependence than ever. Mardonius, however, hoping for Greece as a satrapy for himself, urged him to proceed with his father's original enterprise; and the Pisistratidæ introduced to him the holy mystic, Onomacritus, to encourage him with the sanction of prophecy. This was the same interpreter of the predictions of Musæus, whom Hipparchus had expelled from Athens thirty years before for interpolating these venerated documents; and we are assured that he now recited various glowing passages respecting the triumphant march of a barbaric host into Greece, but suppressed all that related to its final fate. Xerxes was persuaded; and summoning his counsellors, announced his intention of invading Greece, and his confidence that its subjugation would carry with it that of all Europe, making the Persian Empire coextensive with the course of the sun and the ether of Jove. In vain his uncle Artabazus offered some suggestions of prudence and diffidence, adverting particularly to the jealous aversion of the gods towards overgrown human power. The monarch silenced him with impatience, and began to concert his measures.

283. He resolved not only to organise a military power sufficient for the conquest of Europe, but to astonish the world by the display of such an armament as had never been seen before. Every part of the empire was laid under contribution. The fleet was furnished by the Thracians and Ionians, and included 1207 ships of war, besides transports. The land-force was composed of forty-six nations of various complexions, languages, and accoutrements. Besides the regularly accoutred warriors from the

PREPARATIONS FOR A RENEWAL OF THE WAR. 127

various cities of the empire, there were nomade hordes from Asia, armed with daggers and other rude weapons; Libyans, with no other weapons than staffs hardened in the fire; and painted Ethiopians from the Upper Nile, clothed in the skins of wild beasts, and furnished with stone-tipped arrows. Large magazines of provisions for this host were formed at suitable maritime stations along the line of march. But the most stupendous part of the preparation, was the cutting of a ship-canal through the isthmus of Mount Athos, and the construction of a bridge across the Hellespont, where the strait is about an English mile broad. The latter work was intrusted to Phœnicians and Egyptians, who had long been preparing cables of extraordinary size and strength for the purpose—the Phœnicians using flax, and the Egyptians the fibre of the papyrus. Just as the work was announced as complete, a violent storm arose, and utterly destroyed it. The wrath of the monarch was beyond all bounds; the heads of the chief engineers were struck off; the sea, which had dared rebelliously to destroy the bridge, was scourged with 300 lashes, and loaded with a set of fetters thrown into it, while it was addressed in language which the Greek historian characterises as 'nonhellenic and blasphemous.' New engineers were appointed to recommence the work, which consisted of two lines of ships moored abreast across the strait by means of anchors, both at head and stern, with very long cables. Over or through these lines of ships, six enormous cables were stretched from shore to shore, holding them together, and supporting the two bridge-ways of planks which were laid over them.

284. The isthmus through which the canal was cut, was about twelve stadia or furlongs across, and the canal was broad and deep enough for two vessels to sail abreast. Not only the Phœnicians, but the neighbouring Greeks, and indeed all the maritime powers of the empire, were brought together to assist in this labour, and the excavators worked under the lash, though they were not slaves, but freemen, except in so far as they were subject to the Persian monarch.

285. Four years were occupied in these preparations.

When all was completed, Xerxes repaired to Sardis, where he spent the winter, and assembled the whole force in the spring of 480 B.C. In the order of marching, the army was divided into two nearly equal columns, with a space between, which was occupied by the king himself and a select body of Persian troops. First came the baggage, carried by beasts of burden, and followed by half of the infantry of all the nations; next, a select body of Persian cavalry and spearmen, 1000 of each; behind these, ten sacred horses, splendidly caparisoned; then the sacred chariot of Jove, drawn by eight white horses, the charioteer guiding it on foot, as no man might mount; next, the chariot of Xerxes himself, with 1000 chosen horse-guards surrounding his person, and followed by other large detachments of cavalry and infantry, all native Persians. The remainder of the host followed pell-mell. The march was directed to Abydos on the Hellespont; and at the first moment of sunrise, which is specially sacred in the Oriental mind, the order was given to pass the strait. The bridge was perfumed with frankincense, and strewed with myrtle-boughs, the monarch himself making libations, and offering prayers to Helios for the success of his enterprise. The baggage and cavalry crossed on one plank-way, and the other troops, with Xerxes himself, on the other; but notwithstanding the use of the lash to accelerate the progress of the men, the business of crossing occupied seven days and as many nights without a moment's intermission. The strait being cleared, the march was continued along the Thracian Chersonesus; and on reaching the spacious plain of Doriscus, the monarch reviewed and numbered his whole force, the fleet being now in sight. In the entire absence of credible accounts, it would be rash to guess at the amount of numbers; the statement of Herodotus, that they exceeded five millions, is deemed an exaggeration. We are told that, in a spirit of arrogant confidence, Xerxes summoned the exiled Spartan king, Demaratus, who was among his auxiliaries, and asked if it was even conceivable that the Greeks would resist such a force; to which Demaratus replied, that the Spartans assuredly would resist him to the death.

286. The march was continued through Thrace and Macedonia, all subject territory, where magazines had been previously provided for the subsistence of the army, and all was submission to the will of the monarch. Thus did he arrive within sight of Mount Olympus, the northern boundary of what was properly called Hellas.

PREPARATIONS FOR DEFENCE.

287. At the beginning of the winter that Xerxes spent in Sardis, preparatory to his march into Greece, he sent heralds to all the principal cities, except Athens and Sparta, demanding earth and water. Accordingly, these two, knowing themselves to be the special objects of vengeance, united their interests, and jointly convened a federative congress at the Isthmus of Corinth, to organise a plan of resistance. All the dispersed brethren of the Hellenic family were entreated to marshal themselves in the same ranks for the defence of the common hearth and metropolis of the race. This is a new fact in Grecian history, indicating the introduction of habits of co-operation among the inferior states, as well as rival interests among the leading ones.

481 B.C.

288. At the meeting of the deputies on this occasion, it was found necessary to recognise some one commanding state; and though the idea was at first started that Athens should command at sea, and Sparta on land, yet the majority of the allies were averse to any supremacy but that of Sparta, and the Athenians waived their pretensions. This settled, the next preliminary step was to appease all internal dissensions, and the war between Athens and Ægina chiefly claimed their attention, as the most important and dangerous to general unanimity. The Æginetans, though not even now exempt from suspicions of temporising with the enemy, took an active part in the joint measures of defence, and cheerfully consented to accommodate their differences with Athens. The congress proceeded to send envoys to such cities as seemed equivocal or indifferent; and likewise despatched spies to Sardis, to learn the state of the preparations there. The latter soon returned, having been seized,

but released again by the express order of Xerxes, who commanded that they should see the full strength of his assembled armament, and report accordingly to the terror of the Greeks. Doubtless, the step was well calculated for such a purpose; for even to the most patriotic, Xerxes with his countless host appeared quite irresistible, much more to the timid and the treacherous. Scarcely less appalling was the message from the Delphic oracle, which was of course consulted on this occasion. The presages of the priestess were embodied in doleful exclamations, to which, however, was added this perplexing sentence, affording a faint ray of hope, though dark and unintelligible: 'When everything else in the land of Cecrops shall be taken, Jupiter grants to Athens that the wooden wall alone shall remain unconquered, to defend you and your children. Stand not to await the assailing horse and foot from the continent, but turn your backs and retire; you shall yet live to fight another day. O divine Salamis, thou, too, shalt destroy the children of women, either at the seed-time or at the harvest.' When this was reported at Athens, the puzzle was to know what was meant by the 'wooden wall.' Some supposed it the Acropolis, which had originally been surrounded with a wooden palisade; but most of the professional expositors of prophecy maintained that the fleet was indicated; not, however, with the view of a naval battle, but a flight by sea from Attica and for ever. The opinion of Themistocles, however, was that the parties destined to perish at Salamis were not the Greeks, but their enemies, because the gods had termed it not the 'wretched' or the 'fatal,' but the 'divine Salamis.' He therefore encouraged his countrymen to prepare for betaking themselves to their fleet as the 'wooden wall,' with the full determination of fighting and conquering on board.

289. Meanwhile, the congress continued its efforts during the winter, to bring the various states of Greece into united action. Those to the north of Athens and Peloponnesus —as Thebes and most of Bœotia—were either inclined to submit to Persia, or at least cool in the cause of independence. In Peloponnesus, Argos maintained at least an

ambiguous neutrality. Among the islanders, the Cretans refused, on the ground of oracular prohibitions ; while the Corcyræans promised co-operation with the patriots, but without any intention of performance.

290. And now Xerxes was about to pass the Hellespont. Those of the Thessalians who were disposed to resist him, sent envoys to the isthmus, to warn the congress of the necessity of guarding the passes of the Olympian mountains, the most northern entrance of Greece. They offered themselves to aid in this defence ; adding, that if it were not attended to, they should be obliged to make their own separate submission to the invader. Accordingly, a body of 10,000 heavy-armed infantry was sent to co-operate with the Thessalian horse in the occupation of the vale of Tempe.

291. This long, narrow, and winding defile formed then, as it still forms, the only way passable in winter from lower Macedonia into Thessaly ; and here, doubtless, a few resolute men would be sufficient to arrest the progress of a numerous host.

292. But, presently, the Greeks discovered not only that the Persian fleet could land troops in their rear, but that they could make their way by the passes which were practicable in summer, from Upper Macedonia over the mountains, and which open upon Thessaly just about the place where the defile at Tempe begins to narrow. So great was the alarm produced by this discovery, that they abandoned their position, and returned by sea to Corinth. This precipitate retreat served either as a reason or pretext for most of the northern Greeks to make their submission to Xerxes, as, indeed, some of them had already done ; so that when he reached the Thermaic Gulf, within sight of Olympus and Ossa, the heralds whom he had sent from Sardis brought him tokens of submission from a third part of the Hellenic race—the Thessalians, Dolopes, Ænianes, Perrhæbians, Magnetes, Locrians, Dorians, Melians, Phthiotid Achæans, and Bœotians.

THERMOPYLÆ AND ARTEMISIUM.

293. During the six weeks or two months which elapsed between the retreat of the Greeks from Tempe and the arrival of Xerxes at Therma, no new plan of defence appears to have been formed; but the deputies assembled at Corinth pledged themselves by a solemn vow to inflict condign punishment on the recusants, in case of success; only making an exception in favour of those who had been driven to submission by irresistible necessity. But now the danger was imminent, and the Pass of Thermopylæ was fixed upon as the most eligible point of resistance. It defended the widest range of country that could be included with safety; but involved the abandonment of the Thessalians and the other Greeks north of this pass. The fleet was mustered in the northern part of the Eubœan strait, on the line of coast called Artemisium, as it was calculated that in this position they might prevent the Persian fleet from advancing into the narrow strait between Eubœa and the mainland, to disembark troops in the rear of the land-force which defended Thermopylæ.

294. This celebrated pass lies near the town of Anthela,

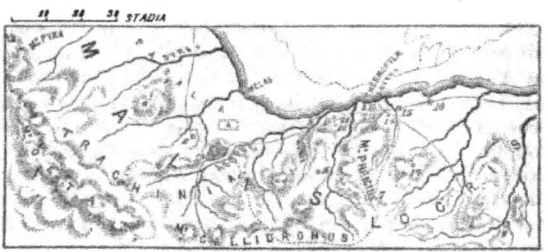

1. Ægonia; 2. Trachis; 3. Heraclea; 4. Tichius; 5. Rhoduntia; 6. 7. Via Anopæa (Persarum); 8. Thermæ; 9. Anthela; 10. Monumt. Spartanorum. 11. Templum Cereris Amphict; 13. 13. Murus Phocensium; 14. Melampygum saxum; 15. Alpenus; 16. Nicæa; 17. Callidromon; 18. Tarphe.

celebrated for the autumnal assemblies of the Amphictyonic Council. Here the northern slope of the long and lofty ridge of Œta approached so near the dangerous morass forming the edge of the Malian Gulf, that it left no more than a single wheel-track between. This was the first gate of Thermopylæ. The road then widened, and about a mile further on another gate was formed by a similar approach of the mountain to the sea-margin. The intervening road abounded with thermal springs, salt and sulphureous, spreading their mud and crust all over the ground; and hence this narrow defile passed in ancient times by the name of Thermopylæ, 'the Hot Gates,' or briefly Pylæ, 'the Gates.' The Phocians, in order to guard against the incursions of neighbouring tribes, had, some time before, endeavoured to direct the water of these springs so as to render the road quite impassable, and, moreover, had built across it a wall, which was now dilapidated. At the gates themselves, the mountains overhung the narrow road in wooded and impracticable steeps. In the rear of the Greek position, the sea-line appears to have been generally marshy, but affording points at which boats could land; so that the Greeks would be able to maintain communication with their fleet at Artemisium, while the town of Alpeni was just behind, to supply provisions. They were to rebuild the Phocian wall, and here await the approach of the invading host.

295. The Greek forces proceeded to occupy the position indicated towards the end of June, when it was known that Xerxes had reached the Thermaic Gulf; the Spartan king, Leonidas, being appointed commander of the land-forces, and Eurybiades, also a Spartan, over the fleet. Leonidas led from the isthmus a select band of 300 Spartans, all citizens of mature age, besides soldiers from other cities to the number of about 3000, with Helots and other light troops in attendance. In their march, they were joined by 700 faithful Thespians and 400 Thebans of somewhat equivocal fidelity. The Phocians also, and the Locrians, who, through fear of the invader, had made submission, now joined the defence in considerable force.

296. It will appear strange, that when the country was menaced by so formidable an invasion, the Greeks should have contented themselves with sending a mere handful of

men in defence. An explanation of this circumstance is found in the national superstitions of this remarkable people. At this critical juncture, they were celebrating the Olympic festival-games on the banks of the Alpheius, and also the festival of the Carnean Apollo at Sparta and most of the other Dorian states; and even at a time when their very existence was at stake, they would not postpone these venerated solemnities. Besides, they reckoned that the detachment of Leonidas would be able to hold the pass of Thermopylæ till the festivals should be over: when the whole force was to assemble in Bœotia, to defend the approach to Attica.

297. When Leonidas reached Thermopylæ, he was told of a mountain-path which was then little used, but which had in former days served the Thessalians after the Phocians blocked up the defile of Thermopylæ. A band of 1000 Phocians now undertook to defend this way; but the Greeks generally were dismayed at the thought of having two entrances to keep with such inadequate numbers, and Leonidas with difficulty persuaded them to remain on the ground.

298. Meanwhile Xerxes, having encamped within sight of Thermopylæ, allowed four days to pass without making any further advance. The Thessalians, who were now his principal guides, together with the king of Macedon, were to endeavour by intrigue to induce the Greeks to leave the spot, and an interval of two or three days might be well bestowed in giving them a chance of success. Xerxes, it seems, persisted in believing that they would disperse without resistance; but on the fifth day he waxed wroth at the presumptuous recklessness of the petty garrison, and sent against them the Median and Cissian divisions, with orders to capture and bring them into his presence as prisoners. It is said that they were first desired to deliver up their arms, and Leonidas desired, in reply, that they should come and take them. They were then told that the Persian host was so numerous, their arrows would darken the sun: 'Then,' said a Spartan, 'we shall fight in the shade.'

299. And so began the ever-memorable battle of

Thermopylæ. Bravely did the assailants maintain the conflict, having nothing but numbers in their favour, and suffering great slaughter, while the loss of the Greeks was small. Bows and arrows were of little use in such a position; and in a hand-to-hand combat, their short spears and light wicker-shields were no match for the long spears, heavy and spreading shields, close ranks, and practised fighting of the defenders. Though constantly repulsed, the attack was as constantly renewed, and the Greek troops were sufficiently numerous to relieve each other, since few could be engaged at once in so narrow a space. Even the Immortals, or 10,000 choice Persian guards, when sent forward on the second day, were repulsed with the same slaughter and disgrace as the rest. At the end of two days' fighting, no impression had been made, and the pass appeared impracticable, when some recusant Greek mentioned to Xerxes the unfrequented mountain-path. At nightfall, Hydarnes, with a detachment of Persians, proceeded to this place, and at daybreak found himself near the summit, within sight of the Phocian guard. A shower of arrows overwhelmed and dispersed them; they abandoned the path to seek their own safety on a higher point of the mountains; and Hydarnes, not troubling himself to pursue them, urged his way down, and arrived in the rear of Thermopylæ soon after mid-day. It was told Leonidas that the enemy were closing in upon him behind; it was evident that Thermopylæ could no longer be defended, and there was yet time for the Greeks to retire. But Leonidas would not hear of retreat: the laws under which he had been trained required him to conquer or die in the post assigned to him, whatever the odds against him; and the 300 Spartans whom he commanded were nerved to a similar course of generous self-sacrifice. The rest of the Greeks, however, withdrew, hoping still to save Peloponnesus by making a stand at the Isthmus of Corinth; the Thespians and Thebans only remaining with Leonidas.

300. By previous concert with the detachment of Hydarnes, Xerxes delayed his attack till near noon, in order that both might fall upon the Greeks nearly

simultaneously. On this last day, however, Leonidas, knowing that he could but sell the lives of his men as dearly as possible, did not confine himself to the defensive, but advanced into the wider part of the road, driving before him the foremost of the Persians, of whom many were trodden down by their own comrades, and many more perished in the morass, besides those who fell by the spears of the Greeks. All the efforts of the Persian officers, seconded by threats and the unsparing use of the whip, scarcely sufficed to keep up their men to the combat. The Greeks fought with desperation, till their spears were broken and Leonidas himself was slain. Now the little band, diminished, exhausted, and deprived of the service of their most effective weapons, retired into the narrow strait behind the cross-wall, and sat together on a hillock, exposed to the main body of the Persian army on the one side, and the detachment of Hydarnes on the other.

301. At this juncture, the Thebans separated themselves, and approaching the enemy with outstretched hands, proclaimed that they were friends and subjects of the Great King, and that they had been brought to Thermopylæ against their will. The Thessalians in the Persian army confirmed their assertion, and they were admitted to quarter, while the devoted band of Spartans and Thespians were overwhelmed with missiles, and slain to a man.

302. The wrath of Xerxes, as he traversed the field after the action, vented itself upon the corpse of the gallant Leonidas, whose head he ordered to be cut off, and fixed on a cross. He now desired to know what resistance remained behind; how many more such Lacedæmonians there were; and how they might most easily be conquered. Upon which Demaratus advised him to send a division of his fleet to make war on the southern coasts of Laconia, so as to divert the Spartans from co-operating with the Peloponnesian force that would be collected to maintain the Isthmus of Corinth. Xerxes rejected this advice, listening to the suggestions of his brother, and confiding in the power of his overwhelming numbers.

303. Meanwhile, these days of battle at Thermopylæ had been passed not inactively by the fleets. It was on

the sea, indeed, that the first blood was shed in this memorable contest. Three cruising vessels of the Greeks fell in with ten of the best of the Persians, and were taken. The rest in terror abandoned the position assigned them, and sailed up the Eubœan strait to Chalcis, as the narrowest and most defensible passage, leaving scouts on the heights to watch the progress of the enemy. The rear of the army at Thermopylæ was thus laid open to the operations of the Persian fleet, which, however, was not destined to reach the spot so easily. A violent storm fell upon it as it lay during the night off the rocky coast formed by the declivities of Ossa and Pelion, and a large number of vessels were dashed to pieces ; the loss of life as well as of property being immense. For three days the storm continued unabated ; but on the fourth, the remainder of the vessels put to sea, doubled the southern promontory of Magnesia, and cast anchor at Aphetæ.

304. The spirits of the Greeks were revived by the news of this disaster to their enemies, and they took courage to sail back to their former station at Artemisium. Though somewhat disappointed at finding the enemy exhibiting a formidable appearance at a few miles' distance, they were persuaded, and indeed bribed by the Eubœans, through the agency of Themistocles, to continue facing the foe. As for the Persians, their only fear was lest the Greeks should escape ; and to prevent this, a detachment of 200 ships was directed to sail round Eubœa, and take the Greeks in the rear. The latter now offered battle, and had gained considerable advantage, when night put an end to the contest. Another terrific storm now fell on the Persians ; it blew all night long against the coast of Aphetæ, causing little disturbance to the Greeks upon the opposite shore, while it not only damaged the main body of the enemy's ships, but utterly destroyed the detachment which was sailing round the island.

305. The courage inspired into the Greeks by this second interference of the gods, as they believed it, was yet further stimulated by the arrival of a reinforcement of fifty-three Athenian ships. Now they would have engaged again, but the enemy was in no condition to fight, and

they were content with destroying some vessels at their moorings. The Persians renewing their efforts, the battle raged furiously the whole of the following day; both parties suffered severely, and the Greek ships were so disabled, that it was doubtful whether they could again renew the combat. Under these circumstances, the Greek commanders decided that they must withdraw the naval force further into Greece; and while they were employed in organising their retreat, they received the disastrous intelligence that the Pass of Thermopylæ was in the hands of the enemy. This news rendered their retreat doubly necessary; they abandoned Artemisium forthwith, sailed up the Eubœan strait, and round the coast of Attica, not halting till they reached the island of Salamis. Themistocles alone delayed at various watering-stations and landing-places, to inscribe on the stones his pressing invitation to the Ionian contingents serving under Xerxes, that they should desert if possible, or at least fight as shyly as they could. He hoped by this stratagem that, if not detached from the Persian side, the Ionians might at least be rendered objects of mistrust, and their efficiency thus diminished.

306. When the withdrawal of the Grecian fleet became certainly known at Aphetæ, that of the Persians proceeded to the north of Eubœa, and took possession of Histiæa, from which many crossed over to view the scene of Thermopylæ. It is said that Xerxes, to impose on spectators, left 1000 of his own men unburied, to make the impression that these were all he had lost; while he had the 4000 Greeks that had been slain, Spartans, Thespians, and Helots, all collected in one heap, undistinguishable from each other, and pointed out as the Spartans who had fallen before his warriors. This trick deceived but few. It was generally believed, and is reported by Herodotus, that the Persians slain were 20,000—perhaps not too high an estimate, when it is remembered that they were three days fighting, with little defensive armour, against the long spears of the Greeks.

307. The Amphictyonic Council afterwards erected monuments near the spot: one inscribed to the effect

that here 4000 Peloponnesians fought with 300 myriads (3,000,000) of Persians; another to the memory of the Spartans alone, with an inscription which has been thus translated:

> 'Go tell the Spartans, thou that passest by,
> That here obedient to their laws we lie.'

A third monument, with a lion, was erected in honour of Leonidas, on the spot where the last stand was made.

SALAMIS.

308. So confident had the Peloponnesians been of the defensibility of Thermopylæ and Artemisium, that though the games were over when the news of the disaster reached them, not a soldier had been put in motion; nor had any plan been concerted for defending the heart of Greece. And now all was disappointment and dismay. The invading force of Xerxes, both fleet and army, was approaching; the loss he had sustained was more than compensated by the fresh auxiliaries he acquired on his march through Greece; his fleet also had received accessions from Carystus and the Cyclades. It was too late to perform the promise made to Athens, of mustering in Bœotia; Xerxes was there already. To defend the Isthmus of Corinth was all the Peloponnesians could now think of; and thither they rushed with all their available population, under the command of Cleombrotus, brother of Leonidas, and now king of Sparta. They began to draw fortifications across the isthmus; bands of 10,000 men each relieving one another, and maintaining day and night the work of collecting materials and constructing the defences. Against a land incursion, it was doubtless an excellent position to secure; but it was no protection against an invader with a fleet which could land troops on any part of the coast; nor could another spot be found like Thermopylæ, presenting a difficult pass, with a narrow strait in its immediate neighbourhood.

309. The case of the Athenians was peculiarly distressing. Trusting that a Peloponnesian army would be in Bœotia, doing all that could be done for the protection of Attica,

they had betaken themselves to the fleet, without providing for the safety of their families or goods. And now, when the conqueror was in full march upon their territory, the Peloponnesians were gone to take care of themselves at their own isthmus.

310. Under these circumstances, they entreated Eurybiades to remain at Salamis to assist them in removing their families, and to give them time to consider what further might be done. And now Themistocles, landing at Phalerum, made his mournful entry into Athens. A proclamation was issued, enjoining every Athenian forthwith to remove all that was dear to him out of the country as he best could; and so short was the time, there were only six days both to circulate the notice and act upon it throughout the whole extent of Attica. By strenuous exertions, however, these few precious days were made to suffice for transporting the whole population, together with as much property as the case admitted. All the vessels were kept employed in this service, but we can form little idea of the misery of such an emigrant population, hurrying, they scarce knew whither, to escape the powerful arm of Xerxes. Some were carried to Ægina, some only to Salamis, but most of them to Trœzen, while the fighting-men remained on board the ships.

311. Either the policy of Themistocles, or the mental depression of the people, gave rise to a report, that even the divinities of the Acropolis were deserting it. In the ancient temple of Minerva, on that rock, there dwelt, or was believed to dwell, a sacred serpent, the familiar attendant of the goddess, and guardian of the sanctuary. A honey-cake was placed once a month for the nourishment of this serpent, and hitherto it had been regularly consumed; but now the priestess announced that it remained untouched—the sacred guardian had set the example of emigration, and it behoved the citizens to follow it. Some few individuals, however, shut themselves up in the Acropolis, along with the officials of the temple; and blocked up the entrance with wooden doors and palisades, according to one interpretation of the oracle about the *wooden* wall.'

SALAMIS. 141

312. In the calamitous circumstances which surrounded them, the Athenian leaders agreed to postpone their political dissensions. Aristides, now in the third year of his ostracism, was recalled, with others who were capable of serving the state, either by their wisdom in council or their valour in fight.

313. Hardly was all this completed, when the troops of Xerxes overran the deserted country, having begun their march towards Attica, under the guidance of the Thessalians, two or three days after the struggle at Thermopylæ. All the people through whose territory they passed tendered their submission, except the Phocians, who perhaps refused only because they hoped for no favourable terms, seeing their bitter enemies the Thessalians so high in the monarch's confidence. Their towns being found deserted, many of them were sacked and burned by the invaders. From Panopeus, Xerxes sent a detachment to plunder the magnificent treasures of Apollo at Delphi, while he himself

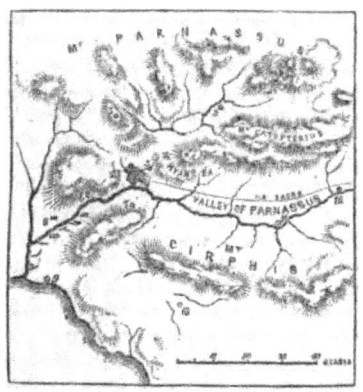

1. Corycium antrum; 2. Lycorea; 3. Alope; 4. Hyampea; 5. Castalia fons; 6. Crissa; 7. Lamiæ antrum; 8. Hippodromus; 9. Cirrha; 10. Cirphis; 11. Cyparissus; 12. Anemorea; 13. Delphi (Pytho); 14. Templum Apollinis.

pursued his way with his main force through Bœotia. Here, also, he found all submission, except at Thespiæ and

Platæa, which, like the towns of Phocis, were deserted—like them, too, committed to the flames—and the host passed on without opposition.

314. Not so fared it with the band which the monarch's cupidity had despatched to Delphi. The inhabitants, indeed, fled; but Apollo declined having his treasures secured by removal, and undertook to defend them himself. So said the priestess. Sixty Delphians ventured to remain in the temple with the religious superior; and when the Persians were making their way along the road, under the steep cliffs of Parnassus, suddenly the dreadful roar of thunder was heard, and two immense crags breaking from the rock fell with deafening noise among them, crushing many to death, and striking the rest with such panic that they turned and fled. They declared, that in this their flight they were pursued, not by the Delphians alone, but by two armed warriors of superhuman stature.

315. No opposition, however, either human or divine, obstructed the march of Xerxes to the foot of the Athenian Acropolis. It was four months since he had left Asia; he had brought with him the Pisistratidæ, confident of their restoration to power, with a few other Athenian exiles attached to their interests. These, eager to save the holy place, implored its little garrison to surrender; but in vain. The Persian soldiers, seeing themselves obliged to take it by force, poured a shower of arrows with burning flax attached to them on the wood-work before the gates. This presently took fire, and was consumed; but when the assailants attempted to mount to the entrance, the defenders rolled great stones down upon them; and it seemed, indeed, as though the Great King would be driven to the slow process of blockade. At length, however, a party of the besiegers, more hardy than the rest, undertook to scale the precipitous rock on the northern side, where it was considered so inaccessible that no pains had been taken to defend it. The scaling-party succeeded in reaching the summit unobserved, and appeared behind the defenders; who then, bereft of hope, threw themselves down from the walls, or fled for refuge to the inner temple. The escaladers opened the gates to their companions, and

the whole Acropolis was at once in their hands. The remains of the little garrison were slain; the temple plundered; and all the buildings, sacred and secular, given to the flames. On the next day but one, Xerxes allowed the exiles to visit the spot, and offer sacrifice amidst the ruins, if so be they might atone for the sacrilege that had been committed. It is said that, while thus engaged, they observed the sacred olive-tree—the special gift of Minerva, which had been burned by the besiegers—sprouting with preternatural vigour, having already thrown out a shoot one cubit long. Another of the exiles beheld the dust, and heard the loud multitudinous chant which usually accompanied the processional march from Athens to Eleusis on this day—the day set apart for the celebration of the Eleusinian mysteries. It was believed that the goddesses themselves were on the march to assist the Athenians.

316. About the time that the Acropolis was taken, the fleet of Xerxes arrived safely in the bay of Phalerum, reinforced by ships from Carystus and the Cyclades. The king himself went down to the shore to inspect its condition, and, after holding a council, decided that an attack should be made next day on the Grecian fleet, now in the narrow strait of Salamis, while the land-force should proceed to Peloponnesus.

317. The chiefs on board the Grecian ships were divided in their opinion as to whether they should await this combat, or remove to the neighbourhood of Corinth, where the land-forces had collected. On the one hand, Salamis was the most favourable position for fighting with superior numbers; besides that the Athenians, Æginetans, and Megarians, whose families were mostly at Salamis, Ægina, and Megara, were naturally unwilling to leave them exposed to a descent of the enemy. On the other hand, the Peloponnesians, and especially the Corinthians, who furnished a large contingent to the navy, apprehended, that if worsted in a naval action, they would be shut up in an island from which there would be no hope of escape; whereas, if at Corinth, they could be assisted by their own soldiers on land. Their influence had almost prevailed, when

Themistocles, despairing of enforcing his own policy by argument, resorted to intimidation, and declared that if Eurybiades removed the fleet, he and the Athenians would emigrate with their families to Siris, in Italy, for their own safety, and leave him to fight the Persians as he could. This was for the time decisive; but a message of expostulation and entreaty from the isthmus renewed the debate, and Themistocles met the desperate emergency by a singular stratagem.

318. He despatched a trusty slave across the strait to the Persian generals, to represent that he at heart wished them success, and advised them that the Greeks were quarrelling among themselves, and meditating flight; so that now the Persians had a splendid opportunity to detain them, and force them to a battle, in which case certainly many would desert the cause of Greece. The message produced the desired impression; and during the night, the strait was closed up on both sides, to prevent the chance of escape, with the view of attacking the Greeks on the morrow. These had not yet come to an amicable conclusion ere daybreak, when Aristides arrived from Ægina, bringing them the intelligence that the entrances were blockaded, and his own vessel had got past only under favour of the night. At first, they scarcely believed; but the arrival of a deserting vessel from the Persians confirmed the tidings, and they prepared at dawn for the inevitable conflict.

319. Xerxes being persuaded that his navy had not done its best at Artemisium for want of his personal presence, now erected for himself a lofty throne on one of the precipitous declivities of Mount Ægaleos, with royal scribes by his side to take down the names both of the brave and the backward. The Greeks rowed forward from the shore with the usual pæan, or war-shout, which was lustily returned by the enemy. But before closing, the Greeks shewed some hesitation, and even backed water for a space; when, as it is said, their retrograde movement was arrested by a supernatural female figure hovering over them in the air, and reproaching their cowardice. The brave Athenian Aminias was the first to obey the voice, and darting

forward from the line, charged with the beak of his vessel full against a Phœnician. The two vessels became entangled; others came to aid on both sides, and the action became general. With the exception of the Ionic Greeks, who displayed little ardour, the subjects of Xerxes conducted themselves with great bravery. But they had no such orderly line and exact discipline as the Greeks, and in the narrow space where they fought, their numbers were a hinderance rather than a help, causing them often to run foul of each other. Those in front could not recede when needful, nor those in the rear advance. The oars were broken by collisions, and the steersmen were unable to adjust the ship's bearing so as to strike that direct blow with the beak which was essential to success in ancient naval warfare. Then, when the day was turned against them, there was no reciprocal attachment or fidelity among them; but every one was ready to desert or even run down his neighbour, to secure his own safety. It is related that Artemisia, queen of Halicarnassus, in Caria, maintained her part with great vigour till the disorder became irretrievable, and she sought to escape. Finding herself closely pursued by Aminias, while full in her way lay a Carian vessel, she ran it down, and sunk it with all its crew. Aminias knowing her ship only as one among the enemy, and seeing it run down one on its own side, concluded it to be a deserter, and allowed it to escape; while Xerxes, believing it was a Greek vessel that Artemisia had destroyed, exclaimed: 'My men have become women, and my women, men.'

320. After some time, the whole Persian fleet was driven back, and became quite unmanageable, so that the issue was no longer doubtful; though some efforts of individual bravery protracted the struggle. The wrath and vexation of the monarch were now beyond all bounds, and he scarcely knew on whom to vent his displeasure. Some of the Phœnician mariners threw the blame on the Ionian Greeks; but Xerxes having observed an exploit of surpassing gallantry by one of them, called these Phœnicians dastardly calumniators, and ordered their heads to be struck off. The rest, alarmed at his menaces—for he had

expected most from them, and vowed vengeance for his disappointment—sailed away at nightfall, and returned home.

321. The presumptuous confidence of the Persian king did not turn to rage and disappointment more quickly than these gave place to alarm for his own personal safety. Great and signal, certainly, had been his defeat; but there still remained as much of his fleet as might have prosecuted the war with vigour, besides a land-force as yet unimpaired. But Xerxes now utterly distrusted his navy, which was composed entirely of conquered subjects; he fancied they could not or would not make any further resistance; and he dreaded lest the Greeks should sail forthwith to the Hellespont, and break down the bridge, to intercept his retreat. Disembarking, therefore, some of the best troops about him, he directed them to make straight for the Hellespont, and guard the bridge till his arrival; after which, he gave orders to the whole fleet to quit Phalerum during the night.

322. Mardonius, while highly approving of this step, knew full well that it would be unsafe for himself to return to Persia with the shame of failure on his head; and he preferred taking on himself the chance of yet subduing Greece. Accordingly, he persuaded Xerxes to leave him at the head of 300,000 chosen troops, with which he pledged himself to fulfil the monarch's vengeance. This was granted, and Xerxes hastened his own return to Asia.

323. It was with no small amount of joyful surprise that the Greeks found their enemies were fled; they pursued them, but without success, as far as the island of Andros; they even desired to push on to the Hellespont, and cut off the retreat, but they were restrained by the caution of their leaders, who represented to them the danger of detaining such a foe, with such a force in the heart of Greece. Again the crafty Themistocles sent a confidential message to the king, intimating that he, Themistocles, had, from motives of personal friendship, secured him a safe retreat by restraining the impatience of the Greeks to cut it off. The terror of Xerxes was

naturally increased by this intelligence, and his journey hastened.

324. The sufferings of the Persian army in this retreat were dreadful. The magazines which had been stored for them when on the advance, had been exhausted; so that they had now to seize upon the corn and other productions of the country which they traversed—an inadequate resource, which they were obliged to eke out by culling leaves, grass, the bark of trees, and other wretched substitutes for food. Plague and dysentery aggravated their misery, and many were left behind sick in the cities through which, they passed. After a march of forty-five days from Attica, Xerxes reached the Hellespont, where his fleet had arrived some time before him. The bridge had been lashed to pieces by a storm, but the troops were transferred to Asia on shipboard.

325. Meanwhile, the Greeks, thus happily delivered from.the presence of the enemy, passed from the extreme of terror to ease, security, and self-gratulation. In the division of the booty, the Æginetans were adjudged the best lot, as having distinguished themselves most in the action; while the second was voted to the Athenians. The prizes of valour thus adjudicated, it was resolved to determine those of skill and wisdom. Each of the chiefs deposited two names on the altar of Neptune, according to the prescribed mode; and when these came to be examined, it was found that every man had voted the first prize to himself, and most of them the second to Themistocles. The result was, that none could claim the first; and as there was no first, there could be no second. The general renown of Themistocles was probably not the less, though he was disappointed of his reward. When he visited Sparta shortly afterwards, the people crowned him with laurel, as they had done their own Eurybiades, and paid him honours such as never were rendered before or afterwards to any foreigner.

PLATÆA AND MYCALE.

326. The hurried and disastrous retreat of Xerxes produced less disaffection among his tributaries than might have been anticipated. The king of Macedon, the Aleuadæ of Thessaly, and the chiefs of Bœotia, remained faithful to Mardonius; nor among all the Greeks north-west of Attica and Megaris, were there any, except the Phocians, whose fidelity appeared questionable. In the Chalcidic peninsula, several of the towns declared themselves independent; and Potidæa succeeded in repelling the force sent to reduce it again.

327. Before putting himself in motion for the spring campaign, Mardonius sought to establish a separate peace and alliance with Athens against the Peloponnesians. 479 B.C. He sent to consult several of the Bœotian oracles, and circulated the report, that it was predicted the day was approaching when the Persians and Athenians together would expel the Dorians from Peloponnesus. The way was thus paved for sending the king of Macedon as an envoy to Athens with the most seductive offers, including the promise of reparation of all the damage done in Attica during the last campaign, and a large accession of new territory, on condition of an equal and independent alliance. It was certainly a great temptation. It found the Athenians just re-established in their half-ruined city, suffering privations of the severest character, as they had lost the harvest of the past summer with the seed of the autumn; their ruined houses and temples required to be restored; and in case of continued war, they still lay exposed to Mardonius, without any such protection as Peloponnesus enjoyed in its isthmus. The Lacedæmonians were so much afraid of their yielding, that they sent envoys to offer assistance during the existing poverty of the city, with entreaties that they would remain faithful to Hellas. The Athenians delivered their reply to the envoy of Mardonius in terms which their descendants were wont to repeat with delight: 'Cast not in our teeth that the power of the Persian is many times greater

than ours; we know that as well as thou; but we love freedom well enough to resist him with all our might. Urge not the vain task of talking us over into alliance. Tell Mardonius, that as long as the sun shall pursue his present path, we will never contract alliance with Xerxes, but we will combat him in our own defence, trusting in the aid of those gods and heroes to whom he has shewn no reverence, and whose temples and statues he has burned. Come not thou again to us with such proposals, nor persuade us, even in the spirit of kindness, into unholy proceedings. Thou art the guest and friend of Athens, and we would not that thou shouldst suffer injury at our hands.'

328. To the Spartans, the Athenians protested their unconquerable devotion to the common cause of Hellas, promising that no temptations whatever should induce them to desert the ties of brotherhood, common language, and religion. While declining the offers of aid with reference to their present privations, they earnestly desired the immediate presence of a Peloponnesian army in Bœotia, to assist in repelling Mardonius from the borders of Attica.

329. This fidelity of the Athenians to the general cause of Hellas, appears to have been hailed only as a relief from danger, and repaid by a selfish and ungenerous neglect. The Peloponnesians redoubled their exertions about the fortifications of the isthmus; and deeming themselves safe behind their own bulwark, thought little of their obligation to join the Athenians in Bœotia. Besides, the omens were unfavourable. Cleombrotus, who commanded the force at the isthmus, was in the act of sacrificing to ascertain the disposition of the gods with reference to the coming war, when an obscuration of the sun filled him with such terror, that he retreated with the main force to Sparta, where he soon after died. And yet further, the Spartans were engaged in celebrating the festival of the Hyacinthia, and it was their paramount object, says the historian, to fulfil 'the requirements of the god.'

330. Meanwhile, Mardonius put his army in motion from Thessaly, joined by all the Grecian auxiliaries, and

reinforcements from Thrace and Macedonia. On his march through Bœotia, he was advised by the Thebans to try the efficacy of bribes to disunite the Greeks, rather than military operations against their united force. But Mardonius, eager to repossess himself of Attica, rejected their advice, entered the country without resistance, and again established the Persian head-quarters in Athens. Before his arrival, the Athenians, disappointed 479 B.C. of Spartan assistance, and unable to make head against the enemy alone, had again removed their families to Salamis. The migration was less distressing than that of the preceding year; but there was the bitter thought, that it might have been obviated if the Spartans had executed their covenant. Mardonius, still anxious to conciliate the Athenians, abstained from injuring either the city or the country, and despatched a second ambassador to Salamis, to repeat his offers. The refusal was still resolute; the envoy was permitted to depart in peace; but an unfortunate senator, Lycidas, who ventured to recommend acceptance of the propositions, was stoned to death; nor only himself—the Athenian women in Salamis, hearing what had occurred, entered the house of Lycidas, and stoned to death his wife and children.

331. While giving such renewed proofs of their steadfast attachment to the cause of Greece, the Athenians sent to remonstrate with the Spartans on their backwardness and breach of faith, invoking them, even thus late, to come forward and meet Mardonius in Attica; and intimating, that if they were thus deserted, they would be forced, however unwillingly, to make terms for themselves. After some hesitation and delay, the Spartans suddenly and vigorously joined the defence, sending 5000 citizens, each attended by seven Helots. Throughout the whole course of Grecian history, there is no other instance of a number at all approaching this being sent at one time on foreign service. But besides, there were also despatched 5000 Lacedæmonian soldiers, each attended by one light-armed Helot; and other Peloponnesian cities following the example, a large force was now assembled under the command of the Spartan Pausanias. The Argeians, who

were at this time in secret correspondence with Mardonius, and had promised to arrest the march of the Spartan auxiliaries, were so alarmed at the suddenness and the extent of the assistance they were bringing, that they could only send their swiftest courier to apprise the Persians of the fact.

332. Mardonius, who had hitherto abstained from injuring either the city of Athens or the surrounding country, in the hope that the Athenians would listen to his propositions, now devoted some days to burning and destroying whatever the army of Xerxes had spared, and then withdrew into Bœotia, as a country every way more favourable for carrying on the war. He took up a position in the plain, on the left bank of the Asopus, not far from the town of Platæa; and here he constructed a fortified camp, of ten furlongs square, with wooden walls and towers. With the fortified city of Thebes in his rear, and a friendly region whence to draw provisions—moreover, with a plain favourable for the operations of his cavalry, there was everything in his situation favourable to success. But his troops were neither hearty in the cause, nor confident of victory. Most of the Grecian allies, except the Thebans and Bœotians, were cool, if not wavering, in their fidelity; even the native Persians, disheartened by the flight of the monarch, were full of melancholy forebodings.

333. After the full force of the Lacedæmonians had reached the isthmus, and been joined by the other confederates, they numbered about 38,700 heavy-armed troops; but there were no cavalry, and very few bowmen; and the total force, including the Helots, and others called light-armed, amounted to about 110,000 men. Pausanias, who acted as regent for the infant son of Leonidas, kept his own army on the mountain declivity near Erythræ, not choosing to venture upon the level ground; while the Persians, who were expert in the management of missile weapons, charged in successive squadrons, overwhelmed them with darts and arrows, and contemptuously taunted them with their cowardice in maintaining the high ground. The Megarian contingent was hardly pressed by the Persian cavalry under Mesistius, but were

succoured by a body of Athenian troops; Mesistius was overpowered and slain; and notwithstanding the furious charge of the Persian cavalry to obtain possession of the body, it was carried off in triumph by the Greeks, and paraded round the army. The grief in the camp of Mardonius was manifested by wailings so loud, as to echo all over Bœotia, while the hair of men, horses, and cattle was cut in token of mourning.

334. Encouraged by this success, Pausanias now ventured to quit the protection of the mountain-ground, which was too scantily supplied with water, and to occupy a position in the plain beneath, interspersed only with low hillocks. Perceiving this, Mardonius drew his army up opposite to them, on the other side of the Asopus. In this position they lay, each expecting an attack, while the sacrifices on behalf of each were offered up. But the prophets appointed to ascertain the dispositions of the gods, delivered the same report on both sides—favourable for resistance if attacked, but unfavourable for offering battle. For eight days, little was done, except that considerable annoyance was inflicted on the Greeks by the Persian cavalry, under the guidance of the Thebans. The impatience of the Persian general became uncontrollable, and it was in vain that Artabazus endeavoured to dissuade him from offering battle, and advised him that the only successful policy would be that of corrupting and disuniting the enemy. Mardonius repudiated the counsel as cowardly, and gave orders to prepare everything for a general attack on the morrow. This order was made known to the Greeks by a secret visit from the king of Macedonia, who rode up to the advanced posts in the middle of the night; and having obtained an interview with the generals, announced his name, and warned them to prepare for the events of the coming day; 'And if ye succeed in this war,' said he, 'deliver me also from the Persian yoke; for I, too, am a Greek by descent, and have thus risked my head, because I would not see Greece enslaved.'

335. With the combat thus immediately in view, Pausanias begged the Athenians to change places with the

Lacedæmonians in the line, and stand opposite to the Medes and Persians; 'for we,' said he, 'have never contended with them, while ye fought and conquered them at Marathon.' This was done—the Lacedæmonians taking the place opposite the Bœotians and Thessalians, with whose mode of warfare they were more familiar. These arrangements were scarcely completed, when the day broke; and Mardonius, perceiving what had happened, ordered a corresponding change in his own line; upon which Pausanias changed places again with the Athenians; and Mardonius executed a second movement, which replaced both armies in their original order. Meanwhile, neither side ventured anything like a general attack; and the Greeks, finding that the enemy both intercepted their convoys of provisions, and choked up the spring which supplied them with water, resolved to remove during the night. The spot selected was a place improperly called 'the island,' about half-way between their present position and the town of Platæa. It was a piece of ground about three furlongs in breadth, lying between two branches of the river Oeroe, which, after running nearly parallel for a time, united in one stream, taking a north-westerly direction to the Gulf of Corinth. In the retreat, however, there was some misunderstanding, and the central troops, composed chiefly of Megarians and Corinthians, marched on to the town of Platæa, where they took up a position on a declivity protected by buildings. The right wing, composed of Lacedæmonians, was next to follow; but Amompharetus, one of the captains, who considered this retrograde movement as unworthy of Spartan courage, refused to stir. The left wing, afraid to move without ascertaining whether the right wing was really preparing to march, despatched a mounted messenger, who found Pausanias and the other Spartan generals in warm dispute with this refractory captain. Meantime the day began to dawn; there was no time to lose; the order was given to march, and the Lacedæmonians slowly ascended the hills, while the Athenians marched round them to gain the appointed spot. Happily, when Amompharetus found that his comrades had really departed, he overcame his scruples, gave orders to follow, and overtook them at their first halt.

336. When the day dawned, the Persian cavalry were astonished to find the Greek position deserted. They pursued and attacked them with disorderly impatience, crossing the Asopus, running at their best speed pêle-mêle, shouting for victory, and not dreaming of having to meet any resistance.

337. Pausanias had not got further than the spot where he had halted to take up Amompharetus, when he was overtaken by the Persian cavalry, closely followed by Mardonius with his main body. The Athenians, to whom he sent a horseman, were themselves engaged with the Thebans, and unable to come to his assistance. Accordingly, the Lacedæmonians and Tegeans were compelled to encounter the foe single-handed. The Persians formed a kind of breast-work, by planting in the ground the spiked ends of their *gerrha*, or long wicker-shields, and from behind this they poured a shower of arrows from their immense bows. Notwithstanding the distress to which the Greeks were thus subjected, Pausanias would not lift a hand in defence till the battle-sacrifice was offered ; and the victims exhibiting unfavourable omens, he would not give orders for advancing and engaging. Meanwhile, many were slain, and many more wounded, until Pausanias raised his eyes to the Heræum of the Platæans, now conspicuous to his view, and invoked the aid of Juno to remove his difficulties. Immediately the victims became favourable, the order was given to charge ; the wicker breast-work was soon overthrown, and the Persians having no defensive armour, had to maintain the fight against the long spears and well-shielded persons of the Greeks. In vain their individual courage would have compensated for the want of discipline and united movement ; though they threw themselves upon the Lacedæmonians, seizing hold of their spears, and sometimes breaking them, they were no match for the well-disciplined Greeks. Mardonius was slain ; the 1000 select troops who formed his body-guard nearly all perished around him ; and the courage of the remaining Persians being thoroughly

broken by the death of their general, they turned their backs and fled, nor stopped till they got into the wooden camp behind the Asopus. The Asiatic allies caught the panic, and fled without striking a blow.

338. Meanwhile the Athenians had sustained a serious conflict with the Bœotians, who were at length driven back with considerable loss. They retreated in good order to Thebes, being protected by their cavalry from the Athenian pursuit. None of the other Greeks in the Persian service took the least part in the conflict, so that the only troops who really fought were the native Persians and Sacæ against the Lacedæmonians, and the Bœotians against the Athenians. Nor did all even of the native Persians engage in the conflict. Artabazus, the second to Mardonius in command, had been displeased not only with his nomination as commander-in-chief, but at his obstinacy in risking an engagement. Accordingly, when Mardonius rushed on with headlong impetuosity after the retiring Greeks, Artabazus, with his division of 40,000, followed somewhat more leisurely, and did not arrive at the scene of action till the discomfited troops of the commander-in-chief were on their way back. Without making the least effort to rally them, or renew the battle, he ordered his own division to retreat, and returned neither to Thebes nor yet to the fortified camp, but straight home by Phocis, Thessaly, Macedonia, and the Hellespont.

339. The central troops of the Greek army, which, as we have said, had gone on to Platæa, knew nothing of the battle till they heard that the Lacedæmonians were victorious. Anxious to participate in the honour, they rushed to the scene of action, and in thorough disorder overtook the Theban horse, who were checking the pursuit of the victorious Athenian hoplites. They were vigorously charged, and driven back to the high ground with considerable loss; but this partial success on the Persian side in nowise mitigated the ruin of the general defeat.

340. Following up their pursuit, the Lacedæmonians, reinforced by the Athenians as well as the Corinthians and Megarians, attacked, stormed, and plundered the

fortified camp, slaughtering its defenders without mercy and without limit. The tent of Mardonius afforded a rich spoil; and his silver-footed throne and scimitar, along with the breastplate of the gigantic Mesistius, were sacredly preserved in the Acropolis of Athens. Respecting the numbers lost on both sides, only a vague estimate can be made; probably not fewer than 1360 of the Greek hoplites were slain; little account being made of the light-armed troops, who seem to have taken no share in the conflict. On the Persian side, it is said that only 3000 men survived out of the 300,000 left by Xerxes under the command of Mardonius, besides the 40,000 who retired with Artabazus. Whatever their numerical loss, the defeat was total and ruinous: probably many individuals were spared, and sold into slavery; while other fugitives might find means of joining the retreat of Artabazus. So rapid was the march of this general, and so strict his silence about what had taken place, that it is said he arrived safely in Asia before the news of the defeat had reached the countries through which he prosecuted his march.

341. The burial of the dead and the distribution of the spoil fully occupied the Greeks for ten days after the victory. The dead body of Mardonius being found among slaughtered heaps, Pausanias treated it with respect, disdaining to retaliate upon it the conduct of Xerxes towards the corpse of Leonidas; but on the morrow, it was found to have been secretly carried away and buried, by whom was never certainly known. The booty was rich and multifarious, including gold and silver money, implements and ornaments, besides splendid accoutrements, horses, camels, &c. When the whole was collected by the Helots into one spot, a tithe was set apart for the Delphian Apollo; a munificent offering likewise for the Olympic Jove and the Isthmian Neptune; besides a handsome share for Pausanias, as commander-in-chief; after which, the remainder was apportioned among the contingents of the army, according to their respective numbers.

342. On the eleventh day after the battle of Platæa, Thebes was summoned to surrender the medising leaders, as those were called who negotiated with Persia; and

the summons was followed up by a vigorous battering of the walls, and devastation of the surrounding country. After twenty days, the obnoxious leaders voluntarily surrendered themselves for the sake of their fellow-citizens, and were carried off to Corinth, where they were put to death immediately, without discussion or form of trial. It would seem Pausanias feared that their wealth and that of their friends might purchase votes for their acquittal, if any delay or consultation were permitted.

343. It is doubtful whether there was any positive vote taken respecting the prize of valour at the battle of Platæa, but the general opinion recognised Pausanias and his Lacedæmonians as bravest among the brave, because they had routed the best troops of the enemy, and slain their general. There was one Spartan, however, who surpassed all even of his own compatriots. This was Aristodemus, the sole survivor of the troop of Leonidas at Thermopylæ. On that occasion, he had been absent on leave from the detachment, suffering from a severe ophthalmic attack. A comrade, who was similarly situated, demanded his armour, ordered his attendant Helot to lead him to his place in the ranks, and fell, fighting as he could. But Aristodemus, overcome by physical suffering, had allowed himself to be carried home to Sparta, where he was denounced as a coward. No one would speak to him, or even afford him a light for his fire; and now, after a year of bitter disgrace, he stepped forth single-handed from his place in the ranks at Platæa, performing deeds of heroic valour, and resolved to regain the esteem of his countrymen. His heroism, or rather recklessness, soon obtained for him the death he sought, and in some measure retrieved his honour; but the Spartans considered that the previous taint having rendered life undesirable to him, there was no such virtue in his rashness as to raise him to a level with their other distinguished warriors, and they refused to assign him equal funereal honours with them.

344. The market-place of the town of Platæa was selected as the scene for the solemn sacrifice of thanksgiving which was offered by Pausanias to Jupiter

Eleutherius, or the 'deliverer,' in the name and presence of the assembled allies. The local gods and heroes of the Platæan territory, who had granted their soil as a propitious field for the conflict, were likewise included; the citizens were invested with the honourable duty of commemorating the victory by a periodical sacrifice, and also that of guarding the tombs of the fallen warriors, and rendering religious service there. Besides, they were to celebrate every fifth year a grand public solemnity, to be called the Eleutheria, with gymnastic games like the other great festivals of Greece. In consideration of the discharge of these duties, and of the sanctity which now must be attached to the ground, the allies solemnly bound themselves to guarantee the independence of Platæa, and the inviolability of her territory, thus emancipating her from the bond of the Bœotian federation. Besides all this, the allies renewed their defensive league against the Persians, and rendered it permanent; the aggregate force to be furnished for the purpose of carrying on the war was agreed to; the proportion which each state should furnish was specified; and it was arranged that an annual meeting should be held at Platæa, where deputies from each city were to assemble.

345. On the same day with the battle of Platæa, the respective fleets of Greece and Persia were engaged in a conflict, hardly less important, at Mycale, on the Asiatic coast. The remnant of the Persian fleet which had conveyed Xerxes and his army across the Hellespont, had wintered at Cyme and Samos, and early in spring had reassembled to the number of 400 sail at the naval station of Samos. The Greek ships, to the number of 110, assembled at Ægina, in the spring, under the Spartan king Leotychides, and advanced as far as Delos; but all the persuasions of the Ionian envoys, with promises of revolting from Persia, could not prevail upon Leotychides to venture near the Ionian coast, or hazard any aggressive enterprise. When at length, however, three Samians, one of them named Hegesistratus, came on a similar mission, Leotychides, having learned it, replied: 'I accept Hegesistratus [army-leader] as an omen; pledge, then, thy

faith to accompany us, and let thy comrades prepare the Samians for our reception.' He of the ominous name remained accordingly to conduct the fleet, while the other two envoys were sent forward to Samos to make preparations. Before they reached the appointed place, however, the Persian commanders, not desiring to engage in a sea-fight, had withdrawn their ships from the island to the promontory of Mycale, near Miletus. Here, being under the protection of a land-force of 60,000 men under the command of Tigranes, the vessels were dragged on shore, a rampart was erected to protect them, and the defending army lined the coast. The Greek fleet pursued them hither, and discovered, to their disappointment, that the Persians had abandoned the sea, and would fight only on land. Leotychides now sailed along close to the coast, and employed a herald of powerful voice to invite the Ionians among the enemy to desert, calculating, as Themistocles had done before, that, even if they did not comply, the Persians, apprehending that they might do so, would mistrust them. He then disembarked his troops, and marshalled them for battle on land; while the Persians, surprised by his daring, and suspecting the Ionians, ordered the Samians to be disarmed, and the Milesians to retire to the mountain-passes. We are told that at the moment when the Greeks were advancing to the charge, a herald's staff was floated towards the shore by the western wave, while a sudden, simultaneous, and irresistible impression was made upon the minds of all, that their countrymen in Bœotia had defeated Mardonius. The army, filled with joy and confidence by this divine message, charged with redoubled energy; the Persians, as at Platæa, formed a breast-work of their wicker shields; but the Greeks eventually succeeded in demolishing it, and driving the enemy into the interior of the fortification. This last rampart, too, was carried, and the Persian allies fled; but the native Persians prolonged the struggle, nor yielded till the Lacedæmonian part of the army, hitherto retarded by the hilly ground they had to traverse, joined the attack, and rendered the defence hopeless.

346. The finishing-stroke was put to this ruinous defeat

by the desertion of the Ionians. The Samians, and others
in the camp, with the Milesians, guarding the passes in the
rear, joined the assailants; and when the Persians were
obliged to fly, those Milesians whom they trusted to guide
them to the summits of Mycale, betrayed them into wrong
paths, threw them into the hands of their pursuers, and
even fell upon them themselves. The Persian land-force
was irretrievably dispersed, and both the generals slain,
together with a large number of native troops. The
remnant which gained the heights of Mycale was immediately ordered to Sardis; so that the Greek cities, even on
the continent, were for the time practically liberated from
the Persian supremacy. The inhabitants of the islands
were in a position of still greater safety; for all the ships
had fallen into the hands of the Greeks, and were burnt.
The islanders were, therefore, now admitted to the protection and reciprocal engagements of the Greek alliance;
and it is presumed that the despots of Chios and Samos
were expelled.

347. There was greater difficulty in guaranteeing a
similar independence to the continental cities, as it might
have required constant and exhausting efforts to uphold
them against the inland power of Persia. Accordingly,
the Peloponnesians proposed to transplant their inhabitants
to European Greece, and to make room for them by
expelling those who had sided with the enemy; but the
Athenians would not allow their colonies to be thus
abandoned, and undertook themselves to see to their
safety.

348. Having settled these matters on the Ionian coast,
the Grecian fleet proceeded to the Hellespont, for the
purpose of breaking down the bridge of Xerxes. So
tardy at this time was the transmission of intelligence,
that they believed this bridge to be in passable condition
in September 479 B.C., though Xerxes had found it broken
and useless ten months before. Having ascertained the
fact, the Peloponnesians returned home; but Xanthippus,
with the Athenian part of the fleet, remained to expel the
Persians from the Thracian Chersonesus. A large part of
this peninsula had been in Athenian possession for forty

years before the suppression of the Ionic revolt; but since that time, had been so entirely under Persian influence that no Athenian could live in it with safety. The Athenians were naturally eager both to re-establish the influence of their city, and to regain possession of large estates which were the private property of their leading citizens. The Persian garrisons, surprised and terrified at this movement, concentrated themselves in Sestus, the strongest place in the peninsula, but without providing means either of subsistence or of prolonged defence. It was resolved to besiege this town; and the Greek inhabitants of the country gladly lent their assistance. The garrison held out, though by painful shifts, till a late period in the autumn, when their privations became intolerable; the commanders Artayctes and Œobazus stole away with a few followers, letting themselves down from the wall at a place where it was imperfectly blockaded; and the inhabitants of the city immediately surrendered it. Œobazus made his way to Thrace, where some of the natives seized him, and offered him up as a sacrifice to one of their gods. Artayctes was pursued by the Greeks along the shores of the Hellespont, made prisoner, and brought back, with his son, in chains to Sestus. His crying sin was, that when Xerxes was on his march across the Hellespont into Greece, Artayctes had, by a stratagem, obtained his authority for plundering the wealthy temple of Protesilaus, and had even turned cattle into the grove, and ploughed and sowed it in the spirit of wanton outrage against the feelings of the people. It was in vain that he now offered a handsome compensation to the sacred treasury, and a further sum as ransom for himself and his son. No money could atone for his sacrilege; he was compelled first to see his son stoned to death, and was then himself hung up to a lofty board, and left to perish on the spot where the bridge of Xerxes had been fastened.

349. Towards the commencement of winter, the Athenian fleet returned home with their plunder, along with which they carried the great cables of the Xerxean bridge, as a trophy to adorn the Acropolis of Athens.

HERODOTUS.

350. To the conflicts between Persia and Greece, we owe the development of historic talent in Herodotus, celebrated as the father of Grecian history. The first attempts at recording national facts seem to have been made in the time of the Pisistratidæ, when prose-writing was only beginning to be cultivated. The style of these annals bordered on that of mythical poetry, consisting chiefly, like the poems of Hesiod and the cyclics, of genealogical lists, early traditions, and isolated details. It remained for Herodotus to conceive the idea of a history in the sense we now attach to the term.

351. Herodotus was born at Halicarnassus, in Caria, in the fourth year after Xerxes brought his hosts into Europe, and consequently the struggles we have described in the foregoing pages, were among the earliest events that filled the imagination of the boy. The historic feeling was probably awakened and fostered by the work of Hecatæus of Miletus, who about the same time composed a narrative of the Ionic revolt. The compass of intellectual vision was extended by the connection now established between the east and the west ; and the mind of Herodotus rose to the idea of a universal history, of which the great focus should be the wars of the Greeks with the Persians. He would penetrate and unfold the original causes of these contests between Greeks and Barbarians ; and finding the scanty materials of the earlier annals insufficient for his purpose, he must travel himself into other lands, to learn the nature and effects of various climates, and the manners of various peoples. Egypt—then supposed to be the cradle of the human race, and the great repository of wisdom and knowledge—was the first object of his curiosity ; after which he visited the coasts of Libya, traversed the whole of Greece Proper as far as Thrace ; penetrated the land of the Scythians, and made himself acquainted with Asia as far as Babylon.

352. On his return to his own country, he found it

distracted and unhappy; he therefore betook himself to Hellas Proper, and, it is said, read his history to the assembled Greeks at the Olympic games. We need scarcely remind the reader that those were not the days of circulating a literary work by printed copies, or even numerous transcriptions; public recitation was the only mode.

353. The work of Herodotus sets out with a promise to narrate the origin and history of the Greeks and Barbarians; but it does, in truth, comprise an account of the whole world, so far as he knew it, a description of various countries and their natural products, as well as of the people inhabiting them. The whole is sketched with a deep poetical and religious feeling, the great work of time is unfolded, and a pervading idea serves as a point of unity to centralise the otherwise isolated narratives. This idea is, that an all-ruling, all-directing Deity guides the system of the world; that no earthly might or majesty can contend with the Almighty arm, or frustrate his decrees. Hence a great part of the history refers to the oracles as organs of divinity, connecting the world below with the world above in a palpable, and, as was then believed, an infallible manner. The mass of history which Herodotus lays before us, seems to have been moulded in the depths of his soul upon this principle, and brought out as a perfect whole. On this account, he has been called the Homer of historians, and his work a historical epic.

354. The veracity of this historian has often been questioned, and at one time it was fashionable to regard his work as an amusing collection of incredible tales, slightly founded on fact. But much that was once rejected as fabulous in his descriptions of places and peoples, has been since confirmed by investigation; and the more our knowledge of those regions improves, the more is the veracity of the old historian established.

THIRD PERIOD.

478—404 B.C.

FOUNDATION OF MARITIME POWER AT ATHENS.

355. THE Athenians, on returning from Salamis after the battle of Platæa, found but a desolate home to receive them. Their country lay waste; their 478 B.C. fortifications were in heaps; their houses for the most part burnt or otherwise destroyed, except the few which the Persian officers had made their quarters. Their first task was to bring home their families and effects from their temporary asylums; and after providing what was necessary for their immediate wants, they began to rebuild their city and its fortifications on a scale of considerable enlargement. The allies now took the alarm, and preferred complaints to Sparta, urging her to arrest the work. The Spartans, quite disposed to sympathise with the jealousy and uneasiness, had, besides, a dislike to fortifications, and would have been glad to see all the other cities of Greece as defenceless as their own. There was some difficulty, however, in forbidding the exercise of a right common to every independent city; and they contented themselves with sending an embassy, to offer a friendly remonstrance at Athens against the refortification of the city. They suggested that, in case of a future Persian invasion, it would be a dangerous advantage to the enemy to find any fortified city outside of Peloponnesus to aid his operations, as Thebes had recently done; and they proposed that the Athenians should even assist in demolishing the defences of other cities north of Peloponnesus. At the same time, they promised shelter within the Isthmus to all these parties in case of necessity.

356. Themistocles was not to be thus imposed upon;

but he saw that the Spartans could prevent the work if they chose, and he laid his plans to circumvent them. He induced the Athenians to dismiss the Spartan envoys, with the message that they would send men of their own to explain their views. Accordingly, he was himself presently despatched as one of three ambassadors who were to explain matters at Sparta. But by previous concert, his two colleagues were tardy in arriving; and he, while affecting surprise at their delay, made it an excuse for not even demanding an audience. Meanwhile, the whole population of Athens, men, women, and children, were labouring without intermission at the walls; neither private dwellings nor sacred structures were spared to furnish materials; and such was their ardour and industry, that the wall had attained a tolerable height before the two lingering envoys appeared at Sparta. The watchful and jealous Æginetans sent positive intelligence to Sparta of the rapid advance of the defences; but Themistocles peremptorily denied it, and was for a time believed. When fresh messengers with similar news arrived, Themistocles advised the ephors to send an embassy of their own to Athens, and satisfy themselves of the fact. They were simple enough to act upon his recommendation; and he transmitted at the same time a private message to Athens, desiring that these envoys should be detained till he and his colleagues had effected a safe return. Then, as soon as Aristides and Abronychus joined him at Sparta, and announced that the wall was now of a height at least above contempt, Themistocles threw off the mask, and avowed his stratagem. He told the Spartans that Athens was already fortified sufficiently to insure safety and freewill to its inhabitants, and its citizens were in a condition to define their own duties, and vindicate their own rights, in reference to Sparta and the other allies.

357. Mortified as the Spartans were to find that they had been outwitted, they were at the same time overawed by the decisive tone of Themistocles. Whatever success they might have hoped for in endeavouring to arrest this operation beforehand, it would have been perilous in a high degree to deal by force with the deed actually

accomplished; and they therefore affected to accept the communication without any symptom of offence. The envoys on both sides returned home, and the Athenians completed the works without hinderance.

358. But Themistocles had conceived plans of a much wider and more ambitious range. Accordingly, the moment that the walls of the city were finished, he called the attention of his countrymen to those wooden walls which had recently served them as a refuge, and he prevailed upon them to provide for these a harbour at once safe and adequate. This was done by the enlargement and fortification of the Piræus, an enterprise which had been commenced two or three years before, but was now resumed on a scale far greater than Themistocles could then have ventured to propose. This noble structure served other purposes besides its direct use as a harbour for military marine: its strong fortifications, and the protection afforded by the fleet, were calculated to reassure those *metics*, or resident foreigners, who had been frightened away by the invasion of Xerxes, and also to attract new immigrants of a similar description, as they saw in the fortified ports and the navy both new securities and new facilities for trade. The presence of numerous metics was highly profitable to the Athenians, as much of the commercial, professional, and handicraft business was in their hands; and the great increase in their numbers from this period forward, does much to explain the extraordinary prosperity of the city, and the excellent cultivation of the country.

359. The execution of these stupendous works did not prevent Athens from taking a part in the expedition which was prosecuted by the allies under the Spartan Pausanias, the year after the battle of Platæa. They sailed first to Cyprus, where they delivered most of the 478 B.C. Grecian cities from the Persian yoke; next, they undertook the siege of Byzantium, on the Thracian Bosporus—a post, like Sestus in the Chersonesus, of great importance as well as strength, occupied, moreover, by a considerable Persian force, with several people of distinction, and even kinsmen of the monarch. This place was taken, and the line of

communication between Greece and the Euxine Sea was thus cleared.

FALL OF PAUSANIAS.

360. In connection with this expedition, we have to notice the deplorable liability of the Grecian mind to be spoiled by prosperity, as already noticed in the case of Miltiades. Pausanias, who, as commander-in-chief at Platæa, had acquired both riches and renown unparalleled in the previous history of Greece, could no longer brook either the prescribed austerity of Spartan life or the necessary control of the authorities at home. Throughout the whole of the expedition of 478 B.C., he had behaved with great arrogance, but it was not till after the capture of Byzantium, that his haughty ambition merged into treason against his country. He now entered into a secret correspondence with Xerxes, in which he proposed to marry the daughter of that monarch, and bring the whole of Greece into subjection to him, with the understanding, of course, that he himself should exercise a subordinate rule as despot. Meanwhile, as pledge of his sincerity, he sent back the valuable prisoners that had been taken, and desired that a trusty man might be sent down to the Asiatic coast to carry on the correspondence. Xerxes, in reply, urged him to spare no expense in the execution of his project, and immediately sent Artabazus to the satrapy of Dascylium, as his future correspondent. Happily for Greece, the childish impatience of Pausanias rendered his designs apparent. He dressed himself in the costume of the now luxurious and effeminate Persians; traversed Thrace with a body of Median and Egyptian guards; and imitated the Persian lords, both in the luxury of his table and the looseness of his morals. Intelligence of this outrageous behaviour was transmitted to Sparta; he was summoned home, to render an account of himself; and though acquitted of the positive charges against him, yet the presumptive evidence of collusion with the enemy was so strong, that he was not reappointed to the command. He now went out in a trireme, under pretence of aiding as a volunteer,

but really to carry on his treasonable designs, and renew his negotiations with Artabazus. The Athenians expelled him by force, and he retired to Colonæ, where he busied himself in striving to form a Persian party, despatching emissaries to distribute Persian gold in various cities of Greece. At length the Spartan authorities sent a herald to bring him home; and in the first moment of indignation, the ephors committed him to prison, which it seems they were competent to do, even had he been king instead of regent. He demanded to be liberated, accused, and tried; and he was set free with this view, but no one appeared against him; amidst a long concatenation of actions, carrying conviction when taken in the aggregate, there was no single act of treason sufficiently demonstrable to condemn him; so that he remained at large, still audaciously persisting both in his intrigues at home, and his negotiations abroad. Suspected, yet unchecked, he had brought his plans to the very brink of consummation, when he was detected in the following manner:—

361. He had written a letter to Artabazus, intimating that all was ready for action, and claiming the immediate performance of the engagements concerted between them. The letter was intrusted to a favourite and faithful slave, who, on receiving it, recollected with some uneasiness that none of the previous messengers to Artabazus had ever returned. His undefined suspicions prompted him to open and read the letter, and he found that it contained an express injunction that the bearer was to be put to death. To avoid this fate, his only alternative was to deliver the document to the ephors. Partly, however, from the suspicion which in those days always attached to the testimony of slaves, and partly from the difficulty of dealing with so exalted a criminal, the ephors declined proceeding on this evidence, and laid a plan for obtaining more tangible proof. They directed the slave to fly as a refugee to the sacred precinct of Neptune, near Cape Tænarum, under the shelter of a double tent or hut. Pausanias being informed of the circumstance, hastened to the temple, and demanded the reason. The slave confessed his knowledge of the contents of the letter, and

complained bitterly that, after long and faithful service, he should be consigned to the same miserable fate as the previous messengers. Pausanias made no attempt to controvert the facts, but endeavoured to quiet the fears of the slave, giving him a solemn assurance of safety if he would but quit the sanctuary and proceed on the journey, in order that the measures in progress might not be retarded.

362. The ephors, concealed in the adjoining apartment, heard, and were satisfied. It was determined to arrest the traitor immediately on his return to Sparta; but as they met him in the public street not far from one of the temples, he discovered their purpose, either from the menacing looks of all, or a telegraphic sign from one; and he immediately fled to the temple. Placing himself there, in a narrow-roofed chamber belonging to the sacred building, he was safe from violence; but the ephors took off the roof, built up the doors, and kept watch till he was on the point of death by starvation, 467 B.C. when they brought him away in time to expire outside; thus avoiding the desecration of the temple.

ADVENTURES OF THEMISTOCLES.

363. The treasonable projects of Pausanias implicated a far greater man—the Athenian Themistocles, whom he had sought to enlist as his accomplice. In the letters brought to light, there was evidence of the collusion of Themistocles; in consequence of which, the Lacedæmonians sent to Athens, preferring a formal charge of treason against him, and insisting that he should be tried as a panhellenic criminal before the synod of the allies. Joint envoys were, accordingly, sent from Sparta and Athens to arrest him, of which he no sooner heard than he fled to Corcyra. The islanders, not daring to protect him against the two most powerful states in Greece, sent him to the neighbouring continent, where he was still tracked by the envoys. He was now driven to seek protection from a man personally his enemy—Admetus, king of the Molossians.

At the moment of his arrival, Admetus was not at home; but his wife, moved to sympathy at the condition of the fugitive, put her child into his arms, and placed him on the hearth, in the position of a suppliant, against her husband's return. On the appearance of Admetus, Themistocles revealed his name, explained his position, and appealed to the generosity of the Epeirotic prince not to take revenge on a man now incapable of defending himself. Admetus raised him from the hearth; engaged to protect him; and finally parted with him only on the expression of his own wish to visit the king of Persia. He arrived in safety at Ephesus, and proceeded to the capital, where he presented himself, and was accepted as a deserter from Greece—moreover, as one who had actually served the monarch, in his communications respecting the intended retreat of the Greeks from Salamis, and also respecting the contemplated destruction of the Hellespontine bridge.

364. The escape of Themistocles and his adventures in Persia afforded a favourite theme for the fancy of authors a century afterwards. They mention, for instance, that the delighted Xerxes offered an immediate sacrifice to the gods; indulged himself in unwonted conviviality; and was heard repeatedly crying out in his sleep: 'I have got Themistocles the Athenian!' Certain it is, the traitor now directed his ingenuity to the formation of schemes for the subjugation of his native country; and that he was rewarded with a Persian wife, large presents, and finally the government of Magnesia, with a considerable revenue, near the coast of Ionia. Here he was joined by his family, and lived we know not how long, but that he died at the age of sixty-five— probably a natural death, though it was rumoured that he took poison, to avoid being obliged to fulfil his engagements to the monarch with respect to the subjugation of Greece.

ATHENS THE LEADING STATE OF MARITIME GREECE.

365. At the time that Pausanias was summoned home from Byzantium, he seems to have left no Spartan authority behind; to have brought home with him even the small Lacedæmonian contingent of ships, while the other Peloponnesians also retired. In these circumstances, the Athenian generals were urged by the allies to assume the command; and such good use did they make of their time, that when Dorcis arrived from Sparta to replace Pausanias, he found them in full supremacy. He had no sufficient force to attempt compulsion, and therefore returned home.

366. This incident was the first open renunciation of the authority of Sparta as the presiding state among the Greeks. We have seen that there had long been a tendency, not very powerful, yet steadily increasing, towards a confederation under her; we have also seen her formally installed as the chief of a pan-hellenic union, at the moment when the town of Platæa was set apart as a consecrated neutral spot for an armed confederacy against Persia, with periodical solemnities and meetings of deputies. But now Athens enters into rivalry as a kind of leader of opposition, possessing in a remarkable degree that capability of comprehensive policy in which Sparta was deficient, besides the actual maritime force which was the want of the day. Here, therefore, a bifurcation commences. The maritime states, newly enfranchised from Persia, gravitate towards Athens; while the land states, which had formed a large proportion of the confederate army at Platæa, cling to Sparta. Henceforward, these rivals divide the Grecian world between them, and bring a much larger number of its members into combination either with one or other, than had ever appeared in league before.

367. The departure of the Spartan Dorcis with the other Peloponnesian allies, not only left the prosecution of the war to Athens, as chief of the newly emancipated

Greeks, but it left them at liberty to organise the confederacy which they had been chosen to conduct. The Ionic allies stood in obvious need of protection against Persia, and had no further kindness to expect from the Peloponnesians. A new confederation was therefore organised; a definite obligation, either in ships of war or money, was imposed on each city; and conditions were regulated in a common synod of the members appointed to meet periodically in the temple of Apollo and Diana at Delos. This had been of old the spot sacred to the religious festivals of the Ionian cities, and it was at the same time a central situation for the members.

368. While there are chroniclers both for the Persian invasion and for the times before it, no one seems to have cared for the events immediately succeeding; so that we are left in almost entire ignorance of the proceedings of Athens as head of the newly established confederacy. The first ten years appear to have been spent chiefly in active warfare against the Persians, who had still many commanders and garrisons in Thrace and the Hellespont. The battles of Salamis, Platæa, and Mycale, had driven the Persians out of Greece by overpowering their main force; but it had not removed them from all the various posts which they occupied in Thrace and throughout the Ægæan. The expulsion of these appears to have kept the Greeks tolerably busy from the year 477 to 466 B.C. There is every reason to believe that, during this period, Athens, according to the power intrusted to her, exacted from every member the regulated quota of men or money, employing coercion with those defaulters who would have desired to enjoy protection without bearing their share of the burden.

477–466 B.C.

369. But after a few years, several of the confederates became weary of personal service, and prevailed upon the Athenians to provide ships and men in their place, in consideration of an adequate payment in money. The plan of commutation gradually gained ground, being a welcome relief to the unwarlike, the indolent, and the self-indulgent; while to the Athenians, patient of labour and anxious for

the aggrandisement of their country, it was a welcome boon. But it tended fatally to degrade the allies, and to extinguish the original feeling of equal rights, and a communion of danger as well as of glory. The Athenians, in time, considered them as a body of tribute-paying subjects, whom they were bound to protect against foreign enemies, and at the same time entitled to hold under their own dominion.

370. When those motives of alarm which had at first stimulated the maritime Greeks to the confederacy became further removed, several of them grew tired even of paying their tribute, and attempted to secede. Athens, apparently in conjunction with the synod, repressed these attempts one after another during successive years, conquering, fining, and disarming the revolters; and thus the allies slid unconsciously into subjects, while Athens passed from a chief into a despot, and became feared and hated accordingly.

371. It is probable that the same indisposition to personal exertion which prompted the confederates of Delos to prefer pecuniary payments to military service, induced them also to neglect attending the synod; but we do not know the steps by which this assembly gradually dwindled into a mere form, and then disappeared.

372. Meanwhile, the democratic spirit was gaining ground at Athens, and her domestic affairs demand a short notice.

PERICLES AND CIMON.

373. Aristides died three or four years after the ostracism of Themistocles. We know little of the manner of the event, except that he died absolutely poor—a fact most honourable to his integrity. And now appeared upon the stage of Athenian politics one of the most remarkable men that Greece ever produced. The political career of Pericles began about the time when Themistocles was ostracised, and Aristides was retiring from the stage. He soon displayed a character which combined the integrity of the one with the comprehensive views of

the other, superadding a command of temper never disturbed, sound discretion, literary education, and an eloquence such as no one had either heard or imagined before. He cordially embraced the democratic party—the party of movement against that of resistance; or, as we say in modern times, of Reformers against Conservatives; yet he was particularly free from the low arts of the demagogue, and disregarded almost to excess the airs of popularity.

374. The Clisthenean constitution, though somewhat enlarged by Aristides after the return from Salamis, had become unpopular with the poorer citizens, and inadequate to the keener democratical feeling which ran through Athens and Piræus.

375. The principal assistant of Pericles in his attempts to satisfy this feeling was Ephialtes, who devoted himself particularly to check the practical abuse of the power vested in the magistrates in judicial cases. After repeated efforts, Ephialtes and Pericles determined permanently to abridge this power, and introduce a new system. Through their influence, the judicial power, civil as well as criminal, was transferred to numerous dicasts, or panels of jurors chosen from the citizens, and regularly paid. Six thousand were annually drawn by lot, and after being sworn, were distributed into 10 panels of 500 each, the remaining 1000 being reserved to supply vacancies. The magistrate, instead of deciding and punishing by his own authority, was now obliged to submit each particular case to the judgment of one or other of these numerous dicasteries; and which of the ten he should take was determined by lot, so that no one knew beforehand by what dicastery any particular cause would be tried. As a still further precaution against either corruption or intimidation, the votes of the jurors were taken by private ballot. The magistrate still retained, however, the power of deciding cases which called for no greater penalty than a small fine. So also the civil judicature which the archons had exercised between man and man, was transferred to these dicasteries under the presidency of an archon.

376. The next attack of democracy was against the senate of Areopagus, which exercised powers immense as well as undefined, not derived from any formal charter, but resting upon immemorial antiquity, and sustained by general awe and reverence. From the character of this court, it naturally served as a rallying-point to the oligarchical or conservative party, including probably the majority of rich and old families, who desired to preserve the constitution of Clisthenes unaltered, and to maintain both the individual magistrates and the collective Areopagus in the judicial authority they had hitherto enjoyed. Of this party, Cimon was the most conspicuous leader, and his success as a military commander did much to strengthen his political influence at home. In taste, in talent, and in character, he was the opposite of Pericles —a brave and efficient general, lavish in expenditure and distribution, convivial in his habits, incapable of close attention to business, limited in his literary education, and endued with a perfectly Spartan aversion to rhetoric and philosophy.

377. Such were the two men who represented the party contest at Athens, between the expanding democracy of the present generation, and the stationary democracy of the past. The political opposition between them was hereditary, since Xanthippus, the father of Pericles, had been the accuser of Miltiades, the father of Cimon. The controversy ran so high, that it was necessary to remove one of the leaders; a vote of ostracism was resorted to, and Cimon was banished. Now Pericles and Ephialtes carried out their scheme of judicial reform; and besides introducing the jury-system we have described, deprived the court of Areopagus of all jurisdiction except in cases of homicide—this being so bound up with religious feeling, that no reformer might attempt to disturb it. The stationary party denounced the curtailments proposed by Ephialtes as impious innovations; and so fierce was the collision of feeling, that they caused him to be privately assassinated—a crime rare in the political annals of Athens.

378. From this point may be dated the administration

of Pericles, who now became the leading adviser of the Athenian people. His first years at least were marked by a series of brilliant successes, to which the reader's attention will presently be invited.

379. Another important political change must be noticed. Shortly after the return of the expatriated Athenians from Salamis, Aristides had seen the necessity of rendering every citizen legally eligible to offices of state, instead of confining them to the three wealthier classes of the Solonian scale. But it would seem that little change actually took place, and that rich men were still most generally chosen. The democratical sentiment, however, had gone on steadily increasing; and about the time of the rivalry between Pericles and Cimon, though we are not sure that it was a proposition of Pericles — the choice of archons and various other magistrates was determined by lot, with the view of equalising the chances of office to every candidate, poor as well as rich.

DIFFERENCES BETWEEN ATHENS AND SPARTA. —PROGRESS OF ATHENIAN POWER.

380. From the confederacy of Delos, 477 B.C. till 463 B.C., the Athenians seem to have been almost entirely occupied in maritime operations, chiefly against the Persians. But now interests nearer home demanded a share of their attention.

381. Of the incidents which occurred in Central Greece during the twelve or fifteen years after the battle of Platæa, we have scarcely any information. Sparta continued inimical to aggregations of cities; and in her desire to keep the little communities separate and independent, she sometimes became the protector of the weaker states against compulsory alliance with the stronger; except in the case of Thebes, which she assisted to regain her ascendancy, through fear of the growing power of Athens.

382. A terrible earthquake which occurred at Sparta, destroying a large portion of the town, and 464 B.C. a vast number of lives, was supposed to be a judgment of

Neptune—the earth-shaking god—for a recent violation of sanctuary at Tænarus, whence certain Helots had been dragged forth to punishment. The feelings of the Helots, at all times easily excited against their masters, now broke out in open revolt. The insurgents, aided by some of the Periœci, marched upon Sparta, which they had nearly mastered. When repelled, they betook themselves to the hill of Ithome, the ancient citadel of their Messenian forefathers. Here they fortified themselves, and made a long and obstinate defence. The Spartans, after vainly besieging them for two or three years, called in their allies, and the Athenians among the rest. But the means of attacking walls in those days were very imperfect, and the Spartans saw with surprise that the Athenians were not more successful than themselves. This surprise presently merged into mistrust and apprehension, and the Athenian allies were summarily dismissed, while the rest were retained—a mistrust this which appears to have been groundless, and a dismissal which excited the utmost indignation. The Athenians immediately renounced the alliance of Sparta, and sought that of her enemies; among whom the most important was Argos, now recovering from the effects of the defeat she had suffered thirty years before from Cleomenes. This rupture came in good time for the Megarians, who, finding themselves encroached upon by their powerful neighbours the Corinthians, and having no hope of assistance from Sparta in its present distracted condition, applied to Athens, and were cordially received. In order that the maritime arm of Athens might reach the inland city, a novel expedient was resorted to. Two lines of wall, near and parallel to each other, were erected to connect the city of Megara with its port Nisæa, almost a mile distant; and the two were thus formed into one continuous fortress, in which a garrison was maintained, and by which the succour of the fleet could always be available. These 'long walls' were afterwards copied, as we shall see, on a larger scale. The alliance of Megara opened up to the Athenians the whole range of territory across the outer Isthmus of Corinth, and put them in possession of the passes of Mount

Geranea, by which they could obstruct the march of any army out of Peloponnesus. It was of course, therefore, considered a wrong by the Lacedæmonians, and gave deadly offence to Corinth.

383. The Athenians now having reason to apprehend a numerous host of foes, began the stupendous work of connecting their city with the harbours of Piræus and Phalerum, by means of long walls, as they had done at Megara. The wall to Piræus was forty stadia (equal to four miles and a half) in length, and that to Phalerum thirty-five stadia. A measure so alarming bestirred the Lacedæmonians, and a considerable force was marched into Bœotia, where a conflict took place at Tanagra. Victory declared for the Peloponnesians, but they gained little by it, except a way of retreat over the passes of Geranea.

384. An interesting circumstance connected with this battle must be recorded. As soon as the Athenian army had passed beyond their own frontier, the exiled Cimon presented himself, and begged to be allowed to fight in his place as a hoplite, or heavily-armed soldier. He was refused, as it was feared he might be an accomplice of certain malcontents known to be among the Athenians, and to be intending to co-operate with the enemy in case of success. Persisting in his patriotism, he conjured those of his personal friends who were in the ranks to conduct themselves so as to wipe away this reproach. Accordingly, they kept his panoply; put it in the place which Cimon himself would have occupied in the ranks; entered into the fight with desperate resolution; and fell to the number of a hundred. This unshaken patriotism of Cimon and his friends, put to shame the conspirators who had entered into correspondence with the enemy, and at the same time awakened a repentant admiration towards the exile himself. The happy result was a generous spirit of compromise among the contending political parties; Cimon was recalled at the suggestion of Pericles himself; and a renewed fraternisation took place among the general body of the citizens.

385. So powerful was this fresh burst of patriotism and unanimity, that the Athenians were soon in a position to

undertake an aggressive march into Bœotia, where they proved completely victorious. Becoming masters of Thebes, as well as of the other towns, they reversed all the arrangements that had been made by Sparta, establishing democracy in the governments, and forcing all opponents into exile. Phocis and Locris also were presently added to the list of their dependent allies; and thus was the influence of Athens extended from the borders of the Corinthian territory to the Pass of Thermopylæ. Ægina, which had, of course, sided with Sparta, was starved into submission, and was then admitted to capitulation only on condition of destroying its fortifications, surrendering its navy, and paying tribute as a dependent ally.

386. At this point in Grecian history Athens was at the summit of its power; at a height from which there was no variation, except towards decline. As a counterbalance, however, to the successes of this energetic people, they experienced a severe defeat in Egypt, whither they had sent a great armament to assist the natives in attempting to shake off the yoke of Persia. About the same time, the Lacedæmonians brought their domestic war to a close; the Helots and Messenians at Ithome capitulating on condition of being allowed to retire with their families from Peloponnesus. Though thus left untrammelled, the Lacedæmonians did not prosecute the war against Athens. They remained inactive for three years, and then concluded a truce for five years longer, which left the Athenians at liberty to prosecute their war against the Persians in Cyprus and Egypt. Here Cimon either died or was killed, but the Athenians concluded, on the whole, victoriously in these their last hostilities against Persia. A convention was entered into, in which the Great King on his part promised to leave the Asiatic Greeks on the coast untaxed and undisturbed, and to send no ships of war into the waters of the Ægæan. Athens, on her part, promised to forego all further aggressions against Cyprus, Phœnicia, Cilicia, and Egypt—a treaty which did little more than recognise the existing state of things.

387. Athens was now at peace, both at home and

abroad, with a great empire, a great fleet, a great accumulation of treasure, and the great Pericles as her leader. The common fund of her confederates, originally deposited at Delos, had been transferred to the Acropolis at Athens; the confederates themselves had been transformed into tributary subjects, Chios, Lesbos, and Samos alone retaining their original footing. Besides, she had acquired a great many new allies, some tributary and defenceless, like Ægina; some armed and free, like Chios; but all strangers to the confederacy of Delos, which passed insensibly into matter of history.

THE THIRTY YEARS' TRUCE—SPLENDOUR OF ATHENS.

388. It has been mentioned that the governments of the Bœotian, Phocian, and Locrian cities had been broken up by the Athenian conquerors, and the previous leaders banished. These exiles joining all their forces, and being aided by partisans in the interior, succeeded in taking possession of Orchomenus, Chæronea, and some other places in Bœotia; whereupon Tolmides undertook a rash and hasty march against them with an insufficient force, and was completely defeated.

389. The united exiles, emboldened by this success, proceeded similarly to enfranchise Phocis and Locris; after which they carried the flame of revolt into Eubœa. But a still more formidable danger appeared at home. A revolt had taken place among the Megarians also; the passes of Geranea were thrown open, which greatly altered the position of Athens, rendering its territory vulnerable on the land-side. The people were so disheartened by the series of misfortunes which had overtaken them thus rapidly and unexpectedly, that they were induced to accept an inglorious peace, the terms of which were, that Athens should altogether abandon Peloponnesus. The truce was concluded for thirty years from the beginning of 445 B.C.

390. This amnesty was not destined to last half that

time; but during the fourteen years which elapsed between its commencement and the breaking out of the Peloponnesian war, Athens enjoyed a high degree of prosperity. Her maritime empire was little disputed, and never with success; while her public treasures, arising chiefly from the contributions of her allies, had accumulated to a sum equal to above two millions sterling. As she did not deem herself accountable to those allies for the use made of this money, so long as she faithfully performed the implied condition of defending them against foreign enemies, a large sum was laid out in public works, both useful and decorative. A splendid arsenal and docks were constructed in Piræus; and the town of Piræus itself was laid out anew, with straight streets intersecting each other at right angles. Among the works at Athens, those most worthy of mention are the theatre called the Odeon, for musical and poetical exercises at the great Panathenaic festival; then the splendid temple of Minerva, called the Parthenon, adorned with a colossal statue of the goddess, 47 feet high, of ivory and gold, and other master-pieces of decorative sculpture and reliefs; lastly, the costly portals called propylæa, which adorned the entrance of the Acropolis, and through which the solemn processions, peculiar to some of the festivals, were to be conducted. Phidias, the celebrated sculptor, was the great director of the ornamental parts of these works; the architects of the Parthenon and other buildings laboured under his superintendence; and he had, besides, a school of pupils and subordinates, to whom he confided the mechanical part of his labours, while his own unrivalled chisel was the glory of the city. When we learn the impression which these works produced on spectators of a later age, we may judge how great was the effect upon the generation which saw them both begun and completed. For it would seem that the celerity with which these miracles of art rose into view, was the most remarkable circumstance connected with them; and that a sensation was produced throughout the whole of Greece, which was exactly what Pericles, the great originator of these works, had intended. In the year 480 B.C., Athens had been utterly ruined by the occupation of Xerxes; but ere the lapse of eight-and-forty years, her walls, docks, arsenals, temples, statues, paintings, had stamped her as the imperial city of Greece; the splendour of her outward appearance investing her with a moral ascendancy far beyond the range of her direct power. This imposing display appeared especially a singular contrast to the old-fashioned simplicity of Sparta, so lately the leading city of Hellas.

391. Several important colonial establishments were likewise founded during this period; chiefly Amphipolis, in Thrace, and Thurii, on the Tarentine coast of Italy, near the site of the ancient Sybaris.

392. The subject allies of Athens appear to have suffered little positive hardship from her supremacy. Doubtless, there was more or less dissatisfaction and uneasiness arising from that instinctive desire of autonomy which seems to have been inherent in every Greek with reference to his own city; and from the sense, too, that the condition of a subject ally of Athens was regarded as one of degradation by all the independent states of Hellas. The oligarchies in the various cities were indeed very generally desirous of shaking off the yoke, but the people were rarely willing to incur the risks, or make the sacrifices which the effort would have involved. How great those risks were, and how hopeless the effort of any single state, may be judged from the case of Samos.

393. This island appears to have been the most powerful of the allies of Athens, and one of the least dependent, standing on the same footing as Chios and Lesbos—that is, paying no tribute-money, but liable to furnish ships and men when called upon; and retaining, subject to this condition, its separate organisation, its oligarchical government, its fortifications, and its military force. In the sixth year of the truce (that is, 440–439 B.C.), a quarrel arose between the Samians and the Milesians, about a town which lay between their respective territories; and the Milesians being worsted, appealed to Athens. The Samians refused to plead their cause before Athens as an umpire; a manifestation of insubordination which the haughty city

proceeded to avenge. In vain the Samians implored the aid of the Spartan confederacy. It was decided by a majority of votes, that it would be a violation of the truce for either of the two great aggregate bodies to intermeddle with the other in its efforts to restrain or punish its own refractory members. The satrap of Sardis, however, lending his aid to the islanders, they were enabled to maintain a long and doubtful contest; but in the end Samos was conquered, disarmed, dismantled, reduced to the condition of a tributary, and obliged to make good all the expenses of the struggle.

OPENING OF THE PELOPONNESIAN WAR.

394. Corinth, as we have seen, had been maritime, commercial, and colonising from a very early period. She seems generally to have been on terms of perfect amity with all her colonies except Corcyra, where habitual ill-will had sometimes broken out into open war. One of these quarrels was destined to occasion extensive hostilities. The Corcyreans appealed to the Athenians, who, after hearing envoys on both sides, concluded a strictly defensive alliance with Corcyra, engaging to preserve her territory, if attacked, but not to assist in any aggression on Corinth, which would have been a manifest infringement of the truce.

395. A great naval battle soon followed—great from the extent of the armaments on both sides, albeit the tactics were not commensurate with the numbers. It was a fierce hand-to-hand combat between the troops on board each vessel, all being conducted upon the old system of Greek naval warfare, without any of the improvements which had been adopted by the Athenian navy during the last generation. When the day turned against the Corcyræans, and the Corinthians pressed their victory, the Athenians, who had hitherto only looked on, could no longer keep aloof, but attacked the pursuers in earnest, changed the face of affairs, and compelled the Corinthians to retreat in serious alarm. The latter carried off numerous prisoners, however, of whom the majority were

sold as slaves; while the rest were detained, and kindly treated, with the view of rendering them instruments against the island at a future day.

396. The Corinthians from this time considered the Thirty Years' Truce as broken, and an opportunity was soon found for them to aim a blow at Athens through one of her dependent allies. Potidæa, on the coast of Macedonia, a colony of Corinth, but a tributary of Athens, was instigated to revolt, under promise of aid from the Spartan confederacy. But the vigorous measures of Athens proved equal to the occasion; and after a complete victory over a Corinthian and Potidæan force outside the walls, the refractory city was closely blockaded. Its capture was now only a question of time; and it held out for two years. Meanwhile, the truce had been undeniably broken; and the opportunity which the Peloponnesians had so long desired for direct war with Athens was afforded.

397. The Corinthians, now exasperated against Athens, lost no time in rousing the Spartans, and inducing them to call an assembly of the confederates to allege their various wrongs, and consider whether Athens had not violated the truce. Besides the blockade of Potidæa, there was a complaint that, on a very slight pretext, the Megarians had been forbidden, on pain of death, to attempt trade, or even intercourse, with any port of the Athenian Empire; an exclusion utterly ruinous to their commerce. The Æginetans complained that Athens had withheld from them that autonomy to which they were entitled; and after all these and other grievances had been duly set forth, the Corinthians vehemently protested that if Sparta did not bestir herself against the common foe, they would seek other allies. The Athenian envoy implored them to adjust all differences by amicable arbitration, according to the provisions of the truce; but the assembly by a large majority decided on war.

398. No immediate steps, however, were taken by Sparta to carry this determination into effect—no formal declaration of war was made; but various propositions were sent to Athens, in which the demands were multiplied, and the grounds of quarrel enlarged. First, the

Athenians were required to banish the Alcmæonidæ, still supposed to be infected with the hereditary taint of the sacrilege of their ancestor Megacles, two centuries before. This was their plan for depriving the Athenians of the counsels of Pericles, whose mother belonged to that family. Then they were desired to withdraw their troops from Potidæa, to restore Ægina to its autonomy, and to repeal their decree of exclusion against Megara. Finally, they were required to leave all the Greeks independent.

399. The Athenians, by the advice of Pericles, conceded nothing to these demands. They reminded Sparta that she, too, had an amount of sacrilege uncleared, in the matter of the Helots at Cape Tænarum, and of Pausanias at Sparta. They would admit the Megarians to their harbours, only when Sparta discontinued her summary expulsions; they would leave the Grecian cities independent, if they were so when the truce was made; and, finally, they would not begin war, but would vigorously meet it if begun.

400. The Athenians were indeed exceedingly averse to a rupture; they had no hope of positive gain from it, and the certainty of immense loss and severe privation. They could, indeed, hold Peloponnesus under siege by means of their navy; but they had no means of repelling the immense land-force with which the enemy could invade and devastate their country; and this was a consideration the more painful, as many of the citizens resided permanently in the various demes of Attica, of which the farming operations, the comforts, and the ornaments, had been restored from the ruin of the Persian invasion, and brought to greater perfection than ever.

401. A few weeks passed in restricted and mistrustful intercourse, without any formal declaration of hostilities. The Thebans took advantage of this ambiguous interval to surprise and overpower the little town of Platæa in the night, and during the celebration of a religious festival, an oligarchical faction within the walls espousing their cause. The adventurous band which conducted this enterprise was but small, and a larger force was to join it at daybreak. This reinforcement was retarded by a heavy rain having swollen the Asopus; and ere it arrived,

the Platæans, becoming aware of the real numbers of the enemy, had in turn surprised the intruders, who were all either slain or captured ere the expected troops arrived.

402. Neither complaint nor discussion seems to have been thought of by either party with reference to the affair at Platæa; it was evident that the war was begun, and that the only thing to be thought of was the means of carrying it on. The Athenians had, for this purpose, a large military and naval force, and a great amount of accumulated treasure, notwithstanding the reduction it had suffered from the recent improvements in the city, and the operations at Potidæa. The Peloponnesian allies had few ships, few trained mariners, no funds, and little power of organisation or leadership, such as Athens boasted in the talents of Pericles; but they had an overwhelming and irresistible land-force; never had so powerful a body of confederates been brought together—not even to resist the progress of Xerxes. With this the Peloponnesian army, under the Spartan king Archidamus, undertook the invasion of Attica.

403. By the advice of Pericles, the Athenians confined themselves to purely defensive measures. They gathered within the walls all the country residents, with their movable property; conveyed the sheep and cattle to some of the neighbouring islands; and looked on, not without impatience and even exasperation, while the enemy laid waste the fertile plains around the city. When Archidamus had remained in the country thirty or forty days—long enough to exhaust his provisions, and to satisfy himself that the Athenians would not hazard a battle—he quitted Attica by way of Oropus, and entered Bœotia.

404. Meanwhile, the Athenian fleet sailed round Peloponnesus, ravaging the coasts, and enrolling some towns of more or less importance as members of the Athenian alliance. Another armament, after devastating the Locrian territories, proceeded to transfer the inhabitants of Ægina to the Peloponnesian shores; after which the island was made over to a body of Athenian cleruchs, or citizen-proprietors chosen by lot.

405. The Megarians, who had been likewise zealous in kindling the war, were destined next to experience the vengeance. Towards the end of September, the whole land-force of Athens marched into the Megarid; the territory was laid waste even to the city-walls; and for years afterwards, a similar destruction was inflicted at least once, often twice, every twelvemonth. Not merely were the field-crops and fruit-plantations destroyed, but even the garden-vegetables round the city were rooted up, the port of Nisæa being blockaded at the same time; so that the Megarians were reduced to the straits of a city under siege.

A NEW CALAMITY—THE PESTILENCE.

406. Notwithstanding the damage which had been mutually inflicted by the belligerent parties, nothing decisive had been accomplished on either side at the close of the first year of the war. A second devastation of Attica was, however, commenced in spring, when the Peloponnesian army carried the work of destruction east, west, and south over the whole territory. They found it, as before, deserted, the people having retired within the walls, adhering to the defensive policy recommended by Pericles, and now apparently convinced of its necessity.

407. But a new calamity diverted the attention of the Athenians from the ravages of the invader. An epidemic disease of the nature of eruptive typhoid fever, which had been raging for some time about the shores of the Mediterranean, broke out unexpectedly at Athens. Its progress was as rapid and fatal as its appearance had been sudden; and the extraordinary press of population within the city and long walls, was but too favourable to the contagion. This was further aggravated by the increasing heat of summer, and the mental depression of the people, arising from the destruction of their property in the country. A large proportion of the sufferers expired on the seventh or ninth day after the attack; others, surviving this period, sunk at a later stage under incurable diarrhœa; while in other cases, both these stages were survived, and

the distemper fixed itself permanently in some particular member of the body, which was rendered useless for life; or on the mind, occasioning a total loss of memory. The surgeons and physicians were completely at fault, no treatment appearing to produce any beneficial effect except in accidental cases, while charms and incantations were alike inefficacious. Among various causes assigned for the malady, the wrath of the gods, and especially of Apollo, was very generally believed in; prophets were accordingly consulted, and supplications, with solemn procession, were used at the temples—but all to no purpose.

408. When it was found that priest, prophet, and physician were alike powerless to retard the spread or mitigate the intensity of the disease, the people abandoned themselves to despair and demoralisation. The family sympathies, which at first prompted friends and relatives to minister to the sick, yielded to the desire of self-preservation; few except convalescents were found willing to tend the sufferers; many a patient was left to die alone and unheeded; and even the nearest relatives neglected those sepulchral duties to the dead which were above all others sacred in the eyes of a Greek. The dead and the dying lay piled upon one another in the public roads, and even in the temples; the dogs that devoured the unburied corpses died in consequence; and no vultures or other carrion-birds ever ventured near the spot. Those bodies which escaped entire neglect, were burned or buried with unseemly haste, and without the customary mourning. The restraints of law and of morals became relaxed amidst the total uncertainty of life; men embraced with avidity the immediate pleasures of sense, and eagerly grasped at such unlawful gains as could be made the means of procuring them, without a thought of honour or permanent advantage. Life and property were alike ephemeral; and every one was eager to snatch a moment of enjoyment, before falling a victim to the outstretched hand of destiny.

409. For three years, but with some intermission, Athens was desolated by this calamity, and the public loss was incalculable. No efforts of the enemy could have

done so much to ruin the state, or to bring the war to the termination they desired.

410. Shortly after the first appearance of this terrible malady, Pericles equipped a naval armament, and led it to the coasts of Peloponnesus; but unhappily the infection was not left behind, and it desolated the fleet as it had done the city. Meeting with some reinforcements, the expedition effected some ravages on the coast, and then proceeded to press the siege of Potidæa, which was still under blockade. But here the distemper assumed a more aggravated character than before, and spread from the new-comers to the troops they had found before the city, cutting off above a fourth part of the hoplites within forty days. In this melancholy condition, Pericles conducted the armament back to Athens, leaving the reduction, as before, to the slow process of blockade.

411. On his return, he found the people exasperated by the ravages of disease within the city, and of the enemy without. They denounced him as the cause of all that they were enduring; and either with or without his consent, they sent envoys to Sparta to negotiate for peace. But the Spartans turned a deaf ear to the proposal, and this humiliating disappointment rendered the Athenians still more furious against Pericles. His political enemies, who had again and again endeavoured to impeach his character, seized the opportunity of the prevalent irritation to bring against him a public charge of pecuniary malversation. This time they carried their point, and the veteran statesman was both fined and deposed from his office as strategus or general. A reaction, however, soon took place in the feelings of the people, and Pericles was not only re-elected, but fully reinstated in public confidence. It was with difficulty, however, that he was persuaded to resume the direction of affairs, being bowed down and almost broken-hearted by domestic calamity. The prevailing epidemic had carried off his elder son, his sister, several other relations, and his best political friends; and now the death of his favourite son Paralus left him without any legitimate heir, and his house without a representative to administer the sacred family rites.

Everything was done, however, to meet the case, and he was even permitted to legitimatise one of his natural sons, and inscribe his name in his own gens and phratry. Pericles lived about a year after this, maintaining his influence as long as his health permitted, and sinking at last under the wasting of lingering fever. His political career had been long beyond all parallel in the history of Athens, reaching to almost forty years, during which his influence had been continually on the increase.

412. The military operations of Athens languished under the depression of disease and death; nor did their enemies make much progress, though their efforts were more vigorous. They were too inferior in maritime force to undertake any formal expedition against Athens; but their single privateers did considerable injury, not only to her commerce, but to that of neutral cities, whose merchant-vessels they captured without scruple, putting the crews to death. An opportunity of retaliation soon occurred. A party of Peloponnesian envoys, on their way to the Persian court, were induced by Aristæus, the Corinthian general, to visit the Thracian king Sitalces, who was a stanch friend of the Athenians, and to endeavour to detach him from that alliance. But Sitalces seized the whole party, and sent them to Athens, where they were put to death without even the form of trial, and their bodies thrown into the clefts of the rocks, after the manner in which the Lacedæmonians had treated their marine prisoners.

413. After the death of Aristæus, Potidæa was left to its fate; and after unheard-of sufferings during a blockade of two years, it was admitted to terms of capitulation. The whole population, with their Corinthian allies, were permitted to retire unmolested, and a body of a thousand colonists was sent from Athens to occupy their places.

PROGRESS OF THE PELOPONNESIAN WAR.

414. At the close of the second year of the war, nothing decisive had been effected; and the Peloponnesians, in commencing the third campaign, did not repeat their

march into Attica, but devoted their force to espouse the Theban quarrel against Platæa. Marching against this city with a large army, Archidamus summoned it to surrender, and offered to spare it, if it would give up its alliance with Athens, and remain neutral. This the Platæans alleged they could not do without the consent of the Athenians, in whose city their wives and families were at present sheltered. It was then suggested that they should hand over their town and territory for the time being to the Lacedæmonians, who would hold these possessions in trust, and restore them uninjured at the termination of the war. But the Platæans finally resolved, at all hazards, to maintain their union with Athens; and Archidamus, invoking the immortal gods to witness that he was acting righteously, commenced the siege with vigour.

415. The processes described in history appear to us sufficiently rude: the besiegers striving to raise an earthen mound against the wall, by way of scaling it, in one place, and driving battering-rams against it, to shatter it, in another; the besieged undermining the mound by subterranean working, and catching the battering-engines with ropes, to divert their aim; or letting heavy beams fall upon them, to break them in their approach. After three months spent in useless operations, Archidamus resorted to the tedious and costly process of blockade and famine. A double wall of circumvallation was completed in September, and a sufficient force was left to maintain it.

416. In the fourth year of the war, Archidamus again invaded and ravaged Attica, and, as on the former occasions, met with no serious resistance. The Athenians seem to have made up their minds to this continually recurring damage; but while the devastation was going on, they received intelligence of a far more distressing event—the revolt of Mytilene, and of the greater part of Lesbos. It will be remembered that Lesbos, like Chios, had remained upon that footing of equal alliance which had at first been common to all the members of the confederacy of Delos. Mytilene paid no tribute to Athens, but was held bound to furnish armed ships in case of need; it

retained its fortifications, its navy, and its oligarchical government, with full power of administering all its own internal affairs. It was thus all but independent, and so powerful that the Athenians, in their present depressed condition, were exceedingly unwilling to believe the intelligence of its revolt. After sending a friendly message in vain, they determined on stronger measures; and Clippides, who had a fleet ready to start for Peloponnesus, was ordered to change his destination, and proceed forthwith to Mytilene. A reinforcement, with Paches as commander, speedily followed, and the Athenian armament was soon strong enough to surround the city with a wall of circumvallation, blockading it by land as well as sea.

417. The Mytileneans had sent envoys to Sparta, who arrived a little before the great festival at Olympia, and were invited to proceed thither, and plead their cause before all the members of the confederacy there assembled. Their representations, on this occasion, proved completely satisfactory; the Lesbians were declared members of the Peloponnesian alliance, and forty triremes, under Alcidas, were sent for the relief of Mytilene.

418. Meanwhile, Salæthus, a Spartan envoy, contrived to land on the west coast of Lesbos, and encouraged the Mytileneans to hold out, assuring them of the approaching succours; but ere these appeared, the provisions were exhausted. As a last resource, the determination was taken to make a desperate effort against the Athenian blockade; and for this purpose the common people were invested with the full panoply of heavy-armed soldiers. But no sooner did the Mytilenean demos find themselves strengthened and ennobled by the possession of armour, than they refused obedience to the order for sallying forth. They declared that they had no quarrel with Athens— that the revolt had been the work of the oligarchy, for their own selfish ends—and that they would themselves negotiate for a surrender. The rulers thought fit to anticipate this movement by offering capitulation; and it was agreed that the city should surrender, but that its fate and that of its population should be suspended till their

cause should be heard at Athens. At this juncture Alcidas with his fleet appeared on the coast of Ionia; but hearing that the besieged town had capitulated, he made no attempt to interfere, and returned to Peloponnesus.

419. The Athenians were now to decide the fate of these unfortunates, and they entered on the discussion in an extremely wrathful temper. There was no difference of opinion about Salæthus—he was to be put to death at once; but what to do with Mytilene and its inhabitants was a point to be argued. Cleon, a tradesman, represented as a low-born brawler, who terrified his opponents by the loudness of his vociferations and the violence of his gestures, took a leading part in this debate. He proposed that all the male population of military age should be destroyed, and the women and children sold into slavery—the harshest measure tolerated by the customs of war in those days. The decree was passed, and a trireme despatched to put it in execution. But ere the morning, the Athenians had cooled and repented; another assembly was convened, and, despite the perseverance of Cleon, the sentence was recalled. A second trireme was put to sea, to arrest, if possible, the orders of the first, which had a start of twenty-four hours. An intensity of effort, unparalleled in the history of Athenian seamanship, was put forth on the occasion, the oar never resting for a moment till Mytilene was reached; and, after all, it was no more than in time, for the order of death was in the hands of Paches, and his measures were preparing for execution. The general body of the people were thus delivered; but the prisoners sent to Athens as the active revolters were slain; the fortifications of the city were destroyed; the ships of war were seized; and the whole island, except Methymna, which had remained faithful, was newly appropriated. It was divided into 3000 lots, of which 300 were consecrated to the gods, and the remainder assigned to Athenians cleruchs, under whom the Lesbians remained as cultivating tenants.

420. As an appendix to the fate of Mytilene, must be added that of Paches. He had taken possession for

himself of two beautiful women of Mytilene, after slaying their husbands; and when they repaired to Athens, and their case was brought before the dicastery, the guilty commander fell upon his own sword in the open court, not waiting for its sentence.

SURRENDER OF PLATÆA.

421. The surrender of Platæa to the Lacedæmonians occurred soon after that of Mytilene to the Athenians. Here, too, there had been a two years' blockade; but when it had been suffered above a year, about half of the garrison had made a secret exit on a dark December night, amidst rain, and sleet, and storm. Their effort had been successful, and they had reached the friendly gates of Athens in safety. This had made the provisions last longer for the rest; but at the end of another year they were exhausted, and the defenders were on the point of starvation. The Lacedæmonian general, having orders not to go in by storm, invited them to make a voluntary surrender, and submit to the Lacedæmonians as judges; adding the promise that none should be punished unjustly. They surrendered accordingly; and after a few days, there came five persons from Sparta to sit in judgment on their case. The 200 Platæans who formed the remnant of the garrison, with twenty-five Athenians, were put on their trial; but instead of any accusation being preferred against them, they were merely asked one by one whether they had rendered any service to the Lacedæmonians or their allies during the present war. It was to no purpose that the unhappy men remonstrated against this as a mockery of trial and judgment; that they appealed to the Hellenic sympathies of the Spartans; adverted to the Persian war, in which the loyalty of Platæa to the Hellenic cause was no less marked than the treachery of Thebes; and reminded their judges of the victory then gained upon this soil, whereby it had become hallowed under the promises of Pausanias, and solemn appeals to the local gods. The Thebans, in reply, represented that *the* proposals and protestations made before the siege

began, exonerated them from all obligation to regard the sanctity of the place. The question before put was again repeated to each one individually, and on his replying in the negative, he was led away to death. The women were sold as slaves; and the place handed over to the Thebans, who could be satisfied with nothing less than blotting its name from the muster-roll of Hellas. They pulled down the buildings, and used the materials to build an immense barrack about the temple of Juno, 200 feet in every direction, for the accommodation of worshippers. The surrounding territory was let out for ten years to farmers and graziers, who were also permitted to lodge in the barrack. The little city of Platæa, interesting from its patriotism towards Hellas, from its grateful attachment to Athens as its protecting ally, and from its unmerited sufferings in consequence—had now no existence except in the persons of the 200 of its citizens harboured at Athens.

422. At the island of Corcyra, there were scenes still more revolting. It has been mentioned, that in the year before the Peloponnesian war, the Corinthians had taken captive 250 Corcyræans, of the highest rank, and treated them with kindness. These they now sent home again nominally under a ransom of 800 talents, but really with the understanding, that the only recompense desired was, that they should induce their fellow-citizens to withdraw from the Athenian alliance. To this object, accordingly, the liberated oligarchs applied themselves; and when fair means proved unavailing, they resorted to foul. A fearful struggle ensued between them and the demos; first one party, then the other had the upper hand, according as the succours from Sparta or Athens proved most effective. But the appearance of fire-signals, announcing large reinforcements from Athens, induced Alcidas to make the best of his way home, leaving the Corcyræan oligarchs to their fate.

423. A cruel fate it was. The demos, suddenly passing from helpless alarm to a sense of irresistible mastery, gave way to ungovernable revenge. Five hundred of the opposite party contrived to escape to the mainland, but all

that could not or did not flee, were killed wherever they were found. Such was the ferocity of the hour, that in one case a father slew his own son ; and as the flood-gates were open, many private feuds were settled by assassination, under pretence of public vengeance. The escaped oligarchs long harassed the island by predatory incursions, and at length fortified for themselves a position on the mountain called Istone, not far from the city, to carry on this annoyance with greater effect.

SPHACTERIA.

424. In the seventh year, the Lacedæmonian army renewed its ravages in Attica, but was recalled by the intelligence that the Athenians had taken up a 425 B.C. military position at Pylos, in Messenia. It appears that Demosthenes, having a kind of roving commission to make descents on the Peloponnesian coasts, had been driven by a storm on the coast of Pylos, an uninhabited promontory overhanging what is now called the Bay of Navarino, a natural harbour, protected by the untenanted islet of Sphacteria. While the fleet was detained by the weather, the soldiers were seized with the spontaneous desire of making a fort; and though without the usual tools and appliances, they completed it in a rough way. Demosthenes, with a small force, remained to garrison it, while the rest of the fleet proceeded to Corcyra, where their assistance was needed. The contending forces on both sides presently concentrated here. The Lacedæmonians, now commanded by Brasidas, a brave and able leader, attacked the fort with vigour; while Demosthenes, reinforced by the return of his fleet, and succours from other allies, maintained his position, and completely defeated the enemy in the bay. A more important advantage was, that a large body of Lacedæmonian hoplites, who occupied the island 420 B.C. of Sphacteria, were now cut off from the mainland, while the Athenians, sailing round, regarded them already as prisoners. The Lacedæmonians on the mainland were deeply distressed, and begged for an armistice, that they *might* negotiate with Athens for peace. It was granted,

on condition that the Lacedæmonian vessels in the harbour and ports should be meanwhile surrendered, and that no hostilities should be attempted by land or by sea till the envoys should return. The Athenians, on their part, engaged to convey them to and from Athens; to abstain from hostilities; and to allow and superintend the transmission of a certain allowance of food daily to the hoplites and their attendant Helots.

425. The proposition of the envoys was in substance—Give up to us the men in the island, and accept in exchange peace and alliance with Sparta; but Athens, surprised to see the Lacedæmonians bearing the olive-branch in an attitude of humiliation, tossed her haughty head in the confidence that she might make her own terms for these prisoners. Cleon became the organ of this sentiment, and insisted that Athens should now demand back what she had been forced by temporary misfortune to yield at the Thirty Years' Truce—Nisæa, Pagæ, Trœzen, and Achaia. To this the envoys would not consent—could not, indeed—for much of what was asked was not now in the power of Sparta; and they were sent back without any result. The armistice terminated immediately on their return to Pylos; the Athenians found a pretext for refusing to restore their triremes, and hostilities were resumed with energy. The land-army of Sparta began to attack the fortifications of Pylos, while the navy of Athens prosecuted the blockade of Sphacteria. This, however, was soon found to be fraught with more difficulty and privation to the besiegers than to the besieged. They were distressed for want of water; and their provisions were running short; while, in spite of all their vigilance, clandestine supplies were conveyed to the island by swimmers from the adjacent shore, or by merchant-vessels from various ports. Week after week passed without any symptoms of surrender; and Demosthenes, doubting the possibility of maintaining the blockade, sent envoys to Athens, to request such reinforcements as would enable him to carry the place by force.

426. Great was the mortification of Athens when this embassy arrived, for it was expected that Sphacteria had

surrendered long before. Cleon pointed reproachfully at Nicias, who was then strategus, and said, that if the generals were *men*, it would be easy, with a proper force, to sail, and at once take the soldiers in the island. 'This, at least,' added he, 'is what I would do if I were strategus.' There was at once a murmuring reply in the assembly of 'Why should he not?' Nicias, taking up this murmur, urged him to undertake the enterprise, and offered to place at his disposal whatever part of the military force he required. The more Cleon strove to evade the task, the louder became the cry that he should undertake it; his political enemies probably hoping to entangle him in his own net, and his friends believing that he could accomplish the matter in hand. When Cleon saw there was no possibility of receding, he assumed a resolute tone, and declared, that without any of the hoplites from the regular muster-roll, but only the Lemnians and Imbrians now at hand, with some peltasts and bowmen, he would engage either to kill the Lacedæmonians in the island, or bring them prisoners to Athens; and this within twenty days. The Athenians laughed at what was called his looseness of tongue; but he fulfilled his boast to the letter.

427. On joining Demosthenes, Cleon found that he had already made every preparation for the attack, and that the soldiers were eager to engage in it. An accidental conflagration of the trees on the island, under the influence of a strong wind, was highly favourable to the assault, as the garrison could now be surveyed, and plans laid with certainty. A surrender having been refused, the two generals embarked their hoplites by night, and ere daybreak, surprised and slew the advanced-guard of the Lacedæmonians ere they were awake. The lighter troops landed early in the morning, and poured forth their missile weapons as they advanced. Then closing nearer with arrows, javelins, and stones, they rent the air with shouts, that rendered the Lacedæmonian word of command inaudible. The Lycurgean drill had made no provision for this mode of warfare; the Lacedæmonians had no missile weapons; and the efforts of hoplites, heavily armed

with spear and shield, to destroy or even reach their nimble assailants, proved utterly abortive.

428. At length the Lacedæmonian commander gave orders to close the ranks, and retreat to the last redoubt at the extremity of the island, where the rocky heights protected their flank and rear. Demosthenes and Cleon, perceiving that here the light troops were less serviceable, brought up their hoplites to a closer struggle. Meanwhile, a detachment of light troops and bowmen clambered up the cliffs in the rear, and the Lacedæmonians found themselves, as at Thermopylæ, between two enemies, without hope of escape. A few moments more, and they would all have been slain; but the Athenian generals invited them to surrender, to deliver up their arms, and place themselves at the disposal of Athens. Most of them signified compliance forthwith, by dropping their shields and waving both hands over their heads. A conference was entered into; the Lacedæmonian authorities on the mainland declined advising their unfortunate friends as to how they should act; and they made a formal surrender. Of the 292 that thus became prisoners of war, 120 were native Spartans of high families.

429. When the tidings spread that these had surrendered, the astonishment throughout Greece was prodigious and universal; for the deep-struck impression of Thermopylæ was, that they would perish amidst their foes, but would never survive as captives. This impression henceforth was sensibly enfeebled.

430. The assault of Sphacteria is reckoned one of the best specimens of able generalship in the whole of this war, distinguished by the skilful employment of different kinds of troops, and by the care to save the lives of the assailants. The praise of it belongs chiefly to Demosthenes, though Cleon deservedly shared it with him. The return of the generals to Athens within the twenty days was a most exhilarating event, and it was resolved to keep the prisoners as a guarantee against the invasion of Attica, till the settlement of a peace.

431. A considerable part of the fleet which had been engaged at Sphacteria, sailed forward to Corcyra, where

the democracy had been suffering severely from the party upon Mount Istone. This post was stormed, and its garrison forced to surrender, only stipulating for being sent to Athens, and left to the discretion of its citizens. Eurymedon, assenting to these terms, deposited the disarmed prisoners in the islet of Ptychia, till it should be convenient for him to accompany them to Athens; and they were warned that if one of them attempted to escape, the terms of capitulation should be no longer binding. And now the leading men at Corcyra sent false emissaries, under the guise of friendship, to the unfortunate prisoners, assuring them that, notwithstanding the convention, they were to be handed over to the vengeance of their domestic enemies, and inviting them to escape in a boat prepared for the purpose. Some of them yielded; the boat was seized in the act of escaping, and the whole body of the prisoners were handed over to the Corcyræans. They were shut up together in a large building, from which they were brought out in companies of twenty at a time, chained together in couples, and compelled to march between two lines of hoplites, who struck and pierced them till they perished. After three successive companies had been thus destroyed, those left behind ascertained what had passed, and refused either to quit the building or let any one enter it. Whereupon an aperture was made in the roof; showers of tiles and arrows were poured upon them; and the prisoners, yielding to despair, assisted in the work of their own destruction. Before morning, the whole number of these wretched men, probably not fewer than 300, had perished. The women who had been found with them at Istone were sold as slaves.

FROM THE EIGHTH TILL THE ELEVENTH YEAR OF THE WAR—THE HELOTS—BRASIDAS—DELIUM—AMPHIPOLIS—PEACE OF NICIAS.

432. The advantage which the Athenians had gained by the capture of Sphacteria, with its prisoners and the Lacedæmonian fleet, stimulated them to more ambitious operations,

having for their object the recovery of their ascendancy in Megara and Bœotia. Their first enterprise was against the Island of Cythera, important as the only accessible portion of the generally inhospitable coast of Laconia. Its inhabitants speedily surrendered; a few were removed as prisoners, and afterwards distributed for safe custody among the dependent islands; but the remainder were enrolled as tributary allies, under the care of an Athenian garrison.

433. The occupation of Cythera and Pylos by Athenian garrisons produced the greatest alarm at Sparta: especially it was feared that these forts might prove rallying-points for the Helots, whose fear of the power of their masters was now greatly diminished. The measures of precaution which it was thought necessary to take, must be mentioned as an example of singular refinement in fraud and cruelty. In order to single out the most valiant and high-spirited of these bondsmen, the ephors made proclamation that those Helots who considered themselves to have deserved liberty by their services in the war, might present themselves and claim it. A large number availed themselves of the invitation—notably perhaps those who had run serious risks in conveying provisions to the blockaded soldiers at Sphacteria, during the preceding summer. Their claims were carefully examined, and 2000 were selected as worthy of emancipation, which was accordingly bestowed upon them with the usual public solemnities of crowning with garlands and marching in procession to the temples. But presently every one of these enfranchised Helots was made away with, no one knew how. A stratagem so perfidious and murderous stands without parallel in Grecian history.

434. While the Lacedæmonians were in this state, there arose for their help one of those remarkable men so often called forth by the difficulties of the times. This was Brasidas, a man bold in action, fertile in resource, and rapid in movement, possessing in a singular degree the power of stimulating the minds of his troops, and at the same time commanding universal confidence by his incorruptible integrity and good faith. He had already

displayed considerable personal valour, but had never occupied a position of command till now, when, at the solicitation of the Macedonians and Thracians, he was sent to aid their efforts against the power of Athens.

435. If the Athenians had known of the expedition of Brasidas, they might easily have prevented him from making his way into Thrace; but they were wholly occupied with their own plans and prospects of conquest.

436. The whole military population of Athens, including citizens, metics, and even non-resident strangers accidentally found there, were marched into Bœotia, under Hippocrates, and Demosthenes, leaving only a sufficient guard to protect the city. They seized upon the Bœotian Delium, or temple of Apollo, which was strongly situated in a border territory. Setting all hands to work, they fortified it with great rapidity, using the vines and vine-props of the sacred precincts to form their palisading; and this being accomplished, the great mass returned home again, leaving Hippocrates to organise a garrison and issue his final orders for the maintenance of the place. But, meanwhile, the Bœotians had collected their forces, and they now overtook the retreating army, which, after a severe conflict, was broken, dispersed, and put to flight—Hippocrates, with nearly 1000 hoplites, being slain. The garrison at Delium was next attacked; and by the construction of a peculiar piece of fire mechanism, the wooden palisading was set in flames, and the place was easily mastered.

437. Among those who were personally engaged in the battle of Delium, were two men who afterwards made a conspicuous figure at Athens—Socrates, the philosopher, and Alcibiades. Socrates was one of the few hoplites who kept their arms in the retreat, and maintained so firm a demeanour, that the pursuing cavalry found it dangerous to meddle with them, and turned to easier prey in the numbers who flung away their weapons and took to flight. Alcibiades served in the cavalry, and assisted to protect these hoplites in their retreat.

438. The result of this expedition proved a fatal discouragement to the hopes which had previously been

entertained at Athens. But yet more severe disasters attended their arms in Thrace. Brasidas found the governor and citizens of Amphipolis quite unprepared to meet him, and the surrounding territory occupied by residents with their families. After seizing a number of these out-citizens, as a means of working upon those within the walls, he sent proposals for capitulation on the most favourable terms; which being accepted, the city opened its gates. The loss of Amphipolis was the most serious and irreparable that Athens had yet sustained; and the generals Eucles and Thucydides, who, it was alleged, might have saved it by timely precaution, were condemned to banishment. During this exile, which lasted twenty years, Thucydides visited the greater part of Greece, and penned the history on account of which posterity rejoices in the sentence which to himself was but sorrow and disgrace.

439. The capture of Amphipolis, including as it did the possession of the bridge over the Strymon, rendered even the eastern allies of Athens approachable by land. The event occasioned a prodigious sensation throughout Greece, for now a certain insecurity attached to the whole empire of Athens; it was impossible to say which of her subject-allies would next revolt and find assistance from the formidable Brasidas. As he habitually abstained from party-jobbing and cruelty, and from meddling with the internal government of the various cities which he liberated from Athenian bondage, all eyes were turned instinctively towards him; and then his unexampled success put the crown on his talents and virtues, making him an object of universal confidence. So much was now expected from him, so little feared from Athens, that on all hands the subject-allies of that city were impatient for revolt, and transmitted solicitations to Brasidas accordingly.

440. Thus the year closed amid humiliations all the more painful to Athens in contrast with the glowing hopes which had prevailed at its opening; while Brasidas was employing the winter in setting in order the acquisitions already made, and laying plans for further conquests in the spring.

441. The Athenians, on their part, were in positive alarm; and regarding a truce as the only hope of arresting the victorious career of Brasidas, they sent to Sparta, to propose a cessation of hostilities for one year, which was to be employed in settling the conditions of a permanent treaty. This was concluded early in the ninth year of the war; but before it could be made known in Thrace, Scione had revolted to Brasidas; and, by a kind of mutual acquiescence, the war continued in Thrace, while the truce was everywhere else observed. Thus Athens obtained no benefit from the armistice in the quarter where she needed it most, and no progress was made in negotiating for a permanent peace.

442. Cleon and his party were eager for a vigorous prosecution of the war, and especially for making an attempt to recover Amphipolis; while Nicias, who was for peace, gladly transferred to him the command of the expedition which was decided on. Cleon accordingly proceeded to Amphipolis, near which he remained some time, waiting for expected reinforcements. Ascending an eminence near the city to reconnoitre, he was surprised to perceive no appearance of stir or preparation for defence; and believing that there was no enemy prepared to fight, he allowed his men to relax their order, and saunter close about the walls. Presently being warned that there was a sound of mustering troops, he ordered an immediate retreat, believing that he should be quite out of reach before the enemy's force could be organised. But Brasidas had been watching his movements, and availed himself of his false security to prepare for a sally and pursuit. This was executed with such rapidity, that the Athenians were taken completely unawares. Cleon lost his presence of mind, and fled at once, but was overtaken and slain; a similar panic seized his troops, the right wing only offering any determined resistance. So admirably had this movement been conducted, that only seven perished on the side of the victors; but among these was the gallant Brasidas himself, who received a mortal wound, and lived only long enough to learn the success of his exploit.

443. Bitter, indeed, was the sorrow which this event occasioned at Amphipolis. The people, now burning with hatred towards Athens, destroyed the tomb of the Athenian founder of their city, demolished the buildings connected with it, and erased every other visible memento of his name; proclaiming Brasidas their œcist, and consecrating the space in front of his tomb as the great agora of their city. As œcist, or 'founder,' he was henceforth entitled to receive heroic worship, with annual sacrifices and games in honour of his memory.

444. The death of Brasidas converted the defeat of the Athenians into a victory in effect; for there was no man in Sparta that even nearly resembled him, either as a skilful general or a conciliating politician. There was none who could succeed him in the confidence of the Athenian allies in Thrace, or could prosecute the enterprises which he had commenced. The peace-party, under the auspices of Nicias and Laches, being now relieved both from his aggressions and from the belligerent counsels of Cleon, resumed their negotiations with Sparta; and after several debates, it was agreed to make peace on the principle that each party should surrender what it had acquired in the war, excepting those towns which had voluntarily capitulated. By this arrangement, the Athenians could not recover Platæa, but they retained Nisæa, the harbour of Megara. The Lacedæmonians engaged to restore Amphipolis and Panactum, and to relinquish all connection with the revolted allies of Athens in Thrace. The Athenians, on their part, were to restore Cythera, and other acquisitions; the captives were to be released on both sides; and provision was made by special articles, that the autonomy of the Delphian Temple should be maintained, and that all Greeks should have free access by land and sea to the sacred pan-hellenic festivals. This treaty, known as the Peace of Nicias, was concluded and sworn to early in the eleventh year of the war.

ELEVENTH AND FOLLOWING YEARS OF THE WAR—ALCIBIADES.

445. Lots were now drawn to determine whether Sparta or Athens should be the first to make the cessions agreed on; and Athens having drawn the favourable lot, the Spartans began their compliance by releasing their prisoners. They likewise sent ambassadors to the Thracian towns to proclaim the peace, and enforce its observance; especially directing Clearidas, the commander of their forces at Amphipolis, to surrender that town to the Athenians. But the envoys met with the most unanimous and strenuous opposition, both in Amphipolis and out of it; and Clearidas declared, that his force was insufficient to effect the surrender in opposition to the inhabitants; so that all Sparta could do was to order her warriors home.

446. The Spartans were thus placed in a position of serious embarrassment; for, not having fulfilled their part of the treaty, they could not expect the Athenians to execute theirs, and they were likely both to lose their good character and the advantages they had stipulated for. In this dilemma, they determined to enter into closer and separate relations with Athens, at the risk of offending their other allies. Accordingly, a treaty, not merely of peace, but of defensive alliance, was contracted between the two hitherto hostile states for fifty years; each party pledging itself to assist in repelling any invasion of the other's territory; the Athenians especially engaging to aid in repressing any rising of the Helots in Laconia. The treaty was to be inscribed on two columns—one set up in the temple of Apollo at Amyclæ, the other in that of Minerva in the Athenian Acropolis. All the Lacedæmonian captives at Athens were now released; so that Sparta obtained the chief object of her negotiations; while Athens relinquished for mere promises that for which she might have demanded almost anything she chose.

447. The Peloponnesian confederacy was completely unhinged by these arrangements; and the recusants

began to turn their attention to a new leader. Argos had maintained a strict neutrality during the war; her truce with Sparta was expiring, and she was free to start again with her old pretensions, backed by the wealth, power, and population which she had been gradually accumulating during the time that the other states were exhausting themselves by their mutual struggles. The Corinthians invited a congress of Peloponnesian malcontents to Corinth; and a new league was formed, including Argos, Corinth, Elis, and Mantinea. But all these political relations were as yet provisional and undetermined; and the alliance between Athens and Sparta was in a most unsatisfactory state. No vigorous effort had been made to restore to Athens her lost dependencies; and a general feeling prevailed that Sparta had acted with selfish dishonesty, securing her own ends, and leaving the Athenians to obtain as they could the restoration of Amphipolis and other revolted cities.

448. It was at this time, and as the organ of this feeling, that Alcibiades first took a prominent part in Athenian politics. He was little more than thirty years of age, but of an ancient and wealthy family; moreover, endued with singular beauty of person, courtly manners, and the more substantial qualities of bravery in the field and capacity for command. With such advantages, he easily attained a conspicuous position, notwithstanding his want of moral worth; and though the extravagance and unlawfulness of many of his acts excited the fears of the more thoughtful, yet the people in general continued to humour him, verifying the saying of one, that if they chose to keep a lion's whelp in their city, they must submit to his behaviour. At an early age, he is said to have imbibed a passion for distinction from the study of Homer. As he approached to manhood, he won the attachment of Socrates, who lost no opportunity of inculcating such salutary lessons as he might without offending the pride of a spoiled youth, looking forward to the celebrity of public life. When Alcibiades first put himself forward as a party-leader, which was shortly before the Peace of Nicias,

he appeared as a partisan of oligarchical and philo-Laconian sentiment. He not only advocated the peace with Sparta and the restoration of her captives, but tendered her his services as an agent for carrying these measures at Athens. But the authorities at Sparta spurned the idea of confiding important political interests to a youth, known chiefly for his ostentation, profligacy, and insolence; and Alcibiades, deeply offended, threw himself, with all his energies, into the anti-Laconian party. The opportunity was favourable; as the death of Cleon had left this party without a leader, and the conduct of the Spartans in delaying the restitutions due to Athens, gave ample pretext for a change of tone. He now denounced them as deceivers, who had abused the generous confidence of Athens; and he advised his fellow-citizens to form an alliance with Argos.   420 B.C.

Sparta, after turning a deaf ear to repeated remonstrances, was now seriously alarmed, and sent three envoys to Athens to expostulate against this step, and prevent it, by engaging to take whatever measures were deemed obligatory upon her for the satisfaction of Athens. The envoys being introduced first to the senate, explained that they had come with full powers to settle all matters to the satisfaction of the Athenians. A day was appointed for them to have an audience before the public assembly. But Alcibiades, obtaining a secret interview with them on the previous evening, gave them counsel to the ruin of their credit. Professing himself a warm friend of their mission, he told them that they would find the public assembly turbulent and clamorous; and that if they proclaimed themselves as invested with full powers of settlement, they would be urged to make unreasonable concessions. He advised them, therefore, to declare that they had come merely to explain, discuss, and report matters; thus only, he intimated, would their explanations be heard with temper; and he pledged himself to second them with all his might, if they followed his counsel. The next day, when the assembly met, and the envoys were introduced, Alcibiades asked them in the blandest manner to state the extent of their powers. On their answering that they had brought no authority to conclude matters, but had only come to explain and discuss, the wrath of the people was unbounded; and those who had heard their previous declaration, could scarcely believe in the truth of what they heard. There was a unanimous burst of indignation against the faithlessness and duplicity of Sparta, in never saying the same thing two days in succession. Alcibiades was the loudest in his invectives; and he found no difficulty in persuading the people to leave Sparta to herself, and conclude an alliance with Argos. This, one of the first acts of his public life, affords a fair specimen of that shameless contempt for good faith which characterised him throughout.

449. After giving Sparta yet another chance of redeeming her character, Athens concluded a treaty for a hundred years with Argos, Mantinea, and Elis; but without Corinth, which refused to join. The words of the treaty were to be engraved on four stone pillars; one for each of the cities, and on a brass one to be erected at Olympia.

450. The Olympic festival, which took place a few weeks after this treaty, was the first that had occurred since the conclusion of the peace, the leading clause of which expressly guaranteed to all Greeks the liberty of access to the great pan-hellenic temples. For eleven years, Athens, with all her numerous allies, had been excluded from sending their Theory or sacred legation to the games; but now the Elean heralds again trod the soil of Attica, and the expected Athenian visit excited unusual interest. Alcibiades took care to confound those who surmised his native city would make but a poor figure, impoverished as she must be by the long war. He had already signalised himself in the local festivals and liturgies of Athens, and now made a display more imposing than had ever appeared before. The Athenian body, of which he was a member, was equipped with the amplest display of golden ewers, censers, and other accessories for sacrifice and procession. At the games, he appeared as competitor at his own cost, with seven chariots for racing, each with a team of four horses. One of his chariots gained a first, and another a second prize; so that Alcibiades was

twice proclaimed by the herald, and twice crowned with a garland from the sacred olive-tree. Nor was this all. Besides the handsome tent provided by the Athenians for their countrymen, Alcibiades had a separate one fitted up in the most splendid manner, for a public banquet to celebrate his triumph.

451. This festival was distinguished by a still more striking novelty—the exclusion of the Lacedæmonians, who had no sacred legation or any recognised place on the ground. This arose from the new political relations of the Eleans, who were the privileged administrators of the festival, and who alleged that the Spartans had been guilty of a sin against the majesty of Jove, by invading their territory after the proclamation of the Olympic truce. Connected as the Spartans were with Olympia, by an ancient and peculiar tie, which had never yet been broken, the affront of this interdict was extreme; and the comparative degradation into which they had fallen was marked in the presence of assembled Greece.

452. The new alliance which the Athenians had contracted, made a vigorous demonstration in the ensuing spring. They were persuaded by 419 B.C. Alcibiades to let Thrace alone for the present, and seek to strengthen themselves by force of arms in the interior of Peloponnesus. Alcibiades commanded this expedition in person, while the Spartan forces were headed by their king, Agis. The crowning conflict of this campaign was a battle at Mantinea, in which the Spartans gained a decisive victory. This event at once wiped out the stain upon the honour of the Spartan arms, and restored her to her old position of military pre-eminence in the eyes of Greece. It also put an end to the political speculations of Alcibiades in Peloponnesus; but it led to a struggle, with various success, for the alliance of Argos; the oligarchs of that city seeking a union with Sparta, while the democracy invited the assistance of Athens. The details of these squabbles possess little interest; and we hasten to notice an expedition which changed the whole face of the war.

THE SYRACUSAN EXPEDITION.

453. The feuds between Greek and Greek, kindled by the Peloponnesian war, had extended to the western colonies. A quarrel broke out between Syracuse, the chief Dorian city of Sicily, and Leontini, one of the Ionian settlements, in which the latter was worsted, its citizens expelled, and the ground taken possession of by the enemy, while Athens was too much pressed at home to be able to send succours. And now Egesta, a non-Hellenic city, was sorely harassed by Selinus, a Hellenic one, aided by Syracuse; and it sent to represent to the Athenians that there would soon be nothing left in Sicily but an all-powerful Dorian combination, allied to Peloponnesus, and ready to aid it in any scheme against Athens. At the same time, the Egestans engaged to provide the funds, if Athens would send to their rescue an adequate armament. The ambition of the Athenians, and especially of Alcibiades, kindled at the idea of conquest in Sicily; of acquiring Syracuse; perhaps humbling Carthage itself. Nicias in vain reminded them, that they had enemies enough nearer home to cope with; and that while talking of redressing the wrongs of Egesta, they had not yet repaired their own in Thrace. The Athenians were tired of Thrace; and the climate was too cold for Alcibiades: nothing would please them but an expedition to Sicily.

416 B.C.

454. As a measure of prudence, it was thought proper to send envoys to Egesta, to form an opinion of its apparent wealth and the general state of affairs. The cunning Egestans devised means to dazzle these envoys with a great display of wealth. They shewed them the treasures of the temple of Venus, which were of inferior metal, gilt, not gold. They collected all the private property in plate belonging to the citizens, and even borrowed some from other towns; the envoys were invited to successive banquets at the houses of various citizens, and at each the host displayed this array of plate as his own—the stock being transferred from house to house for each occasion.

To complete the illusion, sixty talents were placed in the hands of the envoys, as the first instalment towards the expenses of the war.

455. The report of all this wealth appeared perfectly satisfactory at Athens; and it was determined to send sixty triremes, under the command of Nicias, Alcibiades, and Lamachus. They were to hold it in view, first, to relieve Egesta; second, to re-establish Leontini; and third, to further the interests of Athens in Sicily in any other way that appeared feasible.

456. Nicias made another attempt to dissuade his fellow-citizens from the enterprise, by representing that it required no mere fleet to cope with such powers as Syracuse and Selinus on their own soil; that little aid could be expected on the spot; and that it would demand a very large force of hoplites, bowmen, and slingers, an ample stock of provisions, and above all, a considerable sum of money—for he did not believe in the promises of Egesta. The effect of this representation was exactly the reverse of what the speaker intended. The people took him at his word, applauded his frankness, voted a hundred triremes instead of sixty, and unanimously agreed to provide everything he deemed necessary. The whole mind of Athens appeared to be thrown into the enterprise; men of every class and age pressed forward to put down their names for active service; vessels were sent for to the nautical allies; hoplites were invited from Argos and Mantinea; bowmen and slingers were hired elsewhere; and such was the confidence of success, that many prepared to carry on commerce as well as conflict. The religious omens and prophecies were generally favourable; and the only exceptions to the tone of sanguine anticipation, were the forebodings of Socrates the philosopher, and Meton the astronomer.

457. In the midst of this cheerful bustle, an event occurred which cast a fearful gloom over the city. It must be explained that one of the distinguishing features of Athens was the great number of Hermæ, or busts of Mercury, as god of commerce, placed on quadrangular pillars, to about the height of the human figure. They

were placed at the doors of temples and private houses; at the intersections of the streets; in the public agora; meeting the eye, in short, everywhere in every scene of social intercourse. During one night, all these statues, with but one exception, suffered a mutilation, shocking in the extreme to the religious feelings of the people. The characteristic features were obliterated, and there only remained so many shapeless masses of stone, bearing no resemblance to anything human or divine. It is exceedingly difficult for us to enter into the intensity of astonishment, terror, and anger, which seized the public mind on the morning after this nocturnal sacrilege. But it may aid us to remember, that the Greeks considered the god to be domiciled wherever his effigy stood; that the companionship, sympathy, and guardian care of Mercury were supposed to be enjoyed wherever his statue was present and well kept; and without the gods, no Athenian hoped for blessings either personal or political. But now it would appear to them that the city had become utterly godless; every man saw the divine guardian at his doorway dishonoured and defaced; the streets, too, the market-place, the porticos, were robbed of their celestial protectors. What was worse still, this had been no accident or disaster from natural causes—the gods had been deliberately insulted, and they must have gone away with wrathful and vindictive sentiments against the city where they had been so used. Hence the inference, not less natural than terrifying, that some heavy calamity would surely fall on the place.

458. There was yet another aggravation of this calamity. The mutilation of the Hermæ must have been the deliberate act of an organised and not inconsiderable body of conspirators; and it was generally felt they must have had a design to overturn the constitution—perhaps to establish a despotism. Active measures were taken, and large rewards were offered for their discovery, but nothing satisfactory was elicited. Informations were indeed laid of a collateral nature, shewing that the ceremonies of the Eleusian mysteries had been mockingly performed in private houses by drunken revellers; and that Alcibiades

himself had been thus guilty. Just as the fleet was ready to sail, an accusation of this kind was laid against him, and he desired that the charge might be investigated immediately. His accusers, however, evaded this, and he embarked without any clearing up of the matter.

459. The enthusiasm of the people about the Sicilian expedition was all renewed when the moment arrived for its departure. The number of the vessels—though more were yet to join—their equipments, the display of wealth and power, combined with the brilliant expectations of conquest, were calculated to excite the liveliest interest. Nearly the whole population, native and foreign, accompanied the warriors to Piræus. When all were on board, silence was proclaimed by the sound of a trumpet; and now the herald invoked the gods, and sung the pæan, followed by the voices of all the crews in every ship, and the multitude of the people on the shore; while on every deck the officers poured out libations of wine to the gods from gold and silver goblets. This done, the final signal was given, and the fleet sailed from Piræus in single file.

460. The armament was joined at Corcyra by contingents from maritime allies, and ships for luggage and provisions. The whole, when complete, included 134 triremes, with two Rhodian pentekonters, 5100 hoplites, 480 bowmen, 700 slingers, and 120 exiles of Megara, serving as light troops. Besides this, which constituted the armed force, there were 500 vessels of burden, carrying provisions, implements of war, bakers, carpenters, &c., and numerous private ships following for purposes of trade.

461. Three fast-sailing triremes were despatched in advance to prepare Egesta for the arrival of the succours, and to ascertain what other towns in Italy and Sicily would welcome their approach. As the main body reached the Italian shores, their reception was far from encouraging. Then the vessels returning from Egesta reported that the wealth formerly displayed was entirely fictitious; and that no more than thirty talents could be got together for the expense. In these circumstances, Nicias advised merely to sail to Selinus, obtain the best terms that might be for Egesta, and return home. Lamachus was for falling at

once on Syracuse, while as yet its people were unprepared, and not even disposed to believe that any Athenian force was at hand. This bold counsel—probably the best, however—was rejected for that of Alcibiades, which was to beat up the Greek cities of Sicily for allies, and then attack Syracuse and Selinus. He himself proceeded to secure the co-operation of Naxos, and took forcible possession of Catana as a suitable situation for head-quarters.

462. Meanwhile, public alarm and anxiety had been kept alive at Athens in reference to the yet unexplained sacrilege, connected as it was more and more believed to be with designs of revolution, and the establishment of tyranny in the state. The people could not rest without knowing who were the guilty parties; and the large rewards offered soon produced informers. The ferment thus continually increased; no man knew which of his neighbours might be a traitor; nor could he tell whether himself might not next be denounced as such. At length, Andocides, a young man of rank, having been arrested on information, was induced by his fellow-prisoners to make a disclosure which pointed out twenty-two citizens as the mutilators of the Hermæ, himself having been unwillingly drawn into their counsels, and unable from an accident to take any active part. Such of these citizens as did not escape by instant flight, were taken and put to death: the informer was spared, and even thanked; the prisoners who had been in custody on suspicion, were released; the people believed they had got to the bottom of this terrible mystery; and the public mind subsided into comparative tranquillity. Still, the more discerning part of the community did not consider the evidence at all satisfactory; and historians record it as a mystery which was never fully unravelled.

463. The restored confidence was but partial and temporary. The various alleged profanations of the Eleusian mysteries remained unexpiated; and the enemies of Alcibiades found, in the renewed uneasiness of the public mind on this score, a favourable opportunity for reiterating the charge against him. A formal impeachment

having been preferred, it was moved that he should be recalled from Sicily to take his trial. A Salaminian trireme was accordingly despatched for him; but the trierarch was cautioned not to seize his person, or use any violence, for fear of offending the troops under his command; but to allow him to return in his own vessel.

464. This grave requisition met Alcibiades at Catana, and his resolution was speedily taken. Professing ready obedience, he departed in his own trireme, in company with that which had been sent for him and those which conveyed his companions in the accusation. But as they sailed along the coast of Italy, he gave them the slip, and disappeared. The Salaminian trireme was obliged, after a fruitless search, to return home without him; and the Athenians, on his non-appearance, condemned him to death, with confiscation of his property; while the official conservators of the Eleusian mysteries pronounced him accursed by the gods, and recorded this condemnation on a leaden tablet. On hearing this sentence, Alcibiades is said to have exclaimed: 'I will shew them that I am alive!'

465. The proceedings against Alcibiades gave great offence to the troops in Sicily, and slackened their zeal; while it transferred the incensed exile to the side of the enemy, to work all the mischief in his power against his native Athens. Landing on the Italian coast, after quitting the company of the Salaminian trireme, he found means of crossing to Peloponnesus in a merchant vessel, and soon received an invitation from Sparta, with safe-conduct thither. Here, burning with revenge, he stirred up the Lacedæmonians to send help to Syracuse, and freely tendered his own services.

466. Not the least of the evils to Athens consequent on the recall of Alcibiades was, that it left the army in Sicily almost entirely under the control of the timid Nicias, who, in pursuance of the policy he had before advocated, now set about investigating the quarrel between Egesta and Selinus. When the taunts of the enemy at length shamed him into attempting something, he stole a march on Syracuse, fought a battle with success, and returned to Catana,

where he passed the winter, and did little except send home for reinforcements, which were readily accorded.

467. The Syracusans availed themselves of this respite to improve their defences and summon their allies. A new wall was constructed from the Great Harbour to the Bay

1. Thapsus; 2. Leon; 3. Trogylium; 4. Port. Trogyliorum; 5. Turris Galeagra; 6. Hexapylæ; 7. Euryalus; 8. Theatrum and Amphitheatrum; 9. Acropolis Dionysii; 10. Pentapylæ; 11. Portus minor sive Laccius; 12. Latomiæ; 13. Templum Minervæ; 14. Fons Arethusæ and Templum Dianæ; 15. Magnus portus; 16. Palus Lysimelia sive Syraco; 17. Polichna; 18. Dascon (Heracliun); 19. Latomiæ; 20. Cyanæ fons; 21. Olympium; 22. Plemyrium; 23. Castrum Labdalum.

of Thapsus, rendering any process of blockade much more difficult than it would have been before. This wall fronted the slope of the long ridge of high ground called Epipolæ, the only side from which Syracuse was now assailable. It was intended to occupy the summit of this ridge with troops, and thus obstruct the few and narrow passes over it; but ere the forces mustered for this purpose had begun their march, they learned that the Athenians were already in possession of it.

468. Next morning, Nicias and Lamachus descended the hill, and offered battle near the Syracusan walls, but it was not accepted; and there was left no alternative but that of blockading the city according to the mode of

warfare at that time. Descending to a new position about midway down the slope, they constructed as quickly as possible a walled enclosure called the Circle, to be a centre from which the blockading wall was to stretch northward to the sea at Trogilus, and southward to the Great Harbour. In vain the Syracusans endeavoured to interrupt these works—first, by offering battle, which themselves were the first to decline when the troops were marshalled for fight; then, by building cross-walls to traverse the space along which the Athenian circumvallation must pass. The Athenians fell first upon one, then upon the other of these intersecting walls, pulled up the palisading, and carried away the materials to build their own circumvallation. In one of these encounters, Lamachus was slain, though the result of the day left the Athenians completely victorious.

469. The Syracusans now began to view their situation with great despondency: they found they were no match for the superior discipline of the Athenian troops; and many of the Sicel tribes, hitherto wavering, were now tendering their alliance to the prosperous side; while the Italian Greeks generally furnished the invaders with provisions in abundance. Things had at length come to that pass, that a public assembly was to be held immediately to sanction the terms of capitulation. At this critical juncture, the Corinthian admiral reached the city, announcing that a fleet from Corinth, and a land-force, headed by the Spartan Gylippus, were on their way, and could not be far distant. The tidings were received with enthusiasm, and all idea of capitulation was discarded.

470. Nicias took no effective measures to intercept Gylippus by sea, regarding him as a mere privateer, with four ships. And stranger still, though he knew, or might have known, that the Spartan was levying forces at Himera, and that he could approach Syracuse only through the mountain-passes, in the Athenian rear, yet these passes were left unoccupied and undefended. The consequence was, that the relieving army drew on without opposition. As Gylippus descended the slopes of Epipolæ, the whole force of Syracuse issued forth to

welcome his arrival, and accompany him to the city. Gylippus well knew the importance of turning to immediate account this new tide of feeling; and hardly had he joined the besieged, when he marshalled the united force, marched up to the Athenian lines, and offered battle. Struck with amazement, they, too, formed their ranks, and he then sent a herald to offer them five days to collect their effects and begone from the island. Nicias disdained to reply; but still he shewed no disposition to fight; and when Gylippus, not choosing to attack him by his fortifications, led his army day after day into the open ground away from the walls, he declined following. When at length the Athenians were induced to fight on the lope of Epipolæ, they underwent a thorough defeat, and were obliged to take shelter behind their defences.

471. Meanwhile Gylippus had been running a counter-wall from that of the city to cross the intended line of Athenian blockade, and he now pushed it on to the edge of the cliff; so that Syracuse was safe as long as this counter-wall could be defended. New hope was also inspired by the safe arrival of the Corinthian fleet; and Gylippus encouraged his allies to form aggressive plans against the Athenians even on the sea. Nicias, blocked up as in a besieged city, except for his ships, yet not daring to quit his position without orders from Athens, sent home an undisguised statement of his critical position, soliciting either new reinforcements or instructions to withdraw and return home. The Athenians resolved on the former alternative, and prepared a new and formidable armament under Demosthenes and Eurymedon, to set out at the earliest opening of spring.   414 B.C.

472. The winter of 414-413 was a season of busy preparation on both sides. While Eurymedon sailed to Syracuse with his ten triremes even in the dead of winter, Demosthenes was collecting a second armament for spring; and twenty galleys were despatched round Peloponnesus, to prevent succours for Syracuse from sailing out of the Corinthian Gulf. On the other hand, there was an extensive levy of hoplites throughout Peloponnesus, and the Corinthians prepared a strong convoy for the transports

which carried them. Gylippus was not less actively engaged in stirring up Sicily to take a decisive part in the coming struggle.

473. The most important proceeding of the opening year, however, was the renewed invasion of Attica. Twelve years had now elapsed since she had felt the hand of the destroyer; but now she was to see her plains again laid waste by the marauding foe. A large army was despatched for this purpose under Agis, king of Sparta and son of Archidamus. After ravaging the lands round Athens, these troops proceeded to the main object, to fortify a position for themselves at Decelea, which was situated about fourteen miles from the city, on an outlying eminence. Doubtless, the Peloponnesians thought, by this movement, to force the Athenians to keep Demosthenes and his army at home for their own defence; and we read with amazement that even in these perilous circumstances, the citizens allowed their enthusiasm for the war in Sicily to prevail over all the dictates of prudence in reference to themselves; and that they permitted this force to depart, besides a fleet of thirty triremes under Charicles, to harass the coasts of Peloponnesus.

474. About the same time that Agis invaded Attica, and Demosthenes sailed from Piræus, Gylippus returned with reinforcements from the interior of Sicily to Syracuse. He surprised and captured the fort of Plemmyrium, so that the Syracusans obtained complete command of the mouth of the harbour, being in possession of the ground on both sides of it; while the Athenians were cramped up in the north-west corner of that harbour, adjoining the fortified lines of their land-force. For some time, this bay was the scene of much desultory conflict, which, however, gradually became more general and more decisive in favour of Syracuse.

475. The citizens, animated by recent success, thought of nothing less than the utter destruction of their enemies in the harbour. Their calculations, however, were suspended by the arrival of the formidable and imposing armament under Demosthenes and Eurymedon, entering the port in full array, with showy decorations and sound of music.

The Syracusans were struck with dismay as well as wonder; the Athenians revived with hope and courage. Demosthenes judged that one great and decisive blow might now be struck on the strength of this impression—of fear on the one side, and hope on the other. This he attempted by a night-surprise of the garrison on the highest point of Epipolæ. But the result was a humiliating defeat; his troops coming back with fearful loss and broken spirit to shelter within their own lines. He now declared it loss of time and money to stay longer, and especially when the presence of an efficient army was so greatly needed at home. But Nicias would face any danger from the enemy rather than the reception to be feared at Athens; nor would he consent even to remove from the Great Harbour of Syracuse to Thapsus or Catana.

476. Three or four weeks passed in consulting and lamenting, but without either acting or retiring; until Gylippus had beat up the interior again, and returned with fresh troops. When the Athenians saw him marching in with these over the heights of Epipolæ, all scruples gave way; and Nicias himself consented that their troops should privately and quietly depart. Orders were sent to Catana to forward them no more supplies here; the signal for departure was to be hoisted in the morning; but, lo! during the night an eclipse of the moon took place; and the prophets declared they must not stir till after the lapse of thrice nine days—that is, a full circle of the moon. This decision seems to have gone along with the general feeling; and even Demosthenes did not dare to contravene, on principles of worldly wisdom, what seemed the express will of the gods.

477. During the interval, Nicias strove by prayer, sacrifice, and expiatory rites, to appease the supposed displeasure of Jove; while the Syracusans, learning that the eclipse alone had prevented their enemies from making good a furtive retreat, determined to crush them in the harbour, and not permit them to occupy any other post in Sicily. Accordingly, Gylippus drew out both his naval and land forces; defeated the Athenians in a general, close, and desperate action; and then proceeded to blockade

them, by closing up the mouth of the harbour. This was nearly a mile across; and here he anchored vessels of every description, placing them obliquely, and chaining them together.

478. As the Athenians had few provisions left, and had counter-ordered any further supplies, some immediate step was necessary; and it was resolved at last to make an effort to break out of the harbour. All hands prepared for a desperate struggle.

479. When the triremes were fully manned, and everything was ready, the agony of Nicias became irrepressible. He had already, according to usage, delivered a stirring address; but now he broke out afresh, appealing by name to the trierarchs individually, adjuring each in the name of his wife, his children, and his ancestral gods; and pressing every motive that could touch his affections, awaken his patriotism, or revive his courage.

480. Very different were the burning words in which Gylippus reminded his Syracusans of the mischievous designs which had brought these invaders to their shores; congratulated them on the progress which their valour had made in subduing them; invited them to crush this their last despairing effort; to put the finishing-stroke to their ruin, and taste the sweets of a just revenge.

481. The Syracusan fleet was skilfully disposed, so as to guard the barrier, and fall upon the enemy's vessels from different sides as soon as they approached. Besides, the surface of the water swarmed with the light craft of youthful volunteers from among the citizens. The surrounding shore, only excepting that part occupied by the Athenian station, was crowded with Syracusan warriors looking on, while the walls of Ortygia overhanging the water, were lined with the feebler population of the town— the aged men, the women, and children. The day was sacred to Hercules at Syracuse; and the prophets assured the people of victory, if only they forbore to attack, and assumed the defensive.

482. The Athenian fleet at once made an impetuous attack on the barrier, and were attempting to sever its chains, when the Syracusans crowded in upon all hands,

and compelled them to desist. The battle soon became general, and the fiercest courage was displayed on both sides. The issue was long doubtful, for the Athenians were superior both in the number of their vessels and their skill in managing them, though acting at a disadvantage from the narrow space in which they were enclosed. At length victory declared for the Syracusans, who, as soon as they perceived the enemy slackening, redoubled their own exertions, and drove them back towards the land. Presently the Athenian triremes abandoned all further resistance, and were thrust ashore on their own station like shipwrecked vessels, amid shrieks of agony and terror; while maddening shouts of joy burst from the throng that encircled the harbour, in response to their victorious comrades on shipboard. Thus closed one of the most fearful and heart-stirring conflicts that history records.

483. It is difficult for us moderns to appreciate the depth and intensity of feeling which accompanied military warfare in those days. The Greek who fought and the Greek who looked on, were not soldiers separated from the rest of the community, trained in routine duty, and rendered mere machines of war, but citizens instinct with all the sympathies of social and political life—themselves the parties most deeply interested in the result of the struggle.

484. So utterly were the minds of the vanquished paralysed by what they had suffered, and what they feared yet to suffer, that no man thought of picking up the floating corpses, or asking for the usual burial-truce. Terror and despair made it the one anxiety how they, the living, were to escape. They would have decamped overland that very night, but that their enemies persuaded them, by means of false friends, that all the roads and passes were guarded. Whereas the truth was, that such was the wild mirth and jollity, and feasting and mutual congratulation among the citizens, their leaders knew it would be useless to order any one out on such duty. Ere the vanquished Athenians did begin their retreat, all the posts convenient for obstructing them were fully occupied.

And now the full measure of their wretchedness was made manifest. Marsh-fever had prevailed among them for some time; and between the effects of this disease, and want and grief, the march of these 40,000 miserable creatures looked like the pouring forth of the population of a large town after a lengthened blockade. The dead must be left unburied; and though the soldier shuddered at the thought, there was no one to resist the dreadful necessity. But the sick and wounded, too, must be abandoned; and this might not be done without a harrowing appeal. The living sufferers clung around the knees of their comrades, implored them not to desert them, and crawled along the line of march till their strength was exhausted. The clamour of unsuppressed grief took the place of the silent sorrow of the previous day; and it was with the utmost difficulty that the army could be induced to move on, notwithstanding the dreadful necessity.

485. The generals did their best to support the sinking spirits of the men: Nicias, in particular, appears to have displayed unwonted energy and heroism, himself commanding the foremost division, while Demosthenes brought up the rear. But their indefatigable enemies hunted their retreat through whatever zigzag course they pursued; and overtaking first one division, then the other, made prisoners of about 10,000 men, with the two generals. These they led back in joyous procession to the city: the two generals were put to death; the rest were placed, for safe custody, in the stone-quarries of Syracuse—deep narrow hollows with precipitous sides, and open to the sky overhead. Here the miserable captives were huddled together without any protection or convenience, a scanty supply of food being let down to them. Many, having arrived sick and wounded, died in a short time; but no pains were taken to render the sufferings of the living less intolerable, by removing the dead from among them. Seventy days they thus remained, probably serving as a spectacle for the gratification of the triumphant population, till the effluvia became intolerable to the citizens themselves. The survivors seem to have been then sold as slaves; perhaps some got back to Athens on ransom;

and we are told that those who became the property of private individuals, gained in many cases the affections of their masters, by their elegant demeanour and polite accomplishments. Especially, it is said, that those who could repeat portions of Euripides, received generous and humane treatment, if not the boon of freedom.

486. Never, in the history of Greece, had an expedition been sent out so extensive, so costly, so efficient, and so full of promise, as that against Syracuse ; and never was ruin so complete and so disgraceful. The consequences were felt from one end of the Hellenic world to the other, as we shall presently see.

CONSEQUENCES OF THE DEFEAT AT SYRACUSE— THE FOUR HUNDRED.

487. It has already been mentioned, that when the armament of Demosthenes sailed for Sicily, the Spartan king Agis was not only ravaging Attica, but fortifying Decelea for the occupation of a permanent garrison. The previous invasions of the country had been but temporary, lasting for five or six weeks in spring, and leaving comparative repose during the remainder of the year. But now, with permanent quarters so advantageously situated, the work of devastation was carried on with much greater vigour. The fields were kept lying waste ; the sheep and cattle were destroyed ; the artisans and slaves received in great numbers as deserters. And while the citizens were suffering severe privation from these causes, they were obliged to keep watch day and night along the whole extent of the wall which enclosed Athens and Piræus. The public finances were so exhausted, that they were obliged to dismiss their Thracian mercenaries ; and the decline of their naval power was manifested in an indecisive battle with the Corinthians near Naupactus. These were reverses hard enough to bear ; but the cup of sorrow was not full till the tidings arrived of the destruction of the army in Sicily.

488. According to Plutarch, a stranger arrived at Piræus, and entering a barber's shop, began to speak of

it as a topic which must of course be the all-absorbing one in the city; and the barber ran up directly to Athens, to make known the fearful tidings. But when his authority was demanded, and he could not find his informant again, he was treated as a fabricator of rumours to disturb the public tranquillity, and was even put to the torture. Deep, of course, was the affliction when the conviction of the fact was forced upon the people; for there was not only the private mourning for friends and relatives, but utter despair as to the public safety. After a burst of grief and anger, venting itself against the orators who had advocated, and the prophets who had encouraged the ill-starred expedition, they began to look their affairs in the face, and the energy of desperation revived. A board of ten elderly men, under the title of Probuli, was appointed to examine the expenditure, and suggest measures of economy. The splendour of the choral and liturgic ceremonies was consequently reduced; the garrison stationed on the Laconian coast was ordered home; timber was collected for the construction of new ships; and Cape Sunium was fortified for the protection of the transport vessels which brought provisions from Eubœa.

489. But the same intelligence that stimulated Athens to these exertions, proved a signal to all her enemies to redouble their activity. The leading men of Eubœa, Lesbos, and Chios applied to the Spartans to assist them in a revolt. The Persian satraps Tissaphernes and Pharnabazus likewise sent to seek the alliance of Sparta against the power of Athens in Asia Minor. So rapid and energetic, however, had been the rally of this city, that she was able again to maintain a tolerable struggle, though with diminished resources, and on a merely defensive system, against enemies emboldened by success, and more numerous than ever.

490. In the course of a few months, the Spartans began to lose confidence in Alcibiades. Erelong, he was openly denounced as a traitor, and saved his life only by flight. His next refuge was with Tissaphernes, the Persian satrap at Magnesia, into whose confidence he soon ingratiated himself. And now he began to play a completely

anti-Hellenic game, suggesting to Tissaphernes that he should not lend such effective aid to either the Athenian or the Lacedæmonian party, as to enable one to crush the other, but that he should feed and prolong the war, keep the rival states weakening each other, and then rise on the ruins of both. The satrap accordingly slackened his efforts on the Spartan side ; reduced the pay of the men ; paralysed the exertions of the commanders by false promises of reinforcements, and even restrained them by liberal bribes. Meanwhile, Alcibiades coquetted with Athens, representing that his influence would procure for its people the powerful alliance of Persia, on condition of their receiving him again, and substituting an oligarchical government for the democratic, which the Great King could not trust. The repugnance of the Athenians to sacrifice the democracy was both unanimous and wrathful ; but it was overborne by the imperious necessity of the case ; and Pisander, who had chiefly advocated the measure, and organised the clubs to support it, was now appointed with ten others to negotiate further with the exile. Alcibiades had promised what he was quite unable to perform ; and it seems never to have occurred to the Athenians, that they had no warrant but his word, which, it was well known, was of little value. But the renegade extricated himself by one of his characteristic manœuvres. Receiving the Athenian deputation in the presence of the satrap, he made such extravagant demands on behalf of Persia, that the envoys indignantly broke off the conference, and withdrew.

491. The oligarchical revolution, meanwhile, had proceeded too far to be arrested by this termination of the Persian negotiation ; and Pisander, on his return, completed the work in connection with five of his companions, while the other five were sent to effect similar changes among the dependent allies. The propositions which he made and carried were—that the existing magistracies should be abolished ; that no civil functionaries should be salaried ; and that a committee of five persons should be appointed, who were to name ninety-five more ; each of the hundred was to choose three persons, and the body of Four

Hundred thus constituted was to sit in the senate-house, and carry on the government with unlimited powers. They were, however, to convene a select body of 5000 citizens whenever they thought proper.

492. The Four Hundred having been constituted, marched in armed procession to the senate-house, and commanded the senators to depart, tendering them, at the same time, the amount of pay due to them for the remainder of the year. The senators were in no condition to resist; and the Four Hundred found themselves triumphantly established without bloodshed or even serious opposition. Thus ended the democracy of Athens, after an existence of nearly 100 years since its establishment by Clisthenes. We pass rapidly over the events of the next few months.

493. The Four Hundred, having solemnised their installation by prayer and sacrifice, put to death some of their political enemies, banished others, and conducted everything with a rigour unknown under the old constitution. The fugitives from Athens carried tidings of these doings— possibly with exaggeration—to Samos, where the same party had effected a similar revolution; and the men composing the Athenian navy—which, it will be remembered, made Samos its head-quarters—were filled with indignation. At the instance chiefly of the commanders Thrasybulus and Thrasyllus, they took an oath to oppose the Four Hundred at Athens, the people of Samos joining with enthusiasm, and overturning the new party in their own city.

494. The Athenians, thunderstruck at the resolution of their fleet, and utterly powerless without it, sent to Samos an embassy, which was indignantly dismissed. They then sent to Sparta to purchase peace almost at any price— even to admit a Spartan garrison to defend Athens. The Lacedæmonians would not treat; and now a Peloponnesian fleet appeared near the coast, making for Eubœa, which it enabled to revolt, and thus cut off from the Athenians the main source of their supplies of food.

495. Amidst the excitement of these disasters, and while the invasion of Piræus itself was hindered only by

the timidity of the Spartan admiral, the leaders of the late revolution were impeached as traitors to the state, for bringing the fleet of Sparta to aid in enslaving the citizens. The constitution of the Four Hundred, which had lasted four months, was abolished; its authors were condemned to death; and the democracy, under the name of the Five Thousand, was restored.

THE WAR ON THE ASIATIC COAST.

496. While these events had been passing at Athens and Samos, the connection between Tissaphernes and the Peloponnesians had made the coasts of Asia Minor the seat of the war. Here the Spartan force under Mindarus was amused and tantalised rather than aided by this satrap, but found a true friend in Pharnabazus at the Hellespont; while Alcibiades reinforced Thrasyllus the Athenian, who had defeated the Peloponnesians at Cynossema. 411 B.C.

497. In the spring of 410 B.C., Alcibiades himself led the Athenian forces against the united Lacedæmonians and Persians, whom he put to the rout, slaying Mindarus, and capturing the whole of the Peloponnesian fleet, except the Syracusan ships, which were burned by Hermocrates. The Spartans offered peace on the terms of both parties standing just as they were, and on both sides withdrawing their garrisons, and exchanging prisoners; but the Athenians, elated with success, and advised by Cleophon, a demagogue in high repute among them, rejected the proposal.

498. Gathering all the strength of the Greek towns on the Chersonesus, Alcibiades proceeded from conquest to conquest, taking Chalcedon, Selymbria, Byzantium; and Pharnabazus, weary of bearing all the brunt of the war for the benefit of the Peloponnesians, made a truce with the Athenians, gave them a safe escort for envoys to submit proposals to the Persian king at Susa, and himself made a covenant of personal friendship with Alcibiades.

LYSANDER AND CYRUS THE YOUNGER—BATTLE OF ÆGOS-POTAMOS—THE DECARCHIES—HUMILIATION OF ATHENS.

499. A new phase now opened in the Peloponnesian war. The Persian monarch, displeased with the vacillating policy of his satraps, sent down to the coast his son Cyrus, generally called Cyrus the Younger—a prince of strong will, great bodily activity, and a fair share of talent. He was invested with the satrapies of Lydia, Phrygia Major, and Cappadocia, besides the military command of all the forces which mustered at Castolus. This young man set out from Susa, carrying in his bosom a fresh and hearty hatred to Athens, with full authority to embody that feeling in action. On his way to the coast, he met with Pharnabazus and the Athenian envoys, proceeding to Susa in the fond hope of effecting an alteration in the policy of Persia. Their calculations were speedily overthrown: the prince forbade their further proceeding, and ordered them to be detained in Cappadocia, so that no information might be conveyed through them to the Athenians.

500. The arrival of Cyrus at the coast at once overruled the treachery of Tissaphernes and the weariness of Pharnabazus, while it supplied the Peloponnesians with an ample supply of Persian gold when their resources were beginning to fail.

501. Of scarcely less moment was the fact that Lysander, the third of the eminent Spartan commanders elicited by this war, had just come out to supersede the former admiral. The talents of this young man were of a high order; his disposition thoroughly Spartan, making little account of wealth, or pleasure, or intellectual accomplishments, in comparison of the projects of public and private ambition; his morality reckless as that of Alcibiades on the score of integrity; with a dash of cruelty which could not be imputed to the elegant Athenian.

502. As soon as Cyrus arrived at Sardis, Lysander,

who was waiting at Ephesus, went to pay his respects, and was received with distinguished favour. The young prince assured him that he had come to prosecute the war with the utmost vigour. He had brought with him for the purpose, he said, 500 talents : if this were insufficient, he would resort to his own private purse ; and if still more were necessary, he would coin the gold and silver of the throne on which he sat. He refused, however, to raise the men's pay from the rate fixed by the treaty and the king's orders, to that which Tissaphernes had originally promised. When, however, the envoys were feasted at a banquet, and Cyrus, pledging the wine-cup with Lysander, desired him to ask what he most desired, the immediate reply was : 'To grant each seaman an additional obolus.' The prince at once complied, bound in honour to do so, and filled with astonishment and admiration at the disinterested request. With his Persian and princely notions of winning adherents by largesses, a man above looking for presents was a perfect phenomenon; and from this hour Lysander became the object of his implicit confidence.

503. Returning to Ephesus, Lysander was able to put his ships in better order, and to diffuse a spirit of satisfaction and confidence through the armament by paying all arrears, and raising the rate for the future. He likewise summoned from each of the Asiatic cities a few leading men, and organised them into clubs or factions to correspond with him, and use their influence against Athens, promising that, in the event of success, they should be invested with the government of their respective cities.

504. While Cyrus and Lysander were employed in these preparations for effective warfare, Alcibiades had accomplished the delicate step of re-entering his native city. His reception was much more favourable than he had ventured to anticipate. The people flocked down to Piræus to greet his return, and joyfully escorted him to the city. The sentence which had been passed against him was cancelled, and the record of it destroyed ; the Eumolpidæ were directed to revoke their curse, and the leaden tablet on which it was engraven was thrown into the sea ; his property, which had been confiscated, was

restored; he was elected general, with full powers, and authorised to prepare a large military force for future operations against the enemy.

505. It is not necessary hence to infer that the people had utterly forgotten the former misdeeds of Alcibiades. But while the distant past exhibited him as a foe and a traitor, the recent past exalted him as a patriot and a valuable servant of the state; and it was determined that he should have a fair chance of prosecuting his new and better career.

506. Alcibiades, accordingly, set out for the coast of Asia Minor, amid the ardent hopes of his fellow-citizens. It was in vain that he would have instilled into Cyrus the doctrine of feeding and protracting the war, so as to wear out both the Grecian parties; such policy was most uncongenial to the vehement temper of the young prince, and yet more repugnant to him since he had known Lysander.

507. While Alcibiades, hard pressed for money, went to levy contributions in the dependent territories, and to concert measures with Thrasybulus at Phocæa, he left the command of the fleet at Samos to his pilot Antiochus, with strict orders not to venture on an action. But, in spite of these injunctions, Antiochus provoked a battle with Lysander, was defeated, and lost his life. Hastening back to Samos, Alcibiades sailed with the fleet to the mouth of the Ephesian harbour, and challenged Lysander to meet him in battle. But the Spartan would not give him the opportunity of wiping off the late dishonour.

508. Three months had now passed, and nothing had been accomplished. Alcibiades had relapsed into his former dissolute habits, and selected for confidential posts the companions of his revels, like Antiochus, instead of seeking for men worthy to fill them. His men became dissatisfied; and so many complaints were lodged at Athens against him, that he was removed from the command, which was vested in ten generals, with Conon at their head.

509. The year of Lysander's command expired about the same time; but his successor Callicratidas was ill

received by the seamen, and even treated with contempt by Cyrus. Despite the difficulties thus created, he took the principal cities of Lesbos from the Athenians, and repulsed the fleet under the command of Conon. He was, however, assailed near the rocky isles of Arginusæ, where he had a very inadequate force. The struggle was long and fierce; but at length the brave Callicratidas perished, and the Athenians gained the day.

510. Through the influence of the Spartan allies, and especially of Cyrus, Lysander was again appointed to the command of the Spartan fleet in 405 B.C., but nominally as secretary to Aracus, as it was contrary to Spartan usage to appoint any man admiral twice. On receiving this office, Lysander repaired to the court of Cyrus, where he not only obtained large supplies 405 B.C. of money, but was intrusted with the care of his satrapy and revenues during his own absence in Media, whither he was called by the illness of his father.

511. Thus invested with an unprecedented command of Persian gold, and seconded by factions in all the allied cities, Lysander proceeded to the Hellespont, which had been left unguarded, and where he immediately attacked and took by storm the wealthy city of Lampsacus, on the Asiatic side of the strait. The Athenian fleet came up too late to save it, and then took its station upon an open beach directly opposite. The spot, called Ægos-Potamos, or Goat's-River, had neither houses nor supplies; and, armaments in those days having no organised commissariats, the men were obliged to go for their meals to Sestus, nearly two miles off. The generals hoped to force Lysander to an engagement. Daily they sailed across the strait, found his ships ready manned and in battle-array, with the land-force drawn out on shore to co-operate, but all with strict orders not to stir till attacked. On each successive day after this abortive effort to draw out the Spartan, the Athenians became more remiss on their return, dispersing as soon as they got to shore. On the fifth day, Lysander sent scout-ships to watch them as usual, and now desired them to hoist a bright shield as soon as the Athenian vessels were at anchor, and the

crews gone to dine. Then, as soon as this signal appeared, he ordered his whole fleet to row swiftly across, and the land-force to march along the strand. All the enemy's triremes were thus caught at their moorings, some utterly deserted, others very partially manned, and only twelve out of 180 in a tolerable state of preparation. The surprise was complete and decisive; the utmost Conon could do was to escape to Cyprus with a few vessels; all the rest were captured by Lysander; and this without the loss of a single ship, almost without the loss of a single man. There could scarcely be imagined a victory more complete in itself, more disgraceful to the vanquished, and more overwhelming in its consequences than that of Ægos-Potamos. The maritime power of Athens was now utterly broken; and the remaining struggle was for bare existence.

512. Lysander, secure of final triumph, was in no hurry to invest the enemy's capital. Having himself the key to the Euxine, he knew that few supplies could be conveyed to Athens—none to enable it to hold long against a blockade, when he should see fit to establish one. He therefore occupied himself first with the dependencies; and having mastered Chalcedon, Byzantium, and Mytilene, he placed a garrison in each of them, and constituted an oligarchy of ten native citizens, chosen from his own partisans, and called a Decarchy, to govern in conjunction with the harmost (military commander) of the garrison. The same he did in all the cities that successively fell under his power; while Eteonicus made similar arrangements in the cities of Thrace. Samos refused to admit either Lysander or his revolutionary changes; but every other city hitherto in alliance with Athens submitted to both.

513. Thus was Athens stripped of all her dependencies; and, to make matters worse, not only were all her cleruchs or out-citizens deprived of their properties, and driven home, but the garrisons and leading men in the cities attached to Athens were not suffered to repair anywhere but to the capital; Lysander calculating that the numbers congregated there would prove not strength, but weakness, when the match was against hunger.

514. The Athenians prepared as they best could for an honourable resistance; but the best devised measures could do little to meet the paramount difficulty—that of providing food for the population. Some small supplies may still have been reaching the city; but now—that is, about November 405 B.C.—Lysander came with the whole naval force of the Peloponnesians, and completely blockaded the harbour of Piræus, while the army encamped in the precincts of the Academeia, at the very gates of Athens. All hope was at an end; yet the pride and resolution of the citizens forbade them to make either speedy or ignominious proposals. Even when some were dying of hunger, they offered only to become allies of Sparta, retaining their walls and fortifications; but this was rejected with disdain. When the sufferings of the people became more intense, and no one knew what terms to offer, Theramenes offered to go, not with powers to conclude a peace, but to ascertain the intentions of Sparta, and report. He remained above three months in the society of Lysander, who detained him, as he alleged, and only acquainted him after so long a delay, that the matter was in the hands of the ephors at Sparta. By the time he returned to Athens, so terrible was the pressure of famine, that he was desired immediately to go back and procure peace on any terms.

515. Theramenes, thus empowered, was allowed to proceed to Sparta, where the assembly of the Peloponnesian confederacy was to determine the conditions of peace. Some of the allies, as Corinth and Thebes, were for blotting out the name of Athens, and selling the population for slaves. But the Lacedæmonians refused to annihilate or enslave a city which had done so much for the deliverance of Greece at the time of the Persian invasion. The terms finally agreed upon were :—That the Athenians should abandon all pretensions to foreign possessions, and confine themselves to their home-territory; that they should surrender all their ships of war; that they should demolish their fortifications; that they should receive back all their exiles; and that they should follow the leadership of Sparta

both by sea and land, having no friends or enemies but hers.

516. As Theramenes re-entered the city, he was met and surrounded by a miserable throng, who feared nothing but that his mission might have failed. When he announced the terms, there was found a high-spirited minority, who declared for starvation in preference to such submission; but the large majority decided that peace at any price must be deemed a boon, when the dead and the dying were so numerous. The acceptance was made known to Lysander, who triumphantly entered the city with the Athenian exiles, and remained till the conditions were fulfilled. The unfinished 404 B.C. vessels in the dockyards were burnt, the arsenals reduced to ruins, and only twelve ships allowed to remain. A certain number of days was allowed for the demolition of the Long Walls and the fortifications of Piræus; the Lacedæmonians themselves exultingly lent their aid, while the women danced around them, crowned with garlands, and playing the flute. There, too, were the exiles, and other remains of the faction of the Four Hundred, now assuming the attitude of conquerors, and viewing the prostrate condition of Athens as matter of satisfaction for the past, exultation for the present, and high anticipation for the future.

THE THIRTY TYRANTS—RESTORATION OF THE DEMOCRACY—DEATH OF ALCIBIADES.

517. While yet the work of demolition was going on at the walls of Athens, the oligarchical party began to organise itself under the leadership of Critias, one of those believed to have been concerned in the mutilation of the Hermæ; and erelong they were embodied as a board, known in history as the Thirty Tyrants, the counterpart of the decarchies constituted by Lysander in the other cities.

518. All the political and judicial institutions previously existing were abolished, to leave the administration

entirely in the hands of the Thirty, who procured a Lacedæmonian garrison to support their measures, and kept an organised band of youthful satellites and assassins, to dispose of those round whom the oppressed people might be disposed to rally. Still further to secure themselves, they disarmed the citizen hoplites, with the exception of 3000 who were attached to their interests ; and then they gave full play to their malevolence and rapacity. As a still further stretch of tyranny, they would crush the intellectual vigour of the people ; and for this purpose issued an edict for the suppression of the higher class of teachers or professors—that is, those who taught the arts of logic and rhetoric, of literary criticism and composition, and of handling those political and moral topics which were ordinary matter of conversation.

519. This reign of terror continued unchecked for about eight months, reckoning from the capture of Athens by Lysander; during which, it is said that 1500 persons were executed on the simple fiat of the Thirty. The measure of their iniquity was now full. Things had come to such a pass, that no man could reckon himself safe in Attica ; and multitudes, in poverty and destitution, resorted to the neighbouring territories of Megara, Thebes, Oropus, Chalcis, Argos, and wherever they could find reception. A striking revolution of feeling towards the Athenians had taken place in a few years. At the moment when the long war was brought to a close, the reigning sentiment in Greece was hatred to Athens, and exultation at her downfall. But as soon as she was humbled and rendered innocuous, the fear of her power, which had been the bond of union among the other states, disappeared, and was gradually superseded by jealousy of Sparta. A feeling this, for which Lysander had given some cause. Instead of fairly dividing the valuable spoils of the fallen foe, he had kept all ; and he continued to seek the aggrandisement of Sparta without any attention to the interest of her allies. Instead of that freedom throughout Greece which had been proclaimed as the object of the war, there was in reality a Spartan empire wielded by Lysander by means of the

decarchies. Besides, even at Sparta itself there began to arise a dislike to the overweening insolence which Lysander was beginning to display in his personal demeanour.

520. It was from Bœotia that the first sign of deliverance appeared. Thrasybulus, an Athenian emigrant, with a small band of companions — probably not above a hundred at most—took possession of Phyle, a frontier fortress—found probably dismantled—on the road between Thebes and Athens. The little band increased; they successfully resisted an attempt of the Thirty to dislodge them, and the weather was unfavourable for blockading. Shortly after, they surprised a company of soldiers during the night, slew them, and carried off abundance of arms and stores. The most violent of the tyrants now trembled for their safety; and the adherents of Thrasybulus having continually multiplied, he marched by night to Piræus, where he took up a strong position. He defeated the enemy in an engagement which proved fatal to Critias; upon which the more violent of the oligarchical party retired to Eleusis, and the more moderate succeeded in constituting a new oligarchy of Ten. The war between Athens and Piræus continued, with increasing advantage to the latter, which maintained the offensive. The Ten now applied for succour to Sparta, and it was there determined that Pausanias, one of the kings, should repair to Athens, and settle its affairs.

521. As soon as he arrived, the voice of complaint against the recent tyranny was violent and unmeasured; the orphans of those who had been its innocent victims appealed to him for justice, and all eyes were turned to him for sympathy and redress.

522. After vainly requiring the people at Piræus to disband, Pausanias made a show of fighting with them, and having the advantage in the second conflict, he entertained their overtures for peace. It was finally decided that they should be re-admitted to Athens; that the oligarchs should retire to Eleusis, and the Lacedæmonian garrison be withdrawn, leaving the Athenians free to govern themselves as they would; and that there should

be a general amnesty for all that was past. The terms were proclaimed, accepted, and confirmed by oath on both sides; and Pausanias, with all the Lacedæmonians, evacuated the territory of Athens. Thrasybulus and his followers now ascended the Acropolis, where they offered sacrifice and thanksgiving for the deliverance; after which an assembly of the people was convened, and the democracy was restored, with its archons, its senate of 500, its public assembly, and its dicasteries, as they had stood before the victory of Lysander. This restoration took place in the spring of 403 B.C.—a memorable year, which took its name from Eucleides, the man drawn by lot as first archon.

523. The oligarchs at Eleusis again threatened the peace of the city; but finding themselves likely to be worsted, the most obnoxious of them fled from Attica, and the rest came to an honourable accommodation, which incorporated Eleusis again in the Athenian community.

524. Far different, probably, would have been the conduct of the Athenians if Alcibiades had been the author of the restoration instead of Thrasybulus. But Alcibiades was now no more. Shortly after the disaster at Ægos-Potamos, he had retired from the Thracian Chersonese, and sought shelter with Pharnabazus, who assigned him a residence and revenue in Phrygia. But the Lacedæmonians, now in close alliance with Cyrus, and the decarchies, the creatures of Lysander, were uneasy at seeing him again in action amid so many unsettled elements; and the joint influence of Lysander and Cyrus having been enlisted, Pharnabazus was commanded to put him to death. The armed band sent on this errand, not daring to force their way into the house, surrounded it, and set it on fire. Alcibiades rushed out with a dagger in his hand, and none of the assailants ventured to close upon him; but they poured in darts and arrows, till, having no protective armour, he perished under the missiles.

525. Thus fell Alcibiades in the vigour of his life, not having yet attained his fiftieth year. He had never, during his whole career, suffered a single defeat, either

by sea or land; and whatever party he had espoused—Athenian, Spartan, Persian—oligarchy or democracy—each had in turn prospered so long as he was its leader. Yet he had never inspired any of them with confidence, and each had in turn cast him off. Few men have ever possessed such capacities for public life; in few have these been so marred by moral obliquity.

HUMILIATION OF THE ELEANS AND MESSENIANS.

526. When Sparta became mistress of Greece, one of the first uses which she made of her power was to avenge herself on the citizens of Elis, who had not only excluded the Spartan theory from the Olympic festival in 420 B. C., (see page 210), but had since refused to aid in the war against Athens, and declined allowing the oracle to be consulted respecting it. Agis, the Spartan king, now devastated their territory; and when they sued for peace, it was granted only on terms that they should demolish their fortifications, surrender their navy, recognise the independence of the neighbouring towns, and enter the Spartan alliance.   401 B.C.

527. This triumph emboldened the Spartans to root out the remains of their old enemies the Messenians, whom they now compelled to leave the peninsula entirely. Most of them found shelter in Sicily and at Cyrene.

LITERARY RETROSPECT.

528. The literary history of the fifth century B.C. is characterised chiefly by the development of the drama. It had arisen, indeed, at an earlier period, when, in addition to the chorus sung at the Bacchanalian feasts, there was added, first, a monologue in iambic verse; then a dialogue; and, finally, a regular plot requiring three actors. Afterwards satyrs were introduced as companions of Bacchus; and from their goat-like appearance, the entertainment obtained the name of Tragedy. The subjects were always taken from the ancient myths, and the three authors who chiefly excelled in the composition of these

plays were Æschylus, Sophocles, and Euripides. Comedy came to maturity later than tragedy, and differed from it in representing the characters and events of the day, instead of those celebrated in mythic story and tradition.

SOCRATES.

529. Through the drama, as an intermediate stage, appeared the rhetorical and dialectic arts, which were also developed in the period under review. The men who taught these arts in connection with the other more primitive branches of Athenian education, were called Sophists, or Wise Men—a term which was afterwards used to signify men who exercised their talents in verbal quibbles and captious reasonings, indicating that such was too often the mode in which rhetoric and dialectics were misapplied by these, the authorised teachers of the day. In the midst of them arose Socrates, the first that turned his attention entirely to the study of men and morals. Unlike the Sophists, whose boasted wisdom he confounded, he gave his lessons without fee or reward, and always in the way of familiar conversation, instructing his hearers chiefly by putting such questions as elicited from their own minds the truths he desired to impress; while, by a similar process of catechising, he confounded the pretended wisdom of the Sophists. Out of the intellectual school formed by Socrates arose all the leaders of speculative philosophy in Greece for the next half-century; and they called themselves philosophers, or lovers of wisdom, representing themselves as modest inquirers after truth, in contrast to those who claimed the denomination of Sophists, or Wise Men.

530. Socrates, of course, made himself many enemies; but he seems to have been long sheltered from any serious injury by the numerous individuals who had enjoyed his instructions. In his old age, however, he was accused of introducing religious novelties and corrupting the youth of the city. He took no pains to defend himself, and was sentenced to drink the cup of hemlock, which was the usual mode of executing distinguished criminals.

FOURTH PERIOD.

404—371 B.C.

THE TEN THOUSAND GREEKS.

531. The narrative of the Ten Thousand Greeks, their march into the heart of the Persian Empire, and their still more celebrated retreat homeward, is a matter lying apart from the main stream of Grecian history, yet so illustrative of Greek character, and so important in the effects it produced on Grecian affairs, that it demands a place here.

532. The death of Darius Nothus, the father of Cyrus the Younger, took place about the beginning of the year 404 B.C., a little after the battle of Ægos-Potamos, which proved the ruin of the Athenian power. Cyrus, though younger than his brother Artaxerxes, seems to have calculated upon succeeding to the Persian throne; but as Darius had died without making any such declaration in his favour, Artaxerxes was proclaimed, and took possession. Nor was Cyrus merely disappointed of the kingdom: he was seized by his brother's orders, on suspicion of having conspired against his life, and was saved from a cruel death only by the all-powerful intercession of his mother. It was deemed best to send him back to his satrapy on the Ionian sea-board, rather than allow him to remain nearer the capital; and the young prince returned to Sardis, burning with anger, and resolving to dethrone his brother.

533. Cyrus had formed a high opinion of the superiority of the Greeks, both as soldiers and politicians, in comparison with the native Asiatics; and he resolved to enlist them in his service. He had already a certain number of Greek mercenaries in the various garrisons of his satrapy; and he directed the officers in command to strengthen these forces by adding as many Peloponnesian

soldiers as they could obtain. Besides those which he collected in Asia Minor, he raised large levies in European Greece, chiefly through the instrumentality of Clearchus, a Lacedæmonian officer of great ability, and others who had contracted a personal friendship for the prince during the late war. The moment was highly favourable for such operations. There were numerous Greeks who, during the long Peloponnesian War, had acquired such military tastes and habits, that they could not easily settle to prosecute the arts of peaceful industry; others had been driven into exile by the establishment of the Lysandrian decarchies in the various cities; and hence there were plenty of competent recruits to be had for a well-paid service like that of Cyrus; so that it was not long till a force of above 10,000 heavy-armed Greeks was collected, besides two or three thousand peltasts. The king Artaxerxes was deluded into the belief that these new levies were intended for private warfare between Cyrus and Tissaphernes; while the Greeks were led to suppose that they were engaged for an expedition against the mountaineers of Pisidia, who harassed the cities of the Asiatic coast. Cyrus further collected a force of 100,000 native Asiatics. With respect to all, he took great pains to conciliate their friendship and engage their confidence; while from all, except Clearchus, he kept his designs a profound secret. The entire host assembled at Sardis, whence the expedition set out in the summer of 401 B.C., under command of the prince in person. Xenophon accompanied the expedition in the character of a volunteer, and afterwards wrote an account of it, which is still extant, and admitted to be one of the finest pieces of narration ever composed.

534. The march was directed through Lydia and Phrygia, and thence through Lycaonia to Dana, south of which lay the pass into Cilicia over Mount Taurus. At Issus, the last town in Cilicia, the army met the fleet, which brought them reinforcements; and after marching through the defile known as the Gates of Cilicia and Syria, which they found undefended, they struck off into the interior, over Mount Amanus, and reached Thapsacus

on the Euphrates. Here the Greeks were informed, on the authority of the prince, of what they had long suspected—that they were marching to Babylon against the king of Persia. The first announcement excited an outburst of dissatisfaction; but the reluctance to proceed was overcome by liberal pay, and still more liberal promises, added to the consideration, that it would now be difficult to get back. After several days' march, through what may be called the desert, the troops found themselves entering the fertile plains of Babylonia. They had now advanced above 1500 miles from Sardis without meeting any serious opposition; but presently there were symptoms of a hostile force before them, and in the neighbourhood of Cunaxa, about a day's journey from Babylon, they learned that the whole force of the Persian king was approaching. Cyrus immediately drew up his army in battle-array, posting the Greeks on the right, while himself, surrounded by a select body-guard of Persian cuirassiers, took his place in the centre. It was long, however, before the army of the Great King appeared in sight. At first, its approach was intimated only by a vast cloud of dust; but as it drew nearer, the flashing arms and extended ranks were indistinctly perceived, and at length the magnificent array of the royal host was fully revealed. In the van were 150 chariots, armed with scythes, projecting in various directions; and behind these were distinguished the white corselets of the cavalry, the wicker bucklers of the select infantry, the tall wooden shields of the Egyptians, and the numerous columns of light-armed troops, collected from among the various nations that owned the sway of Persia. Tissaphernes was on the left wing, opposite the Greeks, while Artaxerxes himself commanded the centre, which extended beyond the left of Cyrus. When they were about half a mile distant, the Greeks charged them with the usual war-shout, and the Persians did not wait to meet the conflict, but turned and fled, Tissaphernes and his cavalry alone offering a momentary resistance. The centre and right of the Persians, however, remained unbroken; and Artaxerxes, not aware that his left wing was routed, ordered the right to wheel, and surround the army of Cyrus. The prince now charged the centre with great impetuosity; and having broken and dispersed the royal body-guard, he perceived the king himself. The sight filled him with such a paroxysm of rage, that he lost all thought of safety or prudence, and crying out : ' I see the man !' he rushed forward to attack him with a mere handful of companions. Now hurling his javelin at his brother, he wounded him in the breast, but was himself speedily overpowered by superior numbers, and slain. His head and right hand were immediately cut off, by order of the king, and conspicuously exhibited—a proclamation which was understood by the Asiatic troops of Cyrus, who at once deserted the field, and fled.

535. Meanwhile, Clearchus had pursued the enemy upwards of three miles; when, hearing that the royal troops had been victorious in the left and centre, he returned, and again routed the Persian troops in their endeavour to intercept him. Thus terminated the battle of Cunaxa, and with it the life as well as the ambitious hopes of the prince Cyrus. Doubtless, Hellas had no cause to regret his fall; for had his enterprise succeeded, he would probably have striven, and not in vain, to subjugate all the Greeks to himself, both in Europe and Asia.

536. The Greek troops, though disappointed and dismayed on learning the death of Cyrus, were yet unwilling to abandon an enterprise of which they had formed such magnificent expectations; and they endeavoured to induceAriæus, on whom the command of the Asiatic troops had now devolved, to continue the war; promising him an easy victory, and the throne of Persia as its reward. But Ariæus declined their flattering offers, and persuaded them rather to accompany him in the retreat which he commenced immediately towards Ionia.

537. It was impossible to return by the way they had come, for want of provisions, which had been on the point of failing during their upward march, notwithstanding the preparations made by Cyrus for supplies. Ariæus promised, however, to guide them by a new route; longer, indeed, but better provisioned. They pursued their way,

accordingly, in the morning, towards some villages of the Babylonian territory, but found they had been plundered by the enemy, and afforded nothing. This movement struck the Persians with alarm ; and mutual explanations took place. The Greeks said that they had no hostile purposes against the king ; that Cyrus had led them on under false pretences ; but that they had been ashamed to leave him in the midst of danger, especially as he had always treated them generously ; that he being now dead, they desired not to fight against the king, and would rather return home, if they might do so in peace.

538. The reply was, that they should enter into a convention, the terms of which should be, that they should march peaceably to the coast, under the guidance of Tissaphernes, and be furnished with provisions on condition of paying for them, and abstaining from plunder. The offer was gladly accepted ; and after twenty days, the satrap returned with his army ready for the march.Ariæus now withdrew himself from the Greeks, and united his troops with those of Tissaphernes. Clearchus and his soldiers, mistrustful of them all, kept at a distance of some miles in their rear, having guides for themselves, and always maintaining their encampment apart. On the banks of the Great Zab, the suspicions of the Greeks became so aggravated that Clearchus sought an explanation with Tissaphernes. The wily satrap gave him the most unbounded assurances of sincere friendship, denounced in the strongest terms the mischief-makers who were striving to put enmity between the two parties ; and, finally, invited Clearchus and the other generals to dine with him on the following day, promising that he would then disclose to them the hidden springs of this mistrust. It was not without some misgiving, which the confidence of Clearchus overruled, that the other four generals, with some inferior officers and soldiers, repaired to the quarters of Tissaphernes. The generals were immediately seized, and put in chains, to be carried to the Persian king, who put them all to death, except Menon, who escaped on this occasion by professing to have been instrumental in entrapping his colleagues. The soldiers who accompanied the generals had been

all cut down; but one of them contrived to run wounded to the camp of the Greeks with tidings of the murderous treachery of Tissaphernes. The Greeks put themselves in an attitude of defence, but they were not attacked, only summoned to surrender. This they indignantly refused, though utterly at a loss what to do to save themselves. They were in the midst of a hostile empire, 10,000 stadia from home, hemmed in by impassable mountains and rivers; without guides, without provisions, without cavalry to protect their retreat; and, above all, without a single man among them invested with authority to give orders, or with responsibility for taking another step.

539. An inspiration now happily filled the mind of Xenophon, whose own account of the matter is, that snatching a short sleep on that night of sorrow, he dreamed that a burning thunderbolt fell on his father's house and enveloped it in flames. Though not seeing clearly what was foretold by this dream, Xenophon believed that at least it was a message from Jupiter the king of thunders warning him to bestir himself.

540. Without a moment's delay, he called together the lochagi, or captains who had served under his late friend Proxenus; and implored them to prepare for a vigorous defence. 'Let us,' said he, 'take the lead, and communicate the stimulus to others. Do you shew yourselves more worthy of being generals than those we have lost. Begin at once, and I will gladly follow you. But if you order me to take the lead, I will not plead my youth as an excuse for disobeying, but account myself of mature age when the object is to save myself from ruin.'

541. All the lochagi cordially agreed except one, who insisted upon submission to the Persian monarch as the only hope of deliverance, and was for his cowardice degraded from his rank, and made a slave to carry baggage. The rest of the officers, numbering about 100, were then convened, and chose from among themselves the necessary number of generals; after which, the whole army was convoked in a general assembly.

542. It was now the task of Xenophon to set forth the case at length—to work up the feelings of the soldiers to

that pitch of resolution which the emergency demanded, and, above all, to annihilate in their minds every disposition to listen to proposals from the enemy. It was determined that Cheirisophus, a Lacedæmonian, should lead the van, while Cleanor and the other senior officers should command the flanks, and Xenophon himself, with Timasion, being the two youngest of the generals, should take charge of the rear-guard.

543. The first part of the march, which was up the course of the Tigris, was harassed by the Persian troops. They had then to ford that river, and fight their way through the warlike tribes inhabiting the mountainous country beyond. They reached the high table-land of Armenia in December, where they forded the Euphrates, to traverse plains deeply covered with snow ; and thus they held on their way, obtaining supplies from the villages by fair means or foul, just as the inhabitants shewed fight, or fled, or entered into amicable relations.

544. Arriving at length at the Greek maritime city of Trapezus or Trebizond, on the Euxine, they enjoyed, for the first time since leaving Tarsus, a secure repose of thirty days, during which they recovered in some degree from the effects of the severe hardships they had undergone. Here they discharged the vow they had made in the hour of their distress, by sacrificing abundantly to Jupiter the preserver, to Hercules the conductor, and various other gods. Games followed as usual, the skins of the victims being bestowed as prizes to the successful competitors.

545. The adventurers had still to track their way among the Greek colonies on the Euxine, and through the regions of Thrace, ere they could reach their home. Sparta was now mistress of the whole Grecian world, and almost all the cities were governed by decarchies, or ruling ' councils of ten,' with a Lacedæmonian harmost and garrison to maintain their authority. Being again and again disappointed of the pay and supplies which they had been led to expect from these authorities, they were driven to acts of violence for their own support, and were in danger of being denounced as a band of hostile marauders, to be resisted instead of welcomed throughout their native

Greece. Under these circumstances, Xenophon accepted the proposals of Seuthes, a Thracian prince, who desired the assistance of the Cyreian army to reconquer some revolted tribes. Seuthes not only made liberal offers of present remuneration, but promised to afford the warriors a permanent right of settlement in his dominions, in case they should incur the displeasure of Sparta by joining him. Besides, he engaged to give to Xenophon the possession of his best point on the coast, and his daughter in marriage. Even had the promises been less favourable, the troops had no alternative, for they were without even present supplies. The sacrifices likewise being propitious, they concluded the bargain, and remained two months in the service of Seuthes, who, through their assistance, soon found himself in the possession of an extensive dominion, a large native force, and a considerable tribute. The pay, however, which he had promised, was never liquidated; and Xenophon himself, far from realising the splendid prospects which had been set before him personally, seems not to have received his pay as one of the generals.

546. It is hard to say what would have become of this gallant army, had they not been extricated from their difficulties by a change of policy on the part of the Lacedæmonians. Sparta had now declared war against Tissaphernes and Pharnabazus, and her authorities became extremely anxious to enlist the Cyreian army in an expedition against them. The proposal was joyfully accepted; and the band, now reduced by losses and dispersions to 6000 men, crossed over into Asia. Xenophon was persuaded to remain in command till the troops joined those of Thimbron, the commander appointed by Sparta, after which he took leave of them. He returned to Athens after an absence of about two years and a half, a few weeks subsequent to the death of his beloved friend and preceptor Socrates. His feelings on this subject, together with the altered condition of his native city, now subject and quiescent—the habits he had contracted during the term of his military peregrinations—all probably combined to render his residence at Athens distasteful, so that next spring we find him

rejoining his former companions in Asia, to fight his old enemy Tissaphernes.

LYSANDER AND AGESILAUS.

547. In resuming the thread of general Greek history, it is scarcely necessary to remind the reader that the supremacy of Sparta was now complete and universal. It must be told, too, that her empire, which worked badly for the dependent cities, did no better for her own character, and for those internal institutions which had long been her pride and her safety. Sparta was now wealthy as well as powerful. Not only did Lysander bring home a large quantity of gold and silver from the war which he prosecuted against Athens, but he had imposed a much higher tribute upon the dependent cities in connection with numerous appointments of harmosts, which afforded abundance of illicit gains.

548. Agis and Pausanias were the two kings nominally reigning at the close of the war; but Lysander, the commander of the fleet, was for the time greater than either. Whether from the promptings of his own ambition, or the suggestions of the sophists and poets, who loaded him with flattery, he came to conceive the project of breaking the line of royal succession, and himself grasping the crown. Knowing that this could scarcely be accomplished without supernatural interference, he made several efforts to elicit from the oracles an injunction favourable to his views. This failing, he employed his influence to obtain the sceptre for one under whom he hoped for a great increase of his already too extensive power. The king, Agis, dying in 399 B.C., his brother Agesilaus, prompted by Lysander, stood forward to claim the throne for himself, on the ground of some doubts which had always hung over the parentage of Leotychides, a youth fifteen years of age, the reputed son of Agis. Agesilaus had passed through the unmitigated rigour of Spartan drill, and was highly distinguished for all the Spartan virtues—exemplary obedience to authority, intense emulation, extraordinary courage, unremitting energy and

capacity for enduring hardship, combined with perfect frugality and simplicity in his personal habits, and extreme sensibility to the opinion of his fellow-citizens. He possessed also an intellectual culture which raised him far above the narrow-mindedness of the earlier Spartans, and which doubtless was the result of the increased intercourse with other states which had for some time been permitted. His manners were popular, and his countenance pleasing, though he was of mean stature, and lame in one leg.

549. His mature age and high reputation went for much in comparison with the untried youth of his competitor; but his personal deformity was a matter of natural repugnance to the Spartan mind, and, moreover, had been, it was declared, special matter of divine warning. There was an ancient oracle which had been invoked on a former occasion, warning Sparta that 'with all her pride, she must not suffer a lame reign to impair her stable foundations, else unexampled suffering and ruinous wars would long afflict her.' Lysander explained this to refer, not to a bodily defect in the king, but to a hitch in the Heraclid succession; and the preponderating feeling already in favour of Agesilaus led the majority to accept his explanation, and nominate the lame candidate to the throne. Agesilaus conducted himself in a highly popular and conciliatory manner, which, combined with his singular talents, secured to him more real power both at home and abroad, than had ever fallen to the lot of a king of Sparta. And now he displayed some new dispositions hitherto latent in his character. While, like Lysander, he despised money, luxury, and all the outward show of power, carrying his simplicity of personal habits almost to affectation—like Lysander, too, he delighted in the exercise of dominion, and rarely scrupled to uphold factions of partisans in their career of injustice and oppression. Though having no disposition to tyranny, and still less to plunder for his own benefit, he thus made himself the willing instrument of both for the benefit of his friends and coadjutors.

AGESILAUS IN ASIA.

550. The attention of Sparta was now drawn to Asia Minor, where the war had been vigorously prosecuted by Dercyllidas, the successor of Thimbron in command of the Lacedæmonian troops. An armistice had been concluded, of which the satrap Pharnabazus availed himself to make active preparations for a renewal 397 B.C. of the war. He not only obtained large reinforcements of Persian troops, but organised a fleet in Phœnicia and Cilicia, and gave the command of it to the Athenian admiral Conon, who, it will be remembered, had been defeated seven years before at Ægos-Potamos, and thence fled to Cyprus.

551. The news of these preparations reaching Sparta, Agesilaus volunteered to assume the command of a land-force to meet the Persians in Asia. He proposed to take with him only thirty fully-qualified Spartan citizens or peers, as a sort of council of officers, with 2000 neodamodes, or enfranchised Helots, and 6000 hoplites from among the allies. He was to be accompanied by Lysander, who expected to be the leader of the thirty Spartans, and virtually the commander of the whole expedition.

552. The king sailed for the coast of Asia 396 B.C.; and while his army remained inactive at Ephesus, waiting the ultimatum of Persia, the insolence of Lysander became intolerable to the superior officers, and most of all to Agesilaus himself. Agesilaus was resolved to uphold his dignity, and subjected Lysander to so many humiliations, that the latter sought to come to an explanation. Agesilaus firmly answered him that he would humble those who desired to appear greater than himself; and the mortified admiral was glad to beg that he might be sent on some mission apart. He was accordingly despatched to the Hellespont, where he did valuable service against the Persian foe.

553. Agesilaus now made preparations as though to fall upon Caria; and having thus put the enemy on a false scent, he suddenly made for Phrygia, in the satrapy of

Pharnabazus, and ravaged a portion of it. While he was ever ready to grant his army the plunder of any territory over which they carried victorious arms, he was always careful to prevent cruelty and wanton destruction. The most valuable spoil generally consisted of the adult natives, of both sexes, who were sold as slaves; but Agesilaus was vigilant in protecting them from anything like ill-usage. Another circumstance which affords an insight into the social state at this time is the following:—
It was the practice of poor people to sell to itinerant slave-merchants such of their own children as they could not maintain; and these merchants, in their haste to get out of the way of the plundering army, left numbers of such children by the wayside to perish. Agesilaus picked them up on his march, and gave them in charge to those aged natives that were not worth carrying off.

554. Next spring, he gave out that he should march against Sardis; and Tissaphernes, believing that this was another feint, and that the real object of hostilities would be Caria, concentrated his forces there. But this time, Agesilaus was as good as his word. He plundered the country with little opposition, carrying his ravages to the very gates of Sardis, and defying Tissaphernes to come out and fight. The inhabitants now complained loudly that the satrap had left them unprotected, out of anxiety for his own residence at Caria; the Persian monarch was displeased that nothing had been achieved by the large reinforcements he had sent to effect the expulsion of the Greeks; the queen-mother, Parysatis, added her influence against the satrap, having never forgiven him for his part in the death of her son Cyrus; and an order was sent down from court to depose him, and put him to death.

555. Tithraustes, the successor of Tissaphernes, immediately opened negotiations with Agesilaus, and persuaded him to remove his troops to the satrapy of Pharnabazus, giving him thirty talents towards their maintenance. The Spartan king, accordingly, proceeded northward, advanced into the province of Pharnabazus, found himself victorious in every direction, ravaged the greater part of the satrapy,

and soon mastered the whole. Pharnabazus first concentrated his forces at Dascylium; but Agesilaus took up his abode in the immediate neighbourhood for the winter; and the satrap, fearful of being taken, left his quarters to hover about the country, carrying his valuable property with him, and keeping the place of his encampment secret. Agesilaus, however, found him out, defeated and put him to flight, gaining a large amount of spoil. He then spent the remainder of the winter at Dascylium.

556. Ere the spring was available for new enterprises, a personal interview was brought about by a third party between the victorious spoiler and the hunted satrap. Xenophon, who probably was present, has preserved an interesting account of it. First came Agesilaus, with his thirty Spartans, and sat down on the grass to wait. Presently, Pharnabazus arrived with a splendid retinue; and his attendants were beginning to spread elegant carpets, when he perceived how the Spartans were seated, and for very shame sat himself down on the turf beside Agesilaus. As the elder of the two, he was the first to proffer the right hand, and begin the conversation. He reminded the Spartans how he had befriended them in their war with Athens; appealed to them if he had ever played them false by word or deed; then represented how, in return, he had been so reduced by their devastations, that he could not have a dinner in his own territory but by picking up their leavings; and he asked, in conclusion, whether they counted this requital holy and just.

557. The Spartans were covered with shame; and the king, after a long pause, replied by referring to the necessity they were under to treat as hostile every country owning the sway of the king of Persia, since Sparta was at deadly war with him. But professing personally no enmity to the satrap, Agesilaus offered to become his friend and ally, if he would set up for an independent ruler, renouncing allegiance to the Great King. The high-minded reply of Pharnabazus filled them all with admiration. 'If the king,' said he, 'shall send any other general, I shall willingly be your ally; but if he imposes the duty of command on me, the point of honour is so strong, that I shall continue

to fight you with all my might. Expect nothing else.'
Fain would Agesilaus have had him for a friend instead
of an enemy; but as this could not be, he assured him
that he would at once quit his province, nor ever turn
his arms against him while another Persian foe remained.
As the satrap rode away, his son lingered and exchanged
pledges of friendship with Agesilaus—pledges which were
not afterwards forgotten on either side.

558. The plans of Agesilaus were now all laid for
penetrating further into the interior; but as he was on
the point of setting out, he was summoned home to Sparta.
While he had been gathering laurels in Asia, distresses
had been crowding round his native city, which now
required his succour.

COMBINATION AGAINST SPARTA—
BŒOTIAN WAR.

559. The hatred with which the empire of Sparta was
regarded, had not escaped the notice of the Persians; and
Tithraustes had been using it to stir up a war against her
in Greece itself. The island of Rhodes had just revolted
from her, and now Timocrates, a native of that island, was
despatched to those of the principal cities that seemed
most hostile to Sparta, taking with him fifty talents, with
instructions to gain over the leading men, and to exchange
solemn oaths of alliance with Persia for common hostility
against Sparta. No positive union, however, had been
brought about with any of these cities, when hostilities,
kindled by an accident, broke out as a Bœotian war
between Thebes and Sparta separately.

560. The Phocians had disputed with the Opuntian
Locrians about a strip of border territory, and commenced
hostilities. The Locrians, being allies of Thebes, claimed
her protection, while the Phocians threw themselves on
the strong arm of Sparta. The ambitious Lysander, who
had long hated the Thebans, was foremost in advising
an expedition against them, and was himself appointed to
an important command. A small force was committed to
him, and he was to increase it by mustering the various

dependent populations in the neighbourhood of Mount Œta; then taking up the Phocians in his way, he was to invade Bœotia from the north. On a given day, he was to reach Haliartus, and under its walls, to meet Pausanias, who was to approach in another direction with the main force of the Lacedæmonians and their Peloponnesian allies.

561. The Thebans thus threatened, implored succour from their ancient and deadly enemies, the Athenians, who, enfeebled as they had been by the Peloponnesian War, had not now, for eight years, been called upon to decide on any question of foreign policy. They now at once consented, resolved to break the chain by which they were held as mere units in the regiments of Spartan allies, and to begin a new life as a self-acting and primary power.

562. The first approach of Lysander, with his army of Heracleots, Phocians, and others, was truly formidable. To render it more so, Orchomenus, the second city to Thebes in the Bœotian confederacy, broke off, joined Lysander, threw open to him the way into Bœotia, and conducted him into the district belonging to Haliartus. Pausanias had not yet arrived; and Lysander, fearing that the enemy would gain by delay, began the attack without waiting for him. But while he was engaged close by the gates, examining where an entrance might be effected, a fresh division of Thebans was seen rapidly approaching; and the besieged, encouraged by the sight, threw open their gates, and made a sally. The besiegers were driven back with considerable loss, Lysander himself being among the first slain. His army, composed of heterogeneous masses, held together by his mere personal ascendancy, disbanded during the night; so that when Pausanias arrived, he found no second army to join him; and seeing little to hope from a battle, he solicited the burial-truce. Contrary to the received practice of Greece, where the victor was considered as bound to grant the burial-truce unconditionally when asked, the Thebans refused to grant it, except on condition that the Spartan army should immediately evacuate Bœotia. And yet so reluctant was that army to fight, that they cheerfully

acquiesced; and as soon as the funeral solemnities were completed, they were led back towards Peloponnesus. The Thebans watched their dejected march with triumphant insolence, and restrained them, not without occasional blows, from straggling into the cultivated fields.

563. Pausanias, not daring to brave the indignation and resentment which burned against him at Sparta, escaped, and took sanctuary in the temple of Minerva at Tegea. He was condemned to death in his absence, and therefore remained for the rest of his days under the shelter of the asylum he had chosen, while his son Agesipolis swayed the sceptre in his place.

564. The enemies of Sparta were now invigorated with fresh hope. An alliance was concluded against her by Thebes, Athens, Corinth, and Argos, which was speedily strengthened by the Eubœans, Acarnanians, the Ozolian Locrians, the Chalcidians of Thrace, and some others. Corinth was appointed as the head-quarters for their councils, and therefore the hostilities which had begun as a Bœotian war, were henceforth denominated the Corinthian.

CORINTHIAN WAR—CORONEA.

565. In the spring of 394 B.C., the allies, having assembled in great spirits, resolved to concoct new and powerful measures against the enemy. On the other hand, Sparta, threatened with the loss of all her extra Peloponnesian dependencies, resolved at once to recall Agesilaus from Asia, and in the meantime, to muster her whole force, and march towards Corinth. A general engagement took place near the city. The Lacedæmonians themselves were completely victorious; but their allies were put to the rout, and returned home in disgust. The confederates had now leisure to concentrate their whole attention on Agesilaus, who had received with great vexation the summons to return to Greece, yet obeyed it with patriotic submission. Though the home-service was an unpromising one for any one to follow him in—being a war against Greeks, with the certainty of hard fighting and little plunder—yet he had persuaded some of the bravest

soldiers in his army to share his lot; and among them, many of the 10,000, with Xenophon at their head.

566. Agesilaus crossed the Hellespont, and proceeded through Thrace, Macedonia, Thessaly, and Thermopylæ, scattering before him the various detached forces that appeared to bar his progress; for there was not, nor could there be in these regions, any combined or systematic resistance. Knowing that most of his soldiers would remain attached to him only so long as they believed the cause of Sparta to be the gaining one, he carefully concealed from them the intelligence, which reached him at Cheronaia, that Pisander, who commanded the fleet, had been defeated and slain in a naval engagement at Cnidus. He assured them that the day had been won though the admiral was dead, and hastened forward to meet the enemy, while his troops continued in good spirits.

567. The conflicting armies met on the plain of Coronea. The collision which took place is said to have been terrific, beyond anything ever known in Greek warfare. The Spartan and Theban hoplites came to the closest bodily struggle, pushing their shields against each other—all the weight of the mass behind pressing on the foremost ranks—so that their shields were stove in, their spears broken, and each man was closely embraced with his enemy, the dagger his only available weapon. Agesilaus himself, whose strength and stature were by no means commensurate with his personal courage, was wounded and trodden down, but saved from death. The Spartans became masters of the field, having driven back the centre and left division of the enemy; though, as far as the Thebans who formed the right wing were concerned, they had the worst of the combat. On the next morning, Agesilaus commanded the polemarch to assemble the troops, to erect a trophy, to offer sacrifices of thanksgiving with the sound of solemn music, according to Spartan custom; making his demonstrations all the more ostentatious, because he was not sure of his claim to the victory. The suspense was removed only by the Thebans sending a herald to solicit the burial-truce—the understood confession of defeat.

568. Being disabled from immediate action, Agesilaus was carried to Delphi, where the Pythian games were going on, and where he offered to Apollo the tithe of all the booty he had gained by his two years' campaigning in Asia. When tolerably recovered, he returned home; was received at Sparta with every demonstration of esteem and gratitude; and continued to be the chief leader of its policy, enjoying greater influence than had ever fallen to the lot of any previous king. Yet he never forgot himself, or by any means relaxed either in the simplicity of his personal habits, or in the exact observance of public discipline.

DESTRUCTION OF THE MARITIME EMPIRE OF SPARTA.

569. The victories of Corinth and Coronea seem to have done nothing towards improving the position of Sparta with respect to her enemies, while the defeat at Cnidus proved to have been pregnant with disastrous events, which followed each other in rapid succession. Pharnabazus and Conon, with the victorious fleet, sailed from island to island, and from port to port throughout the Ægæan, to expel the Lacedæmonian harmosts, and put down the domination of Sparta. But their task had been almost everywhere anticipated. The harmosts, on both sides of the Hellespont, had deserted their posts, and fled at the mere news of the defeat at Cnidus. Pharnabazus and Conon were received in all the towns as liberators; they engaged that each city should enjoy its own genuine autonomy, and that no foreign force or governor should be introduced. The consequence was, that the maritime empire of Sparta was dissolved without a blow, by the almost spontaneous movement of the cities themselves; and Pharnabazus landing at Ephesus, marched northward to his own satrapy. Here he found a solitary exception to the general feeling. Abydos maintained its attachment to Sparta under Dercyllidas as harmost, who also secured Sestus, and held both for the Lacedæmonians, in defiance of the wrath of the satrap.

570. As soon as spring appeared, Pharnabazus, with a powerful fleet, directed his course to various islands of the Cyclades; then to the coasts of Laconia and Messenia; and, finally, sailed up the Saronic Gulf to the Isthmus of Corinth, where he assured the allies of his strenuous support against Sparta.

REBUILDING OF THE ATHENIAN WALLS BY CONON.

571. The appearance of a Persian satrap with a Persian fleet, as master of the Peloponnesian sea and the Saronic Gulf, was a strange sight to Grecian eyes. No Persian tiara had been seen near this gulf since the battle of Salamis, nor could anything short of the intense personal hostility of Pharnabazus have brought him into this position.

572. Conon availed himself of this feeling, and as the satrap was about to return home, entreated him to leave the fleet under his care, to assist in the great work of restoring the Long Walls of Athens, and the fortifications of Piræus. This, he affirmed, would be the severest mortification that could possibly be inflicted on the Spartans; and such was the irritation of the satrap, that he not only gave leave for this use of the fleet, but left a considerable sum of money towards the works. Conon, therefore, returned, as a second Themistocles, to restore the lost strength and independence of 393 B.C. his country. All hands were set to work. The Bœotians and other neighbours, who, eleven years ago, had danced to the sound of joyful music at the demolition of the former walls, now lent their aid as volunteers, and the work was completed before winter without any opposition. The Spartans had no power to hinder, for by sea the Persian fleet was more than a sufficient protection; while on the land-side, they were barred out by the confederate force being in possession of the Isthmus of Corinth.

CAMPAIGNS OF AGESILAUS IN THE CORINTHIAN TERRITORY.

573. During the remainder of this year, and the whole of the year following, the hostilities were carried on chiefly in the territories of Corinth, the Spartans having taken up their head-quarters at Sicyon, whence they ravaged the fertile plains. Erelong they mastered the Long Walls of the city, and made the port of Lechæum a permanent post of hostility, occupied by a Lacedæmonian garrison.

574. Another feat of Agesilaus was a sudden attack on Piræum, which he captured, together with the Heræum, or sacred territory of Juno, whither the inhabitants had fled with their property. A large booty thus fell into the victor's hands, besides prisoners; and so triumphant now was his position, that the confederates were all in alarm, and sent fresh envoys to solicit peace. Agesilaus, gratified at seeing the Thebans thus humbled, and desiring to increase their mortification, treated their envoys with marked contempt, affecting not even to see them when they stood close by. But a sudden change came over the aspect of affairs.

575. Iphicrates, the Athenian, by a change of equipments, together with careful training, had made a most effective body of the hired peltasts, hitherto made little account of in comparison with the hoplites of Greece. As Agesilaus was sitting in a pavilion on the border of the lake adjoining the Heræum, a man galloped up at full speed on a foaming horse; and springing to the feet of the king, informed him that a Lacedæmonian mora, or military division, 600 strong, had been destroyed almost to a man by the insignificant peltasts under Iphicrates. Ere the bodies of the slain could be picked up for burial, this horseman had started off to inform Agesilaus, who sprang up, seized his spear, ordered the troops to follow, and set out for the spot. He hoped to reach the field in time to contend for possession, and escape the humiliation of asking for the burial-truce;

but before he had gone far, he met other horsemen, who informed him that the slain were already buried under truce asked and obtained. Nothing like this had occurred since the capture of Sphacteria ; and the event produced the greatest sensation, especially reviving the desponding spirits of the Athenian confederation, while it was welcomed with ill-suppressed satisfaction even by the allies of Sparta.

576. And here we are to mark a fact highly characteristic of Spartan training. The news of the defeat filled the city with mourning, and the immediate friends of the survivors were especially overwhelmed with shame and dismay ; but the near relatives of those who had fallen, strutted about with a cheerful and even triumphant demeanour, rejoicing that their friends had not lived dishonoured.

577. Agesilaus, after vainly defying Iphicrates to a battle, marched as quietly as possible back to Sparta, avoiding exposing his army by daylight to the gaze of those populations that would have been likely to manifest their gratification at the recent defeat. His withdrawal was the signal for renewed enterprise on the part of Iphicrates ; and he retook Sidus, Crommyon, Piræum, and Œnoe, thus clearing Corinth of enemies on the east and north-eastern sides.

PEACE OF ANTALCIDAS.

578. There is little interest in following out the details of the struggle between Sparta and the allied forces, in which neither party gained decisive superiority. Whatever advantages Sparta obtained on land, were fully counterbalanced by the success of Athens at sea ; and the Spartans saw no way of putting a stop to the progress of their enemies, but by detaching Persia from their interests. For this purpose, they employed Antalcidas, a dexterous and artful man, to negotiate. The only way of bidding above Athens for the favour of Artaxerxes, was by offering to surrender the Asiatic Greeks to his supremacy;

and even this Antalcidas was ready to do; but for a time he met with little encouragement.

579. In the course of these intrigues, Conon was arrested on false pretences by the Persian satrap of Ionia; and we hear no more of this great man in connection with public affairs. According to one account, he was put to death in prison; but a more probable story is, that he regained his liberty, again took refuge with Evagoras in Cyprus, and died a natural death.

580. When two years had elapsed from the time that Antalcidas first endeavoured to negotiate with Persia, and now all parties were tired of the war, Artaxerxes listened to the proposals of the Spartans; and after bribing the acquiescence of Pharnabazus, by giving him his daughter in marriage, he issued the following edict, which was announced to the contending parties at Sardis :— 387 B.C.

581. 'King Artaxerxes thinks it just that the cities in Asia and the islands of Clazomenæ and Cyprus shall belong to him. He thinks it just also to leave all the other Hellenic cities autonomous, both small and great, except Lemnos, Imbros, and Scyros, which are to belong to Athens, as they did originally. If any parties refuse to accept this peace, I, and those who are of the same mind, will make war upon them by land as well as by sea, with ships and with money.'

582. The Thebans were thus to lose their federal headship among the cities of Bœotia; the Athenians to resign all their distant possessions, except these three islands; and, worst of all, the Greek settlements in Asia Minor were to be for ever cut off from the mother-country; But the agents of the Persian monarch were peremptory, and an overwhelming force would have crushed any single state that refused to accede. Such was the humiliating arrangement called the Peace of Antalcidas.

583. As soon as this peace was concluded, Sparta, as its surety and interpreter, required the restoration of the Corinthian exiles, through whom she became mistress of the isthmus. She then not only declared all the Bœotian cities independent, but proceeded to rebuild the little city

of Platæa—so hateful to Thebes, so dear to Athens—and restore to it the citizens who had escaped from it during the siege formerly described (page 194). The next object of her resentment was Mantinea, a flourishing town in the heart of Peloponnesus, which had shewn strong disaffection towards Sparta during the late war. It was now reduced by siege, and obliged to surrender. The requirement of the conquerors then was, that not only the fortifications, but a great part of the city itself, should be demolished ; that the inhabitants should redistribute themselves into those five villages of which the aggregate city had been formed, each man pulling down his house in the town, and rebuilding it in the village next to his lands ; while a remnant of Mantinea itself should continue to be occupied, but as a village. Each village was placed under oligarchical government, and left unfortified.

584. This sentence was one of the severest that could have been pronounced on free Greeks, in point of dishonour, if not of privation. For, as was observed at an early stage of this history, all the distinctive glory of Hellenism, all that it boasted of literature, philosophy, and the fine arts, of intellectual enjoyment, or of refined social intercourse—depended on the city-appurtenances.

585. It would seem that this proceeding towards Mantinea, was only the most stringent of a series of severities exercised by the Lacedæmonians towards their confederates wherever they had ground of dissatisfaction or mistrust.

OLYNTHIAN WAR.

586. The Greek cities of Chalcidic Thrace, adjoining the kingdom of Macedonia, had been lost to Athens, at least from the time that the fatal disaster at Syracuse had disabled her from maintaining such distant interests. Under these circumstances, Olynthus, the largest of these cities, had not only risen to wealth and influence without exciting jealousy, but had become the centre of an extensive coalition, including many Macedonian as well as Grecian cities, allied for mutual protection against

the Illyrians and other barbarous neighbours, whom the king of Macedonia was not able to restrain. Several of these had joined willingly; others, because they were afraid to refuse; but the two most considerable of them, Acanthus and Apollonia, positively declined. Being threatened with compulsion, they invoked the interference of Sparta, to whom they represented the dangerous ambition of the Chalcidic capital, its alarming growth and brilliant prospects—a picture more than enough to excite Spartan jealousy. The Macedonian king, Amyntas, who, it appears, had in the first instance abandoned his kingdom, leaving the cities to Olynthian protection, and had since been endeavouring to reinstate himself, seconded the application, and besought Sparta to put down this formidable confederacy. The Lacedæmonians eagerly embraced the invitation, and voted 10,000 men, to be commanded by the brothers Eudamidas and Phœbidas, for the assistance of Acanthus and Apollonia; or, in other words, for the reduction of Olynthus. Eudamidas was despatched at once with such troops as were ready; but Phœbidas, who in due time followed with the remainder, was led to employ them in a very different manner from that originally contemplated.

587. The direct way to Olynthus lay through the neighbourhood of Thebes, where there was a political party favourable to Sparta. Leontiades, the leader of this party, now presented himself to the Spartan general, and offered to put him in possession of the Theban citadel—a proposal which was unhesitatingly, if not eagerly, accepted. The time was the most promising that could have been selected for such an enterprise. It was the day of the Thesmophoria, a religious festival celebrated by the women apart, in the Cadmea, or citadel, which was given up to their exclusive use for the time. The senate was sitting in the portico of the Agora, and the heat of a summer noon had driven every one out of the streets, when Phœbidas, under the guidance of Leontiades, conducted his army straight up to the Cadmea, of which he became master without the slightest opposition; nor only of it, but of all the Theban

women—abundant hostages for the submission, however reluctant, of the citizens in the town below.

588. The sudden explosion and complete success of this conspiracy were more than sufficient to crush all spirit of resistance on the part of the citizens. Their first anxiety probably was to regain their wives and daughters from the custody of the Lacedæmonians; and under these circumstances, it was probably easy to procure a vote of the people for concluding an alliance with Sparta.

589. Sparta was now enabled to prosecute the Olynthian expedition with redoubled vigour. Eudamidas and Amyntas gained some advantages; but the conquest of the Olynthians was found to be no easy enterprise; they had a well-organised force, including especially an excellent body of cavalry, and the struggle was protracted for several years. It was ultimately brought to a close by the Spartan king, Polybiades, who blockaded the city so closely, that it was starved into capitulation. The prescribed terms, which the citizens were in no condition to refuse, were, that they should enrol themselves as sworn members of the Lacedæmonian confederacy, with its obligations of service to Sparta.

590. The Olynthian union being thus dissolved, the Grecian cities of which it had been composed were enrolled severally as allies of Sparta; while the maritime towns of Macedonia passed again under the dominion of Amyntas.

PELOPIDAS THE THEBAN.

591. We have scarcely any information in detail respecting the proceedings of the Theban government, which had now been exercised for three years by Leontiades and his partisans, supported by a large garrison in the Cadmea. Doubtless, its spirit was rapacious and cruel, from the circumstances of the case, but in what degree, we have no means of knowing. In vain the exiles who had fled to Athens waited in hopes of some rising at home, or some blow struck from without; and in the third winter after their flight they resolved to take the initiative upon themselves. Among them were found several men of the

highest families of Thebes, and of these the most daring and self-devoted, though one of the youngest, was Pelopidas. His zeal soon communicated itself to a handful of comrades, and a private correspondence with their friends in Thebes assured them of the general sympathy of the citizens there. The first and indispensable step was to destroy the four rulers, Leontiades, Hypates, Archias, and Philippus, of whom the last two were polemarchs. This desperate blow, Pelopidas, and a certain number more, undertook to strike. Of their correspondents in the city, the most effective was Phyllidas, the secretary of the polemarchs, who undertook to gain them access to their persons; with Charon, who promised them concealment in his house till the critical moment should arrive. That moment was determined by Phyllidas the secretary, who invited Archias and Philippus to an evening banquet, promising to introduce to them some women of great beauty belonging to the best families in Thebes. On the day previous to the banquet, the conspirators, disguised as rustics or hunters, and with no other weapons than concealed daggers, got within the gates of Thebes one by one at nightfall, when the latest husbandmen were coming home from their fields, and were all safely housed with Charon.

592. The hour when they were to be introduced had nearly arrived, and they were preparing to act their parts, when a sudden summons arrived for Charon to appear in the presence of the polemarchs. There was, of course, great reason to fear that the plot had been divulged, but it was agreed that he must at once obey. His own worst fear was that the friends whom he had sheltered should suspect him of being the traitor, and he insisted on leaving his son with them as a pledge of his own fidelity. Entering the presence of the polemarchs, he found them half intoxicated, and learned that they had received intelligence from Athens of some plot being afloat, and that they desired to question him as a known friend of the exiles. Aided by the collusion of Phyllidas, Charon had little difficulty in lulling the vague suspicions of the half-drunken men, and he was allowed again to retire. Presently a

dispatch was delivered to Archias, by a messenger who intimated that it related to very serious matters. 'Serious matters for to-morrow!' said the polemarch, putting the unopened letter under the pillow of the couch on which he was reclining.

593. Returning now to their carouse, the guests impatiently reminded Phyllidas of his promise to introduce the ladies. Upon this, the secretary withdrew, and brought the conspirators, who were in female dress, into an adjoining chamber. Then, returning to the polemarchs, he informed them that the ladies would not come in till the domestics were dismissed, which was accordingly done, and the victims were thus left alone with one or two friends at table, all under the influence of wine. Phyllidas now conducted the conspirators into the festive-apartment, three of them attired as ladies of distinction, and the rest as their female attendants ; their long veils and ample robes being sufficient disguise even had the guests been sober. They sat down beside the polemarchs ; the lifting of their veils was the signal for using their daggers : the polemarchs were murdered with little resistance ; and the archon, who had his spear, and tried to defend himself, fell after a short struggle.

594. Immediately three of the conspirators proceeded to surprise and slay the other two rulers in their own houses ; Phyllidas then conducted them to the prison, where they slew the jailer, and liberated about 150 political prisoners, whom they armed from the battle-spoils hanging in the neighbouring porticos ; after which, they felt assured of safety and triumph. Proclamation was now made aloud by heralds that the despots were slain, and that Thebes was free.

595. Meanwhile, tidings of this success had been sent to Attica ; upon which all the remaining exiles, with a body of Athenian volunteers, hastened to Thebes to complete the work. It was resolved to storm the Cadmea before aid could come from Sparta ; and the citizens were already rushing up to the assault, when the harmost proposed to capitulate, and presently surrendered on condition of undisturbed egress from Thebes, with the honours of war.

596. To the feelings of the modern reader, there is something so shocking in the story of these assassinations, and the circumstances under which they were perpetrated, that the other features of the enterprise appear to little advantage. But an ancient Greek had no such repugnance; he saw nothing but matter of admiration in the personal daring of the conspirators, the skilful forecast of the plot, and the sudden overthrow, by a force so contemptibly small, of a government which seemed unassailable but the day before. The thing came like an electric shock upon the Grecian world; and it turned the balance of power which had hitherto been indisputably on the side of Sparta.

THEBAN WAR—EPAMINONDAS.

597. The revolution at Thebes gave rise to a new war. Such was the feeling enkindled by it at Sparta, that though it was the depth of winter, an expedition against Thebes was decreed, and the allied contingents were summoned.

598. The Thebans thus found themselves exposed to the whole force of Sparta and her confederacy, while they had not a single ally to assist them. Their own energy alone could save them, and the emergency called forth the talents of Epaminondas, a man as yet undistinguished in public life, having devoted himself chiefly to private study and the pursuit of knowledge. He coveted neither fame nor riches, and came out in public life merely because his country required his services; but he proved both one of the most accomplished soldiers of his time, and one of the ablest politicians. Such was the man appointed to conduct the affairs of Thebes in concert with Pelopidas, for whom he maintained a strong and disinterested friendship.

599. A foolish and futile attempt on the part of the Spartan general to surprise Piræus so roused the Athenians, that they put themselves forward as the head of a new confederacy on principles similar to that of Delos. The leaders who chiefly organised it were Chabrias, and Timotheus the son of Conon, both able generals; with Callistratus, renowned as an orator, but boasting no military talent. The

wide-spread hatred of imperial Sparta procured for their mission a general welcome. The leading men in Thebes gladly enrolled their city as a constituent member; reserving, however, either tacitly or expressly, her prospective rights as president of the Bœotian federation, as soon as it could be reconstituted. In a short time, not less than seventy sent their deputies; and the general voice was for war against Sparta upon a large scale. In their ardour, the Athenians imposed on themselves a new property-tax; and the Thebans organised the brigade of hoplites called the Sacred Band, composed of 300 youthful citizens distinguished for their strength and courage.

600. Before the end of the year, the Lacedæmonians were entirely expelled from Bœotia; the oligarchical factions were all put down, and the Bœotian confederacy was fully re-established. Orchomenus alone, with its dependency Chæronea, remained attached to Sparta. The Lacedæmonian fleet of sixty sail was completely defeated by that of the Athenians under Chabrias, and the latter were again the undisputed masters of the sea. 374 B.C.

601. The Spartans now had recourse to the same manœuvre that had served their purpose fifteen years before. They sent Antalcidas again to the Persian court, to entreat that it would interfere to enforce the peace which bore his name, which peace they said had been infringed by the re-establishment of the Bœotian confederacy. The Persians, who were at this time renewing their efforts against Egypt, were anxious for the pacification of Greece, that they might obtain from that country a greater number of mercenaries. Athens, too, was becoming more and more disposed towards peace. She had little to hope from the continuance of the war, since the naval power of Sparta had been humbled; the expense was becoming very serious; and chiefly the ancient jealousy between her and Thebes, which had for a time been overlaid by the fear of Sparta, was now fast reviving.

602. A meeting of deputies was now held at Sparta to deliberate upon peace. The peace of Antalcidas was recognised as the basis upon which Athens was prepared to treat; that is to say, Athens and Sparta June 371 B.C.

were to become partners and mutual guarantees, dividing the headship of Greece by an ascertained line of demarcation, yet not interfering with the principle of universal autonomy. The armaments on both sides were to be disbanded, the harmosts and garrisons withdrawn. If any city should violate these conditions, and pursue a career of force against any other, all were to be at liberty to take up arms on behalf of the injured party, but no one was to be bound to do so.

603. On the next day, when the oaths were to be exchanged, Epaminondas refused to swear for Thebes alone, but for Thebes and the Bœotian cities of her confederacy: he maintained that this federal union under the presidency of Thebes was coeval with the first settlement of the country, and that the rights of Thebes in this respect were both as old and as good as the right of Sparta to govern the townships of Laconia. Had Agesilaus been an orator, he might have delivered a harangue in reply. But with scornful abruptness he rose and demanded: 'Speak plainly. Will you or will you not leave to each of the Bœotian cities its separate autonomy?' To which Epaminondas replied: 'Will *you* leave each of the Laconian towns autonomous?' And without another word, Agesilaus struck the Theban name out of the document, declaring them excluded from the treaty.

BATTLE OF LEUCTRA.

604. Immediately after the congress, both the Athenians and Spartans took steps for the performance of its conditions. The Athenians recalled their fleet from the Ionian sea, and the Lacedæmonians sent to withdraw their harmosts and garrisons from the cities still under occupation. With respect to Thebes, and the dispute about the Bœotian cities, Athens was content to allow Sparta to fight it out without her interference; and as Sparta was more than willing, so it was generally believed that she was fully able to reduce Thebes to whatever she pleased.

605. It so happened that while the peace was making, Cleombrotus was at the head of a Lacedæmonian army

including allies. When he heard of the arrangements concluded, he sent home to ask for instructions; and instead of being desired to disband the army, and reconstitute it on the voluntary principle, he was ordered, by a unanimous vote of the Spartan assembly, to march it against Thebes. He made good his entrance into Bœotia by taking a circuitous route, deemed scarcely practicable, over the mountains to the south, and encamped at a place of ever-memorable fame called LEUCTRA.

606. The Thebans were so discouraged at his progress, that it needed all the address of Epaminondas, and all the daring of Pelopidas, to uphold their resolution, and to induce them to go out and fight the enemy, instead of shutting themselves up for a siege. After all, they took the field with a feeling of brave despair rather than of cheering hope—a feeling that it was better to perish in the fight than to live subject to Spartan domination.

607. The Thebans had probably not half the number of the Spartans. But this inferiority Epaminondas would compensate by new and ingeniously conceived tactics. Instead of disposing his troops for fighting along the whole line, as had hitherto been the practice throughout Greece, he thought of bringing a heavy and irresistible mass to bear on the right wing of the Spartan line, where Cleombrotus, with the flower of the Spartan army, would be stationed; and to keep the rest of his line comparatively back from action in the first instance, as he felt assured that, if he were successful on this point against the best troops of the enemy, the rest would offer little resistance. With this view, he marshalled the Theban hoplites, fifty shields deep, on his left wing, with Pelopidas and the sacred band in front; and he ordered the advance to be made obliquely, so that this body should join battle first. Cleombrotus was not prepared for this manœuvre, and he arranged for the usual mode of joining battle at once along the whole line.

608. The plan of Epaminondas proved completely successful. After an obstinate resistance and fearful slaughter, the Spartan right wing was beaten, and driven back to the camp. Cleombrotus himself was

mortally wounded, apparently early in the battle, and around him fell the most eminent members of his official staff. In no other part of the line does there appear to have been any very serious fighting; and very soon the whole force of the Lacedæmonians, with the dying king, was again brought together behind their intrenchments, where the Thebans did not attempt to molest them. The day on which Epaminondas stood victorious on the field of Leuctra was only the twentieth from that on which Thebes had been excluded from the general pacification of Greece.

609. The event electrified every one—allies and neutrals, as well as the victors and the vanquished. Every one now felt that a new military power had arisen, and that the Theban training had proved itself more than a match on a fair field and with inferior numbers for the ancient Lycurgian discipline, which had hitherto been reckoned unparalleled in turning out good soldiers.

610. But there was another species of training in which Sparta never was and never could be surpassed—that of enduring the most poignant grief without betraying emotion. The defeat was calamitous and humiliating beyond all precedent, and aggravated by the fact, that nothing but victory had been anticipated. The messenger who bore the tidings arrived while the solemnities called the *gymnopedia* were celebrating in the theatre; but the ephors would not allow the ceremonies to be either interrupted or abridged. They went through the whole as though nothing had happened, only giving out the names of the slain for the information of the relatives, and ordering that no noise or wailing should be made by the women. On the morrow, as we are told, the friends of the fallen appeared in their best attire in the public places, congratulating each other on the bravery of their kinsmen, while the friends of those who had survived the battle remained for the most part shut up at home, sorrowfully looking forward to the ignominy to which every citizen was condemned who fled before an enemy. So terrible, indeed, was the contempt to which such a one was exposed, that life was scarcely tolerable. Whatever

might have been the justifying or extenuating circumstances under which he had survived a defeat, no citizen at home would speak to him or be seen consorting with him in tent, or game, or chorus; no other Spartan family would intermarry with his; and if he appeared in public with an air of cheerfulness, he was liable to be reminded by blows as well as words of the visible humility which was becoming his degraded position. In the present instance, however, this doom was averted. Whether actuated by a spirit of lenity, or by the consciousness that Sparta could not afford to lose any more of her warriors, Agesilaus decided that the rigour of the law should be mitigated on this occasion. 'Let us,' said he, 'suppose that the sacred institutions of Lycurgus have been asleep during one unfortunate day; but henceforth let them resume their wonted vigour.' His prudent counsel was adopted.

611. The Thebans were anxious to obtain reinforcements before following up the blow they had struck at Leuctra. They therefore sent a herald to Athens, crowned with wreaths of triumph, to invite the citizens to join hands with them. But the Athenian senate received the news with evident chagrin, and dismissed the herald without even a word of courtesy.

612. Another herald was sent to Jason of Pheræ, in Thessaly, for the same purpose; and with a very different result. He at once accepted the invitation of the Thebans; and advancing so rapidly as to forestall all opposition, he joined the victorious army. The Thebans were anxious that he should unite with them in an immediate attack upon the Lacedæmonian camp; but he dissuaded them from the enterprise, advising them not to drive the Spartans to despair, but to allow them to depart under capitulation. He offered himself to negotiate the truce, and, on its conclusion, all parties immediately left the field, the Lacedæmonians returning home after a fashion which shewed they had little faith in this sudden pacification.

FIFTH PERIOD.

371—338 B.C.

PROGRESS OF THEBES—JASON OF PHERÆ.

613. The ascendancy which Sparta had hitherto exercised in Phocis and other places north of the Corinthian Gulf, was now shared between the victorious Thebans and the Thessalian Jason. The Thebans, with their confederates, eager for fresh triumphs, readily submitted to the military training of Epaminondas, and improved rapidly in military tactics. Jason was also becoming more powerful every day. He was one of the most remarkable men of the time. From the position of a mere citizen of Pheræ, he had risen to that of *tagus*, or captain-general of the whole of Thessaly, and not only enjoyed under this denomination the full extent of royal power in his own country, but had its tributary neighbours under complete obedience, with Macedonia in partial subjection. He had at his disposal a numerous force of hardy mountaineers, well paid, and trained to an almost unexampled state of discipline. The personal ability and ambition of Jason, combined with the great power at which he had arrived, inspired universal alarm; for it seemed uncertain whether the Persian king, or the cities of Chalcidice, or the states of Greece, were the most immediate objects of his ambition.

614. This alarm was greatly aggravated when, half a year after the battle of Leuctra, Jason announced his intention of being present at the Pythian festival in August, not only with splendid presents to Apollo, but with a numerous army in his train. It was affirmed that he was about to usurp the presidency and management of the festival which belonged of right to the Amphictyonic Council. It was apprehended, moreover, that he would lay hands on the rich treasures of the temple; and the

Delphians, in alarm, inquired of the god what they ought to do if this were threatened. We are told that Apollo replied, he would himself take care of it, and that he kept his word. Before the day of the festival arrived, Jason was sitting to receive petitioners, when seven young men approached, apparently engaged in warm dispute, and appealing to him for a decision. But as soon as they got near, they fell upon Jason, and slew him. Two of them were killed by the guards, but five escaped. The obscurity which seems to have rested on the motives of the assassins, led many, and Xenophon among the rest, to consider the sudden removal of this ambitious man as the fulfilment of Apollo's promise to take care of his own treasure. His death was felt throughout Greece, and especially by Thebes, as a signal relief; and the fugitive assassins were everywhere received with distinguished honour.

DECLINE OF SPARTAN POWER IN PELOPONNESUS —ARCADIAN FEDERATION.

615. While these events were occurring in Northern Greece, there were stirring scenes also in Peloponnesus. The Spartans had been but slow to execute that part of the treaty which bound them to remove their garrisons from the various cities; but as soon as the tidings of their defeat at Leuctra were spread abroad, the harmosts disappeared at once; and the oligarchies, which could not maintain their authority without the harmosts, became the objects of long-suppressed vengeance.

616. Never did any state fall with greater rapidity than Sparta after the battle of Leuctra; and the·Athenians took advantage of her fall to invite into their confederacy many of the Peloponnesian states which had lost their reverence for her. Nor was this all. There now sprung up two new political powers in the peninsula, which threatened even the independence of Sparta. The Mantineans, deprived of city-life, and condemned to reside in scattered villages, resolved to rebuild their walls, and

resume their political constitution. Other Arcadians lent their aid, and Sparta was not strong enough to prevent the accomplishment of their designs. This success suggested the idea of a political federation of all who bore the Arcadian name, and the assistance of Thebes was invoked.

INDEPENDENCE OF MESSENIA.

617. The application of the Mantineans was just the opportunity that Epaminondas desired; and he resolved not only to support the organisation of Arcadia, but to replace the Messenians in their ancient territory. The region once known, as independent Messenia, governed by its own kings, had for nearly three centuries formed the best part of Laconia, cultivated by Helots for the benefit of Spartan proprietors. Epaminondas would convert these serfs into free Messenians, as their ancestors had been, and invite back the scattered families of the same race who were residing in various parts of Greece, so as to impoverish Sparta by a loss of territory, and also to curb her by the establishment of a bitter enemy at her side. He entered into correspondence with these dispersed Messenians, and by the time of his march into Arcadia, many of them had enlisted under his banner. Agesilaus had retired 370 B.C. before his arrival, and there was no enemy to fight. After ravaging the Spartan territory therefore, and even threatening the capital, Epaminondas devoted himself to the completion of his scheme. It was resolved to build a new city as the Pan-Arcadian capital; a board of œcists from the existing cities and districts was appointed; a convenient site was chosen on the river Helisson; the foundation of the city, to be called Megalopolis, was laid by Epaminondas, in conjunction with the œcists; and arrangements were made for its government and defence.

618. The site chosen for the Messenian capital was Ithome, where the inhabitants had made the last gallant stand against Sparta. The citadel or acropolis was built

upon its summit, while the town itself was situated lower down on the declivity, and connected with its acropolis by a continuous wall. We are told, and it is worth recording as characteristic of Greek usages, that first Epaminondas, who was recognised as the œcist or founder of the city, offered a solemn sacrifice to Bacchus and Apollo Ismenius; then the Argeians, as his principal allies, offered to the Argeian Juno and Jupiter Nemeus; then the Messenians, to Jupiter Ithometas and the Dioscuri. Next, supplication was made to the ancient heroes and heroines of the Messenian race, and especially to the warrior Aristomenes, that they would return and again make their abode in free Messene. After these observances, the ground was marked out, and the building was begun, under the sound of Argeian and Bœotian flutes. The best architects were invited from every part of Greece, to lay out the streets regularly, and secure a proper distribution and construction of the sacred edifices. No less sedulous was the care of Epaminondas for the solidity of the fortifications.

619. A wide area round Ithome, including some of the richest plains in Peloponnesus, was appropriated as territory for the new city of Messene. Besides, the whole country from this to the western sea was cut off from Spartan dominion, to become the property of the Periœci and Helots who had hitherto cultivated it as serfs, and who were now to be Messenian freemen.

620. When the humiliation of Sparta was thus completed, every man's religion suggested to him the cause of it. 'See,' it was said, 'what has resulted from having set at nought the gracious warning of the gods, who bade us beware of a lame reign.' Nevertheless, the energy and bravery of Agesilaus, which had not deserted him even at the age of seventy years, were more than ever necessary to his country, and no one else appeared to be competent to be the chief leader of her affairs.

621. New political combinations, which became more and more intricate, were the result of this enfranchisement of Western Laconia, and the organisation of Arcadia; and these phenomena, highly interesting in themselves,

gave rise to a series of desultory wars of a very uninteresting character. A few of the leading points may be noticed here.

ASCENDANCY OF THEBES—ITS WARS IN THESSALY AND PELOPONNESUS.

622. The two youngest cities of Hellenic name whose birth we have recorded, supported each other in neighbourly sympathy, repelling the assaults of the Spartans, who sought aid from the Athenians. The Athenians, who had been preserving neutrality, threw their weight into the Spartan scale, to counterbalance the predominance of Thebes; while the attention of Thebes was divided between the affairs of Peloponnesus and those of Northern Greece.

623. Alexander, a brutal tyrant, the third successor, as well as the third son of Jason, had inherited a considerable portion of his father's military power, but was unable to retain his hold on Thessaly and its circumjacent tributaries, who sought the protection of Thebes against the despot. Pelopidas, accordingly, entered Thessaly with an army, took several of its cities into Theban protection, and marched onward into Macedonia, which had been torn with intestine divisions. Ptolemy, who was now governing there as regent, had been indebted to Athenian interference for his present position; but he now entered into alliance with Thebes—the superior force of Pelopidas probably leaving him no option—and as guarantee for his fidelity, surrendered to him thirty distinguished hostages; among whom was the youthful Philip, the youngest son of the late king Amyntas. Pelopidas, therefore, returned to Thebes with flying-colours, having extended the ascendancy of his native city over both Thessaly and Macedonia.

624. A victory gained by the Spartans over the Arcadians, and called 'the Tearless Battle,' because no Spartan life was lost in it; and an expedition of Epaminondas into Peloponnesus to add Achaia to the allies of Thebes, took place in the years 368 and 367 B.C. And

now, as the Persian monarch had been regarded as a sort of mediator between the states of Greece ever since the peace of Antalcidas, the Thebans were desirous that his fiat should be obtained as the stamp of their proceedings. Accordingly, Pelopidas, proceeding to Susa for that purpose, induced him to grant a rescript concerning the subjects most in dispute. Amphipolis, which the Athenians were striving to regain, was declared a free and autonomous city, and Athens was ordered to lay up her ships of war, on pain of Persian intervention. The towns of Triphylia, which had been admitted into the Arcadian league, were adjudged to Elis, which claimed them in virtue of an ancient sovereignty; Messenia was pronounced independent of Sparta; and finally, Thebes was declared the head city of Greece, and any city refusing to follow her leadership was threatened with Persian compulsion.

625. On the return of Pelopidas to Greece, deputies were invited from the various cities to hear the decisions of the Great King; but when they were called upon to give in their adherence upon oath, there was a general burst of indignation, and positive refusal. Nor were the Thebans more successful when they attempted to get the rescript recognised by sending it round to the various cities separately.

626. In the course of his efforts to obtain acquiescence in the Persian sentence, Pelopidas, accompanied by Ismenias, undertook a mission to Thessaly and the northern districts. Alexander of Pheræ came, under pacific appearances, to meet them at Pharsalus, when, perceiving them to be unattended by any military force, he seized their persons, and carried them captive to Pheræ. The incensed Thebans despatched an army to recover or avenge their favourite citizen. But the command was given to men inadequate to the task, and the troops were severely repulsed.

627. Epaminondas now undertook an expedition for the recovery of his friend. Avoiding all such extremes as might drive the tyrant to desperation, and imperil the life of Pelopidas, he contrived just so far to intimidate him, that he sent an embassy to apologise for his recent

violence, to propose the restoration of Pelopidas, and to solicit not only peace, but alliance with Thebes; Epaminondas, however, would promise nothing, except to withdraw his troops from Thessaly on condition of the release of Pelopidas and Ismenias, which he obtained. He did not, however, succeed in restoring Thebes to the influence she had previously enjoyed in this quarter. Alexander again became master of the greater part of Thessaly, and maintained a close alliance with Athens.

DEATH OF PELOPIDAS.

628. In the year 363 B.C., Pelopidas led another expedition into Thessaly, in consequence of the continual complaints sent to Thebes of the tyranny of Alexander, seconded probably by his own desire of avenging his personal quarrel with the despot. The hostile armies met on the hills of Cynoscephalæ; the troops of Alexander were driven back; and Pelopidas, perceiving him endeavouring to rally them, was seized, it is said, with such a transport of rage as had possessed the younger Cyrus on the field of Cunaxa. He rushed impetuously forward, challenging his enemy to fight him in single combat. Alexander retired behind his guards; and Pelopidas, plunging among them, was presently slain. His troops, hastening to rescue or avenge him, defeated the troops of the despot, and put them to flight. The grief for the loss of this general was extreme. The soldiers, though warm from their victory, cared not, in many instances, to kindle their fires, or touch their evening-meal, but cut off their own hair, and the manes of their horses, and lay down in sorrow. At Thebes, the feeling was no less strongly manifested. Pelopidas was endeared to his countrymen first as the leader of the devoted band that rescued the city from the Lacedæmonians; he had been re-elected every year since to the office of beotarch; he had taken a prominent part in all their struggles; had been the first to cheer them in the hour of despondency; and had lent himself, with generous patriotism, to second the guiding counsels of Epaminondas. All that Thebes could now

attempt, was to avenge his death. Accordingly, a large force marched into Thessaly, joined the partisans of Thebes in that country, and pressed Alexander so hard, that he was obliged to submit to their terms. These were, that he should relinquish all sovereignty in Thessaly, and confine himself to Pheræ, besides acknowledging the headship of Thebes.

BATTLE OF MANTINEA.

629. Meanwhile the Eleans and Arcadians had been at war, and the Arcadians had quarrelled among themselves, Mantinea siding with the Eleans, and leaning on Sparta for help, while Tegea and Megalopolis held fast by Thebes. In the summer of 362 B.C., Epaminondas undertook his fourth and last expedition into Peloponnesus, while the aged Agesilaus took the field against him with Lacedæmonian forces. A general engagement took place on the plain near Mantinea, where the Lacedæmonians and Mantineans had taken up a position. When Epaminondas came within sight of them, and ordered a halt, they concluded that he was going to encamp, and did not mean to offer battle that day. Under this impression, they left their ranks, unbridled their horses, and took off their breast-plates. Epaminondas marshalled his troops for battle much on the same plan that had succeeded so well at Leuctra; but the enemy heeded not his operations, till he had given the order to 'take up arms,' and was actually in full march upon them. Now, the scattered hoplites ran to their places, and the cavalry hastened to bridle their steeds. Soldiers thus taken unawares, hurried and flustered, were in no condition to withstand the fearful shock of the Theban columns. The charge, both of infantry and cavalry, made by Epaminondas with his left wing, not only defeated the troops immediately opposite, but caused all the rest of the hostile army to take flight. The victorious general, pressing on the retiring enemy at the head of his column, received a mortal wound with a spear in the breast. The handle of the spear broke, and the point was left sticking in the wound. He immediately fell into

the arms of his comrades, and the news spread like lightning through his army. The effect produced is said to have been among the most extraordinary phenomena in the military history of Greece. As soon as he fell, his troops seemed rooted to the spot, without power to follow up the victory. Though the enemy's infantry was in full flight, the Theban hoplites neither killed another man nor advanced another step. Though the cavalry also was flying, yet neither did the Theban horse continue their pursuit, but fell back with the timidity of beaten men; while the light troops and peltasts, who had been mingled with them, being left unsupported, were mostly cut to pieces by the Athenians. As the vanquished, therefore, were allowed to retire unpursued, and perhaps even rallied before reaching the town, they pretended also to have gained the victory, and erected a trophy; yet, as the Thebans were masters of the field, the Lacedæmonians were obliged to solicit the burial-truce.

630. The surgeons who examined the wound of Epaminondas, declared that he would die as soon as the spear-head was withdrawn. He now asked whether his shield was safe, and his shield-bearer produced it. 'He next inquired about the issue of the battle, and was told that the Thebans were victorious. He then begged to see the two generals, on whom he wished to devolve the command of the army; and being informed that both of them were slain, he said: 'Then you must make peace with the enemy;' after which he ordered the spear-head to be withdrawn, and the gush of blood which followed soon terminated his life. He was buried on the battle-field, and a pillar was erected on his tomb.

631. Epaminondas left a name second to none in Greece, by the unanimous verdict of all historians. So rare a union of the soldier, the general, the orator, and the patriot, has seldom been found. Pericles excelled him as a statesman, but fell far behind him as a general; and it is singularly gratifying to meet with such splendid talent combined with lofty disinterestedness, not merely as to the gains of avarice, but to the greater seductions of vanity and ambition. With the sixteen years of his

political life, the ascendancy of Thebes both began and ended. No man arose to fill his place with even a secondary degree of merit; and it would seem, from his dying words, that the only men he deemed capable of succeeding him in military command perished on the fatal day of Mantinea.

632. The peace which Epaminondas had advised was made at once, probably before the army withdrew from Peloponnesus. Nothing was demanded by Thebes except that all things should remain just as they then were, including the recognition of the Pan-Arcadian constitution and the independence of Messenia. All parties consented except the Spartans, who firmly stood out against the last particular, and chose rather to remain without friends or auxiliaries, hoping for better times.

LAST DAYS OF AGESILAUS.

633. The aged Agesilaus was thus compelled to see the dominion of the Spartans irrevocably narrowed, their influence in Arcadia overturned, and the loss of Messene formally sanctioned even by their own allies. The only hope that now remained was from foreign sources. He thought he might yet obtain aid in the shape of money from the native princes in Egypt, and the revolted Persian satraps in Asia, by way of compensation for the services of mercenary troops. Egypt had been for some years in a state of actual revolt, and subject to native princes whom the Persians had vainly endeavoured to subdue; and the Spartans, besides their hope of large pecuniary reward for serving these princes, were not displeased thus to avenge themselves on the Persian king for having sanctioned the independence of Messene. It was under these circumstances that Agesilaus, now above eighty years of age, went to Egypt as a hireling soldier at the head of a band of hirelings. The Egyptians were astonished and disappointed at seeing the man whom they had invited as a formidable warrior appear on their shores a deformed little old man, meanly attired, and sitting on the grass among his troops, without any external appearance of distinction. They declined to invest

him with the supreme command, and recognised him only as general of the mercenary land-force ; while Chabrias, the Athenian, was over the fleet, and Tachos, the Egyptian, himself commanded in chief. Though discontented and indignant, Agesilaus accompanied Tachos in an expedition against the Persians ; but when a competitor for the throne of Egypt appeared in Nectanabis, he went over to him, and so vigorously maintained his cause as to place him firmly on the throne, while Tachos was obliged to take flight. As winter approached, Agesilaus prepared to return, carrying with him 230 talents, as a public donation from Nectanabis to Sparta. But he did not live to present it, being overtaken by death on the way home.

634. The conflicts of these forty-four years, from 404 to 360 B.C., left Greece more disunited, and more destitute of any presiding Hellenic authority, than she had been at any time since the Persian invasion had led the various states to make common cause. Thebes, Sparta, and Athens, had all been weakening each other, while neither had done much to strengthen herself. The maritime power of Athens was now indeed considerable, but its foundations were unsubstantial ; and there was no more either the energy or imperial feeling which dignified her under the administration of Pericles. It was under these circumstances, so untoward for defence, that a new aggressor arose from an unexpected quarter.

PHILIP OF MACEDON.

635. It has already been mentioned that the youthful Philip, the son of Amyntas, and younger brother of Perdiccas III., was one of the hostages received by the Thebans as security for the treaty made by Pelopidas. He remained in Thebes at least from his fifteenth till his eighteenth year, residing with one of the principal citizens. Here he acquired such command over the Greek language as made him no contemptible orator in after-life. He may also have received some instruction in philosophy ; and it is believed that he made the personal acquaintance of Plato ; but the first man whom he learned

to admire, and whom he strove to imitate in his subsequent career, was Epaminondas, the victor of Leuctra. During the last years of his brother's life, Philip resided in Macedonia, where he governed a district in subordination to the king, and organised a military force of his own, at the head of which he probably served in his brother's wars.

636. In the year 360-359 B.C., Perdiccas perished in the flower of his age, leaving an infant son heir to a throne beset with pretenders, and surrounded by enemies. Of the pretenders were Pausanias, supported by the king of Thrace; Argæus, backed by the Athenians; besides three half-brothers of Perdiccas and Philip, sons of Amyntas by a different mother. The surrounding enemies were the Illyrians, Pæonians, and Thracians, who were always ready to invade and plunder Macedonia in any moment of intestine weakness.

637. Philip first assumed the government as guardian of his infant nephew; but so formidable were the difficulties to be encountered, that the Macedonians induced him to assume the crown in his own name, and he was not long of proving his ability to extricate himself. He put to death one of his half-brothers, and the other two fled. Next he bought off the Thracians, so that the competition of Pausanias for the throne became no longer formidable. He then detached Athens from the cause of Argæus by withdrawing the Macedonian garrison from Amphipolis—that jewel which Athens had so long desired to recover—and expressing a desire for alliance with the Athenians. After this, falling in with Argæus, who was supported by a body of mercenaries and a few Athenian volunteers, he totally defeated him, and treated the Athenians who fell into his hands with the utmost kindness, sending them home with conciliatory messages to their countrymen. Peace was now easily made, Philip renouncing his right to Amphipolis, and acknowledging the town as a rightful possession of Athens. His hands were now free to deal with the Illyrians and Pæonians, whom he completely defeated.

638. During the year or two that Philip was thus

occupied, Amphipolis was left to itself, the Athenians taking no vigorous measures for regaining it—perhaps from their being wholly absorbed in vexatious operations in the Chersonese. But now, Philip having humbled his enemies in the interior, and collected a force competent for aggressive operations on the coast, would no longer leave them the opportunity they had let slip. Towards the close of 358 B.C., therefore, he himself laid siege to Amphipolis, assailing the walls with battering-rams and other military engines. The inhabitants, besides defending themselves with vigour, applied even to Athens, their ancient enemy, for aid against the Macedonian prince. But Philip counteracted their application, by assuring the Athenians that he only wished to take the place in order to get rid of a population that had annoyed him, and that he would at once hand it over to the Athenians as the rightful owners. His assurances were received with confidence; the envoys from Amphipolis were refused; and Philip, partly by his military prowess, partly through the treachery of some within the town, obtained possession.

639. Philip contrived still to persuade the Athenians that he was their friend, and disposed to cede Amphipolis to them; only, he urged that the Athenians ought, in exchange, to give him Pydna, an ancient Macedonian seaport. However, he besieged and captured Pydna for himself, not waiting to receive it in exchange for Amphipolis, which he had not the least idea of resigning.

640. Probably Athens would not have looked on so quietly while Philip was thus aggrandising himself at her expense, but that she was now entirely absorbed in the Social War, which broke out in 358 B.C.

641. It would seem that the Athenian confederacy which had begun in 378 B.C., in a generous spirit, and with a view to common defence, had gradually become perverted, and that Athens had been acting more for her own separate aggrandisement than for the common interests of the confederacy; moreover, that she had tolerated, if not countenanced numerous disorderly and rapacious exactions inflicted on the confederates by her ill-paid mercenaries. The adherence of the larger

confederate states became in consequence more and more reluctant, and, finally, a revolt, the beginning of what is known as the Social War, was concerted by Rhodes, Byzantium, Chios, Cos, and some other allies. The Athenians equipped a fleet to attack Chios, where the joint armament of the revolters was mustered. Chabrias was placed in command of it, and Chares of the land-force which went on board with it. But the Athenian troops were vigorously repulsed, and the revolters were enabled to draw other allies of Athens into the defection. In the course of the conflict, the commanders quarrelled, and Chares accused Iphicrates and Timotheus of betraying their trust, and of deserting him at a critical moment. Timotheus, who had conducted the armies of Athens with such success, and maintained the honour of her name throughout the eastern and western seas, was severely fined, and retired from service. Iphicrates, though acquitted, seems not to have been again employed in military command; and Chabrias had fallen in battle. Athens could ill bear such loss; she had no men fit to succeed them; and in the following year, she was obliged to make peace with her revolted allies, recognising their full autonomy. Such was the termination of the Social War, which seriously impaired the power and lowered the dignity of Athens.

642. The two years of the Social War had been diligently employed by Philip in the advancement of his ambitious projects. He not only improved the maritime conveniences of Amphipolis, which became one of the great bulwarks of Macedonia, but also extended his acquisitions into the gold-regions eastward of the Strymon. In the interior of this region he raised a new city called Philippi, and took such effective measures for the improvement of the mining-works in the neighbourhood, that they presently yielded him a large revenue, to meet the constantly increasing expense of his military establishment.

643. It was during this interval, also, that Philip married Olympias, the daughter of a Molossian prince. She bore him a son, afterwards celebrated as 'Alexander the Great;' and it is recorded that the king received nearly at the same time three several messengers, with

good news—the birth of a son, a defeat of the Illyrians under his general Parmenion, and the success of one of his race-horses at the Olympic Games.

SACRED WAR.

644. The Social War had not yet terminated, when new distractions of a far more formidable nature sprang up under the name of the Sacred War, which rent the very vitals of the Hellenic world.

645. In an early part of the present volume, some account was given of the Amphictyonic Council, an ancient and venerable institution of the Hellenes, religious in its main purpose, and political only by occasion. It would seem that during the century preceding the period at which we have now arrived, this assembly had never meddled, to any important purpose, in the political affairs of Greece. But after the humiliation of Sparta at Leuctra, it began to meet for the despatch of business, and unfortunately displayed its activity in measures fraught with mischief.

646. It seems to have been not long after the battle of Leuctra that the Thebans brought before the Amphictyonic assembly an accusation against Sparta, for having seized the Cadmea during the time of peace. A heavy fine was in consequence imposed upon her, to be doubled after a certain interval of non-payment; but as there were no means of enforcing the sentence, and the Spartans did not voluntarily submit to it, the only practical effect which followed was their exclusion from the Amphictyonic Council, the Delphian Temple, and the Pythian Games.

647. In the year 357 B.C., an accusation was brought by the same parties against their border enemies the Phocians; and they also were fined to such an amount as to be far beyond their means of payment. When a certain time allowed for liquidating this fine had elapsed, a vote was passed in the assembly to dispossess the recusant Phocians, and consecrate all their territory to Apollo. The Phocians, thus driven to desperation, resolved on a vigorous resistance, and readily listened to the counsels of Philomelus, one of their leading citizens, who advised them to seize the

temple of Delphi itself—the administration of which, he contended, originally and legitimately belonged to them, as Delphi and its inhabitants were originally a portion of the Phocian family, though they had severed themselves under the auspices of Sparta, and assumed these lucrative privileges as peculiarly their own. Philomelus offered himself to conduct the expedition, and he was nominated general with full powers. Having obtained secret aid from the king of Sparta, under promise of erasing the sentence which stood against his people, Philomelus suddenly attacked both the town and temple of Delphi, and captured them with little opposition. He fortified the place anew, increased the number of his troops, and proclaimed that he had come to resume for the Phocians their ancient rights. At the same time he pledged himself that the treasures should be sacredly respected, that no impiety of any kind should be tolerated, and that the place should be open as heretofore for sacrifice and consultation. The loud complaints of the Delphians met, however, with a response; and it was decided that an Amphictyonic army should be raised to abase the sacrilegious Phocians. The Spartans and Athenians were in no position to afford any considerable assistance against such a combination. The only resource, therefore, was to levy a large mercenary army; and as there were no adequate funds available for this purpose, Philomelus felt obliged to lay hands on the treasures of the temple, apparently with sincere reluctance, and only intending to take a certain sum as a loan, to be repaid when the emergency was over. However, when the feeling which protected the fund was broken through, it was as easy to take much as little; the claims became more numerous and pressing; the very fact of the spoliation having awakened such a feeling throughout at least half the Grecian world, that the spoilers could have no security except under the continued protection of mercenary troops.

648. With these resources, Philomelus was enabled to enlist large numbers, chiefly, as we are told, men of wicked and reckless character, since no pious Greek would engage in such a service. The war assumed a peculiarly ferocious

character, the Thebans putting all their prisoners to death as sacrilegious wretches, and the exasperated troops of Philomelus retaliating on the Bœotian prisoners. After the struggle had lasted awhile with indecisive result, an engagement took place near the town of Neon, in an unfavourable position for the Phocians, amidst woods and rocks. Here Philomelus was defeated, his army dispersed, and himself severely wounded. Finding himself driven to the brink of a precipice, with no possibility of escape, he threw himself down rather than fall into the hands of the enemy, and perished. His troops, however, rallied after a time under Onomarchus, whose energetic measures retrieved the cause. He employed the treasures of the temple still more profusely than Philomelus had done, coining the precious metals into money for the pay of his soldiers, and converting the brass and iron into military weapons; besides scattering presents or bribes in various directions, to secure influential partisans. He strengthened his hands yet further by seizing such of his own countrymen as had prominently opposed his measures, putting them to death, and confiscating their property.

649. Through such a combination of corruption, allurement, and violence, the cause of the Phocians gained the ascendant; and they began to count as an item of first-rate magnitude among the powers of Hellas. The Athenians and Spartans regarded them as a valuable counterpoise to Thebes, their religious feelings yielding to their political interests so far as to make them more than tolerate the Phocian progress.

650. Such was the position of the Sacred War when Philip was led to interfere in it. He had been extending his military operations in the direction of Thessaly, and was welcomed by its inhabitants as a deliverer from the cruel dynasty of Pheræ, which was now represented by Lycophron. Onomarchus espoused the cause of Lycophron, in order to check the further progress of the Macedonian towards the south; and marched with a large army into Thessaly. It was now to be Philip against the Phocians; and in order to inspire his soldiers with unwonted enthusiasm, he decorated them with wreaths of

laurel, as crusaders in the service of Apollo against the plunderers of the Delphian Temple. A battle was fought somewhere near the southern coast, where the defeat of Onomarchus and Lycophron was complete, and Onomarchus himself perished. His dead body was crucified by the order of Philip; and all the prisoners—amounting, it is said, to 3000—were drowned, as men guilty of sacrilege.

651. This victory was an important step in the career of the conqueror. It not only crowned him with fame as the avenger of the Delphian god, and terminated the power of the Phocians north of Thermopylæ, but it proved the death-blow of the powerful dynasty of Pheræ, and placed the whole of Thessaly under his dominion. He now sought to push his advantage over the Phocians by invading them in their own territory, and with this view, marched to Thermopylæ; but the Athenians, alarmed in earnest, put the pass in such a condition of defence, that Philip did not venture to attack it.

652. The stress of the war was about this time transferred to Peloponnesus, where the Lacedæmonians, aided by the Phocians, had opened a campaign against Megalopolis, which was supported by Thebes. These hostilities were carried on with such undecided result, that at length the Lacedæmonians proposed and concluded a peace, in which either formally, or by implication, they recognised the independence of the hated city, and abandoned for the time their aggressive purposes.

653. The more direct war between the Bœotians and Phocians appears to have slackened, but not altogether ceased during this episode in Peloponnesus. In the partial actions which took place, the Phocians are said to have been generally worsted, and their commander, Phayllus, presently died of a painful disease, which was regarded as a judgment of the gods for his sacrilegious actions. He had despoiled the Delphian Temple to a still greater extent than his predecessors, incurring aggravated odium from the fact, that he sacrificed not only to the exigencies of the war, but to the vanity of his female favourites, some offerings of peculiar magnificence and antiquity which had until now been spared.

654. The position of the Athenians with respect to Philip was becoming more and more embarrassing; the reputation of his superior generalship and indefatigable activity was felt in every direction; the Macedonian phalanx, and other strategic improvements which he had been gradually organising, were displaying their formidable efficiency; and the excellent cavalry of Thessaly had become a constituent element in his army. The king of Macedon, in short, was confessedly the ascendant soldier of the day, hanging on the skirts of Greece, and exciting fear or hope, or both at the same time, in every one of its cities. But besides his land-force, Philip had now become master of a naval power by no means despicable. During the early years of the war, he had gained all the Athenian possessions on the Macedonian coast, and more recently, by the acquisition of Pheræ and Pagasæ, had obtained a considerable fleet, with full command of the Pagasæan Gulf—the great thoroughfare of Thessalian trade. He was therefore in a position at least to annoy Athens by sea, which he did by levying contributions from her insular allies, capturing her merchant vessels in the Ægæan, and making predatory incursions on the islands of Lemnos and Imbros; while Eubœa, the nearest and most important of her allies, was subject not only to the depredations of his marauding vessels, but to the mischiefs of his political intrigues. Though many were the debates held on the insults offered to the maritime dignity of Athens, and on the sufferings of those allies to whom she owed protection, and though loud were the complaints against the misconduct of the generals, and the inefficiency of the mercenary troops, still the recognised public advisers shrank from the duty of pressing on the citizens the necessity of personal service and exertion. It fell to a comparatively youthful orator, as yet possessed of little influence, to press the unpalatable truth, that the citizens must themselves make sacrifices, and endure hardships, if they would stem the torrent of Macedonian conquest, which threatened speedily to overwhelm them. We allude to the celebrated Demosthenes, who now first distinguished himself in his peculiar vocation of stirring up his countrymen against the

Macedonian in those famous harangues known as the Philippics of Demosthenes.

PHILIP AND THE OLYNTHIANS.

655. The relations of the Olynthians, with respect to Macedonia, seem to have worn the aspect of partial hostility, when the two half-brothers of Philip sought and obtained refuge at Olynthus, and their reception served as a pretext for open war.

656. It was the policy of Philip, in all the projects of his ambition, to blend the power of deceit with that of arms, and to corrupt and divide those whom he intended to subdue. In each city of the Olynthian confederacy, there were doubtless men competing for power, and not scrupulous as to the means of acquiring it; and in each of them, therefore, the wily Macedonian could open intrigues and enlist partisans. The seductions whereby he secured the co-operation of a venal and traitorous minority were, however, only preliminary to the direct use of the sword; the work begun by his bribes, was completed by his phalanx, his hypaspistæ, his cavalry, and his excellent generalship. We have no authentic details of these operations; but the startling result was, that during the two years and a half from the middle of 349 B.C. till the end of 347 B.C., thirty-two free Grecian cities in Chalcidice were taken and destroyed, and their inhabitants reduced to slavery—a calamity the like of which had not occurred since the suppression of the Ionic revolt in the time of Xerxes. The Athenians being applied to, accepted the Olynthian alliance, but took no active step to co-operate with their allies in restraining the aggressor. That Demosthenes would fain have stirred them up to this duty, appears in the three still extant orations known as the 'Olynthiacs.' As yet, however, the utmost exertion which the Athenians could be induced to make was that of sending a body of mercenaries. No citizen-soldier was persuaded to go.

657. While these things were going on, the foreign relations of Athens were disturbed by the breaking out of

hostilities in Eubœa, and the result of the necessary expenses was serious embarrassment to the Athenian finances. To meet the emergencies of the moment, it was proposed that the surplus revenue hitherto paid to the theoric-fund for religious festivals, should be devoted to the pay, outfit, and transport of soldiers for the war. Such a measure would not only have been a great sacrifice of pleasure, but a violation of some higher sentiments. This was essentially the church-fund of Athens, and as such, could not be encroached on without impairing in the bosom of every individual that feeling of religious, social, and patriotic communion which made the Athenians a united people. The only mode of avoiding such an extreme measure would have been the imposition of a heavy property-tax, as well as much personal military service; but the same disposition to self-indulgence that made the citizens shrink from the hardships of a campaign, rendered them averse to the sacrifice of either their public games or their private incomes. The urgency of the case was not felt till compliance was too late.

658. After Philip had captured the thirty-two inferior cities of Chalcidice, he marched against Olynthus itself, with the Thracian Methone and Apollonia. In forcing the passage of the river Sardon, his troops were at first severely repulsed, and himself obliged to swim back across the stream, besides losing irrevocably the sight of one eye from the wound of an arrow. How long the siege lasted, is not known; but Olynthus, with all its inhabitants, at length fell into the hands of Philip. Finding his exiled brothers in the city, he put both of them to death. The persons of the Olynthians, men, women, and children, were sold into slavery, and their property handed over to the soldiers. It is recorded that Atrestidas, an Arcadian, received a grant of thirty, chiefly women and children, who were seen following him in a string through the Grecian cities as he travelled homeward. The mastery of Philip over the Chalcidic peninsula was now complete. The towns were all dismantled; the 347 B.C. public buildings, and other visible tokens of Hellenic city-life, were demolished; and the remaining dwellings

tenanted by dependent cultivators, who were to work for the benefit of Macedonian proprietors.

SACRED WAR RESUMED.

659. The Phocians had by this time fallen into dissensions among themselves. As the Delphian treasures melted away, the means of paying the mercenary troops declined, yet they were still strong enough fully to keep their ground against their chief enemies the Thebans; and these, little anticipating the consequences, invoked the intervention of the conqueror of Olynthus. They implored him, in the name of the Delphian god, to assume the character of champion of the Amphictyonic Assembly, and to rescue the temple from its plunderers.

660. It was reported abroad, about September 347 B.C., that a Macedonian army was about to march to Thermopylæ; and the Phocians, in the greatest terror, applied to both Athens and Sparta, imploring the aid necessary to defend it. Again the maintenance of Hellenic freedom was to depend on the Pass of Thermopylæ, as it had done 133 years before, during the invasion of the Persian Xerxes. It was Philip's only path into Greece. It could not be forced by any land-army; and at sea, the Athenian fleet was stronger than his. But the Pass he must have; and his cunning was put in requisition to accomplish what force would have attempted in vain.

661. Pella, the head-quarters of Philip at this time, was the centre of hope and fear and intrigue for the whole Grecian world. There were the Thebans and Thessalians calling upon the Macedonian to proclaim himself the champion of the Amphictyonic Council against the Phocians; and there were the Phocians, Spartans, and Athenians, by their representatives, endeavouring to enlist him in their cause against Thebes. The policy of Philip was to keep alive the hopes of all, and thus prevent the formation of any combination against him. Æschines, the rival of Demosthenes, with others of the Athenian deputation, were won over by bribes to hoodwink the Athenian people. With reference to the contemplated expedition, it was asserted

by some of the Macedonian officers that its express purpose was to conquer Thebes, and reconstitute the Bœotian cities, though, it was added, that Philip could not himself make authentic proclamation of this design, on account of his present alliances.

662. No citizen of Athens or Sparta believed it dangerous to admit Philip within Thermopylæ, when the purpose of his coming was understood to be the punishment of the hated Thebans. The wily Macedonian went so far as to write letters inviting the Athenians to co-operate with him at Thermopylæ—fully anticipating, of course, that they would not join him, but that they would infer from the invitation that nothing hostile to them was intended. The bait took, and he gained his object, which was to deprive the Phocians of their assistance. A body of Phocian envoys accompanied his march, and were treated, if not positively as friends, yet in such a manner as made it appear doubtful whether he leaned most to them or the Thebans.

663. The Pass of Thermopylæ was guarded by Phocians with Lacedæmonian auxiliaries in sufficient force to defend it against Philip by land; but this was of little use without the co-operation of Athens by sea, as nothing but her fleet could prevent the invader from landing troops in the rear of Thermopylæ, and thus making himself master of Phocis from the Bœotian side. The Phocians had watched with trembling anxiety the deceitful phases of Athenian policy for several months past; while they would fain cling to the hope of Philip's friendship, their only way of successfully resisting him hung on the decision of Athens to grant or refuse its maritime protection. When Philip, therefore, summoned them to surrender the Pass, and offered them terms, they declined replying till their last deputation should return from Athens. When it did arrive, and they learned that it had been resolved not to oppose Philip, they perceived no course open to them but to make the best terms they could with the Macedonian. Within three days, a convention was concluded, according to which Phalæcus, the Phocian general, was to withdraw from the territory, with all the mercenary troops and such Phocians

as chose to accompany him. The towns, twenty-two in number, together with the Pass of Thermopylæ, were placed absolutely at the disposal of Philip.

664. The moment that the Macedonian king was thus master of the country, he proclaimed his intention to act entirely in concert with Thebes, to transfer to them a considerable portion of Phocis, to restore them the Bœotian towns which the Phocians had taken from them, and to maintain the rest of Bœotia in their dependence as hitherto.

665. The report of these proceedings gave a dreadful shock to the people of Athens. Not only were they mortified at finding they had been over-reached by Philip, and that they had unwittingly been playing into the hands of the Thebans, but they were smitten with the consciousness of having betrayed their allies to ruin, and of having yielded up Thermopylæ, the defence at once of Attica and of Greece, to the all-grasping, insidious conqueror. Their own danger was immediate ; the road to Athens lay open to the Thebans, aided by a Macedonian army. Nothing now remained but to put the Piræus and the fortresses throughout Attica in a state of defence, and to bring the women, the children, and all the movable property, within these walls.

666. The next step of Philip was to restore the disputed temple to the Delphians, and to convoke anew the Amphictyonic Council. Its deputies assembled, of course, under feelings of fervent devotion to Philip, and strong antipathy to the Phocians. By their first step, they dispossessed the Phocians of their place in the assembly, and conferred it upon Philip. Moreover, they decided that all the towns in Phocis should be dismantled and broken up into villages, none of which was to contain more than fifty houses. Abæ alone was to be spared, for the sake of its oracular temple of Apollo, and because its inhabitants had taken no part in the spoliation of Delphi. The horses of the Phocians were to be sold ; their military weapons given to the flames, or thrown down the precipices of Parnassus ; and they were to pay to the Delphian Temple an annual tribute of fifty talents, till all that had been

abstracted should be made good. The execution of the sentence went far beyond the literal terms, rigorous as they were. The troops quartered in the country gave full scope to their malignant passions, under the mask of holy indignation against sacrilege. The Phocians were in many cases stripped and slain, children were torn from their parents, wives from their husbands, and the statues of the gods from their temples—Philip taking for himself the lion's share of the plunder. Those who had personally assisted in the spoliation of Delphi, had been proclaimed accursed, and liable to arrest: these, therefore, fled at once; and most of the citizens who had means of emigrating did so, the poorer ones only remaining of necessity in the country; so that, two or three years afterwards, when Demosthenes passed through, he saw scarcely any population except old men, women, and little children, amidst ruined houses, poor villages, and half-cultivated fields.

667. Philip had now acquired a new Hellenic rank, with new facilities for predominance in Hellenic affairs. The prestige of his constant good-fortune had been immensely strengthened by this last, the most wonderful of his exploits—that he had acquired possession of an unconquerable pass, got rid of the formidable force of Phalæcus, and become master of the twenty-two cities of Phocis, all without striking a blow. Not only was he extolled as the restorer of the Amphictyonic Council, and the avenging champion of the Delphian god, but he was nominated by that Council to be the presiding celebrator of the Pythian festival of the year 346 B.C.—an honour which ranked among the loftiest aspirations of any of the Grecian despots. It availed little that the mortified Athenians refused to send either deputies to the Council or a sacred legation to the festival; the thing passed with the hearty concurrence not only of Thebans and Thessalians, but of the Argeians, Messenians, Arcadians, and all the rest who reckoned upon Philip as a likely auxiliary against their dangerous neighbours the Spartans. Even Demosthenes was afraid to advise any step which would infringe the recent peace, or give pretence to the

Amphictyons for voting a confederate war against Athens, to be executed by Philip. His fortunes were in the ascendant; and Athens, disgraced as the betrayer both of her Phocian allies and of the general safety of Greece, was forced to acquiesce.

668. The inglorious peace of 346 B.C., which the mistaken impulses of the Athenians, and still more the corruption of their envoys, had led them to conclude, lasted, without formal renunciation, for above six years. But though not renounced in form, it became gradually more and more violated in practice by both parties. There are no materials for a consecutive history of these years : the only guide to the facts which transpired is found in the orations of Demosthenes. From these, we learn that Philip carried on his intriguing and interfering in every part of Greece ; that he enjoined Sparta to renounce all claim upon Messenia ; that he established a footing in Elis, and captured three of its colonies in Epeirus, making them over to his brother-in-law Alexander ; that he again overran and subdued the Illyrians, Dardanians, and Pæonians ; that he established his dominion more firmly in Thessaly ; and that he defeated the Thracian prince Cersobleptes. His power increased from year to year, while the cities of Greece remained passive and uncombined, not recognising any one of their own number as leader. Athens was the only power under whom a combination might have been formed ; and it was the policy of Philip to avoid, or at least postpone, any open breach with her. Yet there was much angry altercation, by letters and envoys, concerning the encroachments that were making probably on both sides. For instance, in Eubœa, some of the towns fell under the influence of Philipising leaders, and became hostile to Athens ; and while the Macedonian troops overran the Thracian Chersonese, the Athenian general made excursions beyond the peninsula in the Thracian territories of Philip. By the advice of Demosthenes, whose influence was now becoming very considerable, an expedition was sent to Eubœa, and was so successful as to remove all anxiety in that direction. He was himself commissioned as ambassador to Byzantium,

where he succeeded in persuading the citizens that it was their interest to unite with Athens in resisting the further progress of Philip.

669. The Macedonian so greatly resented this revolution in the policy of Byzantium, that he shortly afterwards laid siege to Perinthus, bringing his fleet into the Propontis, and protecting it in its passage by causing his land-force to traverse the Chersonese, which was laid waste. At the same time, he let loose his cruisers against the Athenian merchantmen, many of which he captured. These new provocations brought the Athenians to a positive declaration of war, and a formal decree was passed to remove the column on which the peace of 346 B.C. stood recorded. About the same time, Philip, on his side, addressed a manifesto to the Athenians, with a declaration of war, as a just revenge for the many wrongs he had received.

670. In vain Philip brought to the siege of Perinthus an army 30,000 strong, and a stock of engines and projectiles such as Greece had never before seen. The situation of the place was naturally strong; the citizens were brave and determined; the Athenians and Byzantians co-operated; and the Macedonian found all his efforts baffled. He then suddenly appeared before Byzantium, which was unprepared for attack; but the Athenians and the principal islanders of the Ægæan hastened to the rescue with a powerful fleet, and this siege also Philip was obliged to abandon. The position of Athens was materially improved by these successes. But now, unhappily, a new quarrel arose in the interior of Greece, inducing another sacred war, declared by the Amphictyonic Council against the Locrians of Amphissa.

671. It was mentioned in a previous part of this History, that the inhabitants of Cirrha, originally the port of Delphi and of Cissa, were accused of extortion, and other offensive proceedings with respect to the visitors to Delphi, and that an Amphictyonic war was conducted against them; that the place was destroyed, and the territory consecrated to the Delphian god—that is, prohibited from being tilled, planted, or otherwise permanently occupied. However, it was found necessary for the

prosperity of Delphi itself that there should be a town or port at hand for the accommodation of worshippers at the temple, and visitors at the Pythian festival, and the fact was winked at that the town and port of Cirrha had been renovated on a modest scale by the Locrians of Amphissa, on whose border it stood, and that part of the adjacent land was tilled for their support. The fact was not new at the time now under review; but the Amphissians having pointed at the Athenians as abettors of the sacrilegious Phocians, the Athenians, by the mouth of Æschines, retorted by denouncing the inhabitants of Cirrha for their impious occupation of the territory. A resolution was at once passed for assembling the whole population of Delphi at daybreak on the morrow, with implements of demolition. From the place of muster, they marched, with the Amphictyons and Æschines at their head, to the port of Cirrha, where they demolished all the harbour conveniences, and even set fire to the dwelling-houses. The terrified inhabitants fled, and ran to inform their fellow-citizens at Amphissa, who came in haste, and drove away the destroyers. The indignant Amphictyons now resolved that the Amphissians should be punished as offenders, not only against the god and the sacred domain, but against the Amphictyons personally. Thus were kindled the flames of a second Amphictyonic war. Philip was appointed commander of the forces and champion of the god, as he had been on the former occasion.

372. His march to the scene of conflict lay through Phocis, which still continued in the defenceless condition to which it had been condemned by the sentence of 346 B.C., and occupied by a poor and scanty population in small detached villages, without a single fortified town. When Philip reached Elatea, formerly the principal city of Phocis, he halted his army, and began forthwith to rebuild the walls, and convert it into a fort for permanent military occupation. This movement created the greatest surprise and alarm throughout Greece. It was now evident that the Macedonian had some other end in view than merely to avenge the Delphian god. Indeed, he no longer affected to conceal that he had come to make war upon the Athenians;

and to make his victory the more sure, he invited the Thebans to join him. As his march had been both rapid and directed towards a different quarter, the Athenians had made no preparations for defending their frontier; neither their families nor their movable property had yet been lodged within walls, and the enemy was within forty-eight hours' march of them.

673. It was evening when Athens received tidings of the proceedings at Elatea, and the prytanes (senators) were at supper. The repast was broken off; and while some ran to get the public assembly convoked, others cleared out the market-place for it, even setting fire to the booths, as the shortest mode of clearing them away. At the earliest dawn, the place was crowded, and Demosthenes addressed the people. He set before them their imminent danger; and implored them, for their own security, to shake off their old aversion, however well grounded, against the Thebans, and send envoys to offer them unconditionally the whole force of Athens to repel the Macedonian from the Theban frontier; otherwise, he assured them, that the Theban territory would become the high road to Athens, and the inhabitants, whether willingly or unwillingly, the allies of the invader. This counsel, at once so wise and so generous, was adopted without opposition; and Demosthenes was appointed chief of a body of envoys to proceed to Thebes, while the military force of Attica was marched to the frontier. The orator carried his point in the Theban assembly, kindling a flame of pan-hellenic patriotism, and inducing them to accept the alliance of Athens, and brave the hostility of Philip. The Athenian army was invited at once to enter Bœotia, and the mutual jealousies of the two cities were cast aside in cordial co-operation against the common foe.

674. The influence of Demosthenes now impressed a vigour on the councils of Athens which had long been unknown. He prevailed upon them to make all the sacrifices he had formerly urged in vain, even to the sacrifice of the theoric-fund to military purposes.

675. The alliance between Athens and Thebes presented

a serious obstacle to Philip, as well as a severe disappointment; and he again resumed his profession of acting on behalf of Apollo against Amphissa, inviting his Peloponnesian allies, but with little success, to join him for this specific purpose.

676. During the autumn and winter of 339–338 B.C., the war was prosecuted in Phocis and on the Bœotian frontier, the new allies maintaining their ground, and even gaining some advantages. An important proceeding in this campaign was the reconstitution of the Phocians as an independent section of Greece. The exiles, many of whom were at Athens, returned, and were assisted by the Athenians and Thebans to re-occupy and secure their towns.

677. After hostilities had been continued about ten months, the two parties met in a general battle on the fatal plain of Chæronea. We have no distinct details of the events which immediately preceded this conflict; nor do we know the numbers engaged on each side. It seems probable that Philip had brought into Phocis the full strength of the Macedonian army, whose organisation, after twenty years of continued improvement, was now in a high state of excellence. It would appear, also, that he had attacked and taken Amphissa, banishing the leading inhabitants, and restoring the sacred domain. After this, he must have considered himself strong enough to attempt forcing his way into Bœotia; and he is said to have drawn down the allies from the strong position they held into the plain near Chæronea, which was the last Bœotian town on the frontiers of Phocis. *August 338 B.C.*

678. The command of the Greek army was shared between the Athenians and Thebans, its movements being decided by their statesmen and generals conjointly. It was the misfortune of Greece that at this critical juncture, when everything depended on the issue of the struggle, there was neither an Epaminondas nor an Iphicrates at hand. It is said that the oracles were unpropitious, and that some fearful portents were seen; but Demosthenes could see only his numerous army cordially combined

for the defence of Grecian liberty. He treated all such stories with indifference, declaring that the Delphian priestess was Philipising.

679. At the battle of Chæronea, Philip commanded in his own person a select body of troops, opposite to the Athenians; while his son Alexander, now eighteen years of age, directed the other wing, opposite to the Thebans. The sacred band, which formed part of the Theban phalanx, exerted all their strength in a fruitless effort to bear down the stronger phalanx, and longer as well as more numerous pikes opposed to them. After a protracted struggle, they were overpowered and slain, while the phalanx was broken and driven back. Philip was still maintaining a doubtful conflict with the Athenians, when the success of his son stimulated him to redouble his efforts, and the whole army of the Greeks was presently put to flight with severe loss.

680. Of Athenian citizens, 1000 perished, and 2000 were taken prisoners; but of the rest, we do not know the numbers on either side. Unspeakable was the agony at Athens when the defeat was reported; but the number of the slain and the captives was as yet unascertained, and the enemy within three or four days' march of the city. At first, it was apprehended that none except the aged would be left for the defence; but it was soon known that the loss, though severe and terrible, did not amount to total destruction, and the Athenians were not the men to despair. The most vigorous measures were adopted. A decree was passed enjoining every one to remove his family and property into the strongholds; the harbour of Piræus was to be put in a condition of defence; every man, without exception, was placed at the disposal of the generals; and all slaves and disfranchised persons capable of bearing arms were constituted freemen.

681. But the Thebans, being much nearer, had to suffer the vengeance of Philip before Athens could be reached; and he now became doubly exasperated against them. He sold the Theban captives into slavery, and is said even to have exacted from them a price for the liberty of burying their slain. Whether the city of Thebes stood

a siege, we are not told; we are only informed that it fell immediately into Philip's power, and that he put to death several of the leading citizens, banished others, and confiscated the property of all. A Macedonian garrison was placed in the Cadmea, and some at least of the minor Bœotian towns were restored to the condition of free communities.

682. The precautions of the Athenians proved less needful than was anticipated; for Philip began to manifest a disposition to treat them amicably. The ashes of their slain were sent home; their prisoners restored; and Oropus was transferred to them from the Thebans. In return, they were required to recognise Philip as the great pan-hellenic chief, and to support a similar acknowledgment in a congress of all the Greeks to be speedily convened. It was the policy of the Macedonian king not to reduce the Athenians to an effort of despair, but to employ his victory and his prisoners to procure from them a recognition of his headship.

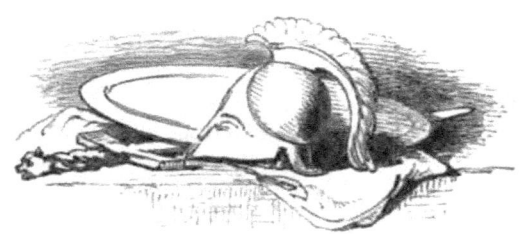

SIXTH PERIOD.

338—300 B.C.

ARREST OF PHILIP'S PROGRESS.

683. Philip next proceeded to carry his arms into Peloponnesus, where the Corinthians, Argeians, Messenians, Eleans, and many Arcadians, submitted to him at once. Sparta was the only city which stood out, refusing to ask for peace, though making no attempt at resistance. We do not know that he attacked the city itself; but he circumscribed the territory, and narrowed its boundaries on all sides.

684. The conqueror next proceeded to convene a panhellenic congress at Corinth, where he announced his intention of leading the united Greeks against the Persian king, avenging the invasion of Xerxes, and liberating the Greeks of Asia. Contingents for this enterprise were to be furnished from the various cities. The Spartans kept aloof from this assembly; and the Athenians were deeply mortified at finding themselves obliged to equip a fleet to serve under Philip, while the maritime states, hitherto confederated under their chieftainship, were enrolled as the dependencies of the Macedonian king. But it was too late to murmur; the peace which they had accepted involved as a necessary result that all the states should pass alike into contributory appendages of Philip. In the spring of 336 B.C., a portion of the army thus raised was sent to commence operations in Asia, and Philip himself was speedily to follow. A different fate, however, was reserved for him.

685. Not long before these transactions, Philip had repudiated his wife Olympias—who is said to have become hateful to him, from the savage impulses of her disposition—and married Cleopatra, niece of the Macedonian

Attalus. This step provoked great resentment among the friends of Olympias, and especially awakened the displeasure of her son Alexander. It was no small aggravation to the outrage, when, amidst the intoxication of the nuptial banquet, Attalus proposed the toast and prayer, that there might soon be a legitimate son from Cleopatra to ascend the throne of Macedon. A violent quarrel ensued; and Alexander withdrew from court with his mother, whom he placed under the care of her own brother Alexander, king of Epeirus. He was afterwards reconciled to Philip, and returned, but Olympias remained in Epeirus.

686. The expedition against Persia had been planned, and actually commenced, when a son was born to Cleopatra; and Philip resolved to conciliate the brother of Olympias, lest mischief should arise from that quarter during his absence from home. With this view, he gave him in marriage his own daughter by Olympias, and prepared a splendid festival to celebrate at once the birth of the son and the nuptials of the daughter. All the species of attraction known to the age—banquets, contests in gymnastics and music, dramatic exhibitions— were accumulated, in order to produce an imposing impression on the Greeks, who from every city sent deputies to offer congratulations. Statues of the twelve great gods were carried in solemn procession into the theatre, with that of Philip immediately after them, as a thirteenth divinity.

687. Amidst the festive multitude, however, there were malcontents; and chiefly one Pausanias, a noble Macedonian youth, to whom Philip had refused satisfaction for some brutal outrage perpetrated by Attalus. He had poured his complaints into the ears of Alexander and Olympias; and she at least, it would seem, vehemently urged him to avenge himself. There is no evidence that Alexander joined; but his partisans, eager to gratify his feelings, and insure his succession, lent their encouragement.

688. Unconscious of the conspiracy, Philip was about to enter the theatre, robed in white, unarmed and

unprotected, when Pausanias rushed upon him with a weapon, hitherto concealed, thrust him through, and fled. The guards and surrounding friends of the king were at first paralysed; but at length some hastened to assist the dying king, others to pursue the assassin. Pausanias was urging his way to the gates, where horses were waiting to assist his flight; but he stumbled over some vine-stocks, fell, was overtaken, and slain on the spot. One of those reputed his accomplices hastened to salute the prince Alexander as king, assisted him to put on his armour, and marched as one of his guards to the regal palace. The unfortunate Cleopatra and her infant were put to death soon afterwards.

689. Thus perished the subverter of Hellenic freedom, at the age of forty-six or forty-seven, after a reign of twenty-three years. The great results of his reign, and the main features of his character, are well attested; but no contemporary historian has recorded the details; and neither his means nor his plans, nor the mode of his interior government, can be ascertained on good authority. Thus much we know: that at his accession his kingdom was a small territory round Pella; and that at his death his dominion was established from the coasts of Propontis to those of the Ionian Sea, and the Ambracian, Messenian, and Saronic Gulfs. Within these limits, all the cities, except Sparta, all the inhabitants, except some hardy mountaineers, confessed his sway, and were enrolled as his appendages. We are assured, and there is no reason for disbelieving it, that among the means whereby he procured this ascendancy, one was corruption, unsparingly used to foment discord among neighbours, and to purchase partisans; that, with winning manners, he combined great deceit, extortion, recklessness in making false promises, and even unscrupulous perjury, when it suited his purpose. Such were the dissolving forces that smoothed the way for an army admirably organised, and generally under his own command. The warmest admirers of Philip's genius stigmatise not only the perfidy of his public dealings, but the dissoluteness of his private life, which was marked by drunkenness, gambling, and excesses of every kind.

These vices he not only indulged in himself, but encouraged in those around him. His body-guard, we are told, was a company in which no decent man could live ; and the number of his wives and mistresses was almost on an Oriental scale.

690. It was the fortune of Philip to fall upon those days in which Greece had no leading city to watch against him, no eminent general to take command, no citizen-soldiers willing to endure the hardships of continued service. We shall find in his son Alexander the like genius working on a still larger scale, and achieving still more wonderful results, while Greece, after a feeble effort, sinks into the nullity of a subject province.

ALEXANDER THE GREAT.

691. As soon as Alexander ascended his father's throne, he took measures for carrying his views into effect. There was some little opposition to his accession, on account of heirs who had more immediate claims, but this was speedily overcome. It does not appear that Philip had seriously intended to set him aside ; and his own personal qualifications were such as would have made it difficult for any one to rival him with success. In the bloom of youth, possessed of an active, handsome, though not athletic figure, with a countenance full of manly beauty, engaging in his manners, and already renowned for feats of military skill and chivalrous valour, Alexander might have won his way to a throne amidst a hundred competitors. One remarkable instance of his tact and readiness in mere boyhood is often adverted to. A fiery horse was on one occasion brought out before Philip and his courtiers ; and no one was able to mount the animal, till Alexander stepped forward and mastered the creature at once and with ease, having perceived that the immediate cause of its unmanageableness was that its head was turned to the sun. The same horse, under the name of Bucephalus, is said to have carried him in many of his campaigns. Alexander had been trained with Spartan simplicity and hardihood, and early inspired with ambitious views of

emulating the heroes of the *Iliad ;* but the most striking circumstance in his education was, that at about the age of thirteen, he was placed under the instruction of Aristotle, for whom his father had the highest veneration. He must, however, have passed out of tutelage at an early age ; for, at sixteen, we find him regent of Macedonia in his father's absence ; and at eighteen, filling an important military position at the battle of Chæronea.

692. The first step of Alexander was to secure the influence of Macedonia in Greece ; and for this purpose he made a journey to Corinth, receiving the submission of the Thessalian states on his way thither. He then convened the Amphictyonic Council ; took his seat as one of that body ; and easily procured from them his nomination to the command with which they had invested his father as captain-general of the Grecian confederacy. He then returned to Macedonia, where his presence was much required. Emboldened by the death of Philip, and encouraged by the king of Persia, the independent tribes of Thrace, with other nations bordering on his territory, had taken up arms, and assumed a menacing aspect. The skill and valour of Alexander suppressed these hostile tribes with little difficulty, and proved to his barbarian neighbours what he had told his own subjects on his accession, that the name only of the king was changed, but the king remained the same.

693. Presently he gave a fearful token to the states of Greece that he was no way inferior to his father. While he was engaged in Illyria, a report of his death was industriously spread in Southern Greece. The Demosthenian party at Athens were elated with the hopes of freedom ; Sparta dreamed of again being the chief of Hellas ; and the Thebans rose and besieged the Macedonian garrison in the Cadmea. The rapidity of Alexander's movements crushed the insurrection in the bud. He marched instantly for Thebes, and reached it in the space of fourteen days ; so that before the Thebans had discovered that the report of his death was false, he was already in the territory of Bœotia. Willing to give them an opportunity for repentance, he marched slowly to the foot of the Cadmea ; but

the leaders of the insurrection, supposing themselves irretrievably compromised, excited the people to the most desperate resistance. The issue was, that Thebes fell into the power of Alexander's army and was utterly destroyed—6000 Thebans are said to have been slain and 30,000 sold as slaves, while the walls and houses of the city were levelled with the ground. In the midst of these severe measures, deemed necessary as an example to the rest of Greece, the conqueror exhibited several traits of humane and honourable feeling. From veneration for literary merit, he spared the house in which Pindar the poet had lived. We are told, too, of a noble lady named Timoclea, whose house had been broken into by a band of Thracians, and herself subjected to the grossest violence by the leader of the troop; after which, on pretence of shewing the wretch some concealed treasures, she induced him to stoop over a well, and threw him in. Being immediately seized, and carried before Alexander, she was asked who she was that ventured on so bold a deed. 'I am,' replied Timoclea, 'the sister of Theagenes, who fell at Chæronea fighting against your father for the liberties of Greece.' The boldness of the reply commanded the respect of Alexander, and he saved her and her children from the doom of slavery.

694. The fate of Thebes struck awe into the inhabitants of Greece, and they were now eager to tender their excuses and their submission. Athens sent ambassadors to congratulate Alexander on his safe return from his northern expeditions, and received a sharp and unpleasing answer, which shewed he was perfectly aware of the hostility of a considerable party to his cause. He demanded the surrender of Demosthenes, and nine other orators, whom he described as the fomenters of disturbance in Greece. The Athenians, in reply, exhibited a perfect readiness to yield their orators; but by some interposition—it is said, of the Phocians—their lives were spared. Moreover, the young king was by this time too much occupied with more important affairs to prosecute his revenge upon the Athenian politicians.

695. Returning now to Macedonia, Alexander entered

upon the long-meditated invasion of Asia. At this time, the possessions of the Persian crown included all the country lying between the Caspian, Mediterranean, and Euxine Seas, and the Persian Gulf, besides nearly as wide a region in Central Asia to the east of Persia. At the head of this great empire was Darius Codomannus, a prince in the vigour of manhood, and not destitute either of courage or ability; but the Persian people had long degenerated from the poor but hardy denizens of the wild who had come into possession of a rich country 250 years before. Their wealth, arising from the revenues of numberless and fertile provinces, had proved fatal to the personal qualities through which their dominion had been acquired; and the Persians were now sunk in sloth, effeminacy, and luxury. Numerous satraps were necessary to hold the wide dominions of this monarchy together, and to make their resources available to the court of Susa. A large standing military force was necessary for the same purpose, because fear was the only bond by which either the satraps or their satrapies could be retained in subjection to the Persian throne. There existed no community of interests, of language, or of religion, to create a more effective union. The expedition of Cyrus, and the retreat of the Ten Thousand, had proved how easy it was for a handful of resolute and well-disciplined men to penetrate into the very heart of such an empire; and we are not, therefore, surprised at the confidence with which Alexander set out on his expedition. Before his departure, he distributed most of the crown-property among his friends; and being asked what he had reserved for himself, replied: '*My Hopes.*'

696. It was in the spring of 334 B.C. that the youthful monarch marched for the Hellespont, at the head of an army of 30,000 foot and 5000 horse. Of the former, about 12,000 were Macedonians, 12,000 more were supplied by the various states of Greece, and the remainder probably derived from Thrace and Illyria; while the cavalry was furnished by Macedonia, Thessaly, and Thrace. The whole army crossed the Hellespont at Sestus, Alexander steering his own vessel with his own

hand towards the very spot where the Greeks were said to have landed when proceeding to the siege of Troy. When half-way across, he propitiated Neptune and the Nereides with the sacrifice of a bull and libations from a golden goblet; and as he neared the shore, he hurled his spear towards the land by way of claiming possession of

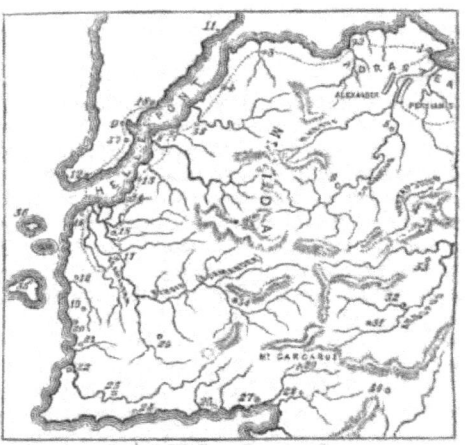

1. Priapus; 2. Parium; 3. Pœsus; 4. Lampsacus; 5. Sidene; 6. Gergithus; 7. Arisbe; 8. Abydus; 9. Koila; 10. Myrrhicus; 11. Callipolis; 12. Elæus; 13. Dardanus; 14. Rhœtium; 15. Ilium, or Troy; 16. Sigeum; 17. Troja Ilium; 18. Sestus; 19. Colonæ; 20. Alexandria Troas; 21. Larissa; 22. Hamaxitus; 23. Pedasus; 24. Assus; 25. Kenchrea; 26. Gargara; 27. Antandrus; 28. Adramyttium; 29. Thebæ; 30. Pionia; 31. Palæscepsis; 32. Soepsis; 33. Caresus; 34. Cebrene; 35, 36. Tenedos Islands; 37. Madytus; 38. Perœote.

Asia. His admiration of Homer induced him to make it his first business to visit the plain of Troy; after which he proceeded to Sigeum, where he crowned with a garland the pillar said to mark the tomb of Achilles, from whom Alexander claimed to be descended. These ceremonies over, he rejoined his army, and marched northwards along the coast of the Propontis.

697. All this while, the Persian king was perfectly aware of the intentions and movement of the Macedonians;

but he left the duty of opposing them, in the first instance, to the satraps of the western part of Asia Minor. Nor were these officers idle. The standing forces of the Lydian, Ionian, and other provinces, were collected near Zelia, on the eastern bank of the river Granicus, a point not above thirty miles distant from the Hellespont. To the Granicus Alexander also came up with his army, and, after a skilful disposition of his troops, began to pass the river in the face of the Persians, himself heading the phalanx immediately behind the cavalry. The Persians behaved with courage, and the cavalry scarcely maintained their ground till Alexander came up, charged into the thickest of the fray, and routed, first the Persians, and then the Greek mercenaries, many of whom were made prisoners. The king himself, conspicuous in the foreground, performed many acts of personal bravery, cutting down with his own hand Mithridates, the son-in-law of Darius, and piercing the heart of Ræsaces, another noble of high rank. His daring would, indeed, have proved fatal to him, but for the interposition of Clitus, who struck off the arm of an enemy as the scimitar which it held was descending upon Alexander's head. The number of Persians who fell in this battle is not well ascertained, but it is said to have been very great, and to have included several satraps and other persons of distinction; while the loss of Alexander was inconsiderable. The conqueror displayed much humanity to his prisoners, and to the wounded of the enemy, as well as to those of his own men who were in the same condition; and he granted immunity from taxes to the families of the slain. Those Grecian mercenaries, however, who fell into his hands as captives were sent to work in the Thracian mines, as a punishment for serving against their country; and by way of conciliating the Athenians, and identifying his expedition with the cause of Hellas generally, he sent to Athens 300 suits of Persian armour, to be placed in the Temple of Minerva in the Acropolis. They were inscribed: 'Alexander, son of Philip, and the Greeks (excepting the Lacedæmonians), offer these, taken from the Barbarians of Asia.'

698. Having by this victory quelled all opposition for

a time in the open field, Alexander proceeded to execute the ostensible purpose of his invasion, by relieving the Greek colonies from the oppression of Persia. Marching first to Sardis, he found an easy entrance, the gates being opened at once, and his friendship implored. His reception at Ephesus was similarly favourable; but Miletus and Halicarnassus closed their gates against him. The last of these occasioned him some trouble, being defended by Memnon of Rhodes, who contrived to shut himself up in a strong castle, which Alexander was obliged regularly to blockade. When Memnon found it no longer tenable, he set fire to it in the night, himself sailing over to Cos; and Alexander razed it to the ground, lest it might again afford a post of advantage to the enemy. His usual mode of proceeding, however, was, if possible, to do no injury either to public or private property; and thus his cause was espoused with ardour in most of the cities and provinces through which he passed. He restored to the Greeks their popular institutions, and gave the Asiatics permission to retain their own hereditary laws.

699. The winter was now approaching, and Alexander sent part of his army, under Parmenion, into winter-quarters at Sardis, allowing those of his soldiers who had been recently married to return to Macedonia and pass the winter at their homes. It was by such considerate measures as these that he became the idol of the army.

700. Finding his fleet utterly ineffective, from the superior numbers of the Persian ships, he gave orders for breaking it up, declaring that by conquering the land he would render himself master of the sea; and with this view, he pursued his march along the coasts, to take possession of all those towns that might afford shelter to a Persian fleet. Having received the submission of the towns and seaports on the Carian and Lydian coasts, he proceeded to Pamphylia. Here he resolved to desist for a time from his pursuit of the coast-line, and to march northward into Phrygia, where he was to be joined in spring by Parmenion, and also by new levies from Greece. Arriving at Gordium, the ancient capital of Phrygia, a

circumstance occurred which was considered prophetic of his future career in Asia. There was in the citadel of Gordium a consecrated chariot or wagon, in which the celebrated Midas, the son of Gordius, had been brought to Phrygia in time of distress, the people having been commanded by an oracle to look for a deliverer in such a vehicle. The car had been reverently kept, ever since, fastened by the yoke to a wall, with a knot so artfully formed of the bark of a cornel-tree, that it was impossible to see where the fastening either began or ended. It was currently reported that an oracle had promised the sovereignty of Asia to the man who should undo this knot. Alexander visited the place, and, according to the story of some writers, being unable to loose the thong, he cut it with his sword. According to another statement, he only wrested the pin from the beam, and said that was enough to make him lord of Asia. Whatever he did, his army and the people of the place believed him to have fulfilled the requirement. A thunder-storm occurring at the time confirmed the impression; and Alexander gave it still further countenance by performing a splendid religious sacrifice, as a tribute of gratitude for the coming glory thus decreed to him.

701. In Phrygia, Alexander met Parmenion, according to appointment, and also a reinforcement of new troops from Greece, accompanying the return of those soldiers who had wintered at home. Here he heard of the death of Memnon, and of the withdrawal of a large portion of marines from the Persian fleet, which circumstances induced him to give orders for again raising a naval armament in Greece. Afterwards he turned his attention to Paphlagonia and Cappadocia, the possession of which was necessary to render him master of all that peninsular region enclosed by the Euxine and Mediterranean Seas. The hereditary prince of Paphlagonia was willing and desirous to acknowledge him, instead of Darius, as lord paramount; so that a treaty was formed here at once. The satrap of Cappadocia had perished on the Granicus, and no successor had been appointed, so that this province was easily overrun. The prudence of Alexander in

securing his conquests was equal to his activity in making them. Wherever he found an existing power friendly to his cause, he left it undisturbed ; where this was not the case, he placed some of his most trusty followers in the vacant office, assigning to them a small military force to maintain their authority.

702. Again directing his course southwards, Alexander had before him the immediate prospect of the severest struggle that he could have to anticipate in Asia. Darius was assembling an immense army on the plains of Babylon, with the view of utterly expelling the Macedonians from his dominions. His reasons for not having earlier appeared personally in the field were of a most unworthy character. He had hoped, and indeed endeavoured, to get rid of his enemy by the treacherous arm of private assassination, and had on one occasion nearly accomplished the design. A Macedonian noble, whom Alexander had loaded with bounties, had been induced by the promise of 10,000 talents to conspire against the life of his benefactor ; but the treason was discovered in time to prevent its execution. Even when Darius took up arms of a more manly kind, and mustered an army of about 600,000 men with which to meet his adversary in the open field, he yet did not desist from the attempt to suborn the followers of Alexander. With this immense force, the Persian monarch, accompanied by his family, and surrounded by all the trappings of Oriental magnificence, advanced slowly from the plains of Babylon into Syria. The Macedonian king proceeded thither also from Cappadocia, only waiting to make himself master of Cilicia, the sole remaining corner of Asia Minor that had not submitted to his arms. While at Tarsus, the capital of this province, he threw himself into a dangerous illness by plunging into the clear but cold waters of the Cydnus at a time when he was heated by rapid marching. The result was a violent fever which threatened his life, and his condition was considered desperate by all his attendants except Philip the Acarnanian, an eminent physician, whose name has been rendered famous by an incident in connection with this illness. While Philip was handing a potion to the king,

a letter from Parmenion conveyed the warning that the physician had been bribed to poison him. Alexander handed the note to Philip while he confidently drank the medicine; and the result proved that his confidence was not misplaced, as he recovered rapidly after the critical draught.

703. Confident in the valour and devotedness of his troops, and eager for the decisive struggle, Alexander, on his recovery, led his army through the maritime pass called the Syrian Gate. He had scarcely done this, when he learned, to his surprise and satisfaction, that Darius, impatient of delay, had left the open country of Syria, and entered Cilicia by the pass called the Amanic Gate— the only other opening in the range of mountains which separates Cilicia from Syria. He had thus got into Alexander's rear, and was moving along the coast to overtake him. The Macedonians now retraced their steps to meet the foe, whom they found encamped on the right bank of the little river Pinarus—a most unfavourable position, since the narrow space between the mountains and the sea afforded no scope for the evolutions of large masses, and especially rendered his cavalry of little avail. Alexander marshalled his troops on the opposite bank of the river, himself taking charge of the right wing, and committing the left to Parmenion; while Darius posted his Greek mercenaries, the portion of his army on which he placed most reliance, opposite to the Macedonian phalanx. These he flanked with his heavy-armed barbarians; but the bulk of his unwieldy army was left utterly useless in the rear, as the nature of the ground admitted of no effective disposition of them. When Alexander came within shot of the Persian bows, he gave the order to charge, dashed gallantly into the water, and was soon engaged in close combat on the opposite side. The Persians were routed at once, but the Greek mercenaries maintained the contest for a time. What chiefly decided the fortune of the day was the cowardice of Darius himself, who, perceiving the defeat of his left wing, took to flight, and was followed by his whole army. Even the Persian cavalry, which had crossed the river, and was

engaging the Macedonian left wing with great bravery, was compelled to follow the example. The retreating Persians were cut down in immense numbers, above 100,000 being left on the field. Darius himself, on reaching the hills, cast aside his weapons and his royal robes, mounted a rapid courser, and was soon out of the reach of pursuit. His camp became the spoil of the Macedonians; but his tent, chariot, robes, and arms, were reserved for Alexander himself. One compartment of this tent was fitted up with a bath steaming with the richest perfumes; another presented a magnificent pavilion, containing a richly spread table for the banquet. From an adjoining tent was heard the wailing of female voices, Sisygambis, the mother, and Statira, the wife of Darius, lamenting his supposed death. The conqueror sent to assure them that their fears were groundless, and ordered them to be treated with the most delicate and respectful attention.

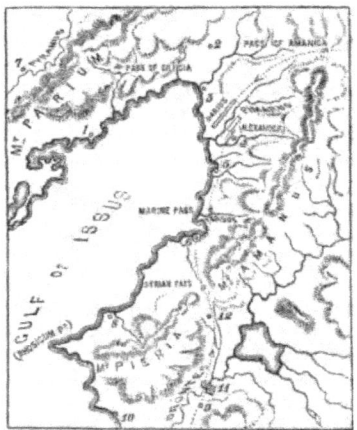

1. Aegææ; 2. Epiphania; 3. Catabalon; 4. Issus; 5. Bajæ; 6. Alexandria; 7. Mopsuestia; 8. Rhosus; 9. Daphne; 10. Seleucia; 11. Antiochia; 12. Pagræ.

704. Such was the memorable conflict called the 'Battle of Issus,' fought in November 333 B.C. The

victory was complete, though the Macedonians incurred severe loss, chiefly in conflict with the Greek mercenaries. Alexander followed up his success by marching along the Syrian coast into Phœnicia, with the view of thus striking at the root of the Persian maritime power. On his way, a deputation reached him from the unfortunate Darius, who had safely arrived at Susa, and now made proposals for a treaty of peace and alliance with his conqueror. Conscious of his power, and displeased with the lordly style of the Persian communication, Alexander rejected the overture, replying that there could be no amicable negotiations except on condition of his being acknowledged sovereign of Asia and lord of Darius.

705. As the conqueror advanced southwards, all the towns of the Syrian and Phœnician coasts hastened to open their gates; even the inhabitants of Sidon hailed him as a deliverer; but Tyre, the greatest and most flourishing of all these seaports, made a reservation which was by no means acceptable. Its inhabitants indeed sent a golden crown for the conqueror, and provisions for his army, in token of submission; but when he announced his intention of visiting their city, and offering sacrifice to Melcart, their tutelary deity, who was considered identical with the Grecian Hercules, the Tyrians had the boldness to say that they could not admit any foreigners within their walls, and that if he desired to sacrifice to Melcart, he might find another and more ancient shrine in Old Tyre on the mainland. Alexander indignantly dismissed the ambassadors, and declared that he would besiege the city.

706. Tyre was naturally a place of great strength, and had been rendered still stronger by art. The island on which it stood was half a mile from the mainland, encircled by deep water, and stupendous walls of solid masonry, which rose above 100 feet from the rocky cliffs of the shore. The city was well supplied with arms, provisions, and fresh water; it was occupied by an intelligent and warlike population, and though the greater part of the fleet was absent in the service of Persia, there was yet a goodly number of vessels in the harbours. The Tyrians,

knowing that Alexander had no naval force at his command, hoped, no doubt, to resist him with success; but they knew not the indomitable energy of the youthful Macedonian. He was resolved to allow no such nucleus of naval strength to remain in alliance with Persia; he would master this island-city at whatever cost; and since other modes of access were beyond his reach, he would construct a causeway from the mainland. His army adopted his views with ardour, and the mole advanced, the labourers being defended by wooden towers and other contrivances. The difficulties increased, however, as the town was neared, both from the deepening of the water and the greater exposure of the workmen to missiles from the walls. At length, seizing the opportunity of a favourable breeze, the Tyrians drove against the work a vessel filled with dry wood, smeared with pitch, and set on fire. The causeway, which was constructed of materials from the forests of Libanus and the ruins of Old Tyre, was thus destroyed; and Alexander became convinced of the necessity of having ships to protect the work which he would begin again on a larger scale.

707. The city of Sidon, and others of the maritime Asiatic states, placed their war-galleys at his service, and these were joined by squadrons from Rhodes and Cyprus, which had been tributaries to Persia, but were now seeking the favour of Alexander. In a little time, he had a fleet of 250 sail, which served to defend the reconstruction of the mole, and to keep the Tyrian galleys within their harbours. Every difficulty was surmounted; the mole carried to the foot of the walls; and the final assault made both from it and from the ships. The Tyrians made a desperate resistance; pouring on the besiegers vessels of boiling tar and burning sand, which penetrated the scales of the armour, and inflicted dreadful torture. After two days, however, they were overpowered, and the city became one wide sea of plunder and indiscriminate carnage. The Macedonians were so exasperated at the difficulties and dangers to which they had been exposed during a siege of seven months, that they granted no quarter. Eight thousand Tyrians are said to have been massacred, and

the rest, to the number of 30,000, reduced to slavery. The Macedonian loss was about 400.

708. During the siege of Tyre, Alexander received new proposals from Darius, offering him his daughter in marriage, with all the country between the Euphrates and the Mediterranean as her portion, to form the basis of a treaty of peace. It is recorded that Parmenion said to his sovereign on this occasion, that he would accept the offer were he Alexander. 'So would I,' replied the conqueror, 'were I Parmenion.' But as he believed himself capable of gaining the whole empire of Persia by his sword, he would not accept a mere instalment of it ; and Darius was obliged to prepare for a desperate resistance.

709. After the fall of Tyre, Alexander bent his course towards Egypt; and in his progress besieged and took Gaza, the only city of Palestine that refused to acknowledge his sway, and which, being a very strong fortress, delayed him three or four months. His career in Egypt was one continued triumph. Its satrap having perished at Issus, the inferior officer now holding the government, with the Egyptian people generally, welcomed the conqueror, and hailed him as their sovereign. He conciliated their affections by the respect with which he treated their national superstitions, holding a splendid festival at Memphis, and sacrificing to their bull-deity Apis. From Memphis, he passed down the principal branch of the Nile, and, observing with surprise that a country so rich in commercial resources was not possessed of one suitable harbour, he resolved upon founding a great maritime capital, which should bear his name, and prove an imperishable monument of his power. With this view, he traced the plan of the city of Alexandria, the site of which was so well selected that it rapidly rose to the condition of a flourishing seaport, and continued for many centuries to be the grand emporium of the trade between Europe, Africa, and India.

710. Alexander next made an excursion, with a small escort, to the Libyan desert, to visit the celebrated oracle of Jupiter Ammon, as his renowned ancestors Hercules and Perseus had done before him. After marching along

the coast for about 200 miles, he struck into the desert; and a five-days' journey, over pathless sands, under a scorching sun, brought him to the fertile oasis which contained the temple. He consulted the oracle in secret, and is said never to have divulged the answer he received.

711. In the spring of 331, the conqueror returned from Africa, taking the direct way to Assyria, where he learned that Darius had mustered an immense force against him. As his march lay chiefly through countries which had already submitted to him, no event of importance occurred till he came within sight of his enemy, near Arbela, a town situated a few days' journey to the east of the Tigris.

1. Acra; 2. Mesyla; 3. Gaugamela; 4. Dasena; 5. Larissa; 6. Birtha; 7. Arbela; 8. Sinna.

The forces of Darius on this occasion were more numerous than those which fought at Issus; but Alexander, too, had increased his army by reinforcements from Europe, and from his dependencies in Asia; so that he had now about 40,000 foot and 7000 horse. These he drew up in the order which he usually observed, with the phalanx in the centre, and himself with the cavalry on the right wing.

Darius occupied the centre of his own army, surrounded by select troops, and preceded by elephants and scythe-armed chariots, while on either side were Greek mercenaries. supposed to number 50,000. The Persians were so fearful of being surprised, that they stood under arms the whole night, and the morning found them exhausted and dispirited. Some of them fought with considerable bravery; but as soon as an accidental gap in their line gave Alexander the opportunity of pushing in a wedge of his phalanx, the fate of the battle was decided, and Darius took to flight as he had done at Issus. The rout became general; the flying enemy was pursued whilst daylight lasted as far as the banks of the greater Zab, where thousands of the Persians perished in attempting to pass the river.

712. Though determined, if possible, to obtain possession of the person of Darius, Alexander forbore the pursuit for the present, till he should have consolidated his power in the provinces which the late victory had acquired for him. He therefore directed his march towards Babylon, whence the greater part of the people came out to meet him, headed by their priests and magistrates, tendering their submission, and offering magnificent presents. The Macedonian entered the city in triumph, riding in a chariot through streets strewed with flowers, while incense smoked on every hand on silver altars, and the priests chanted their hymns of triumph. This was not a display of compulsory obedience; both the priests and the people rejoiced in the downfall of the Persian dynasty, under which the Chaldæan religion had been trampled down and persecuted.

713. Alexander, according to the policy he had observed in Egypt, caused the ruined temples to be restored, and proposed to offer a sacrifice to Belus, under the direction of the priests.

714. The wealth of Babylon enabled the conqueror to bestow large pecuniary rewards on every soldier of his army; and when, after settling the government here, he proceeded to Susa, the accession to his treasury was still greater. Here chiefly the Persian wealth was accumulated,

and the gold and silver bullion which fell into the hands of the conquerors amounted to 10,000,000 of sterling money. In the midst of these riches, the interest of the Greeks was excited in the liveliest manner when they discovered the spoils which had been carried off from their own country by Xerxes, especially the bronze statues of Harmodius and Aristogiton, which were now sent back to Athens.

715. The next movement was towards Persepolis, the capital of Persia Proper, where still further accessions of wealth awaited the victorious army. Here Alexander spent several months, and here he gave one of the first indications of being spoiled by excessive prosperity. At a magnificent banquet, Thaïs, a celebrated courtezan of Athens, proposed to make a bonfire of the splendid old palace of the Persian kings. Alexander, heated with wine, consented, and it would seem that the giddy pair carried torches with their own hands to set the place on fire.

716. Learning that Darius had fled to Ecbatana, and was still there, Alexander quitted Persepolis early in the year 330 B.C., and resumed the pursuit. On reaching the city, he was apprised that the king had departed only five days before with a small body of troops. Alexander immediately followed upon his footsteps, and after a long and difficult march, performed with astonishing celerity, he came near the object of his search, on the borders of Bactria. Here he learned that Darius had been seized and loaded with chains by his own satrap Bessus, who intended to establish himself in Bactria as an independent sovereign. This intelligence stimulated the pursuers to make still greater haste, and at length they perceived the party flying before them. Pushing onwards, they found Darius expiring in his chariot, having been stabbed by the adherents of Bessus. It is related that Bessus had provided a courser, and begged the Persian king to accompany his flight, but that Darius refused, preferring to fall into the hands of the more generous Macedonian; upon which the party of Bessus stabbed him, and took to flight. Alexander, finding him dead, or just expiring, threw his own cloak over the body, ordered it a magnificent

burial, and provided for the education of the children of his former foe. The victor, who had never sought the life of Darius, hunted his murderers with a spirit of keen resentment; and Bessus, being betrayed to him, was brought before a Persian court, and put to a cruel death.

717. The provinces of Bactria, Ariana, and Sogdiana—whose inhabitants receive in ancient history the appellation of Scythians—were not subdued without a series of severe conflicts, extending over a period of nearly three years. Nowhere in his wide career of conquest did Alexander exhibit so much of the soldier and the captain as on these Scythian plains. Not either the extremes of cold or heat, hunger or thirst, toil or danger, wounds or disease, could induce him to forego his purpose; and soldiers will do anything with a commander who can bear these casualties. When he entered Sogdiana in the year 328, he divided his army into five bodies, to scour the country in different directions, while he marched the troops retained under his own command against the fortress called the Sogdian Rock. It was situated on an isolated hill, so lofty and precipitous, that when its defenders were summoned to surrender, they scornfully replied by inquiring whether the Macedonian had brought winged soldiers. But, a small body of the besieging troops having scaled some heights that overhung the fortress, the garrison were terrified, and at once surrendered. Here the conqueror found a lady of surpassing beauty, named Roxana, who had been placed in the Sogdian fortress for safety by her father Oxyartes, a Bactrian. Alexander made her his wife.

718. As Parmenion and other officers had been in the meantime engaged in subjugating Hyrcania and Parthia—two districts of country upon the Caspian Sea—the reduction of Bactriana, Sogdiana, and other Scythian provinces, completed the conquest of all that had composed the Persian Empire. It was towards the conclusion of this laborious task that Alexander was guilty of an act which threw a deep stain on his memory, and proved that his character was deteriorating under the influence of continued success. He had appointed his friend Clitus—the same that

had saved his life at the Granicus—satrap of Bactria, and on the eve of parting, celebrated a festival in honour of Castor and Pollux. The banquet was attended by several parasites and literary flatterers, who magnified the praises of Alexander with unseemly adulation. Clitus sternly rebuked them, and even blamed the king himself for permitting himself to be compared to the gods. The king, flushed with wine, and intoxicated with flattery, rushed at Clitus, to kill him on the spot; but he was restrained by his friends, and Clitus was forced from the apartment. Alexander was no sooner released, however, than he seized a spear, sprang to the door, which Clitus was just about re-entering, and ran him through the body. As soon as the deed was done, he abandoned himself to remorse; threw himself on his couch, and remained for three days in an agony of grief, refusing all sustenance, and calling passionately on the manes of Clitus and his sister Lanice, who had been Alexander's nurse. It was not till his bodily strength began to fail, that he consented to listen to the entreaties of his friends, and to take comfort from the assurances of the soothsayers, who ascribed the fatal deed to a frenzy with which Bacchus had visited him, as a punishment for his having dedicated the festival to the Dioscuri on a day sacred to himself.

719. The ambition of the conqueror increasing with every successive gratification, he now resolved on the conquest of India. Having been joined by new contingents of troops from Europe, as well as by large bodies of Scythians, he set out on this new campaign with a very large army, said to number 120,000 foot 327 B.C. and 15,000 horse. His course was vigorously opposed by the various hardy tribes occupying the district now called the Punjab, and the natural difficulties of the ground proved very troublesome. When he was preparing to cross that tributary of the Indus called the Hydaspes, a powerful native prince named Porus had assembled a numerous and well-appointed army to dispute the passage. Alexander, however, by a skilful stratagem, lulled to rest the vigilance of Porus, and conveyed his army across the river, upon which an obstinate engagement took place.

The Indian army contained many elephants, the sight and smell of which disconcerted the Macedonian cavalry. But when driven into a narrow space, they became unmanageable, and a cause of great confusion among the troops of Porus. After a few vigorous charges, the Indians were completely routed, and Porus himself taken prisoner. Being brought before the conqueror, he displayed his usual majestic bearing, the effect of which was greatly enhanced by the extraordinary height of his stature. Alexander asked how he should treat him. 'Like a king!' was the proud reply. 'Nothing more to request?' 'No; everything is comprehended in that.' Alexander was so struck with this magnanimity, that he not only restored him to his government, but afterwards made him viceroy of his Indian conquests.

720. On the banks of the Hydaspes, Alexander founded two cities, one of which he called Nicæa, and the other Bucephala, in honour of his gallant charger, which died there. He then overran the whole of the country lying among the tributaries of the Indus, as far south as the confluence of the Hyphasis, and stormed Sangala—probably the modern Lahore—the capital of the warlike Cathæi. He was anxious to push his conquests further, having heard of a monarch beyond the Hyphasis reported as still greater than Porus. But his soldiers were worn out, and refused to follow; so, yielding with a good grace, under pretence that the sacrifices were unfavourable to crossing the Hyphasis, he gave orders for the retreat. He determined, however, to proceed by the coasts of the Persian Gulf; and for this purpose collected all the vessels he could procure, and added new ones for sailing down the Indus. The arrangement was, that two detachments of his army, under the command of Hephæstion and Craterus, should march down on the opposite banks of the Hydaspes, while the king, at the head of 8000 men, should go on board the vessels.

721. Several months were spent in the passage to the ocean; the most notable opposition being that offered by the Malli, supposed to have occupied the position of the modern Mooltan. At the storming of their citadel,

Alexander, followed by four officers, was the first to scale the walls. Before a fifth man could mount, the ladder broke, and the king was left alone on the wall, exposed to the missiles of the enemy. In this emergency, he chose, as the least of two dangers, to get down among his foes, rather than venture the much higher leap back to his army; and alighting on his feet, he placed his back to the wall, and kept the enemy at bay till help arrived. When more soldiers scaled the wall, and opened the gates to their comrades, not only was the monarch effectually rescued, but the place was captured, and every living being within it put to the sword. Alexander's life was, however, in great danger for some time, on account of an arrow having pierced his corselet in that fearful encounter.

722. When the mouth of the Indus was at length reached, Nearchus was directed to proceed by sea, and to explore the Persian Gulf and the mouths of the Tigris and Euphrates, with the view of establishing maritime intercourse between India and the Persian dominions. The main army, headed by Alexander himself, set out on the march by land, proceeding through the burning deserts of Gedrosia, towards Persia Proper. The toils of the first part of this march were very severe; but they were lightened to the soldiery by the sympathy of their leader, who himself marched on foot, and patiently endured the same privations and fatigues as the meanest follower in his train. The latter part of their journey presented a very different scene. As soon as they emerged into the fertile province of Carmania, the toilsome march became a triumphal procession, the king himself imitating the conduct ascribed to Bacchus, who is said to have danced and sung with his companions all through Asia. At Harmozia, the main body of the army was directed to proceed under the command of Hephæstion along the shores of the gulf, while the king, with his horse-guards and light-infantry, took a more direct route to Persepolis and Susa. Here he found that several of his satraps, and especially the governor of Persepolis, had been tempted by his long absence to assume independent authority, and oppress the

provinces. By the execution of summary justice on the delinquents, he caused himself to be respected as much for the equity of his administration as for the force of his arms.

723. During his stay at the Persian capital on this occasion, Alexander took to wife Statira, the eldest daughter of Darius—as the customs of Macedonia permitted polygamy—and bestowed the hand of her sister on Hephæstion. Other marriages were celebrated between the Macedonian officers and Asiatic women, to the number, we are told, of about a hundred ; while no fewer than 10,000 of the common soldiers followed the example, and took native wives. As a still further means of amalgamating the Asiatics with his European followers, Alexander admitted numbers of them into his army, and had them armed and trained in the Macedonian fashion. These novel proceedings were regarded with a jealous eye by most of his veterans, who were still further grieved at observing him to be assuming daily more and more of the state and manners characteristic of an Oriental despot. The long-stifled dissatisfaction broke out into open mutiny on the banks of the Tigris, when he proposed to dismiss such Macedonians as were wounded or otherwise disabled ; but his decisive conduct suppressed the incipient rebellion. He first ordered thirteen of the ringleaders to be seized and executed, and then addressing the remainder, reminded them how they had been raised from the condition of wandering herdsmen to be masters of Greece and lords of Asia, and how he had abandoned to them the richest fruits of his conquests, reserving nothing but the diadem to himself, as the mark of his superior labours and more imminent dangers. He then secluded himself for two whole days, exchanging his Macedonian garb for a Persian one, and otherwise displaying his want of confidence in his own people. Overcome by these proofs of alienation, the Macedonians begged with tears to be restored to his favour, and a solemn reconciliation was effected.

724. Soon after these occurrences, Alexander proceeded to Ecbatana, where he astonished the natives by a

splendid celebration of the Bacchanalian rites. But his enjoyment was suddenly turned to bitterness, by the death of his beloved friend Hephæstion, who was a Macedonian noble of his own age, and had accompanied him throughout the whole of his career. Alexander seemed never to recover from the melancholy which this event produced. The memory of Hephæstion was honoured with extravagant demonstrations of public mourning, and his body was carried to Babylon for interment.

725. Alexander entered Babylon in the spring of 324, not only under the influence of great depression, but of considerable reluctance, on account of various prophecies which had pointed to that spot as destined to prove fatal to him. Ambassadors from all parts of Greece, from Libya, Italy, and other regions, were there to salute him, and to do him homage as the conqueror of Asia; the fleet, under Nearchus, had arrived after its long and enterprising voyage; and, in short, all the results and tokens of his great achievements seemed to be collected there to do him honour. A more melancholy monument of his greatness was the funeral-pile preparing for Hephæstion, which was constructed on such a splendid scale, that it is said to have cost 10,000 talents.

726. But the mind of Alexander was not either to be satisfied with past successes, or paralysed by the regrets of friendship. He was now planning the subjugation of Arabia, and several expeditions had been despatched to survey the coasts and explore the seas which must be traversed. The period for commencing the campaign had arrived; solemn sacrifices were offered for its success, and splendid banquets prepared for the departure. Alexander drank deep at these carousals, and at the close of one of them was seized with unequivocal symptoms of fever. During the progress of the malady, the army, as on former occasions of a similar nature, hung about in a state of inexpressible grief and anxiety. When at length all hope was relinquished, his favourite soldiers were permitted to enter his room; and the scene has no parallel in history. Pale and speechless, but perfectly conscious, the dying

chieftain gazed at the warriors as they entered one by one weeping bitterly. He reached out his arm, and each man as he passed the couch kissed the beloved hand. After an illness of eleven days, he died in Babylon, at the early age of thirty-two—twelve years and eight months after he had ascended the throne of Macedonia.

727. Few of the great characters of history have been so differently judged as that of Alexander. Concerning the magnitude of his exploits, indeed, and his title to the appellation of the Great, according to the usual sentiments of mankind, there is but one opinion ; but as to the talents necessary for what he achieved, the motives which prompted his undertakings, and the good or evil that resulted on the whole, there is room for difference. His military renown appears more indebted to the extravagant boldness of his enterprises than to the magnitude of the real difficulties which he overcame. His motives, it must be admitted, appear to have sprung from the love of personal glory and the excitement of conquest, rather than any desire to benefit mankind. Nevertheless, he effected much permanent good. He roused millions from the sleep of barbarism, and became the means of their receiving the language, the arts, and the literature of Greece. On the wide field of his conquests, he founded at least seventy cities, the sites of which were in most instances so happily chosen as to redound to the commercial greatness of the countries in which they were planted. In the measures of his general polity, he was uniformly attentive to the interests of the nations which he subjugated ; and in his private character, he appears to have been liberal, generous, and humane. Fewer odious actions can be laid to his charge than to that of most other conquerors ; but errors and vices did come in the train of his astonishing good-fortune, and one of these—his excessive indulgence in wine—brought him to a premature grave.

SUCCESSORS OF ALEXANDER.

728. Alexander the Great left behind him no legitimate heir to his throne, and there was no descendant of his house capable of holding together his wide and scattered conquests. Aridæus, his natural brother, was a man whose infirmity of mind approached to idiocy; and neither Roxana nor Statira had yet become a mother. His unexpected decease threatened, therefore, to involve both his army and his extensive dominions in the utmost confusion. Each of his great officers, looking round among his fellows, saw none whom he deemed worthy to be his master, and considered his own pretensions as good as any other. At a general council held shortly after Alexander's decease, it was finally determined that Aridæus and Roxana's expected child, if a son, should be joint-successors to the empire; and that Perdiccas, to whom Alexander had given his signet-ring on his death-bed, should be guardian of their persons, and commander of the home-cavalry. The government of Macedonia and Greece was to be shared between Antipater and Craterus; Ptolemy was to preside over Egypt and the countries adjacent; Phrygia Proper, Lycia, and Pamphylia, were assigned to Antigonus; the Hellespontine Phrygia, to Leonnatus; Paphlagonia and Cappadocia, to Eumenes; Thrace, to Lysimachus. None of the parties in this arrangement had any intention that the sovereignty of Aridæus should ever be anything more than a nominal one, while themselves held the real authority under the title of lieutenants or viceroys.

729. The funeral-rites of Alexander were not celebrated till some time after the arrangements were made for partitioning his dominions. The remains were conveyed to Alexandria in a magnificent funeral-car, and deposited in a cemetery, which afterwards became the burial-place of the Ptolemies. In due time, Roxana gave birth to a son, who received the name of Alexander, and was declared joint-heir with Aridæus. Statira, too, had expected to be a mother; but Roxana had decoyed both

her and her sister to Babylon, where they were secretly assassinated.

730. Before further pursuing the history of Alexander's successors, it is necessary to advert to the affairs of European Greece. Sparta, as was formerly mentioned, had preserved a sullen neutrality during the progress of the confederacy under Macedon. Three years after Alexander's departure, Agis, the king, took advantage of Antipater's absence in Thrace to make a demonstration against the power of Macedon. The attempt proved a signal failure. Antipater defeated the Spartans with great slaughter; Agis fell in the battle, and the chains of Greece were riveted more firmly than ever.

731. In the year 325 B.C., Harpalus, one of the favourite captains of Alexander, who had been intrusted with an important charge at Ecbatana, had, like others, betrayed his trust during the expedition of the king to the remoter East. When he learned that Alexander was on his return, and that he had rigorously punished other officers who had been unfaithful in his absence, he determined to seek safety in flight, and hastened to Athens, in the hope of purchasing an asylum there with his peculated gold. At first he was refused, but by contriving to bribe the principal orators, he presently succeeded in securing a reception. The step was, on the part of the Athenians, tantamount to an act of hostility against the Macedonian rule; and accordingly Antipater demanded that Harpalus should be delivered up to him, and that those who had accepted his bribes should be impeached. Demosthenes was among those who were thus brought to trial; a heavy fine was imposed on him, and being unable to pay it, he was thrown into prison, whence he contrived to escape, and resided as an exile at Ægina.

732. When the news of Alexander's death reached Athens, the anti-Macedonian party, now headed by Hyperides, raised their heads again. A determination was taken to strike for freedom, and envoys were despatched to invite the other states to join the struggle. Most of them responded to the call; a considerable army was assembled, and Leosthenes was appointed commander-

in-chief. The Macedonians were defeated in the first engagement in Thessaly; but Antipater retreated in good order, and threw his forces into the city of Lamia, where he defended himself with success. After a time, he made a successful sally, in which Leosthenes was slain, and the Macedonian troops escaped through the midst of their besiegers to join reinforcements which had been sent to their assistance. Soon afterwards, Antipater encountered and defeated the allies, who were compelled to sue for peace, and were treated with one by one as they laid down their arms. The terms were most humbling to the Athenians: they were to bear all the expenses of the war, to receive a Macedonian garrison within the city, and to deliver up a certain number of their orators, among whom was Demosthenes. Such was the result of the contest called the Lamian War.

733. When Demosthenes heard of the conditions of the peace by which his person was compromised, he fled to the Temple of Neptune in the island of Calaurea. Hither he was followed by Archias, who had undertaken the task of luring him from the sanctuary, and delivering him to Antipater. Demosthenes, forewarned, it is said, by a dream, refused to believe his assurances that no injury was intended to him; and when threats succeeded to promises, he begged only for a few moments to write his last injunctions to his family. He then stepped aside, chewed a quill containing poison, and as soon as he felt it beginning to work, desired Archias to lead on, and he would follow. But as he endeavoured to make his way from the sacred fane, which he desired not to pollute with death, he fell down by the altar, and expired. Thus terminated, according to the received accounts, the life of one admitted by the unanimous voice of mankind to have been the greatest orator that ever lived.

734. After the death of Perdiccas, Antipater was appointed his successor in the regency, besides retaining the government of Macedonia and Greece. But he did not long survive the event: he died in the year 318, at the age of eighty, committing the regency to Polysperchon, one of the oldest generals of Alexander, much to the

mortification of his own son, Cassander, who expected to succeed him.

735. One of the first acts of the new protector of Macedonia issued in the death of Phocion, the last of all the Athenians worthy to be ranked with the great men of old. Polysperchon, seeking to conciliate the friendship of the Grecian states, proclaimed them all free and independent, abolished the oligarchies which had been established by Antipater, and gave orders for the dismissal of the Macedonian garrison from Athens. The Athenians were rejoiced at this decree; but the governor of the garrison refused to obey it; and Phocion, being suspected of abetting his contumacy, became an object of popular fury. Neither pausing to inquire into the justice of the charge, nor permitting him to defend himself against it, the Athenians condemned the aged patriot to death, and he was forced to drink the fatal .hemlock. When their momentary and misguided passion had passed away, they remembered his virtues with sorrow; brought back his bones, which had been cast out on the frontiers of Megara, and erected a statue of brass to his memory.

736. About the same time, Eurydice, the active and intriguing wife of Aridæus, determined to throw off the yoke of the regent, and formed an alliance with Cassander, while Polysperchon was joined by Olympias. The hostile armies met, and when the Macedonians perceived the mother of Alexander on the field, surrounded by a train in Bacchanalian fashion, they at once declared in her favour. Eurydice, abandoned by her own troops, fled to Amphipolis, where she fell into the hands of Olympias, who put both her and her husband to a cruel death, and then wreaked her vengeance on the family of Antipater and the adherents of Cassander. Cassander now advanced to Macedonia, and at his approach Olympias threw herself, with Roxana and her son, into Pydna; Cassander laid siege to the place, and Olympias surrendered after a blockade of some months, stipulating that her life should be spared. All Macedonia now submitted to Cassander, who confirmed his power by the destruction not only of Olympias—whose fate was regretted by none—but by the

317 B. C.

cruel murder of Roxana and her son Alexander, then sixteen years of age. By these sanguinary acts, not a single individual claiming kindred with the late conqueror of the world was left alive fourteen years after his decease at Babylon. The men who held the four principal governments assumed the title of kings; and their history continued to be marked by the same ambitious designs, the same quarrels, and the same cruelties that had stained it from the first.

737. On the death of Cassander, his sons preferred conflicting claims to the throne of Macedonia, but it was wrested from them both by Demetrius, the son of Antigonus, who had obtained possession of most of the Asiatic provinces. Demetrius himself was expelled by others, but his son regained the sceptre, and it continued in the family as long as Macedonia remained an independent sovereignty.

738. In the years 280 and 279 B.C., an immense host of Celts or Gauls crossed the Danube, under the command of Brennus their king, made a descent upon Macedon and Greece, and committed fearful devastation. Attracted by the report of the treasures of Delphi—which, however, were now probably little more than an empty name—they attacked the city, and the god, it is said, vindicated his sanctuary by thunderings and lightnings, similar to those that had repulsed the Persians in former days. Certain it is, that the barbarians, including Brennus, perished in great numbers before Delphi; and part of those who remained, passing over into Asia, gave their name to the country called Galatia.

739. One of the few events which shed a lustre on this the declining period of Grecian history, is the rise and progress of the Achæan league. While all Greece, with the exception of Sparta, was prostrate at the feet of Macedonia, this political power arose in the small province of Achaia, of which the very name has scarcely occurred since the heroic age. At a very early period, there had existed a league among its twelve principal cities. But its objects were chiefly religious; it had never assumed much political importance; and it had been finally suppressed by the

Macedonians, who held its cities in complete subjection. When, however, the king Antigonus was obliged, by the affairs of Macedonia, to withdraw his personal presence from Greece, the Achæan cities began to coalesce, and, under the influence of Aratus, one of the most remarkable characters of this period, the league rose into active political existence. It was governed by a strategus, or general, whose functions were civil as well as military ; a grammateus, or secretary; and a council of ten ; but the sovereignty resided in the general assembly, composed of all Achæans above thirty years of age. Through the instrumentality of Aratus, who was again and again elected general, Sicyon, Corinth, Megara, Ægina, Salamis, even Athens, and a great part of Peloponnesus, joined this association.

740. Sparta continued to maintain her haughty independence, but without the shadow of her former greatness. The primitive simplicity of manners had been forgotten ; the number of her citizens had been fearfully reduced ; the kings had become like the condottieri of modern times, hiring themselves to the highest bidder, and squandering in the luxuries of foreign courts the riches thus ingloriously acquired. The young king, Agis IV., who succeeded to the crown in 244, attempted to revive the ancient Spartan virtue in the face of much opposition ; and Cleomenes, who succeeded in 241, carried out these reforms with some success. The land was divided anew ; old debts were cancelled ; the ancient discipline was restored ; the Macedonian mode of warfare was adopted ; and Sparta had good hope of recovering her position, when she became embroiled with the Achæan league. The Achæans called in the aid of Antigonus of Macedon, who demanded, as the condition of his assistance, that he should be nominated head of the league. The demand was acceded to. Antigonus took the field against the Spartans, who were joined by the Ætolians, confederated in a league of tribes rather than of cities; the war was continued in the reign of Philip, his nephew and successor ; and Sparta, which had remained unconquered for many centuries, fell into the hands of the Macedonian. But the

Achæans, though victorious, had lost their independence; they were henceforth obliged to admit Macedonian garrisons; they could undertake nothing without consent of the Macedonian king; and Aratus, whose influence had been so beneficial, had now no power except that of his personal vote.

741. Meanwhile the Ætolians were unsuppressed, and carried on a series of freebooting expeditions in various parts of Peloponnesus. The Achæans could make no head against them without the aid of Philip, who readily listened to their application. The war which ensued was carried on with considerable vigour for three years, when Philip, though on the gaining side, concluded a peace with the Ætolians, being anxious to turn 217 B.C. his arms against the more formidable power of Rome. The Achæans were displeased, and Aratus expostulated; the consequence of which was that Philip caused this excellent man to be poisoned, in order to rid himself of a troublesome monitor.

THE ROMANS IN GREECE.

742. Rome had been gradually increasing in magnitude and importance: one by one, the cities and states of Italy had succumbed to its sway; and the eyes of the Roman people, whose thirst for glory and power knew no limits, had become directed to objects further from home. The people of Carthage were the first enemies who gave a severe check to their grasping ambition; and Hannibal, leading the Carthaginian troops into Italy, seemed on the point of crushing their power for ever. The king of Macedon allied himself with Hannibal, in the hope of afterwards receiving such assistance as would further his own views in Greece. The Romans had no leisure to avenge this while their struggle with Hannibal continued; but after their final triumph over Carthage, they concluded an alliance with the Ætolians, and declared war against Philip. The contest was continued during his life, and ended with the defeat of his son Perseus, who died in captivity to the Romans, the last king of the Macedonian

line. Such was the end of the Macedonian Empire, which was now divided into four districts, each governed by an oligarchical council.

743. After the conclusion of the Macedonian war, the Romans evinced the design of bringing all Greece under their sway. In these views, they were assisted by despots and traitors in various cities, and especially by Callicrates, who denounced above a thousand of the leading Achæans as having favoured the cause of Perseus. These were carried over to Italy, ostensibly to account 168 B.C. for their conduct before the Roman senate, but really with no other view than that of weakening the Achæan league, upon which hung all the hopes of Greece. No opportunity was given them to defend their conduct; they were distributed as hostages among the Italian municipia; and after what may be termed a free custody of seventeen years, the survivors, numbering about 300, were permitted to return. They were chiefly old men, and among them Polybius the historian; yet they employed their declining energies to arouse their countrymen to another struggle with Rome.

744. The final decision of the fate of Greece was brought about by the Athenians, through an obscure quarrel between them and the inhabitants of Oropus. The Oropians being refused protection from the Achæans, bribed the general of the league, who was a Spartan, to procure it. A fresh feud arose, in which Diæus, a furious enemy of the Romans, excited the Achæans to violent measures against Sparta, who, incompetent to resist the attack, appealed to the Romans. The violent and impolitic conduct of Critolaus, now general of the league, rendered all attempts at accommodation fruitless, and war was declared. A Roman army under Metellus marched into Bœotia; Critolaus did not advance in time to make a stand at Thermopylæ, and being defeated near Scarphea, in Locris, was never again heard of. Diæus, who succeeded him, drew together the last forces of the confederacy; but a fresh Roman force under Mummius occupied the Isthmus of Corinth, and in the ensuing battle of Leucopetra, decided the fate of Greece.

745. Three days after the battle, the Roman general entered the now defenceless city of Corinth, and after plundering its treasures, destroyed it by fire. All the male inhabitants were put to the sword; the women and children were sold as slaves. The master-pieces of ancient art, with which Corinth abounded, were partly destroyed, partly carried to Rome.

746. Mummius then employed himself in chastising the whole of Greece; and ten commissioners were sent from Rome to determine its future condition. The consequence was, that the whole country was formed into a Roman province. The Achæan league and all other confederacies in Greece were declared to be dissolved, and an oligarchical government was established in every state.

747. Greece, under the name of Achaia, which was derived from that confederacy which had made the last struggle for political existence, remained for upwards of four succeeding centuries in the condition of an humble dependency of Rome. Though politically one of the least important of all the provinces of the Roman Empire, it retained its pre-eminence in learning and literature. No Roman youth of rank and wealth was held to have perfected his education, without a visit to Athens, and a course of study under its professors. The language of Greece served, in later ages and other climes, to communicate to mankind the civilising influences of poetry and philosophy. Yet even this was not the highest of its destinies. Through the medium of the books of the New Testament, it had the distinguished fortune of imparting to the world the Christian religion, the diffusion of which in early ages was greatly facilitated by the Greek language being so generally understood.

INDEX.

	PAGE
ABRON'YCHUS, the Athenian,	165
Achæ'an league; rise & progress,	338-342
Achæ'ans; their origin, &c.,	40-42, 68
ACILÆ'US, progenitor of the Achæans,	26
ACHIL'LES, a distinguished warrior,	34
———, Alexander the Great claims to be descended from,	314
Acrop'olis,	79, 89-99, 130, 140-143, 180
ARME'TUS, king of Molossians,	169, 170
ADRAS'TUS, king of Argos,	32
Adventures of Themistocles,	169, 170
ÆANT'IDES, despot of Lampsacus,	94
ÆE'TES, king of Colchis,	31
Ægi'na, its fortifications destroyed,	179
Ægine'tans,	114, 123, 124, 129, 165, 184
Ægine'tan scale of weights and measures,	62
Ægos-Pot'amos, battle of,	233, 234
Æo'lian or Bœo'tian emigration,	40-42
Æ'OLUS, son of Hellen,	26
ÆS'CHINES, the Athenian,	296, 302
Æ'SON, uncle of Jason of Thessaly,	31
AGAMEM'NON, king of Mycenæ,	34, 35
AGESILA'US, king of Sparta—	250-262, 271-278, 282-285
AGESIP'OLIS, king of Sparta,	257
A'GIS, of Sparta,	210, 220, 225, 240, 250
——, king of Sparta,	335
—— IV., king of Sparta,	339
A'JAX, a distinguished warrior,	34
ALCÆ'US, a lyric poet,	103
ALCIBI'ADES, the Athenian—	202, 206-216, 226-232, 239
ALCI'DAS's mission to Mytilene,	192-195
ALCMÆON'IDÆ,	80, 89, 91, 94, 95, 99, 185
ALC'MAN, a lyric poet,	103
ALCME'NE, wife of Amphitryon,	27
ALE'TES, son of Hippotes,	40, 45
ALEXAN'DER of Pheræ,	279-282
———, son of the Great,	334; 338

	PAGE
ALEXAN'DER THE GREAT,	305, 308-340
Alexan'dria, foundation of city of,	323
Alliance between Athens and Sparta,	206
Aman'ic Gate, pass of,	319
AMA'SIS, king of Egypt,	104
Am'azons, female warriors,	28, 29
AMIN'IAS, the Athenian,	144, 145
AMOMPHAR'ETUS, the Spartan,	153, 154
Amphictyon'ic Councils—	6, 24, 25, 132, 138, 289, 298, 299, 311
Amphictyon'ic oath,	24
Amphip'olis, capture of,	203-205
———, siege of,	287
AMPHIT'RYON, king of Thebes,	27
AMYN'TAS, king of Macedon,	94
———, king of Macedonia,	265, 266
ANAC'REON, a lyric poet,	103
ANDOC'IDES, the Athenian,	215
ANDRO'GEOS, son of Minos,	29
ANTAL'CIDAS, Peace of—	262-264, 270, 280
ANTIG'ONUS, of Macedon,	334, 338-340
ANTI'OCHUS defeated by Lysander,	222
ANTI'OPE, queen of the Amazons,	29
ANTIP'ATER, of Macedonia,	334-337
ANTOM'ENES, king of Corinth,	46
APOL'LO and DIA'NA at Delos, temple of,	172
APOL'LO ARCHE'GETES, altar of,	53
———, god of Music, &c.,	10-22, 29, 38
———, legends of,	16-19
——— PYTH'IUS,	62
Ara'bia, Alexander plans subjugation of,	332
ARA'TUS, general of Achæan league,	339
Arbe'la, battle of,	324, 325
Arca'dia; its population, &c.,	72, 73
Arca'dian federation,	276
Arca'dians,	40-42, 72
AR'CHIAS, a Theban polemarch,	267, 268

AR'CHIAS; his mission to the Temple of Neptune, . . . 336
ARCHIDA'MUS, king of Sparta, 186, 191
ARCHIL'OCHUS, a lyric poet, . . 103
Ar'chons and magistrates chosen by lot, ... 176
Ar'chons, Athenian, . . 41, 77, 78
Areop'agus, court of, 78, 80, 86, 87, 96, 175
ARGÆ'US defeated by Philip, . 286
Argei'ans, ... 150
Ar'gives, combat of Spartans and, 74
Argonau'tic Expedition, . . 31
Ar'gos, . . 62, 63, 77, 114, 207, 209
ARIAD'NE, daughter of Minos, . 29
ARLE'US, a Persian general, . 245, 246
ARIDÆ'US, brother of Alexander, 334
ARI'ON, a lyric poet, . . . 103
ARISTÆ'US, a Corinthian general, 190
ARISTAG'ORAS, despot of Miletus, 107-110
ARISTI'DES; character and actions— 116-118, 124, 125, 141, 144, 165, 173-176
ARISTODE'MUS, son of Hyllus, 39, 69, 157
ARISTOGI'TON and HARMO'DIUS, . 92-94
ARISTOM'ENES, Messenian general, 70, 71
ARISTO'TLE, the philosopher, . 311
ARTABA'ZUS, the Persian— 152, 155, 156, 167, 168
ARTAPHER'NES, of Sardis, 100, 107-112
ARTAXERX'ES, of Persia, . 242-247, 262
ARTAYCT'ES, a Persian general, . 161
ARTEMIS'IA, queen of Halicarnassus, 145
Artemis'ium, battle of, . . 187-139
Arts, Fine, progress of, . . 52
Asiat'ic coast, war on the, . . 229
A'sia invaded by Alexander, . 313
ASTY'AGES, king of Media, . . 104
Athe'nians, . 26-30, 41, 42, 70, 109-242
——— betray the Phocians, 297, 298
——— rebuild city, &c., . 164, 166
Athe'nians; their noble reply to Mardonius, ... 148
A'thens, ... 77-102
——— and Sparta; differences, 176-180
——— - and Thebes; alliance, . 303
A'thens, foundation of maritime power, ... 164-167
A'thens, humiliation of, . . 235, 236
———; its democracy ended, . 228
———, leading state of Greece, 171-173
——— overreached by Sparta, . 206
———, pestilence in, . . . 189
———, pre-eminence in learning and literature, ... 342
A'thens proposes peace to Sparta; refused, ... 189
A'thens, splendour of, . . 180-183
ATREST'IDAS, an Arcadian, . . 295
AT'TALUS, the Macedonian, . . 308
At'tica, Spartans invade, 186, 191, 220

Bab'ylon, Alexander's entry into, 325
BAC'CHUS, king of Corinth, . 45, 46

BAC'CHUS, god of Wine, . . 15
———, women indulge in rites of, 20
Bara'thrum, pit for public criminals, 114
Battle-sacrifice at battle of Platæa, 154
BE'LUS, sacrifice to, . . . 325
BES'SUS, satrap of Persia, . 326, 327
BŒO'tians, . . . 100, 155, 262
Bœo'tian war, . . . 255-257
Boustrophe'don, mode of writing, . 86
BRAS'IDAS, Lacedæmonian, 196, 201-205
BREN'NUS, king of the Celts, . 338
Brut'tians, ... 61
Buceph'ala founded by Alexander, 329
Buceph'alus, horse of Alexander, 310
Bull of Brass, story of, . . 54
Byzan'tium, siege of, . . . 301

Cadme'a, surrender of the garrison, 268
CAD'MUS, founder of Thebes, . 7, 31
Calamity—Pestilence in Athens, 189
CALLIC'RATES, the traitor, . . 341
CALLICRA'TIDAS, the Spartan, 232, 233
CALLIS'TRATUS, the Athenian orator, 269
CAMBY'SES, king of Asia, . . 106
CA'rians, ... 52
Carne'an Apol'lo, festival of, . 134
CAR'NUS, prophet, slain by Hippotes, 40
Carthagin'ians, ... 55, 56
CASSAN'DER of Macedonia, 337, 338
CE'CROPS, founder of Athens, . 6
Cen'taur; illustration, . . 15
CE'RES or DEME'TER, goddess of agriculture, . . . 14, 20, 21
CE'RES, sanctuary of, . . . 124
CHA'BRIAS, Athenian, 269, 270, 285, 288
Chærone'a, battle of, . . 304-306
Chalcid'ice, destruction of thirty-two free Grecian cities in, . 294
Chalcidin'ians, ... 100
CHA'RES, an Athenian general, . 288
CHAR'ICLES, the Athenian, . . 220
CHARILA'US, king of Sparta, . 63
CHA'RON, the Theban, . . 267, 268
Children, Greek, sold as slaves, . 253
Chi'os, the blind bard of, . . 17
CI'MON and PER'ICLES, . . 173-178
———, son of Miltiades, . . 122
Cir'rha, destruction of, . 301, 302
Clans, Greek, classification of, . 38, 39
CLEAN'DER, despot of Gela, . . 55
CLEAR'CHUS, Lacedæmonian, 243-246
CLEAR'IDAS, a Spartan general, . 206
CLEOM'BROTUS, king of Sparta, 139, 149
———, Spartan general, 271-273
CLEOM'ENES, of Sparta, 95-101, 114, 123
———, king of Sparta, . 339
CLE'ON, an Athenian general— 193, 197-199, 204, 205, 208
CLEOPA'TRA, wife of Philip, . 307-309
CLE'OPHON, the Athenian, . . 229
Cle'ruchs, lot-holders or settlers, 101
CLIP'PIDES, the Athenian, . . 192

INDEX. 345

CLIS'THENES, republicanism of, 95-100
Clisthe'nian constitution unpopular, 174
CLI'TUS saves the life of Alexander; afterwards murdered by that monarch, ... 315, 328
Coast, population of, . . 89, 97
Co'DRUS, king of Athens, . 41, 77
Colonies, early Greek, . . 49-53
Commerce, &c., of colonial Greeks, 51
Congress at Isthmus of Corinth, 129,130
Co'NON, Athenian, 232-234, 252, 259-263
Copper and silver coinage of Argos, 62
Corcyræ'ans, . . . 131, 183, 195
Corinth'ians, 46, 70, 100, 101, 143, 177, 183, 184, 195, 207
Corinth'ians and Corcyræ'ans, naval battle between, ... 183
Corinth'ian territory, Agesilaus in, 261
———— war—Coronea, . 257-259
Cor'inth subdued by Aletes, . 40
CRAT'ERUS, Macedonian general, 329, 334
CRESPHON'TES, son of Hyllus, . 39, 40
Cre'tans, ... 131
CRIT'IAS, the Athenian, . 236, 238
CRITOLA'US, an Achæan general, . 341
CRŒ'SUS, king of Lydia, . 53, 104, 105
Cro'ton, an Italian colonial city, 58-60
Cryptei'a, system of, . . . 76
Cn'mæ, foundation of, . . 53
Cunax'a, battle of, . . 244, 245
CU'PID or EROS, son of Venus, . 13, 14
CY'LON, an Athenian patrician, . 79
———'s followers killed at altar of Fates, ... 80
Cy'me, chief of the Æolian cities, 42
Cynosceph'alæ, battle of, . . 281
Cypri'ans, defeat of the, . . 110
CY'RUS, king of Asia, . . 104-106
———— THE YOUNGER, 230-233, 239-246

DAN'AUS, founder of Argos, . 6, 7
DARI'US CODOM'ANNUS, of Persia, 313-327
————, king of Persia, 94, 106-116, 120
———— NOTHUS, king of Persia, . 242
DA'TIS and ARTAPHER'NES, . 114, 115
Debtor and Creditor, law of, . 82-87
Dec'archies instituted by Lysander, 234
DEIANI'RA, wife of Hercules, . 27
De'lium, battle of, . . . 202
De'los, birthplace of Apollo, 16,17, 29, 30
————, synod of, . . . 173
Del'phian temple; treasures, 290-292, 338
Del'phi, legend of, . . . 18
————, oracle of, 22, 27, 31, 41, 47, 64, 69, 70, 73, 80, 94, 95, 123, 130, 141, 142, 156.
Del'phi, temple and town captured, 290
DEL'PHUSA or TIL'PHUSA, fountain of, 17
DEMARA'TUS of Sparta, 100, 114, 123, 128
Demēs, or townships, . . . 97
DEME'TRIUS, Phalereus, . . 30
————, son of Antigonus, . 338

Democ'racy; Grecian type, 82-86, 96-102
DEMOS'THENES, an Athenian general— 196-202, 219-225
DEMOS'THENES, orator and general— 293-304, 312, 335, 336
DERCYL'LIDAS, a Spartan general, 252
Des'pots, expulsion of, &c., 108, 109, 113
————, short-lived in ancient Greece, ... 49, 57
DEUCA'LION, son of Prometheus, . 26
Dia'crii, or mountaineers, . 82
DIÆ'US, general of Achæan league, 341
Dialects of the Greek language, . 5
DIA'NA or ARTE'MIS, goddess of Hunting, ... 12
Dicasteries, Athenian, instituted, 174
Dictator; his office, . . . 48
DIOME'DES, a distinguished warrior, 34
Dodo'na, oracle of, . . . 22
DOR'CIS, the Spartan, . . 171
Do'rians in Peloponnesus, 39-42, 62, 68
Do'RIEUS, a Spartan prince, . 55
Do'RUS, son of Hellen, . . 26
DRA'CON, an Athenian archon, 78, 79, 87
Drama, development of the, 240, 241

Earth and water, Persian tokens of submission, . . 113, 129
Earthquake at Sparta, great, 176, 177
E'CREMUS, the hero of Tegea, . 28
Eges'tans deceive Athenians, . 211
Egypt; Athenians defeated here, 179
Egyp'tians, revolt of, . . 125, 127
E'lean heralds at Olympic festival, 209
E'leans, humiliation of the, . 240
Eleu'sian Mysteries; legend, 20, 21, 143
————————, profanation, 213
Eleu'sis, importance of this town, . 21
Emigrants, Greek, . . . 49, 50
Envoys from Sparta deceived, . 208
EPAMINON'DAS, the Theban, 269-286
EPHIAL'TES, the Athenian, . 174, 175
Epic authors, old, . . . 6
EPIG'ONI, expedition of the, . 32
EPIMEN'IDES, sage of Crete, . 81, 82
Epip'olæ, defeat of Athenians at, . 219
Epon'ymus = name-giving ancestor, 36
ERECH'THEUS, worshipped at Athens, 28
ETE'OCLES, son of Œdipus, . . 32
ETEONI'CUS, the Spartan, . . 234
Ethio'pians, ... 127
Eubœ'a, expedition to, . . 300
Eubœ'ans, ... 137
Eu'boic scale of weights and money, 51
EU'CLES, an Athenian general, . 203
EUDAM'IDAS, a Spartan general, 265, 266
Bupat'rides, or Athenian nobility, 78
EURO'PA, daughter of the Phœnix, 29
EURYBI'ADES, the Spartan, 133, 140, 144
EURYD'ICE, wife of Aridæus, . 337
EURYM'EDON, the Athenian, 200, 219, 220
EURYS'THEUS, grandson of Perseus, 27, 28

	PAGE		PAGE
Fall of Pausanias,	167-169	Herac'lid family, tradition of,	39
Fates, altar of,	80	Heralds, inviolability of,	114
FIFTH PERIOD: 371-338 B.C.,	275-306	HER'CULES, the great Grecian hero,	26-28
FIRST PERIOD: 776-500 B.C.,	44-103	Her'mæ, or busts of Mercury,	212-215
Fleet, Ionian, victory of,	110	HEROD'OTUS, Greek historian,	162, 163
Four Hundred, constitution of,	227-229	———, quoted, 102, 120, 128, 138	
FOURTH PERIOD: 404-371 B.C.,	242-274	Hero'ic Legends,	25-30
		HE'SIOD, character of his poetry,	37
Ga'za, besieged and taken,	323	HI'ERON, son of Gelon,	56, 57
GE'LON, despot of Syracuse,	55-57	Hier'ophants, a class of priests,	20
Genealogies, Grecian,	25-30	HIP'PIAS and HIPPAR'CHUS—	
Gené, or gentes, definition of, 38,39,85,96		92-96, 101, 107, 113-115, 120	
Gens, poetical, called Homerids,	36	HIPPOC'RATES, despot of Gela,	55
Geometry and Astronomy; origin,	103	———, the Athenian,	202
Gods of ancient Greece,	7-16	HIP'POTES, a descendant of Hercules,	40
—— of Athens destroyed,	213-215	HISTIÆ'US, despot of Miletus,	107-112
———, various sacrifices to the,	278	Historic Ages,	43-342
Gor'dian-knot cut by Alexander,	317	HO'MER; his *Iliad* and *Odyssey*, 36-38,63	
Gor'dium, citadel of,	317	Homer'ic and other poems, Pisis-	
Governments, early,	47-49	tratus's care of,	92
Grani'cus, battle of,	315	Horses, Thessalian, finest in Greece,	45
Gre'cian history; division into six		Hyacin'thia, festival of,	149
periods,	43	HYDAR'NES, a Persian general,	135, 136
Gre'cian states, growth of,	62-68	Hydas'pes, battle near,	328, 329
Greece & Persia, war between,	112-115	HYL'LUS, son of Hercules,	28, 39, 40
——— becomes a dependency of		HYP'ATES, a Theban ruler,	267, 268
Rome,	342	HYPERI'DES, an anti-Macedonian,	335
Greece, geography of ancient,	1-4		
———; its internal resources,	3, 4	*Iliad*, Homer's,	36, 37
———, preparations for defence, 129,131		Immor'tals, or Persian guards,	135
Greek States during First Period,	44-47	In'dia conquered by Alexander,	328-330
Greeks, heroic, resemblance be-		Io'nia, foundation of,	41
tween, and Scottish Highlanders,37,39		Io'nians, 38, 40-42, 50-52, 104-112, 138,	
Greeks, the Ten Thousand,	242-250	159, 162, 172	
GROTE, Mr, quoted,	44	Ion'ic Helle'nes,	77
GYLIP'PUS, a Spartan general,	218-222	—— Revolt,	104-112, 116
Gymnastic exercises,	5	I'ON, progenitor of the Ionians,	26
Gymnopæ'dia, celebration of,	273	IPHIC'RATES, the Athenian, 261, 262, 288	
		IPH'ITUS, slain by Hercules,	27
Halicarnas'sus razed to the ground,	316	I'ra, a mountain-fortress of the	
HAMIL'CAR besieges Himera,	56	Messenians,	71
HAN'NIBAL in Italy,	340	ISAG'ORAS, leader of the nobles, 96,99,100	
HARMO'DIUS and ARISTOGI'TON,	92-94	Is'sus, battle of,	319-321
HAR'PAGUS, General,	106	Is'ter, bridge of boats across,	107
HAR'PALUS, a Macedonian captain,	335	Isth'mian games,	6, 22-24
HE'BE; her attributes,	15, 28	Ital'ian Colonies,	58-62
HECATÆ'US of Miletus,	162	Itho'me, hill of, fortified by Helots,	177
Hecatompho'nia, sacrifice of,	71		
HEC'TOR, son of Priam,	34	JA'SON, a prince of Thessaly,	31
HEGESIS'TRATUS, the Samian,	158, 159	—— of Pheræ,	274-276
HEL'EN; her elopement with Paris,32,34		JOCAS'TE, queen of Thebes,	32
Heliæ'a, assembly of,	86, 89, 98	JOVE, Spartans the priests of,	47
Helle'nes, people of ancient Greece—		JU'NO, wife of Jupiter, 9, 12, 27, 33, 34	
4-7, 42, 44, 45, 61, 72, 76, 77, 112, 129		——, temple of, at Samos,	52
HEL'LEN; Greeks boast descent,	5, 26	JU'PITER ELEUTHERIUS; sacrifice,	157
Hellen'ic cities of Sicily, history of,	54	—— or ZE'US,	8, 9, 21-34
Hel'lespont, bridge across, 127, 146, 147			
He'lots, or slaves, 68, 74-76, 150, 177,185		LA'CHES, the Athenian,	205
———, 2000 emancipated; their fate,201		LA'IUS, father of Œdipus,	31, 32
HEPHÆS'TION, the Macedonian, 329-332		LAM'ACHUS, the Athenian,	212-218
Herac'leids, representatives of		La'mian War,	336
Perseus,	28	Land-force of Peloponnesians, large,186	

INDEX. 347

LATO'NA, mother of Apollo, . 16, 17
Lau'rium, silver-mines of, . . 125
Law of Debtor and Creditor in Attica, ... 82–85
Legends of Apollo, . . 16–19
LEON'IDAS, king of Sparta, 133–136, 139
LEONTI'ADES, the Theban, . 265–268
LEOS'THENES, Athenian general, 335, 336
LEOTY'CHIDES, of Sparta, 123, 158, 159
Letters, use of, from Phœnicians, . 7
Leucop'etra, battle of, . 341, 342
Leuc'tra, battle of, . . 272–276
Lib'yans, ... 127
LI'CHAS, discovers body of Orestes, 73
Literary Retrospect, 102, 103, 240, 241
Luca'nians, ... 61
Lyc'ians; their defence of Xanthus, 106
LYC'IDAS and family stoned to death, 150
LYC'OPHRON of Pheræ, . 291, 292
LYCUR'GUS; his history and polity, 63–68
————, leader of the population of the Plains, . . . 89–91
Lyd'ians; their character, . 52, 53
LYG'DAMIS, despot of Naxos, . 91
Lyr'ic poets, . . . 102, 103
LYSAN'DER, Spartan, 230–239, 250–256

Macedo'nia, king of, . . 148, 152
Mal'li, storming of their citadel, 329, 330
Mantine'a, battle of, . 210, 282–284
———— reduced by siege, . 264
Mantine'ans, ... 72
Maps of battles and sieges—
33, 118, 132, 141, 217, 314, 320, 324
Mar'athon, battle of, . . 118–121
————, Greece after battle, 123–125
MARDO'NIUS, Persian, 112–115; 146–159
Maritime activity of colonial Greeks, 51
———— power of Athens, foundation of the, . . . 164–167
Marriages between Macedonians and Asiatic women, . . . 331
MARS or ARES, god of War, . 11
MEDE'A, daughter of Æetes, . 31
MEG'ACLES, archon of Athens, . 79, 80
————, grandson of archon, 89–91
Megalop'olis, foundation of, . 277, 278
Megar'ians; alliance with Athens, 177
MELAN'THUS, king of Athens, . 40, 41
MEM'NON defends Halicarnassus, 316
Mem'phis, splendid festival at, . 323
MENELA'US, king of Sparta, . 33, 34
MER'CURY or HER'MES, god of Eloquence, ... 11
MESIS'TIUS, Persian general, 151, 152, 156
Messe'nia, independence of, . 277–279
Messe'nian and other Wars of Sparta, ... 68–77
Messe'nians, ... 68–72
————, humiliation of, . 240
METEL'LUS, a Roman general, . 341
Met'ics, or immigrant tradesmen, 97, 166

ME'TON, the astronomer, . . 212
Migrations, early, . . . 39–42
Mile'sians, . . . 159, 160
———— and Sa'mians, dispute of, 182
Mile'tus, conquest of, . . 51, 111
MILTI'ADES; character & actions, 116–123
MIN'DARUS, a Roman general, . 229
MINER'VA, goddess of Wisdom and War, . 12, 13, 33, 34, 79, 90, 91, 140
MI'NOS, king of Crete, . . 29, 30
Min'otanr, fable of, . . . 29, 30
MITHRIDA'TES slain by Alexander, 315
Moon, eclipse of; its effects on Athenians, ... 221
Mountain, population of, . 89, 97
Mount Istone stormed; fate of prisoners, ... 200
MUM'MIUS, a Roman general, 341, 342
My'cale and Plataea'a, battles of, 148–151
Mysteries, nature of the, . 19–21
Myths, poetic, ... 36
Mytile'ne, revolt of, . . 191–194

Naupac'tus, battle of, . . 225
Navy, the Athenian, . 124, 125
Nax'os, in Sicily, foundation of, . 53
NEAR'CHUS, the Macedonian, . 330, 332
NECTANA'BIS, king of Egypt, . 285
Neme'an games, . . 6, 22–24
Neodam'odes = 'recently set free,' 76
Ne'on, battle of; Philomelus defeated, ... 291
NEP'TUNE, god of the Sea, 8–10, 12, 13
NES'TOR, king of Pylos, . . 34
Nicæ'a founded by Alexander, 329
NIC'IAS, Athenian, 198, 204, 205, 214–224
————, Peace of, . 205, 207, 211, 212

O'deon, theatre of music and poetry, 181
Od'yssey, Homer's, . . 36, 37
Œ'cist = founder of a colony, . 50
ŒD'IPUS, king of Thebes, . 31, 32
ŒOBAZ'US, a Persian general, . 161
Oligarchies, first check received by, 48
Oligarchy, introduction, by Bacchidæ, 46
Olym'piad = four years, . . 23
Olym'piads, . . 43, 46, 53
Olym'pian Jove, temple of, . 92, 156
OLYM'PIAS, mother of Alexander the Great, . 288, 307, 308, 337
Olym'pic and other games—
6, 22–24, 40, 54, 59, 62, 79, 134, 163
Olym'pic festival, . . . 209
Olym'pus, Mount, . . 8, 17, 28
Olyn'thians; Philip of Macedon, 294–296
Olyn'thian war, . . 264–265
ONOMAC'RITUS, mystic poet, banished, 92
ONOMAR'CHUS, a Phocian general, 291
Oracles; their nature, . . 22
ORES'TES, son of Agamemnon, . 73
OR'PHEUS, a lyric poet, . . 103
Os'tracism, definition of, &c., 98, 99, 125

HISTORY OF GREECE.

OTHRY'ADES, the Spartan champion, 74
OX'YLUS, an Ætolian, . . 39, 40

PA'CHES, an Athenian general, 192-194
Palla'dium, a statue of Minerva, . 34
Panathenæ'a, festival of, . 13, 92, 93
Papy'rus as a writing-material;
  general use in literature, . . 52
Par'ali, or merchants, . . 82
PAR'ALUS, favourite son of Pericles;
  his death, ... 189
PAR'IS, prince of Troy, . . . 33
PARME'NION, the Macedonian—
                316-319, 323, 327
Parnas'sus, Apollo's temple of, . 17
Pa'ros, siege of, . . 121, 122
Par'thenon, temple of Minerva, . 181
PARYS'ATIS, queen of Persia, . 253
PAUSA'NIAS assassinates Philip, 308, 309
———, king of Sparta, . . 35
———, of Sparta, . 238, 256, 257
———, the Spartan—
              150-157, 166-169, 171
Pedi'eis, or nobles, . . . 82
Pelas'gi, &c., said to inhabit Greece, 6
PELOP'IDAS, Theban, 266-272, 279, 282
Peloponne'sian envoys put to death, 190
Peloponne'sians, 143, 149, 172, 178, 184
———, monument to, . 139
Peloponne'sian war, opening of, 183-187
———, progress of, 190-194
Peloponne'sus, various races occupy, 45
PE'LOPS settles in Peloponnesus, 7, 35
PERDIC'CAS, king of Macedon, . 286
———, regent of Alexander's
  empire, ... 334
PER'ICLES and CI'MON, 178-190, 283
Perin'thus, siege of, . . . 301
Perioe'ci, freemen and citizens, 75, 76
Persep'olis, palace of, burnt by
  Alexander, ... 326
PER'SEUS of Macedonia, . 340, 341
Per'sia & Greece, war between, 112-115
Per'sian invasion, renewal of, . 125
Per'sians, . . . 104-121, 172
Pestilence in Athens, . . 187-190
PHALÆ'CUS, the Phocian, . . 297
PHAL'ARIS, despot of Agrigentum, 54
PHARNABA'ZUS, the Persian—
      226-230, 239, 249, 252-254, 259, 263
PHAYL'LUS, a Phocian general, . 292
PHID'IAS, the celebrated sculptor, 181
PHI'DON, king of Argos, . 62, 65, 68
PHIL'IP, nephew of Antigonus, 339, 340
——— of Macedon, . 279, 285-311
———, the Acarnanian, . 318, 319
PHILIP'PUS, a Theban polemarch, 267
PHILOME'LUS, the Phocian, . 289-291
Pho'cians, . . . 133, 134, 141
———, abasement of the, . 289-299
PHO'CION, death of, . . . 337
PHŒ'BIDAS, a Spartan general, . 265

Phœnic'ians, 54, 56, 106, 110, 111, 127, 145
Phratrē-bond, definition, &c., 88, 39, 96, 97
PHYL'LIDAS, the Theban, . 267, 268
Phylo-Basileus, or tribe-king, . 88
PIN'DAR, a lyric poet, . . 102
———, Alexander's respect for, 312
Piræ'um, captured by Agesilaus, . 261
Piræ'us and Phal'erum, connecting-
  walls, ... 178
Piræ'us, Athenian fleet depart from, 214
———, fortification of the, . 166
PISAN'DER, a Spartan admiral, . 258
———, the Athenian, . . 227
Pisistrat'idæ, . 93-96, 101, 142, 162
PISIS'TRATUS, despot of Athens, 89-92
Plains, population of, . . 89, 97
Platæ'a and My'cale, battles of, 148-161
——— rebuilt by Sparta, . 263
———, siege of, . 191, 194-196
——— surprised by Thebans, . 185
Platæ'ans, ... 191, 194
Plemmy'rium, capture of fort, . 220
PLU'TO or HA'DES, and PROS'ERPINE, 8, 9
Poetry, ancient epic, . . 35-88, 102
Pol'emarch = commander-in-chief, 78
POLYBI'ADES, king of Sparta, . 268
POLYB'IUS, the historian, . . 341
POLYC'RATES, despot of Samos, . 106
POLYDEC'TES, king of Sparta, . 63
POLYNI'CES, son of Œdipus, . 32
POLYSPER'CHON succeeds Antipater, 336
Poor v. Rich in Attica, mutiny of, 82, 83
PO'RUS, a brave Indian prince, 328, 329
Potidæ'a, blockade of, . 184, 189, 190
PRI'AM, king of Troy, . . . 33
Probu'li, an Athenian council, . 226
Progress of Athenian power, . 177-180
PROSER'PINE, wife of Pluto, 8, 9, 20, 21
Protesila'us temple plundered, . 161
Prytane'um, court of, . . 84, 86
Pryt'anies, definition of, . . 98
PSAMMIT'ICHUS, king of Egypt, . 52
PTOL'EMY of Egypt, . . . 334
———, regent of Macedonia, 279
Pyd'na, siege and capture of, . 287
———, siege of, . . . 337
PYR'RHA, wife of Deucalion, . 26
PYTHAG'ORAS; his character and
  philosophy, . . . 59, 60
Pythagore'an order, . . 59, 60
Pyth'ian festival, Jason at, . 275, 276
——— games, . 6, 22-25, 259, 299
PYTH'IA, the Delphian priestess, . 22
Pyth'ii; their office, . . . 47

RŒSA'CES slain by Alexander, . 315
Religious fraternities, first record of, 81
Republicanism in Greece, first form, 48
RHADAMAN'THUS, son of Jupiter, . 29
Romans in Greece, . . 340-342
ROXA'NA, wife of Alexander—
                    327, 334, 337

INDEX. 349

	PAGE
Sacred Band, the Theban,	270
———— War,	289-294, 296-306
Sacrifices to the gods; their nature,	16
Sages, the Seven; their names,	103
SALÆ'THUS, a Spartan envoy,	192, 193
Sal'amis, battle of,	139-147
Sa'mians and Mile'sians, dispute of,	182
SAP'PHO, a Greek poetess,	103
Sar'dis, burning of,	109, 110
SAT'URN or CHRO'NOS, god of Time,	9
Scyth'ian provinces, conquest of,	327
Scyth'ians,	107
SECOND PERIOD: 500-478 B.C.,	104-163
Serfs, cultivation of the soil by,	46
Ses'tus, siege of,	161
SEU'THES, a Thracian prince,	249
Ship-building, improvement in,	46
Ship-canal across isthmus of Mount Athos,	127
Si'cels; their influence on Greeks,	54
Sicil'ian Colonies,	53-57
SIMON'IDES, a lyric poet,	103
SISYGAM'BIS, mother of Darius,	320
SITAL'CES, king of Thrace,	190
SIXTH PERIOD: 338-300 B.C.,	307-342
Social War,	287-289
SOC'RATES, the philosopher—	202, 207, 212, 241, 249
Sog'dian Rock, surrender of,	327
SO'LON; his laws, polity, &c.,82-90, 96,97
Soph'ists, or Wise Men,	241
Spar'ta,	46-49, 61, 63-77
———— and Athens, differences between,	176-180
Spar'ta, destruction of maritime empire,	259
Spar'tan power, decline of, in Peloponnesus,	276
Spar'tan senate and discipline,	64-68
———— training, characteristic of,	262
Spar'tans,	26, 49, 62, 64-77, 95, 101, 114, 120, 123-242
Spar'tans, monument erected to,	139
Sphacte'ria, assault of,	196-201
Sphinx, fable of,	32
States, convocation of, at Sparta,	101
STATI'RA, daughter of Darius, and wife of Alexander,	320, 331, 334
Subject allies of Athens,	182
Successors of Alex. the Great,	334-340
Sun regarded by Greeks as a god, and designated Helios,	16
Syb'aris; destruction of this city,	58-61
Sybari'tic festivals, 5000 horse at,	58
Synchronis'tic Table,	351
Syracu'san Expedition,	211-225
Syracu'sans,	54-57
Syr'acuse, consequences of defeat at,	225-229
Syr'acuse, foundation of,	54
Syr'ian Gate, maritime pass of,	319
Syssi'tia, or public meals of Sparta, 30,74

	PAGE
TA'CHOS, the Egyptian,	285
Tæ'narus, sanctuary of,	177
Tan'agra, battle of,	178
Tar'tarus, place of punishment,	9
Tayg'etus, Mount, Diana's temple,	68,71
Tearless Battle, the,	279
Tege'ans,	78, 74
TEL'ECLUS, king of Sparts,	68, 69
TE'LYS, despot of Sybaris,	60, 61
TEM'ENUS, son of Hyllus,	39, 40
Tem'pe, Vale of; retreat from,	131
THA'IS, a courtezan of Athens,	326
The'bans,	133-136, 194, 195
The'ban War—Epaminondas,	269-271
The'bes, Progress of, 275, 276, 279-281
————, utter destruction of,	312
————, War of the Seven against,	81
THEMIS'TOCLES; his character and actions, 116-118, 124, 125, 130,137-140, 144, 146, 147, 164-166, 169, 170
Theor'ic-fund of Athens,	295
THERAM'ENES, the Athenian,	235, 236
Thermop'ylæ, battle of,	132-138
————, Pass of,	296-298
THE'SEUS, the great Attic hero, 26, 28-31
Thesmopho'ria, a religious festival, celebrated exclusively by females,	265
Thes'pians,	133-136
Thessa'lians, 39, 45, 95, 132, 134, 136, 141
THIM'BRON, a Spartan general,	249
THIRD PERIOD: 478-404 B.C.,	164-241
Thirty Years' Truce—Splendour of Athens,	180-184, 197
THRASYBU'LUS; his defeat,	57
————, the Athenian,	228, 232
THRASYDÆ'US, tyrant of Himera,	57
THRASYL'LUS, an Athenian commander,	228, 229, 238, 239
THUCYD'IDES, the historian,	203
Thyr'ea, conquered by Sparta,	74
TIGRA'NES, a Persian general,	159
Ti'gris, rebellion of Alexander's troops on banks of; suppressed,	331
TIMOCLE'A, a story of her bravery,	312
TIMOC'RATES, a native of Rhodes,	255
Timocrat'ic scale of income,	96
TIMO'THEUS, Athenian general, 269, 288
TISAM'ENUS, king of Peloponnesus,	39
TISSAPHER'NES, a Persian satrap— 226-231,244-253
TITHRAU'STES, a Persian satrap, 253, 255
TOL'MIDES, the Athenian,	180
Traders and artisans encouraged at Athens,	87
Treason of Pausanias detected by a slave,	168
Tribute-paying subjects of Athens,	172
Tri'reme, or three-tiered galley,	46
Troy or Il'ium, siege of,	33-35
Tyrants, the Thirty Athenian,	236-238
Tyre, siege of,	321-323
TYRTÆ'US, a lyric poet,	70, 72, 103

ULYS'SES or ODYS'SEUS, a great warrior, 34, 36, 37	War of the Seven against Thebes, 21
U'RANUS, most ancient of all the gods, 9	Wars of Sparta, 68–77
	Weaving, dyeing, &c., of colonial Greeks, 53
VE'NUS or APHRODI'TE, goddess of Love, 12, 14, 29, 33	Wooden wall of Athens, oracle about, 130
VES'TA, altar of, 50	Writing employed to perpetuate history, 43
—— or HES'TIA, goddess of the Hearth, 9, 14	XANTHIP'PUS, father of Pericles, 122, 160
VUL'CAN or HEPHÆS'TUS, god of Fire, 10, 11	XEN'OPHON, the historian— 243, 247–249, 254, 258
Walls, connecting, of Athenians, 177	XERX'ES, imperial leader of Sicily, 55, 56
—— of Athens rebuilt by Conon, 260	——, king of Persia— 126–151, 156, 158, 161, 167, 170
War-cry, or pæan, of the Greeks, 119	XU'THUS, son of Hellen, 26

SYNCHRONISTIC TABLE OF THE CHIEF POLITICAL EVENTS, AND OF THE MOST EMINENT STATESMEN, GENERALS, POETS, HISTORIANS, PHILOSOPHERS, AND ARTISTS OF GREECE.

Years B.C.	Political Events.	Lawgivers, Statesmen, and Generals.	Poets.	Historians.	Philosophers.	Art and Artists.
?	Mythical times.	Minos.				Dædalus.
?	" "	Rhadamanthus.				
1184	Destruction of Troy.					
1104	Dorians' migration.					
1068	Codrus at Athens.		Homer, 950 B.C.			
1040	Ionians' migration.					
884		Lycurgus.	Hesiod, 830 B.C.			Rhoecus and Theodorus, first Greek brassfounders.
776	Corœbus victor at the Olympic Games.		Cyclic Poets, 776 B.C.			Temple of Diana (Artemis) built at Ephesus by Chersiphron.
743	First Messenian War.					
734	Syracuse founded by Archias.					
721	Sybaris founded by the Achæans.					
700			Archilochus flourishes.			Glaucus invents soldering.
691						
683	Second Messenian War.		Tyrtæus.			
664	Sea-fight (Corinthians against Corcyræans).					
661		Zaleucus legislator over the Locrians.				
660	Cypselus at Corinth.					
658	Byzantium founded by Megarians.		Pisander, epic.			Chest of Cypselus.
648			Stesichorus born.			
640						
624						
612		Dracon.				Lesches.
604	Sedition of Cylon at Athens. Athenians conquer Salamis.					

Years B.C.	Political Events	Lawgivers, Statesmen, and Generals	Poets	Historians	Philosophers	Art and Artists
600	Massilia founded by Phocæans.		Alcæus and Sappho flourish.		Seven Sages of Greece. Thales born 624 B.C.	
597	The Alcmæonidæ banished from Athens.		Stesichorus flourishes.			
596			Mimnermus flourishes.			
594		Solon legislates.				
585	Periander dies at Corinth.		Æsop the Fabulist.		Anaximander.	
572						
570	Pittacus dies.		Anacreon.			
560	Pisistratus at Athens.		Simonides.			
556						
549				Hecatæus.		
548						
544			Theognis, Hipponax.		Anaximenes. Pherecydes. Pythagoras.	Ageladas at Argos. Bupalus and Athenis.
540	Tyranny of Pisistratus.	Pythagoric league at Croton.				
535			Thespis.			
533	Polycrates of Samos.					
528	Hipparchus and Hippias.					
525			Æschylus born.			
524	Cleomenes conquers Argives.					
522			Pindar born.			
514	Hipparchus dies.		Phrynichus gains a tragic prize.			
511						
510	Hippias banished.	Constitution of Clisthenes.				
500	Ionian insurrection: Aristagoras of Miletus.		Æschylus and Epicharmus begin.		Anaxagoras born.	
499						
497	Piræus fortified.		Sophocles born.		Pythagoras dies. Zeno born.	
493	Persian 1st Expedition: failure of Mardonius's fleet.	Themistocles.				
490	Persian 2d Expedition: Battle of Marathon.	Miltiades.				
488			Panyasis.			

485 484	Gelon, tyrant of Syracuse.		Æschylus's first victory.	Herodotus born.	Phidias born.
483 480	Aristides banished. Persian 2d Expedition; Thermopylæ and Salamis.		Euripides born on the day of the Battle of Salamis.		
479 478	Platæa and Mycale. Gelon dies; Hieron succeeds.	Pausanias commands the fleet.	Chœrilus born.		
473 472 471	Themistocles banished; Athenian maritime supremacy dawns.		The Persæ of Æschylus.	Thucydides born.	Empedocles.
470	Cimon's victory by the Eurymedon.	Cimon.			
469 468 464	Pericles begins. Helot insurrection.		Simonides dies. Epicharmus flourishes. Sophocles's first victory.		Socrates born.
461 460 456	Cimon banished. Gorgias, the orator, flourishes.		The Orestes of Æschylus.		Phidias begins. Polygnotus.
457	Ægina's maritime power destroyed.				
455 450	Truce between Athens and Sparta.	Themistocles dies. Cimon dies.	Æschylus dies.		
449 447 444	Peace of Cimon. Battle of Coronea. Pericles at the head of Athenian affairs.	Charondas legislates for the Thurians.			Parmenides.
442 441	Samian War.		Pindar dies. Euripides's first victory.		
440			The Antigone of Sophocles.		Phidias erects the statue of Athena in the Parthenon. The Odeum built.

Years B.C.	Political Events.	Lawgivers, Statesmen, and Generals.	Poets.	Historians.	Philosophers.	Art and Artists.
435	Isocrates, the orator, born.					Olympian Jove by Phidias.
432	Potidæa revolts from Athens, and Prodicus, the orator, appears.					Alcamenes and Aristoeritus.
431	Peloponnesian War begins.		The *Medea* of Euripides.		Hippocrates, physician.	Polycletus and Myron, pupils of Phidias.
429	Plague at Athens.	Pericles dies.—Cleon.			Anaxagoras dies.	
428						
427			The *Daitaleis* of Aristophanes.			
424	Battle of Delium.	Brasidas.		Thucydides banished.		
423						
422	Truce of Sparta and Athens.	Cleon dies.				
421	Sicilian Expedition.					
415	Second Sicilian Campaign.	Alcibiades.		Herodotus dies.	Philolaus the Pythagorean.	
414						
413	Athenians defeated at Syracuse.					
407	Alcibiades returns victorious.	Lysander the Spartan.	Euripides dies.			
406	Dionysius becomes tyrant of Syracuse.		Sophocles dies.	Ephorus born.		Apollodorus.
405	Battle of Ægos-Potamós.		The *Frogs* of Aristophanes.			
"	Sparta, mistress of the sea.					
404	Athens taken by Lysander. Sparta at the head of Greece. Thirty Tyrants of Athens.	Critias. Theramenes.				
"						
"						
399					Death of Socrates.	Zeuxis flourishes.
397						Parrhasius and Timanthes.
396	Agesilaus in Asia.					
394	First Bœotian War.	Cimon. Iphicrates.				
"	Sea-fight at Cnidus.					
392					Theophrastus born.	Scopas.

SYNCHRONISTIC TABLE.

Year				
391	Lysias and Antiphanes, orators, begin. Peace of Antalcidas.		Thucydides dies.	
387			Aristotle born.	
384, 382	Thebes under Sparta. Demosthenes born.			
380				Polycletus the Younger.
379, 378	Liberation of Thebes. Athens' maritime power revives.		Lysias dies.	
376	Battle of Naxos.			
371	″ Leuctra.	Iphicrates, Chabrias, Timotheus. Cleombrotus of Sparta.		
368, 367	Dionysius dies. Demosthenes and Isaeus begin. Pelopidas dies.		Aristotle comes to Athens.	Lysippus. Praxiteles and Euphranor.
364, ″	Alexander, tyrant of Pherae.			
362, 360	Battle of Mantinea. Philip of Macedon.		Theopompus flourishes. Democritus and Hippocrates die.	
357	Social War.	Chabrias dies.	Plato dies.	Apelles.
356	Alexander born. First Philippic of Demosthenes.		Epicurus born.	
347, 346	Olynthus destroyed. Treachery of Aeschines.			Apelles and Diogenes.
341				
340	Panathenaic Oration of Isocrates.		Isocrates dies.	
338	Battle of Chaeronea.			
″	Timoleon liberates Greece.			
336	Death of Philip.			
″	Accession of Alexander.			Dinocrates (architect).
334	Asiatic expedition of Alexander.			
″	Battle of the Granicus.		Ephorus dies.	
333	Battle of Issus.			

Year B.C.	Political Events.	Lawgivers, Statesmen, and Generals.	Poets.	Historians.	Philosophers.	Art and Artists.
331	Battle of Arbela. Agis dies.					Melanthius.
323	Alexander dies at Babylon.				Diogenes, the Cynic, dies.	
"	Samian War.					
322	Sagian War ends.				Aristotle and Demosthenes die.	
317	Demetrius Phalereus at Athens.		Menander and Diphilus.			
310					Epicurus teaches at Athens.	
307	Demetrius Poliorcetes at Athens.					
304	Demetrius besieges Rhodes.					Chares works at the Colossus of Rhodes; Protogenes at the Ialysus.
301	Battle of Ipsus. Pyrrhus of Epirus.					
296	Museum founded at Alexandria.				Theophrastus dies.	
291			Menander dies.			
286						
281	Achæan League originates.				Zeno the Stoic.	
280	Aratus liberates Sicyon.				Chrysippus born.	
243	Agis at Sparta.					
222	Battle of Sellasia.					
216	Aratus dies.				Archimedes dies.	
212	Syracuse taken by Marcellus.					
197	Battle of Cynoscephalæ.	Philopœmen.				
196	Greece declared free at the Isthmian Games.					
167				Polybius at Rome.		
146	Corinth destroyed. Greece a Roman province.					

www.ingramcontent.com/pod-product-compliance
Lightning Source LLC
Chambersburg PA
CBHW020730160426
43192CB00006B/179